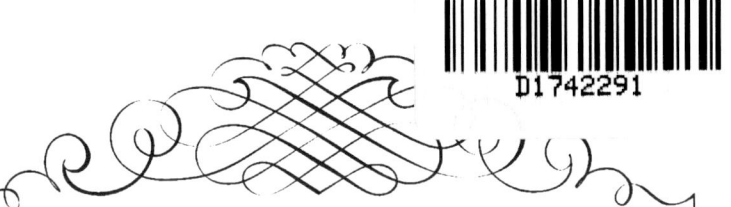

ISBN 978-1-330-35932-7
PIBN 10040012

1 MONTH OF
FREE
READING

at
www.ForgottenBooks.com

By purchasing this book you are eligible for one month membership to ForgottenBooks.com, giving you unlimited access to our entire collection of over 700,000 titles via our web site and mobile apps.

To claim your free month visit:
www.forgottenbooks.com/free40012

Gomes.

HIS HIGHNESS SEYYID KHALIFA-BIN-HARUB, SULTAN OF ZANZIBAR.

[Frontispiece.

ZANZIBAR

THE ISLAND METROPOLIS OF EASTERN AFRICA

BY

MAJOR F. B. PEARCE, C.M.G.

BRITISH RESIDENT IN ZANZIBAR

WITH ILLUSTRATIONS AND MAPS

LONDON

T. FISHER UNWIN, LIMITED

ADELPHI TERRACE

1920

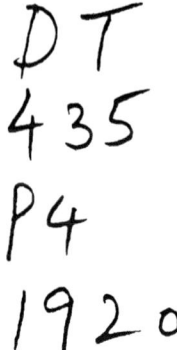

DT
435
P4
1920

First published . . March 1920
Second Impression . . May 1920

PREFACE

ALTHOUGH the name of Zanzibar—that rich spice-island of the African seas—is fairly familiar in the English-speaking world, little has hitherto been written concerning it.

Destiny and duty having led me to its shores, I have been presumptuous enough to write the following pages in the hope that they may engender some interest in the story of this romantic island kingdom.

The first chapters deal with the historical past, and in them I have endeavoured to trace the close political association of Arabia with Zanzibar from the very earliest times : and the references to the Arab kingdom of Omân and its princes will do something, it is hoped, to save from total extinction the memories of Ahmed, the founder of the Albusaid Dynasty, and of Seyyid Said, the ruler of Omân and the maker of modern Zanzibar.

Subsequent chapters recount the advent of Vasco da Gama to the East African seas in 1498, as well as the almost forgotten visit to Zanzibar, a century later, of that famous Elizabethan sea-captain Sir James Lancaster while on his way to the Indies.

The second portion of the book deals with the Zanzibar and Pemba of to-day, and not only gives some account of the Arab, Swahili, and Indian populations, but affords information concerning the clove industry on which the prosperity of the Sultanate so largely depends.

The third and last part describes for the first time the ancient Persian and Arab ruins which lie hidden in the forests of Zanzibar and Pemba. Although these relics of medieval civilisation can claim no place among the great ruins of the world, they are of vital significance in piecing together the history of the island kingdom of Zanzibar ; and while their full exploration remains to be undertaken, the brief description of these old towns—the very names of which have been forgotten—may prove of some interest both to the archæologist as well as to the general reader.

· In conclusion, I wish to express my gratitude to all who have assisted me in my pleasant task.

To His Highness the Sultan of Zanzibar I am indebted for much valuable information. My thanks are likewise due to Dr. W. Mansfield Aders for his interesting contribution on the natural history of the Sultanate ; to Sheikh Saleh-bin-Ali for his ready assistance on many occasions; and to Messrs. A. C. Gomes, the well-known photographers of Zanzibar, for generous permission to utilise some of their photographs.

F. B. P.

September 16th, 1919.

CONTENTS

CHAPTER VIII

CHAPTER IX

PART II

CHAPTER X

CHAPTER XI

CHAPTER XII

CHAPTER XIII

CHAPTER XIV

CHAPTER XV

CHAPTER XVI

CONTENTS

CONTENTS

CHAPTER XXVI

CHAPTER XXVII

CHAPTER XXVIII

LIST OF ILLUSTRATIONS

xi

MAPS

PART 1

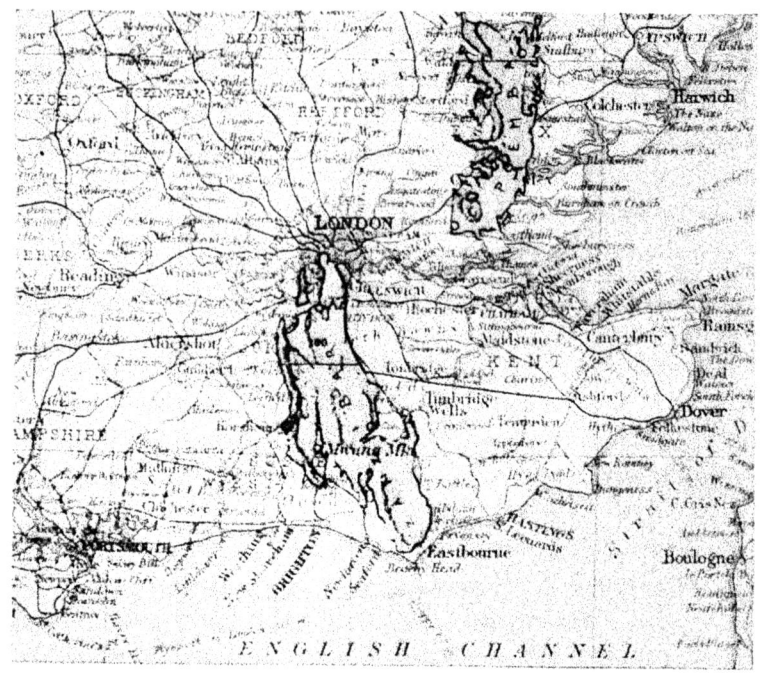

SKETCH-MAP OF S E. ENGLAND WITH ZANZIBAR AND PEMBA ON SAME SCALE
SUPER-IMPOSED TO DEMONSTRATE RELATIVE SIZE.

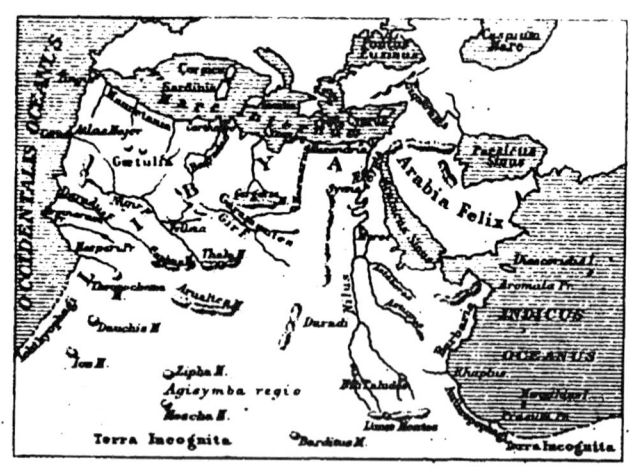

AFRICA ACCORDING TO PTOLEMY, A.D. 150.

CHAPTER I

THE SULTAN'S DOMINIONS

THE Island of Zanzibar is situated in the Indian Ocean about twenty-five miles from the east coast of Africa, 6° 10′ south of the Equator, and in longitude 39° 19′ east of Greenwich.

It lies 118 miles south of Mombasa, 26 miles north-east of Daresalaam, and about 8,000 miles from London.[1]

Twenty-five miles to the north-east of Zanzibar is the sister-island of Pemba, " the place where the cloves come from." These two islands, together with numerous islets, constitute the island dominions of His Highness Khalifa II, the Sultan of Zanzibar, whose sovereign rights and territories are guaranteed by, and are under the immediate protection of, Great Britain.

Zanzibar Island, which is about the size of Hertfordshire, lies with its main axis N.N.W. and S.S.E., and is fifty-four miles in length, with a maximum breadth of about twenty-four miles. Its dimensions will be better realised if it is explained that its length from north to south is equivalent to the distance as the crow flies between London and Eastbourne ; while its breadth from east to west would comfortably fill up the intervening space between Dover and Calais.

The island of Pemba is a little larger than Huntingdonshire, and is forty-two miles long from north to south, with an extreme width of fifteen miles.

---

[1] These distances are to the nearest point of Zanzibar Island. To Zanzibar Town add thirty miles in each case.

The dominions of His Highness also comprise, in addition to the two islands mentioned above, Mombasa Island and a strip of coast ten miles wide and fifty-two miles in length on the mainland of Africa. It may not be generally known that the Zanzibar ensign flies not only in Zanzibar and Pemba, but also over the old Portuguese-built fort at Mombasa. The mainland possessions of His Highness are leased to the Government of the East Africa Protectorate at a yearly rental of £11,000.

The city of Zanzibar, the seat of His Highness's Government, is situated on the west coast of Zanzibar Island, and faces the continent of Africa, which can generally be seen in fair weather. The town contains about 36,000 inhabitants, and is one of the most romantic and picturesque Eastern cities in the British Empire. Any one who has seen Oscar Asche's well-known play, *Kismet*, and remembers the scene depicting the native bazaar, will have a very fair impression as to what some portions of the city of Zanzibar are like. But before we can describe the town, it is desirable to say something concerning the name, the geological formation, and the history of Zanzibar Island.

It is generally accepted that the name " Zanzibar " is derived from the Persian word *zangh*, meaning a negro, and *bar*, a coast. Thus the name in its widest sense signifies " The Negro Coast."

The Arabic form and meaning of the name are similar, except that the hard Persian *gh* is softened into the Arabic letter *jim*, making the name " Zinjbar." The native population call their island " Unguja."

The Arab geographers of medieval times always applied the name of " Zinj " to the whole region of Eastern Africa, and the well-known Arab traveller, Masudi, who commenced his travels about A.D. 912, defines with some precision the limits of the " Negro Coast," or the " Land of Zinj "; but it is evident that he does not apply the name to the island with which we are primarily concerned at the present time.

That a name such as Zanzibar applied in the first instance to a vast region of the African continent should, in the course of the centuries, come to indicate a small island is somewhat strange. Such an application is the reversal of the general rule, for it is quite conceivable that the name of a prosperous port or city might be applied to a region or country of which some port or city was its vital centre. Indeed such cases are not uncommon. The name " Africa " (derived from the Berber name *Ifrikiah*), for instance, which was at first confined, in the times of the Romans, to signify their colony of (modern) Tunis,[1] became eventually applicable to the whole continent. The Cape of Good Hope lends its name to a vast territory; while the Presidency of Bombay borrows its designation from the original island of that name.

Marco Polo, the famous Venetian traveller of the thirteenth century, refers to " Zanzibar " as an island with a compass of 2,000 miles, inhabited by most hideous negroes, and subsequent geographers and cartographers perpetuated the mistake, and we find in old maps made prior to the discoveries of the Portuguese in the Indian Ocean, a very substantial island labelled Zanzibar (or a modified form of the name) stowed away in some convenient corner of the Southern Seas

For instance in Fra Mauro's Chart of the World dated 1459, there is an island shown near the confines of the world labelled " Chancibar "; while on the same map, a region of the African Continent in the neighbourhood of Sofala and " Maabase " (Mombasa) is named " Xengibar."

In this case the cartographer has solved the difficulty by applying the name to an island and to a portion of the mainland as well.[2]

The *Chronicles of Kilwa*, which record the history of the great Persian and Arab State of that name from the tenth to the fifteenth century, refer to the island of Zanzibar, as also do the Portuguese navigators of the early years of the sixteenth century, so it is clear that from the latter period at least the name Zanzibar was definitely applied to the island.

Closely associated with, and suggestive of, the Arab and

---

[1] Sir Harry Johnston, *The Colonisation of Africa*, Cambridge Historical Series, 1899.

[2] Incidentally it may be mentioned that Mauro has confused the Island of Tumbatu near Zanzibar with Timbuktu.

Persian word *Zangh* or *Zanj* is the still more ancient name of Azania, which at the commencement of the Christian era was applied to the continental region lying between the modern Somaliland and Portuguese East Africa.

The word Azania is possibly the Latinised form of the old Arabic word *Ajam* or *Ajem*, used in conjunction with the word *bar* to indicate a non-Arab or foreign country. The term *Bar-Ajam* was applied by the Arabs to a region in much the same manner as the ancient Greeks employed the word " Barbaria."

Thus the author of the *Periplus of the Erythræan Sea*, writing in about A.D. 60, frequently alludes to the east coast of Africa as Azania, while the renowned Greek astronomer Claudius Ptolemy in A.D. 150 tells us that Azania commences south of Ras Hafun ; and he uses both the name Azania and Barbaria to denote the same region. Pliny too speaks of the Azanian Sea as communicating with the Gulf of Arabia : while the Southern Arabians refer to the identical region as " Bar-Ajam."

Azania was one of those names which, like Numidia, Libya, and Mauretania, served to indicate certain regions of the African continent recognised by the Greek and Roman geographers of the first and second centuries of the Christian era.

Azania is an old-world name, venerable with the glamour of the centuries ; it is moreover a pleasant-sounding name, and it is to be regretted that it is no longer employed, in the place of those cumbrous modern expressions British East Africa and " German " East Africa.

May I venture to suggest that the name Azania be again utilised to denote some new colony or group of dependencies in the regions of East Africa, whenever the necessity of finding a suitable designation arises ?

And may I seize this opportunity to submit the proposal that that portion of the Indian Ocean lying to the west of a line drawn from Cape Guardafui to the Seychelles, and thence to Cape Amber in Madagascar, be in future styled " The Sea of Azania " ? By this means an ancient name would be preserved from total extinction, and a most con-venient partition of the Indian Ocean would be effected·

At present it is necessary, in order to specify the sea contiguous to the East African littoral, to refer to " that portion of the Indian Ocean adjacent to the coast of British East Africa," or some such clumsy and ill-defined phrase, whereas a reference to the Azanian Sea would be perfectly explicit and concise.

II

As regards the geological formation[1] of the Sultanate, the islands of Zanzibar, Pemba, and Mafia appear to be a part of the East African Barrier system, formed in a similar manner, but on a much less extensive scale, to the Great Barrier Reef which skirts the north-eastern coasts of the Australian continent.

It is clear that at one time Zanzibar must have been connected with the African continent, as the presence on the island of certain specimens of mainland fauna can be accounted for in no other way, and a reference to the chart of this region will show that the sea-channel which to-day separates the island from the mainland is a shallow strait —seldom exceeding twenty-five fathoms in depth—while the submerged portion of the strait exactly coincides with the extent of Zanzibar Island from north to south.

Pemba Island, while geologically of similar structure to Zanzibar, is separated from the latter island and from the African coast by sea-channels of great depth, which range from 270 fathoms to as much as 400 fathoms : and its former connection with the mainland is therefore less evident.

Zanzibar and Pemba Islands, with their numerous reefs and islets, have a basic structure of hard coralline limestone, upon which is superimposed strata of white and yellow chalky deposits, sand, and red earth. A very soft sandstone is occasionally found, and harder beach-sandstone occurs at a few places on the coast, and in particular near the town of Zanzibar.

[1] For much of the information in this section I am indebted to Mr. Cyril Crossland's *The Coral Reefs of Zanzibar* and *Desert and Water Gardens of the Red Sea* ; to Dr. James Christie's *Cholera Epidemics of East Africa*, and to *The African Pilot*.

The red earth is undoubtedly formed in the same way as in other cases of its occurrence, viz. by the disintegration of coral rock, and the chalky deposits probably have a similar origin.[1]

The steep though low cliffs, which doubtless edged the islands when they were upheaved from the sea depths, have been persistently attacked by wave action, and the substratum of coralline formation exposed. This formation has been, and is at the present time, being undermined and cut down by wave action.

The upper surface of the coralline limestone becomes intensely hard when exposed to rain and the tropical sun, while the lower portion remains comparatively soft, and the consequence is that the coralline cliffs on the sea edge, or when separated from the main island, often assume most fantastic shapes. All this undermining of the limestone cliffs, and the existence of isolated rocks and islets, are evidential of the fact that the main island and the archipelagoes of small islets scattered in the neighbouring waters are slowly but surely being destroyed and broken up by the action of the sea.

It is interesting to realise that the numerous reefs, which are only visible at low tide, in the neighbourhood of Zanzibar Harbour, and other parts of the coast, are the remains of islands which have been destroyed by the same process of disintegration that to-day is attacking the islands of Zanzibar and Pemba.

This transformation of an island into a submerged reef is of course a lengthy process, but evidence shows that one of the existing reefs to the south-west of Zanzibar Town, now known as Nyange, was at the commencement of the nineteenth century known as " Tree Island," from the coco-nut palms growing thereon. At the time of Captain Owen's visit in 1822 this island had disappeared, leaving only two white sandheads visible on the submerged coral reef.

All the other islands, such as Bawé, Grave Island, and Prison Island, which face the city of Zanzibar, are undergoing the same process of attrition. On the other hand the coral organism is busily at work building up other reefs, which

[1] Crosaland.

may in the course of time be upheaved—not necessarily by volcanic action—and form islands.

It is conjectured that there are other causes at work besides upheaval, to account for the height of the fringing coralline islands above sea-level, one being the lowering of the level of the ocean at some remote geological period. Professor Gardiner estimates this lowering of level to have been about fourteen feet, and to this he attributes the formation of many atoll islands. Crossland points out in this connection, that if the ocean returned to its original level, large areas of the eastern parts of Zanzibar and Pemba Islands would be submerged at high tide.

Hills composed chiefly of coral rock only occur in the north, south, and east of the island, the highest of which is Kidoti Hill in the north-west, 250 feet above the sea-level. The extensive coral plains, so characteristic of the eastern areas of the islands, are composed almost entirely of coral-limestone rock, and their continuity is only broken by a few isolated hills.

The sand and chalk formations lie as a rule above the coral, and form most of the surface of the western areas of both islands. The highest hills of the two islands are of this formation, and attain a maximum height in Zanzibar of 440 feet, and in the sister-island of about 380 feet above sea-level.

Neither Zanzibar nor Pemba is known to contain any minerals or precious stones of commercial value. There is a popular idea current that the sea-beaches contain gemstones. This sounds alluring and romantic, but investigations tend to show that the assumption is incorrect, although moonstones, and non-precious stones and minerals, such as garnets, zircons, quartz, epidote, monazite, are sometimes found. In fact garnets are so numerous in some places as to colour the sands a deep claret-red, while the pretty blue fragments found on the sea-beaches, often supposed by optimists to be sapphires, consist of a valueless mineral called kyanite.

Another product which is found strewn along the coasts of Zanzibar in great profusion, especially on the eastern side of the island, is pumice stone. The existence of this material on the sea-beaches of Zanzibar, and indeed along the whole

East African coast as far south as the Zambesi River, must always be regarded as one of Nature's romances, for it almost certainly originated on the other side of the Indian Ocean in the Sunda Straits between the islands of Java and Sumatra, having been ejected from the bowels of the earth in vast quantities at the titanic eruption of Kraktau in August 1883, and carried westward by the great ocean current which sweeps across the southern portion of the Indian Ocean from Asia to Africa.

Parenthetically it may be observed that it is probable the casuarina trees (*Casuarina equisetifolia*) and the pandanus or screw-pines (*Cycas circinalis*), and possibly even the coco-nut palm, which are found fringing the east coast of Africa and its islands, may have sprung from seeds borne from Sumatra, Java, and the Far East across the Indian Ocean by the same current.

The basic coralline foundation of the western halves of the islands of Zanzibar and Pemba is capped with a mass of soil (composed largely of red clay, sand, and limestone in various stages of modification) which has during the centuries been rounded off and moulded by the agencies of Nature into a diverse surface of undulating ridges and shallow valleys running from north to south.

In certain areas, especially in the eastern portion of Zanzibar Island, the basic limestone formation lies entirely bare, or is covered with a shallow layer of soil. Whether this marked variation in the aspect and topography of the western and eastern areas of Zanzibar Island is due to denudation, or to the fact that the infertile coral country of the east is of more recent geological formation than the hilly and diversified western area, is a question which geologists must decide.

III

The islands of Zanzibar and Pemba comprise about 375,680 acres, and 238,080 acres respectively. Off the western coasts of each island numerous small islets lie scattered, some of which are inhabited.

The western halves of both islands are the most fertile, while the eastern regions are composed largely of bare coral rock sparsely covered with vegetation. The western areas are also the most varied orographically, and it is on this side of the islands that such " hills " as Zanzibar and Pemba can boast of exist. The " hills," it is feared, would make a mountaineer smile, for, as already explained, the highest point of either island does not much exceed 400 feet above the sea.

In Zanzibar the highest ridges run from north to south, at a distance of about three miles from the western coast. In Pemba, especially towards the south of that island, the elevated country rises almost directly from the sea-edge, and the island consequently presents a more imposing appearance than Zanzibar does, when viewed from the sea.

In looking at a map of Zanzibar and Pemba, one feature common to both islands is certain to strike the observer. The eastern coastline, against which the full force of the Indian Ocean—free to Australia—is ever pounding, is far more regular in outline than the western coasts, which face the African continent. Under similar conditions elsewhere, the reverse is the case, and a sea-beaten coast is generally broken and irregular in outline, while that contiguous to a narrow sea is smooth and featureless. The coasts of Ireland exemplify this rule clearly. The reason for the anachronism with regard to Zanzibar and Pemba appears to be twofold.

In the first place the greater force of the wave action on the eastern side of the island has cut down more quickly and effectively all outstanding inequalities of the coast. As a result of this action, a hard coral protecting reef has been left, and on this partially submerged flat the wave power expends its force, while the actual edge of the island is protected. On the western coast this process of demolition is less rapid and less violent, owing to the calm and sheltered waters. The second reason which may be adduced for the reversal of the normal rule with regard to coast erosion, is that on the western side the sea is shallow, and the coral builders are thus enabled to throw out their bastions under favourable conditions, while on the eastern side of both islands the sea is of too great a depth close to the shore for the coral organism to thrive except within narrow limits.

Zanzibar is famous along the African coast for its good drinking water. There are several flowing streams in both islands ; but all are insignificant in volume, and are confined to the western and fertile regions.

One of the largest streams—for none really merit the designation of " river "—is the Mwera, which rises in a swamp in the centre of the island of Zanzibar. After flowing above ground for about five miles, it disappears into the earth, and its subsequent course has not yet been traced.

The spring whence Zanzibar city draws its supply, and from whence the whole of the shipping is supplied, is named " Chem-Chem." It is scarcely half a mile from the sea-beach, and wells up from some unascertained source, forming a pool at the foot of a large tree. Many suppose the water, which is of the highest purity, originates from the African continent thirty miles distant.

The natural porosity of the coralline formation of the islands accounts for the numerous cave-wells, from which a very large proportion of the native population obtain their water supply. Some of these caverns are of quite imposing dimensions, and most of them, according to native belief, are the abodes of jinns and spirits ; and women who go to fetch the household supply of water will only descend together in parties. Strips of calico and broken potsherds will always be found near these cave-wells, being offerings of the village folk to the presiding spirits of the place.

The climate of Zanzibar is of course tropical, but the heat is tempered throughout the year by constant sea-breezes, which blow with great regularity, except during the change of the monsoons. The prevailing trade-wind, between April and September, blows from the S.S.W., and from December until the end of February from the N.N.E. These regular trade-winds have in the past, and indeed at the present time, had a tremendous influence over the fortunes of Zanzibar and the east coast of Africa, for they have enabled systematic trade to be carried on with the most remote ports of the Indian Ocean, and vessels venture forth with the certitude that they will perform the voyage with a favourable breeze in both directions.

The maximum mean temperature for Zanzibar is 85·7°,

and the minimum is 77·1°; while the mean temperatures of Pemba are about five degrees cooler than those of Zanzibar.

The rainy seasons are well defined : the heavy rains occur in April and May, and lighter falls take place in November and December. For the rest of the year the weather is one unbroken series of sunny days. The average annual rainfall for Zanzibar is 52 inches, and in Pemba 60 inches.

The climate is not unhealthy, although the constant high temperature which is experienced without relief through the year makes it necessary for Europeans to seek recuperation in Europe at short intervals. Malaria is generally of a mild type, and blackwater fever is almost unknown.

The population of the Protectorate according to the census of 1910 is 197,199, of whom 117,000 live in Zanzibar and 80,000 in Pemba.[1] There are only about 171 Europeans, of whom 140 are British.[2] Zanzibar City contains 36,000 inhabitants, and is of course by far the largest town in either island. The only other Government stations, which for administrative purposes may be regarded as towns, are Mkokotoni in the northern portion of the island, and Chwaka on the east coast of the island. Gauged by the number of inhabitants, both these stations are little more than villages.

Except for the Swahili quarter of Zanzibar town, there are no large native villages in either island, the natives residing generally in scattered hamlets. The chief towns of Pemba are Chake, an old Portuguese settlement with about 2,000 inhabitants, and Weti with a population of about 700 souls. .

The chief modes of travel within the islands are by donkeys, carts, and motor-cars. There are about eighty miles of first-class metalled roads, all radiating from Zanzibar city in various directions. Besides these, there are many miles of subsidiary district tracks which are used for cart traffic, and the whole system is connected by innumerable native footpaths. Zanzibar possesses a small railway, which is largely used by the natives. It is only seven miles in length, and runs from the city to the village of Bububu.

[1] For details regarding the various races which compose the population of Zanzibar see Chapters XV, XVI, and XVII.
[2] Inclusive of women and children.

The chief agricultural produce grown in Zanzibar and Pemba consists of cloves and coco-nuts, with a considerable quantity of chillies, which have the reputation of being the hottest in the world. Besides these main products of the islands, the native population grows a large quantity of foodstuffs, fruit, tobacco, and other growths for home consumption.

It is curious to notice that in spite of the fertility of the soil, the native crops are not conspicuous for their luxuriance · and to any one who knows the quality of native crops on the mainland, those produced in Zanzibar and Pemba are decidedly poor.

The staple food cultivated by the Zanzibari is *muhogo*—the cassava or manioc root. There are two varieties, the sweet which can be eaten raw, and the poisonous which requires washing and drying in the sun before it is fit for consumption. The latter variety is largely used for cattle fodder. Mubogo is a growth specially adapted to the black man's temperament, for it is a very accommodating crop. It requires very little rain, and a minimum of attention on the part of the cultivator. Being a tuber, neither birds nor locusts can injure it, but on the other hand wild pigs are extremely partial to it.

Mtama or millet (sometimes known as " Kaffir Corn ") is also largely grown, and in a lesser degree rice and maize. Rice was formerly grown in large quantities, especially in Pemba, and a considerable export trade was done in this product, but nowadays a large proportion of the rice consumed is imported from India. There are in Zanzibar and Pemba ideal localities for rice growing, and it is to be regretted that much money is lost to the country by the necessity of importing this cereal.

Maize (Indian corn), which in many parts of Africa is the staff of life, is only grown spasmodically. Its quality is poor, partly owing to unsuitable soil, and partly to improper methods of cultivation : any mainland native fresh from a maize-producing region would ridicule the miserable attenuated cobs produced in Zanzibar. It is generally understood that the Portuguese introduced maize into Africa, but, like the coco-nut and orange, it appears likely that it was an importation of the Arabs or Indians long before the Portuguese ever ventured into the Indian Ocean. Its introduction into the African continent was probably the work of the Indian trader, or his Islamised negro agents, for the Portuguese did little in the way of real colonisation in East Africa. The Swahili name for maize is *muhindi*, which is itself suggestive.'

To the above-mentioned crops may be added ground nuts, sesame (*sim-sim*), yams, sweet potatoes, beans of several varieties, vast numbers of oranges, limes, mangoes, bananas, and other kinds of fruit. Tobacco for native consumption is extensively cultivated, especially in the eastern portions of the island; it is plaited into rolls, and large quantities are exported to Pemba.

Sugar grows well, and was at one time the favourite crop, until the development of clove cultivation during the first half of the nineteenth century induced less interest in its production. When the clove industry had been firmly established, attention was again turned to sugar, and in parts of Zanzibar Island ruined sugar-mills, containing thousands of pounds' worth of valuable, but out-of-date, machinery are to be found. It is rather melancholy to see these relicts of a great enterprise given up to silence and tangled creepers.

Sugar cultivation received its death-blow when slavery was finally abolished. It is of interest to note that Duarte Barbosa mentions that the people of Zanzibar in about A.D. 1512 grew much sugar-cane, but were not acquainted with the process of manufacturing sugar.

All cultivation in the islands is effected by means of the hoe. The use of this primitive implement is justified by the fertile zones of both islands being densely covered with coco-nut, clove, and other trees of economic value, and also to the fact that, except in the richest areas, the coral " rag " is never far from the surface, and indeed often projects from the soil.

On the eastern side of both islands it is really remarkable

---

[1] It may be worthy of note that the Chinyanja—that is the language of the Lake people, spoken by the Bantus of the Nyasa region—for maize is *chimanga*. The word *Manga* in Swahili means " Arabia " or " Arab." May it be surmised that maize was introduced into Zanzibar from India, and into Nyasaland by the Arabs ?

what fine crops are produced on what at first sight appears to be bare rock, but which on closer investigation is seen to be interspersed with small pockets of good soil.

Next to agriculture the most important industry is fishing. Nearly every Swahili is a born sailor, and a staple item of his diet is fish. His preference lies in the direction of shark, and if it is a little high he appears to appreciate it the more. Considerable quantities of dried shark-flesh are imported every year from the Somali coast, and meet with a ready sale.

The dried-shark market in Zanzibar town is one of the localities to be carefully avoided !

CHAPTER II

HISTORICAL : BEFORE THE CHRISTIAN ERA

1

THE history of the Sultanate of Zanzibar may be divided into the following epochs :

1. During the first and second centuries of the Christian Era.
2. The Rise of Islam.
3. The Coming of the Portuguese.
4. The Advent of the English.
5. The Sword of Omân.
6. Seyyid Said's Dream of Empire.
7. The Modern Phase.

These divisions are, it must be admitted, somewhat arbitrary; but it will be seen as our story is unfolded that at intervals during the above periods the obscurity which enshrouds Zanzibar occasionally lightens, and enables us to obtain a glimpse of its fortunes, and of the part it has played in the history of the Eastern World.

The east coast of Africa and the western portion of the Indian Ocean were practically unknown to the nations of Europe until the sixteenth century. The interior of Africa too, remained a more or less closed book down to our own times, and the geographical features of the continent portrayed in the atlases of our grandfathers were really little more than copies of Claudius Ptolemy's maps, which had been compiled in Alexandria in about A.D. 150—

> " When geographers on pathless downs
> Placed elephants instead of towns."

But although Europe remained blissfully ignorant of these regions until so recent a period, it must not be assumed that others were equally so. As a matter of fact, we shall be able to produce sufficient evidence to prove that at the commencement of the Christian era, so far from the east coast of Africa (at any rate as far south as Zanzibar) being in the grip of an undeveloped and primeval Nature, a steady and systematic trade existed along its littoral, in which the leading nations of the Eastern World participated; that a series of trading stations, and at least some form of colonial organisation existed on the coast; that the coco-nut palm had found its way to Africa; and that there was already a steady demand in the Far East for African ivory and other local produce.

No matter in which epoch of history the name of Zanzibar appears, we find the island closely connected with the history of Arabia. As it was during the first century of the Christian era, when the east African coast and its islands were under the sway of the ancient kingdoms of South-Western Arabia, so it is to-day, when we find seated on the throne of modern Zanzibar a prince descended from the line of those ancient dynasties, which include such names as Joktan, Hazarmaveth, Jerah, Sheba, Ophir,[1] Saba and Himyar.

The descendants of Joktan (the Arabised form of the name is Kahtan) in about 1800 B.C. entered and conquered South Arabia from the Cushite Adites. Hazarmaveth governed and gave his name to the kingdom of Hadramaut, while his brother Jerah (of which the Arab form is Yarub) was the grandfather of Saba, the founder of the great Sabæan kingdom, and builder of the royal city of Marib or Seba[2] in South-Western Arabia.

Descendants of this royal stock migrated eastward and populated the kingdom of Omân, and out of Omân in due season came the ruler and the Arabs who inhabit Zanzibar to-day.

It can justly be asserted that the past histories of those

[1] *Vide* Genesis x. 26, 28, 29. ". . . and Joktan begat . . . Hazarmaveth and Jerah . . . and Sheba and Ophir and Havilah . . ."
[2] Identical with the Sheba of the Bible. (Professor E. Palmer in his translation of the Koran.)

hoary principalities of Saba and Omân are in a measure the history of Zanzibar.

To fully appreciate the affinity it must be remembered that the people of Saba were the great trade intermediaries of the ancient world. They controlled the trade-routes, both on sea and land, which connected the Eastern and the Western worlds. They were likewise a great maritime nation, and what the Phœnicians were to the Mediterranean and western ocean, the Sabæans were to the eastern seas.

To their ports came the wealth of the East, and to these trade-emporia resorted those who wished to purchase or barter merchandise of every kind, even as the Phœnician sailors of King Hiram—". . . came to Ophir and fetched from thence gold, 420 talents, and brought it to King Solomon. . . "

The ancient kingdoms of Southern Arabia, besides controlling the sea-routes long prior to the Christian era, possessed another source of prosperity and wealth within their own borders. This was the almost complete monopoly in the supply of frankincense and myrrh. The demand for these aromatic gums was enormous in the ancient world, and every nation regarded with jealous eye the Incense Country on the Hadramaut coast, situated a few miles westward of the modern Kuria Muria Islands, and in the region contiguous to the Plain of Dhofar.

> " . . . at sea north-east winds blow
> Sabean odours from the spicy shore
> Of Araby the Blest.   "
>
> *Paradise Lost.*

Sheba or Saba in South Arabia was the emporium for the whole spice-trade. The frequent references in the Bible to Ophir and Sheba clearly indicate the prosperity of these Arabian principalities, which were ruled by the descendants of Joktan, and the ancestors of the Kings of Omân and of the Sultans of Zanzibar.

The Biblical records of the great wealth of these South Arab States are confirmed, and indeed amplified, by the Assyrian inscriptions dated about 700 B.C. By the seventh century before Christ the Sabæans were supreme in Arabia, and dominated not only the sea-trade of the East, but also that of the African coast as well.

The Sabæan and other South Arabian States are referred to by the Greek historians in about the third century B.C. Agatharcides (120 B.C.) comments on the wealth and prosperity of the Sabæans, and somewhat later Artemidorus (100 B.C.) does the same.

Now, the above references dealing with the pre-eminence, the antiquity, and the prosperity of these ancient kingdoms of South Arabia emphasise the fact that for centuries preceding the birth of Christ they were the dominant factors and the great maritime power of the eastern seas. They possessed the monopoly of the incense trade, and much of the carrying-trade of the East was in their hands. The gold from Africa, the slaves, the tortoise-shell, the ebony, and above all the ivory were commodities which the empires of the ancient world demanded in increasing quantities, and these Great Powers—Egypt, Assyria, Chaldea, Iran, Rome, and Byzantium—few of which, strangely enough, possessed any great affinity for the sea—were almost entirely dependent on the maritime nations of South Arabia for the supply of these luxuries.

This being the case, it is inconceivable that the Sabæan merchants and sailors did not extend their commercial enterprises and trade down the east coast of Africa, and to Zanzibar, long before the Christian era.

Zanzibar, the " Menouthias " of the ancient Greek geographers, was, of course, well within the range of Arabian seamen even as it is to-day, and it is highly improbable that during the centuries before Christ, when the Sabæan kingdom was at the zenith of its prosperity and fame, these Arab sailors and merchants had not penetrated to Zanzibar, and laid the foundation of that traditional right to the island, and the adjacent continental coastline, which exists, and is indeed confirmed by actual occupation of their descendants, to-day.

The journey from Omân and from Aden, the chief port of ancient Saba, to Zanzibar and Sofala,[1] was nothing to those

---

[1] The reader will no doubt recall Milton's pregnant line, " Sophala thought Ophir."

sailors of Sheba, any more than it is to their descendants in modern times.

At the present time, directly the north-east trade-winds set in at the commencement of each year, hundreds of picturesque Arab and Persian craft—differing no doubt but little from those of ancient times—set sail, and make their way across the Indian Ocean and along the African coast to Zanzibar.

The journey of over 2,000 miles is little thought of by these hardy Arabs—descendants of the Sabæan sailor of Queen Sheba's time. These vessels hail from almost every port on the Arabian coast, between the Red Sea and the shores of India, and their crews, aggregating in Zanzibar during the height of the dhow season some 3,000 to 4,000 souls, are often of the wildest and most romantic aspect.

On arrival at Zanzibar, they don their best clothes, and roam about the streets of the city decked in coloured silks, with silver-handled swords and daggers in their sashes.   If they dared, they would probably be pirates or slave dealers, but while in Zanzibar they are content to be simple traders, and exchange their dates, spices, coffee, prayer-rugs, antique copper-ware, and dried shark's-flesh for wheat-flour, rice, millet, building timber, calico and other articles of Western manufacture.

By the end of March the south wind begins to blow once more, and in a few days this phantasmagoria of the unknown East, these materialised visions of ancient Sheba, hoist their tapering yards, unfurl their sails to the favouring breeze, and vanish with their ships over the northern horizon, homeward bound to " Araby the Blest " 1

CHAPTER III

-

AMONG the many eminent geographers of ancient times Claudius Ptolemæus (or as he is generally called Claudius Ptolemy) specially appeals to all who are interested in the past history of Eastern Africa and its coast. To him the world is indebted not only for his profound theories regarding the Universe, as expounded in the Ptolemaic System, but for many works on astronomy, and for a series of geographical studies and maps of the world of his day, which include itineraries of the coasts of the continent of Africa.

The knowledge regarding Africa and the sources of the Nile had been greatly extended during the first century of the Christian era, and maps and itineraries of the coasts and interior as far south as the latitude of Zanzibar had been compiled during his lifetime.

In addition to the geographical researches of this philosopher and his predecessors, there has been preserved to us another work of exceptional interest, which affords detailed information concerning the commerce and trade-routes of the Indian Ocean and the countries contiguous thereto, and further includes references to the towns and islands of the east African coasts.

This book is known as the *Periplus of the Erythræan Sea*,[1] or in other words *A Directory of the Indian Ocean*. The name of the author is unknown, but it is generally assumed that he was an Egyptian-Greek, who may have resided at Berenice,

[1] The Erythræan Sea was a name which comprised the Red Sea, the Indian Ocean, and the Persian Gulf.

a seaport on the Egyptian coast of the Red Sea. The *Periplus* is believed to have been written about A.D. 60.

We find, then, that we are in the happy position of being able to refer to two undoubtedly authentic works dealing, *inter alia*, with East Africa, viz. a commercial directory in the form of the *Periplus of the Erythraean Sea*, written about A.D. 60; and the maps and works compiled by the great Alexandrian astronomer Claudius Ptolemy in about A.D. 140.

The general scope of the *Periplus* comprises a list of the ports (with their respective exports and imports) touched at in the journey from the port of Myos-hormus on the Red Sea to the Persian Gulf, to India, and to Zanzibar. Each succeeding port is described in turn, and the list includes Berenice, whence goods were transported overland to the Nile in eleven days; Ptolemais, identified with the modern Port Sudan; Adulis, corresponding to the present Massowa and Avalites, the modern Zeila in Somaliland. In like manner all the ports on the south coast of Arabia are described, as also are the chief harbours of the Persian Gulf, the numerous ports and cities situated on the coasts of Hindustan and Ceylon, and in less detail the countries and commerce of the Far East as far as the land of Ts'in (China). With the ports of Asia we are not in the present instance concerned, and so we shall confine our attention to the description of the African coast which extends southward from Cape Guardafui, or, as Ptolemy and the other ancient geographers named it, " Promontorium Aromata " or the " Cape of Spices."

II

Starting from the Cape of Spices we will now follow the itinerary along the east coast of Africa as recorded by the author of the *Periplus*, and give *in extenso* that portion of the text which refers in any way to Azania or Zanzibar.[1]

[1] The translation used is that by Wilfred H. Schoff in his *Periplus of the Erythraean Sea* (Longmans, Green & Co. 1912). I am also indebted to him for many of his annotations of the text.

The interest of the extracts will be enhanced if the reader bears in mind that this guide-book to the east African coast was written more than 1,800 years ago.

" Beyond this place, the coast trending towards the south, there is the Market and Cape of Spices,[1] an abrupt promontory at the very end of the Berber coast towards the east.

" The anchorage is dangerous at times from the ground-swell, because the place is exposed to the north. A sign of approaching storm, which is peculiar to the place, is that the deep water becomes more turbid, and changes its colour. When this happens they run to a large promontory called Tabæ, which offers safe shelter. There are imported into this market the things already mentioned ; and there are produced in it, cinnamon . . . and frankincense.

" Beyond Tabæ, after 400 stadia,[2] there is the village of Pano.[3] And then after sailing 400 stadia along a promontory, towards which place the current also draws you, there is another market town called Opone [4] into which the same things are imported as those already mentioned,[5] and in it the greatest quantity of cinnamon is produced, and slaves of the better sort, which are brought to Egypt in increasing numbers ; and a great quantity of tortoise-shell, better than that found elsewhere.

" The voyage to all these market-towns is made from Egypt about the month of July, that is Epiphi. And ships are also customarily fitted out from the places across this sea from Ariaca and Barygaza,[6], bringing to these market towns the products of their own places : wheat, rice, clarified butter, sesame oil, cotton cloth, girdles, and honey from the reed called sacchari.[7] Some make the voyage especially

---

[1] Cape Guardafui.
[2] Ten stadia may be reckoned as equal to one English mile.
[3] Identified as Ras Binna, 11° 12′ N., 51° 7′ E.
[4] Generally identified with Ras Hafun.
[5] Among the articles mentioned by the author of the *Periplus* are : flint-glass, dressed cloth, wheat, tin, tunics, cloaks from Arsinoe (Suez), drinking cups, sheets of copper, iron, etc.
[6] This is the north-west coast of India around the Gulf of Cambay, the modern Cutch, Kathiawar, and Gujerat. Barygaza is the modern Broach on the Gulf of Cambay.
[7] Sugar, probably the Indian *jagri.*

to these market towns, and others exchange their cargoes while sailing along the coast.[1]

" This country is not subject to a king, but each market-town is ruled by its separate chief.

" Beyond Opone, the shore trending more towards the south, first there are the small and great bluffs of Azania ; this coast is destitute of harbours, but there are places where ships can lie at anchor, the shore being abrupt ; and this course is of six days, the direction being south-west.

" Then come the small and great beach for another six days' course, and after that in order the Courses of Azania, the first being called Serapion,[2] and the next Nicon[3] ; and after that several rivers and other anchorages, one after the other, separately a rest and a run for each day, seven in all, until the Pyralaæ Islands,[4] and what is called the ' channel '; beyond which, a little to the south of south-west, after two courses of a day and night along the Ausanitic coast, is the ISLAND OF MENOUTHIAS, about 300 stadia from the mainland, low and wooded, in which there are rivers, and many kinds of birds, and the mountain tortoise.

" There are no wild beasts except the crocodiles : but there they do not attack men.   In this place there are sewed boats, and canoes hollowed from single logs, which they use for fishing and catching tortoise.   In this island they also catch them in a peculiar way, in wicker baskets, which they fasten across the channel opening between the breakers.

" Along this coast live men of piratical habits, very great of stature, and under separate chiefs for each place.

" The Mapharitic Chief governs it under some ancient right, that subjects it (the coast) to the sovereignty of the State that is become first in Arabia.[5]   And the people of Muza[6] now hold it under his authority, and send thither

---

[1] Just as they do at the present day.
[2] Generally identified with Mogdishu.
[3] Probably the town of Brawa.
[4] Almost unanimously identified by experts as the islands of Patta, Manda, and Lamu, owing to the Lamu "channel," which is a protected waterway running on the land side of the group of islands in question.
[5] The Himyarite Kingdom, which at the period of the *Periplus* had subdued the Kingdom oi Saba.
[6] The modern town of Mocha in Arabia.

many large ships ; using Arab captains and agents, who are familiar with the natives and intermarry with them, and who know the whole coast and understand the language.

" There are imported into these markets the lances made at Muza especially for this trade, and hatchets and daggers and awls, and various kinds of glass ; and at some places a little wine and wheat, not for trade, but to serve for getting the good-will of the savages.   There are exported from these places a great quantity of ivory, but inferior to that of Adulis,[1] and rhinoceros-horn and tortoise-shell (which is in best demand after that from India), and a little palm-oil.[2]

" And these markets of Azania are the very last of the continent that stretches down on the right hand from Berenice ; for beyond these places the unexplored ocean curves round towards the west, and running along by the regions to the south of Aethiopia and Libya and Africa, it mingles with the western sea."

The interest of the above extract from this ancient work of the first century lies for us chiefly in the references to the island of " Menouthias," and to the trade conditions and existence of towns on the Azanian coast.

It may be remarked at once that although considerable doubt exists as to the identity of many of the places mentioned in the *Periplus*, there is practically unanimity that " Menouthias " is Zanzibar Island.   The identification of the places referred to in the *Periplus*, and in the maps of Ptolemy, has been of course a subject of discussion ever since interest in the Dark Continent revived in the nineteenth century. Hundreds of volumes have been written on the subject, and the whole question has been critically reviewed by experts, so we shall be in safe company if we accept the general opinion subscribed to by such geographers (to name but a few) as D'Anville, Vincent, de Forberville, Guillain,

---

[1] The modern Massowah on the Red Sea.

[2] From a note by the translator it is evident that by " palm-oil " he means " coco-nut oil."   He points out that the word in the text, *nauplios*, is corrected to *margilios*, which is the Sanscrit *narikela*, Prakrit *nargil*—coco-nut ; and " the appearance of the word on the Zanzibar coast is of course a confirmation of Indian trade there," viz. during the first century of the Christian era. (See Lassen, *op. cit.* I. 267.)   This "palm-oil" was from *cocos nucifera*—the coco-nut palm.

Schlichter, Markham, and Burton, that the " Menouthias " of the *Periplus* can fairly be identified with the modern island of Zanzibar.

Other geographers not quite so specific in their decision are ready to agree that Menouthias must be either Zanzibar, Pemba, or Mafia Island.

It will be observed that the distance of Menouthias from the mainland is given in the *Periplus* as about 300 stadia.[1] This may be taken as representing about thirty English miles, and makes it fairly clear that Mafia Island, which is only ten miles from the mainland, cannot be meant. Zanzibar, on the other hand, is not less than twenty-five miles, while Pemba Island is about thirty-five miles from the African coast.

The general description of the island as " low and wooded " might in truth apply to both Pemba and Zanzibar. The latter island as a matter of fact gives the impression of being of less elevation than the former. This is the experience of all who visit both islands, and a visitor from Zanzibar would be inclined to refer to Pemba as " hilly."

We are next told that " there are rivers " : this is true of both islands, but the Zanzibar rivers are certainly more apparent than those of the sister island. There are a number of insignificant rivulets in Pemba, but they are concealed in thickly verdured and deep valleys, and are generally difficult to come to. Many of the streams of Zanzibar, on the other hand, debouch on to the sea-beach.

Zanzibar is famous for its drinking water at the present day, which is supplied in increasing quantities to the shipping which resorts thither for that purpose. It is easily the best water on the east coast of Africa.

The next detail mentioned in the *Periplus* is that there are many kinds of birds in Menouthias. This is a fact as regards Zanzibar, but there are possibly just as many in Pemba, Mafia, and elsewhere, so the information is of too

---

[1] Schoff, whose translation has been used above, points out that three different stadia were in use in the Roman world at the time the *Periplus* was compiled, viz. the Philiterian, 525 to the degree ; the Olympic of 600 ; and that of Eratosthenes of 700. He considers that the last standard has been used in the *Periplus*, and that ten stadia may be taken to represent an English statute mile.

general a character to warrant any deduction being made. The next piece of information is that the " mountain tortoise " exists on the island. There are no such reptiles in Zanzibar at the present date, and no record that any ever existed. The giant tortoise (*Testudo granvieri*) of Madagascar has only become extinct in comparatively recent times, so it is possible that a similar disappearance may very well have occurred in Zanzibar since the author of the *Periplus* visited Menouthias. The small land-tortoise is, however, found in Pemba and Mafia at the present day

" There are no wild beasts, except crocodiles which do not attack men." With regard to this statement, there are wild beasts in Zanzibar, in the form of a few leopards, which confine themselves to the bush-covered coral-country on the east side of the island. That they were more numerous or more widely spread than now, appears likely.

In Pemba there are not known to be any wild animals, except serval cats, and ground vermin such as ferrets, etc.

There are no crocodiles at the present day in either island, although inasmuch as the Zanzibar leopards and other fauna are a legacy derived from the period when Zanzibar was joined to the mainland, so too crocodiles might similarly have been left behind.[1] The fact mentioned in the *Periplus* that the Zanzibar crocodiles were harmless to man, points to the possibility that the author did not refer to the true crocodile, but to the iguana, or giant lizard (*Varamis niloticus,* family Varanidæ), which attain a length of over five feet, and are innocuous to man. They are widely distributed throughout Africa, and exist to-day in Zanzibar.

" In this place there are sewed boats, and canoes hollowed out of single logs." The " sewed boats " of Menouthias are, as pointed out by Burton and others, the native craft known locally as *mitepe*, which ply to-day along the East African coast.

[1] Since the above was penned, a crocodile has been shot on the sea-beach at Chwaka on the east coast of Zanzibar. It was eight feet in length, and was found hiding in a coral cave on the sea-shore. Its tracks led from the sea, and on being cut open there were no signs of food in its stomach. Whence it came has never been discovered, but it is supposed that it was washed over from the mainland. It is on record that a hippopotamus found its way to Zanzibar from the mainland. (*Vide* article on Zanzibar in the *Encyclopædia Britannica*.)

Bishop Steere, of the Universities Mission to Central Africa, thus describes them in his handbook of the Swahili language (1870):

" *Mtepe* (plural, *mitepe*), a kind of dhow or native craft belonging chiefly to Lamu and the coast near it. *Mitepe* are sharp at the bows and stern, with a head shaped to imitate a camel's head, ornamented with paintings and tassels and little streamers. They carry one large square mat sail, and have always a white streamer or pennant at the masthead : their planking is sewn together, and they are built broad and shallow."

Burton's description written in 1857 shows that the *mtepe* " is pegged together, not nailed " ; " the sail is of matting." " The stern is long and projecting, and the swan-throat of the arched prow is necklaced with strips of hide and bunches of talismans. It bears a red head, and the latter as on the Ark of Osiris and the Chinese junk has the round eye painted white." [1]

The *mitepe* are nowadays most frequently seen in Lamu waters, but it is evident that until comparatively recent times they were the common type of vessel both in Zanzibar

---

[1] Burton and Stuhlmann may be correct in identifying the *mtepe* as " the lineal descendant of the sewed boats " of the *Periplus*, and therefore of great antiquity, but they were apparently unaware of the full significance of the camel-shaped prow and the ornaments which make this particular style of vessel so unique. If for no other purpose than to preserve a record of the meaning of the decorations, a brief reference may be made here to these features. Steere is correct in identifying the prow with a camel's head, and the design commemorates, according to Arab belief, the she-camel which, as is narrated in the Koran, was sent from heaven to the Thamud, an ancient Arabian tribe, which, in spite of this sign, refused to accept this divine token and killed it.

The " eye " is of course the camel's eye, and the red colour perpetuates the slaughter of the animal at the hands of the impious Arabs. The tassels which hang pendent from the prow represent those of the camel's rein and the head-stall. All *mitepe* fly three flags on the masthead. The white pennant is the flag of a certain ancient Persian Sultan named Ali, who lived at Shangaya on the east African coast. It is possible that this potentate may be identical with one of the earliest settlers from Shiraz in the tenth century. Below the white pennant is flown an enormously long streamer, known as *utakataka*. Under the streamer is flown the red flag of the Sultans of Shangaya, in ancient times the capital of the Persian settlements on the Azanian coast. The small white pennants on the prow represent, it is said, the sons of the Sultan Ali of Shangaya.

The above references to Sultan Ali are full of interest, for, as will be seen in subsequent chapters of this book, the tradition exists that he was the founder of the great State of Kilwa in the tenth century.

and on the neighbouring coast as far south as Mafia. A
good number still visit Zanzibar during the north-east monsoon, and bring cattle, salt, and other produce from Lamu
and Kismayu. They sail remarkably well close-hauled, and
the huge mat sail is managed most deftly by the crew.

Odd beliefs still centre round the modern *mtepe*. For
instance, no *mtepe* will carry a cargo of coco-nuts. Inquiries
as to the reason of this ban only engender a vague explanation
to the effect that as the planks are tied together with coir
fibre, a cargo of coco-nuts tends to force open the seams of
the boat and make it leak. Some deep-founded superstition
is probably at the bottom of this peculiar aversion to carry
coco-nuts in this style of craft.

Professor Franz Stuhlmann in his *Handwerk und Industrie
in Ostafrika* (Hamburg, 1910) also identifies the "sewn
boats" of the *Periplus* with the *mtepe*, which he considers
originally came from the coast of Arabia, "the land of spices
with its old trade-centres."

Canoes "hollowed out of single logs" are universally
employed throughout tropical Africa. Those at Zanzibar
are hewn from the trunk of mango trees, are fitted with outriggers on both sides, and carry a single mast and a large
triangular sail. Though frail in appearance they are wonderful sea-boats and very fast. They are largely employed in
fishing and catching turtle. When they become soaked with
salt water or overgrown with seaweed, the natives light a fire
of palm fronds under them to dry and harden the wood.

"In this island they also catch them [fish] in a peculiar
way, in wicker baskets, which they fasten across the channel
opening between the breakers."

Fish-traps are of course in common use throughout the
world, but it would seem that the Zanzibar native and
the Swahili of the neighbouring coast use a fish-trap of a
somewhat novel form. The native name of this trap is
dema. Its method of use is precisely as stated in the *Periplus*.
The *dema* is an open-work flat wicker basket of pentagonal
form about 6½ feet high, and 14 inches in thickness. A hole
cunningly wrought to prevent the imprisoned fish from
escaping is made in the centre of one of the sides.

The basket is weighted with stones tied to the outside,

and after being baited with remnants of fish or with a variety of grass-green seaweed which is collected on the rocks at low tide, it is sunk either in deep water or in the channels which are covered at high tide. The *dema* is largely used in Zanzibar, and every fisherman's hut has one or more leaning against the wall, but its use is not confined at the present day to Zanzibar or Pemba.

This ends the actual reference to the island of Menouthias in the *Periplus*, and we proceed now to briefly consider the identity of the lost city of Rhapta, and other points connected with the trade and political status of the Azanian coast as disclosed to us by the author of that work.

III

After describing the island of Menouthias, the author of the *Periplus* makes the following statement :

" Two days' sail beyond, there lies the very last market-town of the continent of Azania, which is called Rhapta."

The location of this town has been the subject of much discussion.

If Menouthias is really Zanzibar, then Rhapta would have been situated on the delta of the Rufiji River. If Pemba is taken as representing Menouthias, then Pangani would reasonably represent the site of the lost town. Opinions appear equally divided as to the site of the ancient Rhapta, but the Rufiji and the Pangani localities are generally considered the most likely.

The author of the *Periplus* explains that the place received its name [1] from the " sewed boats " (*rhapton ploiarion*) which were apparently built there. At the present time, as already stated, Lamu to the north of Mombasa is the town where the *mtepe*—" the lineal descendant " as Burton terms it, of the *rhapton ploiarion* of the *Periplus*—is built.

The itineraries of Claudius Ptolemy, which show the geography of the Azanian coast some eighty years later than the *Periplus*, mark Rhapta as situated to the north-west of Menouthias. The place appears situated some miles

[1] From the Arabic : *rabta* = to bind (Glaser).

up a river of similar name, which has its sources in the eastern ranges of the "Mountains of the Moon." Sir Clements Markham, who considered that Ptolemy undoubtedly obtained his information of the region from the Greek merchants who went from Arabia to Rhapta and Zanzibar, says :

" It seems clear to me that Rhapta is correctly placed on the River Pangani, and the snow-clad mountain of which Ptolemy had evidently heard is the mountain whence the Rhaptus River flows—that is Kilimanjaro." [1]

In any case Rhapta is a lost town. Possibly its ruins lie fathoms deep beneath the alluvial soil of one of the Azanian rivers opposite Zanzibar, or traces of its quays and turreted walls—for it was surely fortified to keep out wild beasts and *anthropophagi*—may still await discovery up some forgotten creek. The number of ruined towns—all unexplored—on the Azanian coast are so numerous, as to make it possible that some signs of Rhapta may yet be found.

To return once more to the *Periplus*. The author is quite specific as to the imports and exports of Menouthias, Rhapta, and the Azanian littoral. The first item consists of spear-heads made at Mocha especially for the African trade. These and the axes and knives were used, no doubt, not only to barter with the natives of the mainland for ivory, tortoise-shell, and rhinoceros horns, but also to arm the hunting parties which killed the elephants. For it is clear that ivory was the main desideratum of the Rhapta trader.

The observation that wine was imported at some of the places " to get the goodwill of the savages " has quite a modern touch, and it is evident that the influence of the gin-bottle over the African chief was as potent 1900 years ago as it is in certain parts of Africa to-day l

One of the most interesting items in the list of exports from Azania is that of coco-nut oil, for it is clear that not only were coco-nuts flourishing on the coast at the commencement of the Christian era, but it almost certainly indicates that a connection existed—even as it does to-day—between India, where the coco-nut palm originated, and Zanzibar and the East Coast of Africa.

Personally I feel it fairly safe to assume that the bartering

[1] From *Journal of the Royal Geographical Society.*

and purchase of ivory, tortoise-shell, and other merchandise at Rhapta was in the hands of the Indian merchant, while the Arabs confined themselves to the shipping of the goods to and from their destinations.

One of the most important items of information accorded us in the *Periplus* regarding Azania during the first century now remains to be considered.

The *Periplus* tells us that—

" The Mapharitic Chief governs it [viz. the East Coast of Africa] under some ancient right that subjects it to the sovereignty of the State that is become first in Arabia. And the people of Muza [Mocha] now hold it under his authority, and send thither [to Azania] many large ships : using Arab captains and agents, who are familiar with the natives and intermarry with them, and who know the whole coast and understand the language."

Here in a few sentences is disclosed the political status during the first century of the trade settlements which stretched along the African coast from Cape Guardafui to Menouthias and Rhapta.

We see at once that the trade and markets which existed in the neighbourhood of Zanzibar were no mere spasmodic undertakings of a few hardy adventurers, but a definite colonial enterprise of one of the great nations of Southern Arabia. This fact is most interesting, and enables us to realise how intimate and prolonged, through a period of 1,900 years at least, has been the hold of the Southern Arab on Zanzibar and East Africa.

The association of the sheikh or chief of Mapharite with Azania is made clear by a further reference of the author of the *Periplus* when writing about the island of Socotra. He explains that " just as Azania is subject to Charibael and the chief of Mapharitis," so Socotra was under the domination of the king of the Hadramaut. Charibael was the king and supreme head of the Himyarite kingdom : the province of Ma'afir (or Mapharitis) was a part of his dominions. By an " ancient right "—ancient, let it be remembered, in the first century of the Christian era—the chief of Ma'afir had the control of the Azanian coast, and at the time of the *Periplus* this right had evidently been leased to the merchants of

Muza, who, as we have already seen, used to send " many big ships " to Menouthias and Rhapta for trading purposes.

The author of the *Periplus* in describing this town of Muza refers to it as being without a harbour, but with a good roadstead. The place is described as " crowded with Arab ship-owners and sea-faring men, and busy with the affairs of commerce " It is also specifically stated that the people of Muza carried on trade with the African coast and with Barygaza (the modern Broach on the Gulf of Cutch).

Muza was the chief port of the province of Ma'afir. The city of Zafar, one hundred miles inland to the north-east of Muza, was the capital of the Himyarite kingdom, and King Charibael, who resided there, had by means of embassies and gifts some intercourse with the Emperors Claudius and Nero in Rome.

There is no doubt that the trade connection and the political association between South Arabia, Zanzibar, and the coastal lands of East Africa existed at the commencement of the Christian era, and there is every probability that for a long period—perhaps centuries—anterior to that epoch commercial intercourse prevailed between these countries, as is indicated by the observation in the *Periplus* concerning the *ancient* right which the sheikh of Ma'afir claimed over Azania and Menouthias.

The remark in the *Periplus* as to the intercourse which then existed between the Arabs and the natives of Azania, and the intermarriage of these two races, is full of interest, for it indicates the period of the genesis of the Swahili race.

CHAPTER IV

HISTORICAL : THE RISE OF ISLAM

I

In the preceding chapters I have endeavoured to demonstrate that during the early years of the world's history, the association of the East African coast (or, as I prefer to call it, Azania), as far south as Zanzibar, with Southern Arabia had been an intimate one, both in a commercial and in a political sense : and it is safe to assume that changes which affected the welfare and prosperity of the parent-state in Arabia, made themselves felt in her African dependencies.

The Himyarite kingdom, which comprised the adjoining kingdom of Saba, was still flourishing at the commencement of the Christian era, and indeed it continued as an independent political entity until the sixth century of that epoch, although it is evident that shortly after the period dealt with in the *Periplus* its pre-eminence began to decline, and the indispensability of its services as a commercial intermediary with other nations became less pronounced.

There were several reasons for this. In the first place, the Roman Empire had pushed its mercantile marine into the eastern seas, and traded directly with India and the East without the mediation of the Sabæan middleman. This change was largely due to the discovery, as related in a previous chapter, by a Roman navigator named Hippalus, of the periodicity of the monsoons in the Indian Ocean—a natural phenomenon which for their own purposes appears to have been kept secret by the South Arabian traders. Egypt too, being a Roman province, made it possible for the Romans to navigate the Red Sea, and to deliver merchandise destined for Rome at Egyptian ports without having recourse to the caravan routes which traversed Arabia ; and moreover the rise of the Roman Power and the consequent development of Europe tended not only to render the old trade routes formerly controlled by the South Arabians obsolete, but to require the opening up of subsidiary lines of supply in other regions.

A domestic affliction likewise overtook the Sabæan and Himyarite States, and to this the Arab historians generally attribute the weakening of the Arabian influence in the world's commercial enterprises. This catastrophe was the destruction of the great dyke and dam of Marib,[1] the royal capital of unknown antiquity of the Queen of Sheba.

This work is reputed to have been commenced by Saba the Great, several centuries prior to the Christian era, and on its efficacy, as a means of irrigation, the welfare of the whole region of South-West Arabia largely depended.

The destruction of this reservoir or barrage seriously affected the interior economy of the country, and eventually caused the abandonment of Marib itself. With the decline of prosperity consequent on diminished trade, the inhabitants began to scatter, some emigrating as far north as Syria, while others found homes in Omân or settled in Azania.

There can be little doubt but that the weakening of South Arabian States adversely affected their trading enterprise on the Azanian coast, although the insistent demand throughout the world for ivory and slaves makes it appear probable that trade in the Azanian Seas never really ceased : and it may safely be conjectured that as the Arab and Greek traders from the Red Sea and Egypt loosened their grip on Zanzibar and Azania, the Indian merchant stepped in and filled the vacancy.

It must be admitted, however, that from the period dealt with in the *Periplus of the Erythræan Sea* until the seventh century, information as to what was happening at Zanzibar and on the neighbouring coasts is of the scantiest.

---

[1] The destruction of the dyke at Marib is an historical event which occurred during the first or second century of the Christian era. The incident is moreover mentioned in the Koran, and is referred to by Mahomed as a divine punishment of the people of Marib or Sheba for their wickedness and covetousness.

The disintegration of the South Arabian States in the sixth century was, however, followed by a profound and tremendous change in the political situation of Arabia, which materially affected her position in the comity of nations.

In about A.D. 622 the Arabian people were moulded and unified into a world-power, under the stimulus of the Islamic Revelation, and for 130 years after Mahomed's death they remained the predominant factor in the Moslem world.

The results which followed the awakening of Arabia are too well known to need reiteration here; suffice it to say that the effect on Africa was of far-reaching import and, as we realise to-day, of a permanent character.

With the invasion of Africa by the Arab hosts, the real history of the Dark Continent may be said to have commenced. The whole of the northern parts of the continent quickly came under their sway, and the influence of Islam westward and southward has never ceased to extend up to the present.

In A.D. 640 Egypt was conquered by the Arabs, and by A.D. 711 the whole of the Mediterranean littoral had succumbed to their arms. This was not, of course, the sum of their success. The conquest of Syria, Persia, Assyria, and the invasion of Europe are matters of history, and had the followers of Mahomed remained united, it is difficult to say where their domination would have ended.

Dissensions, however, arose among them, even as Mahomed himself had foretold, and it was not long before the once irresistible solidarity of Islam was undermined by schisms and disagreements within its ranks.

As already related, the zeal of the Arab was at first the impulse which led Islam to victory, but the revolt of the Shia and Persian Moslems, who maintain that the Caliphate belongs to Ali and his descendants, led to the transfer of the balance of power to Persia : and Baghdad became the capital of the Abbasid Caliphs. This was the Golden Age of Islam, and it culminated in the glorious reign of Haroun-al-Raschid (A.D. 786–809), known throughout the Western world from the references to him in *The Arabian Nights' Entertainments.*

The persecution and unrest resulting from these internecine struggles among the several factions of the Moslem world in Asia caused many to emigrate and seek peace and new homes away from the scenes of strife.

It is easy to appreciate the reasons which induced the people of Western Asia to turn their faces towards East Africa. In the first place Azania was the America of Asia. It was within easy distance of Arabia, and for centuries the dwellers of Arabia and Persia must have regarded it as a Land of Promise—a land of flowing rivers and abundant crops, the source of gold, of slaves, of ivory : a place where the poorest might live in comfort. For centuries had the Arabian and Shirazian people seen their trading vessels return with each succeeding monsoon, deep laden with the produce of Africa, and no doubt the tales brought by sailors concerning these seas and lands assisted to generate in the Arab mind the idea that the Azanian coast was an El Dorado to all who dared to venture there.

Small wonder, then, that both Persians and Arabs in times of stress turned covetous eyes to the rich and placid region which stretched southward so temptingly from the Horn of Africa.

That there were penalties and dangers to be encountered and overcome did not deter the immigrants. The warlike Arab was well able to overcome the indigenous negro population, but the death-rate of the settlers must have been terrible, for they could not have coped with similar ease with the malarial poison of the mangrove creeks.

It is to be noted that the earliest Arab and Shirazian settlements in East Africa were almost invariably on islets lying off the mainland, and such sites no doubt greatly reduced the death-rate of the immigrants, although it cannot be supposed that they were chosen for hygienic reasons. Those Arab and Persian colonists who survived the first year's exposure to the African climate no doubt became inured to its influences, and this immunity was no doubt enhanced in subsequent generations by the intermarriage of the new-comers with the aboriginal populations.

In spite, therefore, of the dangers which residence in the Land of Promise entailed, it is not difficult to realise the readiness, and perhaps the eagerness, with which the victims of some conqueror or of some new religious movement, in Western Asia, turned their faces southward, and undertook the journey to Africa, whither a favourable north-east monsoon would carry them in two or three weeks.

It is a mistake, however, to imagine that these incursions of immigrants from Asia to the East African coasts were on the scale of the exodus of the children of Israel from Egypt.

The specific instances of immigration which are historically on record are very limited in number, but reference to them by authors often engenders the idea that the existence of Arab and Persian sultanates and principalities along the East African coast was the immediate consequence of the few specific instances of immigration which have been noted in Arab records. There appears to be no justification for any such conclusion. Specific persecutions and wars in Western Asia no doubt stimulated emigration to Africa from the particular regions affected, but the building up of Arab and Persian principalities and communities on the east coast during the late Middle Ages was a matter of centuries rather than the result of two or three spasmodic cases of immigration of any particular people at any particular period.

It will be seen, then, that Africa—especially the eastern half of the continent—was affected in a double sense by the rise of Islam. In the first place the stimulus to immigration and to trade, which the initial conquests of the Saracens in North Africa imparted, was supplemented at a later date by a course of settlements, resulting from the persecutions and rivalries of the contending parties in Asia.

The Abbasid Dynasty lasted from A.D. 750 to 1258, when the Mongol hordes under Hulagu captured Baghdad, and the Caliphate came to an end. The Mongols, sweeping on until checked by the Mamelukes of Egypt, retired to Persia, and in due course embraced Mahomedanism. After about a century of comparative tranquillity, the invasion of Persia by Timur (A.D. 1380–1405) again brought chaos to Western Asia.

All these events reacted upon East Africa by causing waves of immigration, and, as we shall presently see, the

Azanian coast became a favourite region for the settlement of Arabs and Persians driven by political and religious stress from their homes in Asia.

Persecution and war in Asia, then, were among the prime causes which led to the establishment on the east coast of Africa, and in Zanzibar and Pemba, of rival Arab and Persian sultanates and chiefships, during medieval times. There was, however, another reason which led to the founding and induced the permanency of these Arab and Persian colonies on the Azanian coast. The reader will not require to be reminded that trading-stations on the East African coast were no new institutions, for, as we have seen, they had existed certainly during the first century, and in all probability for a very long time prior to that epoch.

Valuable commodities, which the civilised world demanded, were to be obtained from the coast, and there can be no doubt, that a regular trade was established from an early date during the Islamic period to exploit the region of East Africa. Ivory, slaves,[1] tortoise-shell, ambergris, were always to be obtained by barter, and the numerous ancient ruins on the coast and in Zanzibar, Pemba, and Mafia Islands all testify that the settlements were not merely the sanctuaries of a few stricken immigrants, but the substantial and permanent abodes of thriving merchants and communities.

Thus trade, as well as war, attracted Arabs, Persians, and Indians to the Azanian coasts, and to its chief islands during the evolution of Mahomedanism.

I need not labour the point, for there exists incontestable evidence, which will be referred to in its appropriate place, that the Portuguese on their arrival in Azanian waters, in A.D. 1497, found large well-built cities, populated by Asiatics clad in silks and jewels, who openly scoffed at the miserable presents offered them by the Portuguese.

---

[1] To indicate the extent to which the traffic in African slaves had attained at an early date, mention may here be made of the important part played by the negro in the wars of Southern Arabia about A.D. 750. A century later the revolt of these slaves shook the whole of Arabia. Under the leadership of an African negro, who went by the nick-name of "Lord of the Blacks," they stormed the fortress of Basra, and were not overcome until the year 883.

II

The chief historical records of events on the east coast of Africa during the period we have now under review are : *The Arab Chronicles of Kilwa*, and the accounts of certain travellers, who visited the settlements on the East coast between the death of Mahomed in A.D. 632 and the coming of the Portuguese in A.D. 1497.

In addition to the above there is the well-known map compiled by the Arab geographer Edrisi, at the court of Count Robert of Sicily in the twelfth century (1154), which embodies the geographical knowledge of the period. Edrisi's representation of Africa shows but little improvement on that of Claudius Ptolemy, except that the port of Sofala is marked, and a place named " Zinj " or " Zenj " is shown on the mainland in about the latitude of Zanzibar. As already explained, " Zinj " is the Arab form of the Persian word *zangh*, meaning a negro, and *bar* in Arabic signifies a coast or country, so Edrisi may be credited as being the first geographer to record on a map, with some approximation of accuracy, the situation of modern Zanzibar,[1] although it appears unlikely that he really referred to the island of that name.

The chronicles of the city and sultanate of Kilwa came into the possession of the Portuguese when they took Kilwa from the Shirazis or Africanised Persians in A.D. 1505. There appear to have been two records originally, but the copy to which reference is generally made is that which came into the possession of Sir John Kirk when he was in Zanzibar, and which he presented to the British Museum. The work in question is believed to be unique. It has of course been translated many times, and in the version which appears in the *Journal of the Royal Asiatic Society* for 1895, and to which I had recourse, a most interesting holograph note by Sir John Kirk himself explains how he became possessed of this important document. I give his own words :

" This MS. given to the British Museum is the copy of

---

[1] Ptolemy marks a " Zingis " on his map of Africa, but far to the north of modern Zanzibar. He, like Edrisi, probably intended to mark in a general way the Region of the Negroes.

an abstract prepared from a larger Arabic history known as *Sinet el Kilawia*, of which no copy is known to exist now, although there (may) yet be one found on the African coast. The abstract came from among the papers of Sheikh Moheddin, they were stolen after his death and fell into my hands as Judge of the Court : before being returned the Sultan [1] had a copy made for me."

In this book we are only concerned with the islands of the Zanzibar archipelago, so there is no intention to weary the reader with a lengthy summary of these Kilwa records, but the fact that Zanzibar Island is mentioned in the chronicles makes some reference desirable.

The Kilwa records give an account of the founding of this great Persian settlement on the Azanian coast in the tenth century of our era ; and as the story of its genesis is probably very similar to that of other Arab and Persian colonies on the islands and coast of Africa, a brief summary of the event may be given here.

The narrator describes how a Sultan named Hasan of Shiraz on the Persian Gulf had six sons. Hasan and his family left their native land in seven ships. The sixth ship came to Kilwa. What happened to the other six ships is not stated, but, presuming they all arrived off the African coast, it is fairly safe to assume that the remainder of the party formed similar settlements either in Zanzibar, in Pemba, or at some other point on the mainland. The tradition of ships having arrived from Shiraz at various periods in the distant past, bringing parties of settlers, is still strongly current among the natives—especially those who claim Shirazian descent—in Zanzibar and the neighbouring coastlands. In many of these independent accounts by modern natives, who certainly have never heard of the Kilwa chronicles, the same names crop up as in the old records, and it is frequently stated that some of the original immigrants stayed at one place, while others of the party proceeded farther south and founded cities at other points on the coast.

[1] Seyyid Barghash, who reigned in Zanzibar from 1870 to 1888. Sir John Kirk was connected with Zanzibar from 1866 to 1887. He was appointed Her Majesty's Consul-General and Agent at Zanzibar in 1873.

To advert to the Kilwa chronicles, and to what happened to Hasan and his party on his arrival at that place. On landing, so the chronicles tell us, the immigrants found " a Muslim already settled at Kilwa with his family, and a mosque." This is a very interesting piece of information, as showing that prior to the advent of the Shirazi immigrants to the East Africa littoral in the ninth century, other Moslems had preceded them, and had settled there. The suggestion that this Mahomedan which the Shirazis found already settled at Kilwa was an Indian engaged in trade will appear probable to all who are acquainted with the conditions on the east coast of Africa.

The chronicles go on to tell us how the son of Sultan Hasan bought the island of Kilwa from the chief of the neighbouring Almuli tribe, at the price of fencing it round with cloth. The new-comers found, however, that Kilwa was only an island at high tide, and the first thing they did, after completing the purchase, was to deepen the channel which dried at low tide.

The narrator informs us that the first sovereign of Kilwa was Ali, who was nick-named *Nguo-Mingi* (Much Calico). His father was the original Sultan Hasan of Shiraz, who apparently was on board one of the other six ships, the fate of which is not related.

King Ali ruled over Kilwa during the middle of the tenth century, and reigned forty years, and he established his son Mahomed as ruler of Mombasa.

After some years Kilwa was overrun by incursions of the neighbouring negro tribes, and the then reigning Sultan— a grandson of the original founder of the city and colony— fled to Zanzibar.

What attraction the island of Zanzibar possessed at this early period besides safety, the chronicler does not say ; but if Zanzibar local tradition is of any value, it would appear that the Kilwa colony was but the offspring of an older settlement founded in Zanzibar, or, to be precise, on the aforesaid islet of Tumbatu, where the extensive ruins of a forgotten town can be seen to-day.

The fugitive sultan was not required, however, to remain in Zanzibar for long, for the chronicle informs us that the

Kilwa people drove out the invading negroes, and that they thereupon sent deputations to Zanzibar and brought back their prince, who reigned fourteen years.

The record then proceeds to give a long list of kings of Kilwa, and the number of years each reigned. Some of the names of these sultans have been identified with those on numerous copper coins which have been picked up in large numbers on the sea-shore of Mafia Island.

The State of Kilwa rose to a position of great influence and prosperity during the eleventh, twelfth, and thirteenth centuries. She extended her sway down to Sofala, whence the gold from the Zimbabwe mines was shipped, and introduced among the Persian settlements on the east coast and its islands a high standard of architecture, and a refined civilisation altogether foreign to Africa. Many of the buildings erected in the past by the Shirazis betoken a high artistic perception, and the grace and beauty of many of their creations, especially the stone doorways and arched entrances, inspire admiration to-day.

Kilwa was the predominant power on the Azanian coast, and, until the coming of the Portuguese, seems quite to have overshadowed the Arab colonies which shared the African littoral with her. The Arabs have remained to this day, while the Shirazian ascendancy is but a memory of the past, evidenced only by some rough but artistic ruins in seaports, the very names of which have been forgotten, and by the proud claim of a large section of the native coast populations —especially in Zanzibar and the isles thereof—that they are of Shirazian descent.[1]

The next glimpse we obtain of Zanzibar in *The Chronicles of Kilwa* refers to an event which, as far as one can judge, occurred during the thirteenth century. A pretender named Said claimed the throne of Kilwa, and he went, we are told, to Zanzibar to beg the Sultan of that island, whose name was Hasan, son of Abu Bakr, to assist him in his designs against Kilwa. The Sultan of Zanzibar consented, and Said and an Emir of Sultan Hasan started for Kilwa with a large force.

[1] It is interesting to note that the chiefs and village head men of Zanzibar are officially styled "sheha," which is understood to be derived from the Persian word *shah*.

Dissensions, however, arose between Said and the Emir, with the result that the latter, and it may be supposed the Zanzibar army, deserted Said, and presumably the designs of the latter came to naught.

From the above account it will be observed that Zanzibar was progressing ! Obviously in the thirteenth century it was an independent State, with a Sultan and an army of its own.

Just prior to the arrival of the Portuguese in East African waters in A.D. 1497, the Sultan of Kilwa was named Fudayl, and his throne was threatened by a person called Hasan, apparently the son of a former ruler of Kilwa. Hasan determined to make war on Kilwa, but the Sultan of Zanzibar sent an ambassador to Kilwa, with the object of promoting peace between Hasan and Fudayl, on the basis of the restoration of the former to his previous title and power. This intervention was ineffectual, and it is related that when the ambassador was returning to Zanzibar, Hasan advanced and attacked Kilwa, but met with a severe defeat.

It was during Fudayl's reign that news arrived of the coming of three Portuguese ships under the command of Vasco da Gama (A.D. 1497).

So much for *The Chronicles of Kilwa.*

It should be understood that the Kilwa immigrants who accompanied Sultan Hasan of Shiraz were not necessarily the first persons to colonise the east coast of Africa. They were in no sense the Pilgrim Fathers of Azania. Prominence is given to their enterprise because a definite record of the events has been handed down to us.

As a matter of fact, it appears probable that the Persians arrived on the east coast as early as the sixth century,[1] and there is no reason to suppose that the Arab settlements were not as early. In fact a record of an Arab incursion exists, and it is especially interesting to those acquainted with Zanzibar, inasmuch as this particular party of colonists consisted of Arabs from Omân.

It is related that in A.D. 684 two brothers, Suleiman and Said, the descendants of Julanda, withstood with their forces

[1] *Handwerk und Industrie in Ostafrika,* by Dr. Franz Stuhlmann (Hamburg, 1910).

the attempt of El Hajjaj, the Governor of Irak, to reduce Omân to submission. At first the Omân forces were successful in withstanding the invaders, but the latter received reinforcements, and finally overcame the defenders. The brothers with some of their followers made good their escape, and fled to East Africa, where they settled.[1]

These few specific records of immigration of Arabs and Persians to Azania in medieval times have been preserved to us, but it is obvious that these isolated cases could not account for, by themselves, the establishment of the numerous sultanates dotted along the east coast of Africa. To name but the most important of these independent Arab and Persian States, we find Mogdishu, said to have been founded in A.D. 908 ; Warsheikh ; Merka ; Brawa ; Kismayu ; Patta ; Lamu ; Malindi ; Mombasa ; Zanzibar ; Mafia ; and of course Kilwa. All these were fortified, and many were surrounded by walls of imposing appearance. Their houses were of stone, and their mosques often displayed a high sense of artistic perception. When the Portuguese arrived on the coast, they were astonished at these well-built and substantial cities, and compared some of the buildings with those of their native land.

III

Masudi[2] was an Arab who lived in Baghdad in the early years of the tenth century, and who spent much of his life travelling. He quitted his native city in the year 912, and has left an account of his journeys to various parts of the world. Among the many countries and regions he described, and possibly visited, was the east coast of Africa. He does not, unfortunately, mention the island of Zanzibar—and his

---

[1] This definite account of the immigration of the Omân Arabs to East Africa is taken from Salil-bin-Razik's work, *The Seyyids and Imams of Omân*, which was translated by Badger. As pointed out by the translator, the account modifies and corrects the usually accepted version, which writer after writer on the subject of Arab immigration to East Africa perpetuates, by reproducing Herr Krapf's version of the advent of some Arab immigrants he calls " Emozaides."

[2] His full name was Abdul-Hasan Ali-bin-Husein-bin-Ali el Masudi. He died in Egypt in A.D. 956.

silence is somewhat suggestive—or any port which can be identified on the African littoral, but he nevertheless affords some interesting information on the subject of trade in the western portion of the Indian Ocean, which confirms the tradition that the people of Omân were even at this early date deeply interested in the commercial enterprises of the Azanian coastlands.

Our Arab traveller informs us that the " Zendjes" or negroes were settled on the coast as far south as Sofala, " which is the most remote frontier of the region, and the limit of the navigation of the vessels of Omân and Siraf in the Sea of Zendj." This sea was bounded by the country of Sofala and the " Wak-wak " (bushmen) a country which produces gold and other marvels in abundance ; the climate is hot and fertile.

The territory of the Zendj, he tells us, abounds in elephants, which are not used by the natives for war, but simply killed for the ivory. He adds that " the ivory so obtained ordinarily goes to Omân, and is forwarded therefrom to China and India." This is a very interesting statement, for it shows that the ivory used in such enormous quantities in the East came from Azania, and that the transport was in Omân vessels. It further indicates that a regular trade existed on the east coast of Africa, and tends to substantiate the supposition that the trading stations, or market-towns, which we saw existed in East Africa, and in Zanzibar (Menouthias) during the first century, were still thriving at the time of Masudi's visit.

A more specific and definite reference is made to the island of Zanzibar by Yakut, an Arab traveller, whose geographical dictionary is mainly a compilation made in the thirteenth century from earlier Arab and Persian writers. The observation, though brief, is the most precise of any ancient writer.

He states that the people of the " island of Tumbat " were Moslems early in the thirteenth century, and that the people of the neighbouring Lenguja (viz. Unguja, the Swahili name for Zanzibar) were wont to go to Tumbat to seek safety from their enemies.

A reference has been made on a previous page to the islet of Tumbatu, separated by a narrow channel from the main island of Zanzibar. On the islet in question are the ruins of an extensive stone-built town. The settlement must have been an important and permanent one. Yakut's remark about the population of this islet leaves little doubt but that the town must have been in existence early in the thirteenth century, in fact it appears probable that the city on Tumbatu was really the first town to be established in Zanzibar, and I surmise that when mention is made in the Kilwa chronicles of "Zanzibar," and the Sultan thereof, the town on Tumbatu islet is really referred to, although the very name of this ruined town is now forgotten. *A propos* of this question, it may be mentioned here, that it is generally accepted, that the modern city of Zanzibar is of no very great antiquity.

Our next Arab tourist is generally known as Ibn Batuta,[1] who left his native city of Tangiers to perform the pilgrimage to Mecca in A.D. 1324, and afterwards visited the East African coast settlements.

He describes Mogdishu as "an exceeding large city." He was entertained by the sheikh there, and gives an account of the food given to him, which was probably typical of that of the other Arab colonies on the Azanian coast.

"Their meat," he says, "is generally rice roasted with oil, and placed on a large wooden dish. Over this they place a large dish of roasted meat, which consists of flesh, fish, fowl, or vegetables. They also eat the fruit of the plantain, and after boiling it in new milk, they then put it in a dish and the curdled milk on another. They also put on some of preserved lemon, bunches of preserved pepper pods salted and pickled, as also grapes which are not unlike apples, except that they have stones. These when boiled become sweet like fruit in general, but are crude before this. In the same manner they use green ginger. When therefore they eat the rice, they eat it after these salts and pickles. The people of Mogdishu are very corpulent : they are enormous eaters, one of them eating as much as a congregation ought to do."

Batuta then visited Mombasa, which he states is a large city abounding with the banana, lemon, and citron. There

---

[1] His full names were Abu Abdulla Muhammad ibn Abdulla ibn Muhammad ibn Ibraham el Lawati el Tanji.

is no grain on the island, " what they have is brought to them from other places." The people are generally religious, chaste, and honest.

After staying one night in Mombasa, he proceeded by sea to Kilwa, which he describes as large, and composed of " wooden houses." The king's name was Abu-el-Mozaffr Hasan, who had obtained great victories over the infidel Zenj. Hasan gave much away in alms. The greatest gift bestowed by the people of these countries is ivory ; and Batuta adds, " they seldom give gold."

Batuta then returned to Arabia. He makes no mention at all of Zanzibar Island, and the translator adds a note, expressing a doubt as to whether Batuta really visited Kilwa and the coast of Zenj.

In addition to the trade from Arabia and India, there is historical proof that the Chinese also visited the East African coast during medieval times. This intercourse between the Far East and Africa is confirmed by the find of numerous Chinese coins at Mogdishu, Kilwa, Mafia, and at other Azanian ports. A number of these coins discovered at the first-named place have been assigned dates by Dr. Friedrich Hirch of Munich as ranging from A.D. 845 to 1163. A Chinese coin found in 1916 at Mafia Island has been examined by the Department of Coins at the British Museum, and stated to be a " cash " of the Emperor Shen Tsung, who reigned between A.D. 1068 and 1086.

From Chinese sources we learn that a Chinese fleet visited Mogdishu for the purposes of trade in A.D. 1430.[1]

It must be admitted that evidence relative to the local history of Zanzibar and Pemba Islands for the 1,500 years subsequent to the birth of Christ is scanty. That both

---

[1] The author extracted from an ancient tomb in Pemba a bowl which the authorities of the Ceramic Department of the Victoria and Albert Museum state is of " cream-coloured Ting ware of the Sung Dynasty " (A.D. 960–1279).

Professor Justus Strandes, in his *Die Portugiesenzeit von Deutsch und Englisch-Ostafrika*, observes : " The fragments of porcelain which are found everywhere in the oldest ruins in East Africa, and some of which is pronounced by experts to be the famous Celadon porcelain, is a further proof of the relations which existed long ago between China and East Africa. The Chinese authors who wrote in the fourteenth century were well aware of this export of their country's products to the Zanzibar coast, which they called Tsangpat or Tseng-po."

4

these islands possess a history is clear from the existence of many ruins scattered on their coasts, and, although specific mention of these two islands in historical records may be wanting, it is evident that they could not have stood aloof from the traffie and history of the Persian and Arab settlements on the adjacent coasts.

Zanzibar is not an island one can easily miss, when sailing along the Azanian coast. The gold fleets from Sofala must have passed it, and probably filled up their water jars at its running streams : the Omân sailors, who we know shipped ivory in such quantities during the tenth century from the negro coast, must have known it well, even as to-day it is the converging point for native craft hailing from Arabia, from the Persian Gulf, and from Hindustan.

And yet one cannot fail to notice that every Arab traveller who visited the coast during the later Middle Ages passes Zanzibar Island by in silence. It may be that the island was shunned as being the haunt of corsairs, who lay in wait and intercepted the richly laden argosies which sailed northwards with their cargoes of gold and ivory, of slaves and ambergris ; or perchance, by the time these Arab travellers came to East Africa, the history of Zanzibar was already past ; for one very characteristic feature of early sea-traffic and colonisation was the selection of islands for trade-depots, rather than sites on a mainland. The object of such a preference is obvious, and one can well understand that on the wild African coast, with its still wilder inhabitants of cannibal negroes, those who first ventured to traffic in the sea of Zenj would see the advantage of having their depots, their refitting and careening stations, on islands which offered safe anchorages, abundant water, and immunity from attack, rather than on the exposed mainland.

In fact such island sanctuaries would appear to have been essential not only during the initial stages of opening up trade connections with the mainland, but subsequently as ports of call for refreshment on the outward and homeward journeys.

The choice of islands by the ancient maritime nations for their towns and trading ports is too well known to need demonstration in these pages. Thus Tyre itself, the great trade-emporium of the Phœnicians, was on an island, so too were Tarshish and Aradus. In the case of the early Greek colonies, Mitylene and Syracuse, both on islets, may be instanced. The early history of maritime trading enterprise chows two phases : firstly the appropriation of the islet or peninsula, and later the settlement on the mainland littoral. Other instances of the choice of islands for settlement will readily occur to the reader : Bombay, Diu, Singapore, Hongkong, for instance, or that islet whose very name was synonomous with the wealth of the East, namely Ormuz, concerning which the Persian poet sings ·

> " If the world was a ring,
> Ormuz would be the jewel in it."

And yet Ormuz was a small arid island, and like Tyre entirely dependent on the mainland for water. On the east coast of Africa we have the island towns of Lamu, Mombasa, Tumbatu, Mafia, Kua, Kilwa, Mozambique, not to mention Zanzibar or Pemba.

So the silence of the early Arab geographers regarding the islands of Zanzibar and Pemba may have been due to the fact that, at the time of their advent, the towns of these two islands in question were even then in ruins.

But, whatever the explanation may be, it is some satisfaction to those who have learnt to appreciate Zanzibar to realise that the despised island, which failed to call forth a single word from the pundits of the Middle Ages, was in the course of the centuries to rise phœnix-like, and become the hub and the metropolis of Eastern Africa !

CHAPTER V

.

WITH the advent of the Portuguese during the year 1497 into the calm seas of East Africa, a new era commenced for Zanzibar and Azania. The sleep of centuries was rudely broken, and the veil which had concealed the mysteries of the Southern Ocean from Europe was permanently drawn aside.

It was not, however, only Zanzibar and East Africa which were affected by the discoveries of the Portuguese, but the world at large, for the growing wealth and power of Islam menaced the very existence of Christendom; and had not the monopoly of Eastern trade been wrested from the Moslem States which controlled it, it is conceivable that the growing ascendancy of the Mahomedan world might have become so assured and consolidated as to seriously menace the future development of Christian Europe.

It must be remembered that at the period of which we are speaking the Moors were still masters of a portion of Spain. In 1358 Ottoman Turks had crossed the Hellespont, and in 1453 they entered Constantinople, and obtained a footing in Europe, whence they have never been ejected. In 1517 Syria, Egypt, and Arabia were added to their dominions, and their fleets were for a long time a scourge to all Christian shipping in the Mediterranean. Farther eastward the ascendancy of the Moslem was marked by the rise of the Empire of the Great Mogul, while in the year 1502 Persia became an independent Mahomedan kingdom.

The discovery of Eastern Africa by the Portuguese was merely an incident in their search for a route to the Indies which was their ultimate goal. With the west coast of Africa they were fairly familiar, but it was not until Bartholomew Diaz had rounded the Cape of Good Hope that the possibility of forestalling their Spanish rivals in the race for the Spice Islands of the Far East by utilising the Cape route developed from an aspiration into a practical project.

From the commencement of the fifteenth century the interest in the exploration of the coasts of the African continent had been encouraged and stimulated by that remarkable man and Prince of Portugal known as " Henry the Navigator."

Born in the year 1395, he was the second son of King John I of Portugal and Philippa, daughter of the English John of Gaunt, and it is no detriment to those wonderful Portuguese explorers of the fifteenth century to attribute the love of the sea, and the zest for exploration possessed by Prince Henry, to the fact that he was by birth half English, and that in his veins ran the proud blood of " old John of Gaunt, time-honoured Lancaster."

Under the stimulus of his encouragement, the Portuguese nation became the paramount maritime nation of Europe, and by his direction a series of expeditions probed far into the unknown waters of the South Atlantic.

Slowly but surely, year after year, the Portuguese expeditions crept farther southward down the west coast of Africa, until by 1446 Cape Verde had been reached, and in 1448 the coast had been explored as far south as Sierra Leone.

On November 13th, 1460, Prince Henry died, but the spirit of adventure he had instilled into the Portuguese survived, and the systematic exploration of the African coast continued with unabated zeal.

A year after Prince Henry's death the coast of the modern Republic of Liberia had been reached, and by 1485 the mouth of the Congo had been discovered. The following year Bartholomew Diaz rounded the Cape of Storms, and sailed as far east as Algoa Bay. The same year a Portuguese named Pero de Covilhao had started from Lisbon and made his way to India via Egypt and the Red Sea. On his return journey he visited the east coast of Africa as far south as Sofala, and the report of his travels on his return to his native country determined King Manoel to dispatch an expedition round the Cape to India via the East African coast.

In 1492 the Spaniards had fitted out a squadron which sailed westward, under the command of Columbus, to discover that El Dorado of the East of which Europe had dreamed for centuries.

Hitherto Europe had been supplied with the spices, silk, and other luxuries of the East through the medium of the Venetians, who obtained the merchandise from Alexandria, to which city it was brought by Indian and Arab ships from the ports of the Persian Gulf, from Azania, and from the coasts of Hindustan. The northern overland routes from the East to the Mediterranean were at this period entirely in the hands of the Turks.

As it was in the days of the old Sabæan dynasties, so it was just prior to the discovery of a sea-route to the East by the Portuguese—Europe was dependent for the luxuries of the Indies on the goodwill and mediation of Asia.

Small wonder, then, that the two great maritime powers of the period—Spain and Portugal—determined to cast off these commercial shackles, and discover for themselves the secrets of the Orient. They were themselves rivals, and it can be understood that when the Portuguese saw Columbus sail westward, as he conceived towards Cathay and its fabled treasures, they were not long in setting out on a similar quest.

Now it was that the work of Prince Henry the Navigator stood them in good stead, for when on July 8th, 1497, Vasco da Gama set sail from the Tagus, he was already acquainted with the southern limits of the African continent, and, thanks to nearly a century of explorations, was enabled, instead of hugging the coast, to strike boldly south into the open Atlantic. His plan was to hold this course until he calculated he was in the latitude of the Cape, then to turn eastward and run towards the land.

His bold project succeeded wonderfully well, for on November 4th, 1497, he made the land, and anchored only 120 miles north of the Cape of Good Hope—not a bad piece of navigation, considering he had been three months at sea, and the actual latitude of the Cape was unknown !

Vasco da Gama's fleet consisted of four vessels : the *St. Gabriel*, the flagship, rated as of 120 tons ;[1] the *St. Rafael*, of 100 tons : a caravel named *Berrio*; and a store-ship which carried provisions reckoned to last the squadron three years. The two first-named ships had been specially built for the expedition.

The number of men in the four vessels is stated variously as 148 and 170 : the discrepancy being probably due to the inclusion and non-inclusion of the officers' servants, or of the criminals who were to be utilised by being sent ashore to acquire information at dangerous places.

On November 22nd da Gama doubled the Cape of Good Hope, and at the modern Mossel Bay, where he remained thirteen days, he caused the store-ship, after transferring her cargo to the other ships, to be burnt.

On Christmas Day da Gama with his squadron, now reduced to three vessels, was off that portion of the African coast which in honour of the Festival he named Natal.

On that momentous day a new page of history was commenced for East Africa and Zanzibar.

On March 1st, 1498, da Gama arrived off Mozambique. This was the frontier town of that long series of wealthy and prosperous settlements which lay scattered along the African coast as far northward as Mogdishu.

These powerful Arab and Persian sultanates, with their extensive and well-built stone cities, filled the Portuguese with amazement. They no doubt expected to meet the wild negro, as they knew him on the west coast. Instead of this they found civilised communities, possessing settled and organised trade connections with India and the East, which had been established for a thousand years or more.

Through the medium of a Portuguese interpreter named Fernao Martins, who had become acquainted with Arabic in one of the Moslem States on the Mediterranean, and who was borne on the flagship *St. Gabriel*, the Portuguese on arrival at Mozambique soon commenced to gather information

[1] For note on the method of reckoning tonnage in Queen Elizabeth's reign, see page 73.

concerning this new country. The main object of their voyage was to find the way to India, and their first endeavour was to engage pilots who would take them there.

Now, there was on board the *St. Gabriel* a certain person, whose name has not been handed down to posterity, who kept a journal of the events of the voyage, and it is to this chronicler that the world is chiefly indebted for its knowledge of this epoch-making voyage of Vasco da Gama from Lisbon to India.

I propose to give such extracts from this anonymous journal as will afford some information as to the conditions prevailing on the east coast at the time of the visit of the Portuguese, and I shall not fail to give every detail which can throw any light upon the islands of Zanzibar and Pemba.

The journalist [1] states that at Mozambique the people were Moslems, and their language Arabic. Their dresses he says were of fine linen and cotton stuffs, with variously coloured stripes, and of rich and elaborate workmanship. They were merchants, and had transactions with the " white Moors " (Arabs) four of whose vessels were at the time in port laden " with gold, silver, cloves, pepper, ginger, and silver rings, as also a quantity of pearls, jewels, and rubies, all of which were used by the people of the country." All the above articles, except the gold, the journalist understood had been brought to Mozambique by these Arabs.[2]

The journalist tells us that the Sheikh of Mozambique visited the flagship, and was presented with some " hats, marlottas (a short dress of silk or wool, worn in India) corals,

[1] *The Journal of the First Voyage of Vasco da Gama*, 1497–1499. Translated by E. G. Ravenstein, and published by the Hakluyt Society.

[2] I venture to think that a considerable proportion of this cargo existed only in the imagination of either the interpreter or of the journalist of the *St. Gabriel*. It seems unlikely that the owners of this treasure would inform complete strangers of the contents of their ships. Martins, the interpreter, may not have been very efficient, and the distinction which appears to be made in the text between the " merchants " and " white Moors," or Arabs, inclines one to think that the merchants were really Indians, of whose language Martins would not know a word. Without discrediting the whole list of cargo, I surmise that the journalist and interpreter, overjoyed at having come, after many weary months, within sight of the Golden East, accepted too readily the rumours which no doubt were flying about the ships.

and other articles." " The Sheikh was so proud, that he treated all we gave him with contempt " : and " asked for scarlet cloth of which we had none."

It must have been distinctly embarrassing for the Portuguese, who naturally wished to make a good impression on their guest and his suite.

The relations between the new-comers and the people of Mozambique soon became hostile, for the latter had at first thought that the Portuguese were Turkish Moslems. As soon as they became undeceived on this point, matters became unpleasant : and when the ships' boats were sent in to get water, they were attacked, and da Gama in retaliation fired on the town and killed some of the inhabitants. However, a peace was patched up, and the Portuguese record that when they left Mozambique on April 1st they took with them " many fowls and goats and pigeons," which had been given them in exchange for " small glass beads." [1]

Our anonymous author on the *St. Gabriel*, referring to the native craft in the harbour, says that they were of good size and decked. There were no nails, and " the planks were held together by cords of coir." The sails were made of palm matting.[2] The mariners, he adds, " had Genoese needles " (magnetic compasses) by which to steer, quadrants and navigating charts.[3]

The Portuguese evidently saw coco-nut palms for the first time, and describe them as yielding a fruit " as large as a melon, of which the kernel is eaten." It has, it is re-marked, " a nutty flavour."

As previously stated, the Portuguese squadron sailed from Mozambique on April 1st, and we begin to scan the records of the voyage more closely to ascertain whether they saw, and landed at, Zanzibar or Pemba, and what they found

---

[1] The question of antique beads found in considerable abundance at many of the ruins in Zanzibar and Pemba is an interesting one, and is discussed on a subsequent page.

[2] The vessels were evidently *mtepe*, still to be met with in Zanzibar waters. See also the description of the " sewed boats " of the *Periplus* in Chapter III.

[3] This account shows that the Portuguese had evidently been on board the native craft. It may be of interest to note that most of the Arab craft which come annually to Zanzibar at the present time are furnished with the same aids to navigation.

there. It may be said at once that, according to the *St. Gabriel* diarist, Vasco da Gama, neither on this outward journey to India, nor when homeward bound a year later, stopped at Zanzibar; and the Portuguese, like the travellers before them, passed it by, not exactly in silence—for, as will be seen, a brief reference is made to both islands—but it is evident that neither place was of sufficient importance to stay them on their course.

After sighting Mafia Island, the journalist records that the ships stood out to sea until out of sight of land. This was at sundown on April 4th, 1498. When the next day broke, there was still no land in sight. They were steering north-west, and during the day were running, without knowing it, parallel to the eastern coast of Zanzibar Island. That same evening (April 5th) the anonymous journalist tells us that they " again beheld the land," which must have been the high land in the northern portion of Zanzibar Island.

After nightfall, the squadron changed its course to north by west, and " during the morning watch " again changed to north-north-west. This means that during the early hours of the night Ras Nyungwe and the northern part of the island was passed, and a course was then steered nearly parallel to the mainland coast. The Portuguese, however, evidently hugged the coast too closely, for the record relates that at about 4 a.m. on April 6th, when sailing before a favourable wind, the *St. Rafael* ran aground two leagues from the African coast, on the shoals opposite Mtangata,[1] which lies due west of Chake-Chake, the chief town in Pemba Island.

" When the tide fell, the *St. Rafael* lay high and dry." On the rising tide, however, the ship was got off " with much rejoicing," with the aid of the boats and many anchors laid out.

On the mainland facing these Mtangata shoals, they saw a " lofty range of mountains, beautiful of aspect " (the

---

[1] That is on the modern Karange Reef, which is a low, narrow island about three miles from the mainland, and covered with scrub. Tangata Reef is the extreme end of the Karange Reef. *The African Pilot*, an Admiralty publication, thus describes the place : " Tangata Reef is the extreme of the coral reef, dry at low water, extending nearly two miles north-eastward from the low peninsula within which is the village of Moarongo. There are mangrove bushes at about half a mile within its extreme."

Usambara Mountains). These mountains they called the "Serras de Sao Rafael," and they gave the same name to the shoals on which the ship had run aground.

While the Portuguese were busily engaged in endeavouring to float the *St. Rafael*, the journalist records that " two canoes approached, one of which was laden with fine oranges, better than those of Portugal." This shows that oranges are no new importation into Zanzibar and East Africa.

Having refloated the *St. Rafael* on Saturday, April 7th, they " ran along the coast," and caught a glimpse of Pemba. The record of this interesting event is as follows :

" They saw some islands at the distance of fifteen leagues from the mainland, and about six leagues in extent.   They supply the vessels of the country with masts.   All are inhabited by Moors." [1]

The squadron arrived off Mombasa the same day, and there is no need to follow the fortunes of da Gama further in detail, except to say that his reception at this place was not cordial. After a great deal of mutual distrust and misunderstanding with the Mombasa people, he proceeded to Malindi, where he was most hospitably received, and the friendly relations which sprang up between the people of this town and the Portuguese were of a permanent character, and lasted unimpaired during the whole period the Portuguese held domination over the East African coast.

At this friendly port, da Gama obtained the services of a pilot from Gujerat, and twenty-two days after sailing from Malindi the Portuguese arrived off Calicut in India.

On his return journey, Vasco da Gama touched at Malindi, and after obtaining " refreshment " for his weary crews, he started in January 1499 on his triumphal return to Lisbon.

We obtain from the anonymous journalist of the squadron one definite allusion to Zanzibar Island.

Owing to the number of deaths among the personnel of the squadron, it was found impossible to navigate the three ships home, so it was determined to beach the *St. Rafael* on

---

[1] Sir John Kirk remarks : " This was Pemba, which, owing to its deep bays, appeared to consist of a number of islands."   The Portuguese sighted the northern half of Pemba, having evidently stood well away from the mainland, after the catastrophe on the Mtangata Shoal.

the Mtangata Shoal, and, after taking everything out of her, to burn her.

This was done, and I dare say that as the Portuguese trimmed their sails for home, there was many a pang of regret in their hearts as they looked back for the last time and saw the smouldering hull on the lonely reef. Vasco da Gama removed the figure-head of the *St. Rafael*, and brought it with him to Portugal, where it was lodged in the church at Belem.

Now comes the first reference to Zanzibar !

After burning the ship, the journal continues :

" On Sunday the 27th (January 1499) we left this place (Mtangata Shoals) with a fair wind. During the following night we lay to, and in the morning (January 28th) we came close to a large island called Jamgiber, which is peopled with Moors, and is quite ten leagues from the mainland. Late on February 1st we anchored off the island of St. Jorge near Mozambique." [1]

Whether they ran down the east or west of Zanzibar is not definitely stated ; but from the fact that the distance from the mainland is mentioned, it appears probable that the two vessels passed down the west coast, between the island and the continent. Pursuing such a course, land would be

---

[1] With reference to the question as to whether da Gama touched at Zanzibar on his homeward journey, Burton points out that Goes declares that da Gama, after calling at Mogdishu and Malindi, arrived at Zanzibar on February 28th, and was supplied by its rulers with provisions, presents, and specimens of country produce. The land is described as large and fertile, with groves of fine trees producing good fruit.

The statement of the *St. Gabriel* diarist, as given in the text above, is so clear and explicit that it seems almost certain that da Gama did not call at Zanzibar during this voyage. In the first place such an incident would certainly have been recorded in the itinerary of the voyage, and secondly, to have reached Mozambique on February 1st would imply that the two ships could not have tarried on the way. From the north of Zanzibar Island to Mozambique is some 700 miles, and to cover this distance in 108 hours would mean good going night and day, for it must be remembered that the ships were old, and certainly foul, while the strong Mozambique current would have been against them part of the way. The wind, on the other hand, for the first part of the voyage, might during February have been favourable. It may further be presumed that the Portuguese had no desire to loiter on their way to Lisbon, and Zanzibar, it must be confessed, was, as will be seen later, of no very great consequence at the time of the Portuguese visit to East Africa.

visible at intervals on either hand—Zanzibar on the portside, and the African mainland on the starboard.

But here at any rate is a definite mention of the island of Zanzibar, and it is evident that in 1499 the name " Zanzibar " was applied definitely to the island, rather than in a general sense to the whole coastal region of Equatorial Africa.

II

The success of Vasco da Gama's voyage to the Indies induced great activity in fitting out further expeditions for the purpose of not only consolidating the Portuguese influence in East Africa and in India, but of imposing on these distant regions the Christian religion.

It is beyond the scope of this book to detail these various enterprises, but as a consequence of this more frequent intercourse with Eastern Africa, fuller and more detailed information became available, and references to Zanzibar are more numerous in contemporary works.

For instance we learn that Ruy Lourenço Ravasco, the commander of one of the ships of the Portuguese squadron which had left Portugal in 1503, under Antonio da Saldanha the discoverer of Table Bay, became separated from his admiral, and that after waiting at Mozambique and at Kilwa in vain, sailed for the island of Zanzibar, off which island he employed himself for two months by capturing a large number of Arab vessels.

His action was of course one of pure piracy according to modern ideas, but the dread of the Moslem peril to Christian Europe was, at that period, so pronounced as to make the destruction of Mahomedans and their property a meritorious act, and the duty of every devout Christian.

When Ravasco wearied of destroying dhows, he dropped anchor before the " town of Zanzibar,"[1] and attacked it. The

---

[1] The question as to the identity of the town of Zanzibar is dealt with in fuller detail in subsequent chapters, but it may be stated here that from the time of the arrival of the Portuguese until about 1650, the " Zanzibar " referred to in contemporary records was the " Unguja Kuu " (Big Zanzibar) of the present day. This native town was situated about fifteen miles to the south of the

" town of Zanzibar " must have been the modern " Unguja Kuu," for there is no doubt that the site upon which the modern city of Zanzibar now stands was not occupied until the middle of the seventeenth century.

Some details of Ravasco's exploit have come down to us. It appears that he approached and anchored off the town after dark, and it was not until next day that the inhabitants of old Zanzibar became aware that the notorious European, who for months past had been sinking their vessels, had paid them an unwelcome visit. Delegates from the Sultan, or as the Portuguese invariably termed these potentates of the coast, the " King " of Zanzibar, went out and remonstrated with Ravasco, but as they obtained no satisfaction, they returned to shore. Shortly afterwards Ravasco sent a ship's boat and two native craft, full of men and armed with two cannon, to attack the Zanzibaris, who had assembled on the beach to the number it is said of 4,000. As this estimate was made by Ravasco, who claimed a great victory, it is possible that the number has been exaggerated. As Ravasco approached the shore, one of his cannon was fired, and killed thirty-five Zanzibaris on the beach, among them being the son of the " King of Zanzibar." A short fight ensued after the Portuguese had landed, but the Zanzibaris were no match for so well armed a force, and quickly sued for peace. Ravasco imposed a yearly tribute of one hundred meticals of gold [1] (about £57), and thirty sheep to be paid to the King of Portugal. Of the four ships he found in the harbour, two were given to the son of the friendly King of Malindi, who apparently was in Zanzibar when the attack took place, one vessel was allowed to ransom itself, and the fourth with its cargo was taken as a prize for the King of Portugal.

modern city. To-day no remains of the old settlement exist except a masonry well, a few stones stated to have been a mosque, and a mound or two which may or may not have once been buildings. In one of these mounds several gold coins were discovered in 1866. They bore Cufic inscriptions, and could not have been less than 600 years old.

[1] The " metical " was the gold standard on the Azanian coast at the time of the arrival of the Portuguese. It was not a coin, but a specific quantity of gold dust. Like all weights and measures its value varied from time to time and in different places, but it may be taken to have been worth about eleven shillings and sixpence. This value is the average of a series of transactions referred to by Portuguese writers of the sixteenth and seventeenth centuries.

Thus Zanzibar came under the dominance of Portugal in about 1503. Before we consider the extent of that domination, some idea of the relative importance of Zanzibar on the east coast of Africa in the sixteenth century may be gathered from amounts levied as tributes by the Portuguese on the capitals of the other sultanates and towns, which were subjugated about the same time as Zanzibar, and it will then be understood why Vasco da Gama did not consider it worth his while to call at Zanzibar on his first voyage.

Thus the tribute exacted from Kilwa, the predominant State on the east coast was 2,000 meticals of gold (about £1,100), Brawa had to pay an annual sum of £223, and Lamu £268, while in 1528, when Nuno da Cunha destroyed Mombasa, the tribute imposed on that city amounted to 1,500 meticals.

It is evident from the above that the day of Zanzibar had not yet dawned!

We next hear of Zanzibar in the year 1509 when a Portuguese named Duarte de Lemos with one ship visited the ports on the east coast to collect the tribute due. Ravasco's unprovoked assault on the town had not increased the popularity of the Portuguese, and it is scarcely surprising that the landing of de Lemos was opposed at Zanzibar. Resistance, however, was soon overcome, and the unfortunate people fled to the interior of the island, while de Lemos and his men plundered the town.

In about the year 1512 a Portuguese named Duarte Barbosa wrote an account of the East African coast and of Malabar, and he refers in his book to both Zanzibar and Pemba ; but reading between the lines, it may be surmised that he had not personally visited either island.

This is what he says :

" Penda, Manha, and Zanzibar.

" Between this island of St. Lorenzo (Madagascar) and the continent, not very far from it, are three islands which are called one Manfia, another Zanzibar, and the other Penda : these are inhabited by Moors : they are very fertile islands, with plenty of provisions, rice, millet, and flesh, and abundant oranges, lemons, and cedrats. All the mountains are full of them : they produce many sugar canes, but do not know how to make sugar. These islands have their kings. The inhabitants trade with the mainland with their provisions and fruits : they have small vessels, very loosely and badly made : all their planks are sewn together with cords of reed or matting, and their sails are palm-mats.

" They are very feeble people with very few and despicable weapons. In these islands they live in great luxury and abundance : they dress in very good clothes of silk and cotton which they buy in Mombasa of the merchants from Cambay [Gujerat] who reside there.

" Their wives adorn themselves with many jewels of gold from Sofala, and silver in chains, earrings, bracelet and ankle-rings, and are dressed in silk stuffs : they have many mosques, and hold the Alcoran of Mahomed."

Barbosa might have given us a better account. He wrote as if the population comprised one race, whereas it would seem that there were various communities as at present. For instance there was evidently the raw native with his " badly made canoe," who took his oranges over to the mainland for sale. Then there was a portion of the popu- lation who dwelt in ease, and " wore very good clothes of silk," purchased in Mombasa. Then there is the account of the ladies' costumes and jewels of gold and silver, which savour of India.

The statement that there were many mosques gives us no clue as to the state of advancement of the people. Barbosa may have been referring to a large town " with many mosques " or simply to the insignificant wattle-and-daub hut which serves the purpose of a mosque in every hamlet.

It is when we read Barbosa's account of the cities of Kilwa and Mombasa that we can gauge the relative insignificance of poor Zanzibar in A.D. 1512.

This is what he says of the former town :

" It is composed of handsome houses of stone and lime, and very lofty, and their windows are like those of Chris- tians . it has streets, and these houses have their terraces, and the wood worked into the masonry with plenty of gardens. This island has got a king over it, and from hence is trade with Sofala with ships which carry much gold, which is dispensed thence throughout all Arabia Felix. . . . When the King of Portugal discovered this land, the Moors of Sofala, Zuama (Zambesi) and Angoche and Mozambique were all under obedience to the King of Kilwa, who was a great King among them."

Barbosa continues : " And there is much gold in this town, because all the ships which go to Sofala touch at this island (Kilwa) both in going and coming back.[1] These people are Moors, of a dusky colour, and some of them are black and some white : they are very well dressed with rich cloths of gold and silk and cotton."

Of Mombasa, or Bombaza, Barbosa refers to it as a city of the Moors, " very large and beautiful, and built of high and handsome houses of stone and whitewash, and with very good streets like those of Kilwa. . . . It is a town of great trade in goods, and has a good port, where there are always many ships, both of those which sail for Sofala, and those that come from Cambay, and Malindi, and others which sail to the islands of Zanzibar, Manfia, and Penda."

The next glimpse of Zanzibar afforded us is in the year 1522, when we find the Sheikh of the island complaining bitterly to the Portuguese about the rebellious conduct of the inhabitants of the Kerimba Islands,[2] which appear to have been under the domination of the Arab ruler of Zanzibar. The Kerimba islanders had refused to pay tribute to Zanzibar, and the Sheikh of the latter island pointed out to the Portuguese that unless he received the tribute due to him from Kerimba, it was impossible for him to meet his own tribute obligations of £57 and thirty sheep for the King of Portugal.

It is evident that between the years 1509 and 1522 the

---

[1] Kilwa and Mombasa both exploited for their own advantage the Sofala gold trade, and they levied very heavy rates on all merchandise going to Sofala, and on all gold brought back. These levies on the gold trade formed the mainstay of their wealth and prosperity.

Barbosa's remark that there was much gold in Kilwa in 1512 is exactly the opposite to that of Ibn Matuta made two hundred years before.

There seems an inevitable tendency for explorers to exaggerate the possible mineral resources of a new country. This has been evident with respect to all the latest acquired Protectorates in Africa. The coal measures turn out to be shale, and the gold is found to be iron pyrites. It is possible that the Portuguese suffered from similar delusions !

[2] The Kerimba Islands consist of a chain of islets situated close to the African coast between Mozambique and Cape Delgado at the mouth of the Rovuma River.

Portuguese and the people of Zanzibar had become more or less reconciled to one another, and the bad impression which the attacks of Ravasco and de Lemos had engendered had in a measure been eradicated.

The fact no doubt was that by the latter year the Portuguese began to realise that the maintenance of their supremacy on the East African coast was likely to be a costly and troublesome matter, and, though their general attitude to the native races was not conciliatory, it must have become more and more apparent to them that it was simply foolish to set the whole coast against them by wanton acts of aggression.

Mombasa from the first had been hostile to them, so had the neighbouring island of Pemba. Malindi to the north of Mombasa, on the contrary, had always been friendly, and, although there was not much to be obtained from Zanzibar, it was obviously politically and strategically sound to possess at least one friendly point south of Mombasa which could be used as a base from which to watch over that turbulent and rebellious town.

Throughout the whole history of the east coast during the occupation of the Portuguese, Zanzibar, except during the first years, appears to have been always well disposed to Europeans, and indeed this conciliatory attitude is apparent on other occasions, as for instance when the English first arrived in Zanzibar in 1591—an event to which we shall refer in greater detail later—and placed on record that the Zanzibar people received them in a friendly spirit. However, to return to the ruler of Zanzibar and the contumacious people of Kerimba.

The complaint of the Sheikh did not fall on deaf ears, partly because no doubt the Kerimba people happened to be amicable with Mombasa, the most inveterate enemy the Portuguese possessed on the coast. Any hostile action against an ally of Mombasa was always readily undertaken by the Portuguese, whenever they had adequate forces. So the Portuguese dispatched an expedition against Kerimba, and duly reduced it again to the subjection of Zanzibar.

Six years later, we find the Zanzibar people again asking for assistance from the Portuguese. In this instance the complaint was against the truculency of Mombasa, and, as explained above, the Portuguese did not need much inducement to make things unpleasant for that city. Unfortunately for the Portuguese, Mombasa was a powerful enemy, and operations had to be undertaken against her with care and circumspection.

In the present instance to which we have referred, the Zanzibar Sheikh had chosen an opportune moment to lodge his complaint, for at the time Nuno da Cunha was *en route* to assume the Governor-Generalship of India, and he happened to touch at Zanzibar with his fleet.

Finding himself delayed by an unfavourable monsoon, he determined to teach Mombasa a lesson, and with the assistance of native levies from Zanzibar, Malindi, and other places, he took the town and for the time brought Mombasa and its people into entire subjection. He imposed upon them an annual tribute of 1,500 meticals of gold, and required them to deposit 12,000 meticals in addition as security for their future good behaviour.

The enemy temporised, however, for they became aware that the Portuguese were suffering much from sickness, and that Nuno da Cunha wished to proceed without delay to India. They temporised, however, a little too long, for the Portuguese commander before his departure burnt Mombasa to the ground, after destroying many of the coco-nut plantations of the enemy.

This salutary lesson inflicted on so formidable a foe as Mombasa raised the prestige of the Portuguese among the people on the African coast, and so impressed the Mombasa inhabitants that they remained quiet and well conducted for a long time.

In fact little of importance appears to have happened during the fifty years which followed the destruction of Mombasa by Cunha. The Portuguese consolidated their position on the coast, and the fact that a Portuguese ship made use of Mombasa as a port of call in 1554 may be regarded as proof that that city was still on its good behaviour, and under Portuguese control.

In 1571 we witness another example of the amicable relations which existed between the Portuguese and the

Zanzibaris. Francisco Barreto, a soldier of European reputation, had been appointed Governor-General of Mozambique, and shortly after assuming his command he made a tour of the several places and States over which he had jurisdiction. While at Zanzibar he was enabled to do the Sultan of the island a service by quelling a revolt among a section of the population. This timely assistance so gratified the Sultan that he permitted the Portuguese to export certain produce from the island. This concession was evidently regarded as of great importance, for Barreto officially reported the matter to Lisbon, where it is on record in the State archives. Barreto comments too on the great fertility of the island, and on the extraordinary succession of crops produced throughout the year, and he opines that no one could starve in this wonderful island. Among other products he mentions sugar, coco-nuts, gum-copal, and quantities of valuable timber.

With regard to subsequent events along the east coast, it may be as well to remember that in 1580 Portugal became subject to Spain, and remained so until 1640. Spain herself at this period was engaged in a life-and-death struggle with Islam in the Mediterranean, and there can be little doubt but that these events in Europe tended greatly to weaken the position of Spain and Portugal in Eastern Africa, and at the same time inclined the subject races to foster hopes of liberation from the Christian yoke.

It is not surprising, therefore, to learn that subsequent to 1580 a series of most disquieting events occurred, which demonstrated how insecure the hold of the Portuguese over the Azanian region really was.

Some of the events are of the greatest interest, not only because they include the arrival of the first English ship in Zanzibar, but also because they are connected with the revolt of Pemba against the Portuguese, and the manner in which the rebels of that island were dealt with.

All went well until the year 1586, when there suddenly appeared off the east coast a Turkish corsair or adventurer known as Ali-Bey. The mere fact that he was a Turk was sufficient to stir the hearts of, and to create unrest among, the Moslem communities on the coast and the islands.

The world was at this period divided into two armed camps, one representing the Christians, and the other comprising those who fought under the Crescent of Islam. The growing power of the followers of Mahomed had long been a cause of alarm and anxiety to Christian Europe, and there is little wonder that the appearance of Ali-Bey in the Azanian Seas, which presaged according to him the arrival of a great Turkish Fleet, raised hopes of deliverance in the hearts of the Moslem communities of East Africa.

With the exception of Malindi, and apparently Zanzibar, the whole of the coast revolted against the Portuguese, and to restore their authority, a squadron of eighteen vessels was dispatched from India, and the rebellious States were brought again into subjection. But only for a time, for three years later, that is in 1589, Ali-Bey again appeared on the coast with a squadron of five vessels, and proceeded to Mombasa, where he commenced preparations for the subjugation of the faithful Malindi.

To counter this new aggression, the Portuguese dispatched a fleet of twenty sail to East Africa, which duly arrived off Mombasa, and prepared to attack the forces of Ali-Bey, who of course had been warmly welcomed by the people of Mombasa.

But a very remarkable condition of affairs presented itself to the newly arrived Portuguese, for they found Mombasa besieged from the land side by a horde of cannibal savages, known as the Zimbas, or Wazimba. These terrible foes, it appears, originated from the interior of Africa, and had in the first instance attacked Kilwa, into which city they gained entrance one night through the treachery of a Moor, who thought to save his own life by his perfidy. The wretched inhabitants, taken entirely unawares, were slaughtered without mercy by the Wazimba, and thousands of prisoners were taken, and utilised, it is said, for food by the victorious savages.

Elated by their success at Kilwa, the Wazimba swept northwards, devastating as they went, until they found themselves opposite Mombasa, just as the Portuguese fleet, under Thome Coutinho, was preparing to attack Ali-Bey and the Mombasa rebels.

The people of Mombasa found themselves between two fires, and imprudently accepted the offer of the Wazimba chief to assist them against the powerful force of Portuguese opposed to them. No sooner did the Wazimba gain entrance to the city than they immediately turned against the forces of Ali-Bey, and indiscriminately killed, with terrible carnage, the whole population. The miserable inhabitants fled from the savages, and flung themselves into the sea, hoping to find some security with the Portuguese; but although some prisoners, including Ali-Bey, were taken, the majority who escaped death at the hands of the WaZimba were slain by the swords and muskets of the Portuguese.

So ended the adventures of Ali-Bey, who was taken as a prisoner to Lisbon, where he turned Christian and eventually died.

These series of events had a most disturbing influence on the whole coast of Africa, and in about 1587, after the first appearance of Ali-Bey, the people of Pemba determined to rebel and rid themselves of the Portuguese yoke. So one night they attacked the Portuguese residing in the island, and massacred men, women, and children. The Chief of Pemba was strongly pro-Portuguese, and the rebels thirsting for his blood endeavoured to kill him while in his house, presumably at Chake Chake,[1] but this man managed to escape accompanied by a few Portuguese, and eventually found safety at Malindi.

Throughout its history Pemba Island has always been regarded as an appanage of Mombasa, and it evidently held the same political views as that important city : whereas Zanzibar, somewhat beyond the range of Mombasa influence, readily accepted the not very onerous domination of the Portuguese.

The Portuguese authorities no doubt took steps to restore their influence in Pemba, and they promised to reinstate into his former position the pro-Portuguese chief of the island, who had so narrowly escaped with his life ; but it

---

[1] The older form of this name appears on the Portuguese charts as Chique Chaque, which seems perpetuated also in the modern name of Kishi Kashi, a haven to the north of Weti in Pemba. The remains of a Portuguese fort exist at Chake Chake.

appears that the Pemba people again rose in rebellion, and gave their over-lords clearly to understand that they would not render obedience to this particular individual. It is related that he thereupon retired to Mombasa Fort, where he turned Christian, and married a Portuguese orphan who had been sent out with other girls from Lisbon.

These are not the only occasions that Pemba, no doubt at the instigation of Mombasa, revolted against the Portuguese ; but in order to keep to the sequence of events, it is necessary to leave contumacious Pemba, and to turn our attention to the event which of all others in the history of Zanzibar and East Africa should appeal most strongly to Englishmen.

I allude to the first appearance of an English ship at Zanzibar in the year 1591.

This is stating the case very baldly, for the arrival of that vessel on the east coast of Africa was the initial step, undertaken in the spacious days of Queen Elizabeth, which resulted in the establishment of our great eastern empire, and was one of the events which led to the predominance of the British race as a world-power.   •

If we wish to mark the road of our ascendancy through the centuries, then let the year 1591, when the " tall ship " *Edward Bonaventure*, dropped anchor in Zanzibar Harbour on her way to the Indies be not forgotten.

Fortunately there has been preserved to us the actual account of this momentous voyage, written in the delightfully quaint phraseology of the Elizabethan era. From this account full extracts will be given of all that concerns Zanzibar ; but so that the full significance and importance of this voyage of the *Edward Bonaventure* may be appreciated, it is necessary to go back a few years, and briefly record what the English and other nations had done to find a way to the Far East.

CHAPTER VI

I

THE Portuguese were not destined to enjoy a monopoly of the Cape route to the Indies for long. Rivals were soon on their trail, and although the Portuguese did their best to keep to themselves the secret of the Southern Seas, other nations quickly found their way to the Spice Islands of the Far East.

The French appear to have been the first to have followed the Portuguese round the Cape. Some of these French vessels were merely pirates which cruised about the Mozambique Channel, and intercepted the homeward-bound Indiamen. The earliest record of such a capture was in 1507. Other French enterprises of a purely mercantile character sailed from Dieppe in about 1527, and subsequent years, for the East via the Cape route, but the French do not seem to have ever seriously contested the trade supremacy of the Portuguese until the middle of the seventeenth century.

The Dutch were the most dangerous rivals to the Portuguese in the East, and it was this nation rather than the English which really possessed themselves of the Eastern trade which the Portuguese had so carefully fostered. We can, however, leave further mention of the Dutch until later, as they were never associated with the African possessions of the Portuguese north of Mozambique, and in any case they appeared on the east coast subsequent to the voyage of the *Edward Bonaventure*, the first English ship to drop anchor off Zanzibar.

The English, strange to relate, were somewhat slow to avail themselves of the Portuguese discoveries of the Cape route to India, and it was not till 1580 that Sir Francis

Drake in the *Pelican* rounded the Cape of Good Hope on his homeward voyage after having circumnavigated the globe from east to east. The *Pelican* was the first English ship to sail round the world.

Drake did not touch at any African port, but he records his passage past the Cape of Good Hope in the following words, which have a pleasant English ring about them :

" We ran hard aboard the Cape, finding the report of the Portuguese to be most false, who affirm that it is the most dangerous cape of the world, never without intolerable storms and present danger to travellers who come near the same. This cape is the most stately thing, and the fairest cape we saw in the whole circumference of the earth, and we passed it on the 18th of June."

In 1586 Thomas Candish equipped a small flotilla at his own expense, with the object of learning the secret of the road to India. The squadron, composed of the *Desire* of 120 tons,[1] the *Content* of 60 tons, and the *Hugh Gallant* of 40 tons, set out from Plymouth, and after entering the Pacific Ocean via the Magellan Straits, visited the Philippines, Java, and in fact penetrated into the very heart of the spice region. They returned to England via the Cape of Good Hope. Caudish had during the voyage made the most elaborate notes as to the routes followed, and he was enabled with this mass of material at his command to amend the Portuguese charts, to correct and amplify the existing knowledge as to distances, winds, soundings, currents, dangers, and anchorages, and to point out to his fellow-countrymen the vast possibilities of the Indian trade.

[1] The question as to how the tonnage of vessels of the Elizabethan period was reckoned is lucidly explained in E. Keble Chatterton's work, *Sailing Ships and their Story* (Sidgwick & Jackson, Ltd., London, 1909), as follows :

" Up to 1628 it (the rule of tonnage measurement) had been far from reliable, being reckoned by the capacity for storing so many tuns of wine. From the time of Henry V and long after," ton," as applied to shipping, denoted the capacity to hold a barrel measuring 42 cubic feet in the hold below deck. Therefore a vessel of 900 tons was capable of holding 900 such barrels. As the barrels were circular, and could not be packed close together, the tonnage was really greater than what was given. From 1628 it was to be estimated from the length of the keel, leaving out the false post (a piece bolted to the after edge of the main sternpost), the greatest breadth within the plank, the depth from that breadth to the upper edge of the keel, and then to multiply these and divide by one hundred."

As a direct result of this pioneer voyage, the merchants of London determined to dispatch a trading expedition to the East Indies by the Cape route, and " three tall ships," namely the *Penelope*, the *Marchant Royall*, and the *Edward Bonaventure*, sailed from Plymouth on April 10th, 1591, for the Indies via East Africa.

This expedition was a most important one, as it was the first commercial venture made by the English to capture the Indian trade, and the direct result of the voyage was the establishment of the East India Company in 1600, which eventually absorbed into its control the whole of the Indian Peninsula.

To anticipate events a little, it may be mentioned at this point that the *Penelope*, the flagship of the squadron, was lost off the Cape, and the command devolved upon that famous Elizabethan sea-captain James Lancaster, who was afterwards knighted by Queen Elizabeth in recognition of his services. He was a director of the East India Company, a great promoter of voyages of discovery, and his name was immortalised by William Baffin, the explorer, naming one of the great waterways of the Arctic Ocean after him.

Of the " three tall ships " which originally composed the squadron, the *Marchant Royall* was of 400 tons, and had fought against the Spanish Armada : while the *Edward Bonaventure*, the vessel in which we are now especially interested as having been the first English ship to enter Zanzibar harbour, was of 160 tons.

The introductory note to the original narrative [1] gives a succinct summary of the itinerary of this momentous voyage, and is as follows :

" A voyage with three tall ships—the *Penelope*, Admirall : the *Marchant Royal*, Vice Admirall : and the *Edward Bonaventure*, Rear-Admirall—to the East Indies, by the Cape of Buona Speranza to Quitagone, ncere Mosambique, to the Iles of Comoro and Zanzibar on the backe-side of Africa, and beyond Cape Comori in India, to the Iles of Nicubar and of Gomes Pulo, within two leagues of Sumatra, to the Ilands

---

[1] *The Voyages of Sir James Lancaster, Kt., to the East Indies.* Edited by Clements Markham, C.B., F.R.S. Published by the Hakluyt Society, London, 1877.

of Pulo Pinaom, and thence to the maine land of Malacca, begunne by M. George Raymond, in the yeere 1591, and performed by M. James Lancaster, and written from the mouth of Edmund Barker of Ipswich, his lieutenant in sayd voyage, by M. Richard Hakluyt."

As already related, the fleet of three tall ships above-named " departed from Plimmouth the 10th of April, 1591." They crossed the " equinoctial line on the sixt of June," and just previous to the event we are informed that the squadron took " a Portugal carawel laden by marchants of Lisbon for Brasile, in which carawel we had some 60 tunnes of wine, 1,200 iarres of oyle, and about 100 iarres of olives, certaine barrels of capers, three fats of peason, with other divers necessaries fit for our voyage : which wine, oyle, olives and capers were better to vs than gold."

Many of the crew fell sick, and two died before crossing the line, from the effect, so the narrator informs us, of "those hote climates " which " be wonderful unwholesome."

The squadron followed the usual sailing course towards the coast of Brazil, and then turned eastward towards the Cape of Buona Esperansa. On July 28th they sighted the Cape, but owing to contrary winds and to " our men being weake and sicke in all our shippes, we thought good to seek some place to refresh them."

They finally dropped anchor in the modern Table Bay, at that time called Agoada de Saldanha, from the Portuguese commander who discovered it.

" The first of August being Sunday we came to an anker in the baie sending our mĕ on land, and there came upon them certaine black salvages, very brutish, which would not stay." For twenty days they could get no supplies, " onely foules, which wee killed with our pieces, which were cranes and geese ; there was no fish, but muskles and other shellfish, which we gathered on the rocks."

However, they at length procured a good supply of seals and penguins from Robben Island, a few miles distant, and at last, through the intervention of a negro, got into com-munication with the natives. After a week, forty natives appeared with forty cattle and as many sheep, and it is satisfactory to know that these Devonshire lads treated the negroes so fairly that they brought another forty oxen for barter, of which the sailors bought twenty-four. " We bought an ox for two knives, a stirke for a knife, and a sheepe for a knife." There was also plenty of game, and " other great beasts unknowen to us. Here are also great store of ouergrownen monkeis."

The number of sick was so large that it was determined to send the *Marchant Royall* back to England with the worst cases, " as it was thought good rather to proceed with two ships wel manned, than with three evill manned : for here we had of sound and whole men but 198 of which there went in the *Penelope* with the admiral 101, and in the *Edward*, with the worshipful M. Capitaine Lancaster, 97."

Six days after the *Marchant Royall* had sailed for England, the *Penelope* and the *Edward* set forth on their journey eastward, and appear to have made good progress, for by September 14th they were in the vicinity of Cape Corrientes. Here a great catastrophe occurred, for " we were encountered with a mighty storme and extreme gusts of wind. This evening we saw a great sea breake ouer our Admirall, the *Penelope*, and their light strooke out : and after that we neuer saw them any more." [1]

The flagship *Penelope* had been overwhelmed by an enormous sea, and had sunk with all hands. Thus early were the seas strewn with English dead !

The *Edward Bonaventure*, after cruising about, in the hope of finding some trace of, or survivors from, the flagship, at length proceeded on her way : but misfortune was not at an end, for " foure days after this uncomfortable separation [2] in the morning toward ten of the clocke, we had a terrible clap of thunder, which slew foure of our men outright, their necks being wrung in sonder without speaking any word, and of 94 men there was not one untouched, whereof some were stricken blind, others were bruised in their legs and

---

[1] From the account of the voyage written by Henry May, who served in the *Edward*, and who wrote the account of his adventures on his return to England. This account is much shorter than that of Lieutenant Barker, which we have hitherto followed. Both are included in the Hakluyt Society's publication already referred to.

[2] " An uncomfortable separation " appears nowadays a strangely inadequate phrase to use in connection with the total loss of the flagship and her crew !

Gomes

OLD ARAB MANSIONS ON THE SEA-FRONT, ZANZIBAR.

THE BRITISH RESIDENCY, ZANZIBAR.

arms, and others in their brests, so that they voided blood two dayes after, others were drawen out at length, as though they had been racked. But God be thanked! they all recovered, saning only the foure which were slaine outright. Also with the same thunder our maine maste was torne very grievously from the head to the decke. . . . "

After this mishap they passed to the north-west of " the mighty island of St. Laurence " (Madagascar), where they were in imminent danger of running ashore, but managed to escape this peril, and missing Mozambique, they came to a place called Quintagone about ten miles to the north of Mozambique. Here they " tooke three or foure barkes of Moores, which barkes in their language they call pangaias, laden with millio, hennes, and ducks, with one Portugal boy, going for the prouision of Mozambique."

They next arrived at the Comoro Islands, where another misfortune overtook them. The narrative tells us that the island was " exceeding full of people, which are Moores of tawnie colour and of good stature, but they be very treacherous, and diligently to be taken heed of."

" The king came aboard our ship in a gowne of crimosine satin, pinked after the Moorish fashion down to the knee, whom we entertained in the best manner." They then commenced to replenish the ship with water, and had nearly completed their task when " our master William Mace of Radcliffe . . would needes goe himself on shore with thirtie men, much against the will of our captaine," to obtain a further supply of drinking water. While they were on shore they were set upon by the Arabs, and " in our sighte for the most part slaine, we not being able for want of a boat to yeeld them any succour." [1]

" From hence with heavie hearts we shaped our course for Zanzibar, the 7th of November [1591], where shortly after wee arrived, and made us a new boat of such boards as we had within boord, and rid in the road until February 15th, where during our aboad, we saw diners pangaias or boats, which are pinned with wooden pinnes, and sowed together with

---

[1] It appears strange that the *Edward* only possessed one boat. It may be presumed that their other boats had met with mishap, possibly in the storm when the flagship was lost.

palmito cordes, and caulked with the huskes of cocos shels beaten, whereof they make occam [oakum].

" At length a Portugal pangaia coming out of the harborow of Zanzibar where they have a small Factorie, sent a canoa with a Moore which had been christened, who brought us a letter wherein they desired to know what wee were, and what we sought. We sent them word that we were Englishmen with which answere they returned, and would not any more come to us. Whereupon not long after we manned out our boat and took a pangaia of the Moores, which had a priest of theirs in it, which in their language they called a sherife, whom we used very courteously : which the king tooke in very good part, haning his priests in great estimation, and for his deliverance furnished us with two moneths victuals, during all which time we detained him with us.

" These Moores informed us of the false and spiteful deal-ings of the Portugals towards us, which made them believe that we were cruel people and man-eaters, and willed them if they loued their safety in no case to come neere us. Which they did onely to cut us off from all knowledge of the state and traffique of the countrey. While we road from the end of November until the middle of February in this har-borough, which is sufficient for a ship of 500 tuns to ride in, we set upon a Portugal pangaia with our boat, but because it was very little, and our men not able to stirre in it, we were not able to take the said pangaia, which was armed with ten good shot like our long fouling pieces.

" This place for the goodnesse of the harborough and watering,[1] and plentiful refreshing with fish, wherof we tooke great store with our nets, and for sundry sorts of fruits

---

[1] The watering facilities at Old Zanzibar must be admitted to be indifferent according to modern ideas. The supply is from wells : but people were not so particular about their water in the sixteenth century. If by " goodnesse " the narrator meant " convenience," his remark would call for little comment, for at Unjuga Kuu there happens to be an ancient stone-built well within twenty yards of the landing beach, and one can well understand that a water supply so handy to the shore, which did not require the water casks to be rolled or transported far, must have been a great boon from a sailor's point of view. The well in question is in good repair, and lies within thirty yards of the spot where the ancient gold coins were unearthed in 1866. It is more than probable that it was from this very well that Sir James Lancaster and his crew obtained their water supply during their three months' stay at Zanzibar in the year 1591-2.

of the countrey, as cocos and others which were brought us by the Moores, as also for oxen and hennes, is carefully to be sought for by such of our ships as shall hereafter pass that way.

" But our men had need to take good heed of the Portugals : for while we lay here, the Portugal admiral of the coast from Malinda to Mozambique came to view and betray our boat, if he could have taken at any time advantage, in a gallie frigate of ten tunnes, with eight or nine oares on a side.   Of the strength of which frigate and their trecherous meaning, we were advertised by an Arabian Moore, which came from the king of Zanzibar diners times about the deliuerie of the priest aforesayd, and after by another which we carried thence along with us. .

" Moreover here againe we had another clap of thunder which did shake our foremaste very much, which wee fisht and repaired with timber from the shore, whereof there is good store thereabout of a kind of trees some fortic foot high, which is red and tough wood, and as I suppose a kind of cedar.[1]

" Here our surgeon Arnold, negligently catching a great heate in his head, being on land with the master to seeke oxen, fell sicke and shortly died, which might haue been cured by letting of blood before it had been setled.

" Before our departure we had in this place some thousand weight of pitch, or rather a kind of grey or white gumme like unto frankincense,[2] as clammie as turpentine, which in melting groweth as black as pitch, and is very brittle of itselfe, but we mingled it with oyle, whereof we had 300 iarres in the prize which we tooke to the northward of the equinoctiall, not far from Guinie, bound for Brasil.

" Sixe days before we departed hence, the Cape marchant of the factorie wrote a letter unto our captaine in the way of friendship as he pretended, requesting a iarre of wine and a iarre of oyle, and two or three pounds of gunpowder, which letter he sent by a negro, his man, and a Moore in a canoa : we sent him his demands by the Moore, but tooke the Negro along with us, because we understood he had bene in the East Indies and knew somewhat of the countrye.   By this negro we were advertised of a small barke of some thirtie

[1] Possibly the Casuarina.
[2] Probably gum-copal, which is imported from the mainland.

tunnes (which the Moores call a junco), which was come from Goa hither laden with pepper for the Factorie and seruice of that Kingdome.

" Thus having trimmed our shippe as we lay in this road, in the end we set forward for the coast of the East India, the 15th of February aforesayd. .   "

We need not follow the subsequent adventures of the *Edward Bonaventure* in detail, except to record that variable winds and currents carried the ship to Socotra before they were able to shape their course to India. They rounded Cape Comorin in May 1592, and sailed towards Sumatra. They picked up several prizes, but continued sickness so reduced their strength that by the end of the year there were only " left thirty-three men and one boy," and of these only twenty-two were fit for work. The mortality on these long voyages was terrible : the record of the present voyage states that at one place the *Edward Bonaventure* lost twenty-six men, and from the narrative of Captain Kidd's voyage in the Indian Ocean, to which reference is made elsewhere in this book, we learn that the famous pirate lost no less than fifty of his crew in one week.

To return to the voyage of Captain Lancaster. The remnant of the crew eventually became discontented and mutinied, and Lancaster was obliged to turn homewards in December 1592. Misfortune followed them, for instead of making England, calms and contrary winds forced them to shape their course to the West Indies, where the *Edward* was wrecked, and it was only after many adventures and hardships that Captain Lancaster and the survivors of his crew reached Dieppe in a French ship, and landed at Rye in Sussex on May 24th, 1594.

Unfortunately the information afforded in the narrative concerning Zanzibar is meagre. The visitors were evidently impressed with the commodious harbour,[1] the good water

---

[1] The *Edward* no doubt rode at anchor in the roadstead opposite the town of Old Zanzibar (Unguja Kuu). The statement in the narrative that a ship of " 500 tunnes " could use the harbour tends to confirm this opinion, because the harbour of modern Zanzibar can accommodate the largest of modern steamers. The remark, too, that a Portuguese boat " came out " of the harbour to the *Edward* riding outside is quite consistent with the topography of Unguja Kuu. The harbour at Old Zanzibar lies up a creek at the back of the town.

supply, the plentiful stocks of fruit and provisions, and on the whole they seem to have got on very well with the Moors of Zanzibar.

It would appear that Zanzibar during the ninety-five years which had elapsed since the first visit of Vasco da Gama to East Africa had gained a certain amount of local importance, for the arrival of a ship from Goa laden with pepper, as also the fact that the *Bonaventure* chose Zanzibar rather than any of the other coast towns to await the change in the monsoon, point to the growing importance of the place. It is clear, however, that at the time of Lancaster's visit no fort existed, and there was evidently no Portuguese garrison. The extent of the Portuguese occupation of the island consisted in the establishment of a factory or trade-depot, where produce was purchased and collected for shipment to Mozambique, whence African cargoes were picked up by the returning Indiamen bound for Lisbon. In other respects the affairs of the island were managed by the local " king," the predecessor of the Mwinyi Mkuu of Dunga.

The next glimpse of the Zanzibar Islands afforded us is the visit in 1608 of Captain Alexander Sharpeigh, who commanded the *Ascension*. This vessel with the *Union*, commanded by Captain Richard Rowles, formed the fourth East Indian expedition dispatched from England by the newly formed East India Company. The venture was rather unfortunate, for the two ships were separated off the Cape, and the *Ascension* was eventually wrecked off Cambay, while the *Union* after great tribulation was found in a parlous condition at Madagascar by Sir Henry Middleton, who commanded the sixth voyage to India in 1610.

Our first reference must be to Captain Sharpeigh.

Having failed to obtain a supply of water at the Comoro Islands, he came on to Pemba, but why he passed Zanzibar without calling is not stated in his narrative.[1]

He tells us that at first the people of Pemba appeared quite friendly, but the Portuguese in the island, jealous of

---

The account of his voyage to Pemba is from a record written by himself, supplemented by the report of the journey in the India Office archives. The extracts are from the Hakluyt Society's publication, *The Voyages of Sir James Lancaster, Kt., to the East Indies*.

the advent of the English to the east coast of Africa, induced
the natives to attack a party of seamen from the *Ascension*,
who had been sent on shore to fill the water casks, no doubt
from the stream which runs at the back of the town of Chake
Chake. One man was killed, another wounded, and a third
was missing. No tidings could be obtained of the latter,
and a force landed the following day to seek him. Whether
he was found is not quite clear from the narrative, but at any
rate when the search party returned the *Ascension* at once
put to sea, having evidently had enough of Pemba.

The following year, that is in 1609, the *Union* under the
command of Captain Rowles arrived at Zanzibar. It will
be remembered that the *Ascension* and the *Union* had left
England in company, but had become separated off the Cape
of Good Hope. The *Union* fared little better at Zanzibar
than the *Ascension* had done the previous year at Pemba,
but the visit to Zanzibar had better be related in the words
of one Nicholas Downton, the second-in-command to Sir
Henry Middleton, who commanded the sixth expedition to
India. Middleton's squadron discovered the *Union* anchored
in St. Augustine's Bay at Madagascar, and learnt that after
losing sight of the *Ascension*, the *Union* had followed after,
and " put into Zanzabar, an iland bordering on the Abexin
[Abyssinian] coast, where the Portugals made show of
favour and trade, inticing them to land wth their boat, where
they betrayed and took three of their men : the rest seeing
their dainger fled wth the boat unto the ship, who proceeded
on their journey, till owing to contrary winds they were
enforced to return to Madagascar."

Another reference to this incident at Zanzibar is given in
the India Office records, which state that the *Union* when
discovered in St. Augustine's Bay " had road there six
weekes. And she was in great distresse for want of vittles :
so wee relieved hir, for shee was homeward bound, laden
with peper, having in hir one merchante whose name was
Mr. Bradshawe, for the rest of the merchantes with the
Captayne was betrayed at a place caled Zensebar."

It is evident that since the visit of Sir James Lancaster
in the *Edward Bonaventure*, the " Portugals " had become
seriously alarmed at the number of English ships which were

finding their way to India; and in fact at the period the *Union* visited Zanzibar, there were clear indications that their trade supremacy in the East was already doomed.

II

In 1622 Portuguese prestige received a staggering blow when Ormuz, that island of fabled wealth in the Persian Gulf, was taken from them by a Persian force assisted by English ships. Ormuz was the key of the Persian Gulf, and had been captured by Albuquerque in the year 1511. The island itself was merely a barren waste of sand and salt, but its strategical position and transit trade were so important that its possession was regarded as of the very greatest importance by the Portuguese. It is stated that at the time of its capture by the Portuguese, the town contained 30,000 soldiers of whom 4,000 were Persian archers. There were said to have been no less than 400 vessels in the port, of which 60 were of considerable size.

Ormuz was close to the small kingdom of Omân, and in due course the coveted island was captured by the Omânis from the Persians. Three of the great Portuguese bronze guns which had been taken from the Portuguese by the Persians at the capture of the island in 1622 are now in Zanzibar, having been brought hither by the Omân Arabs in the nineteenth century.

In 1650 the Portuguese were driven from Muscat, the capital of Omân, and from that date the ascendancy of the Omân Arab on the east coast of Africa and in Zanzibar may be reckoned to have commenced.

But in order to adhere to the due sequence of events in Zanzibar, it is necessary to retrace our steps a little.

After the visit of the *Union* to Zanzibar in 1609, nothing of very pronounced interest occurred until 1627, when a most serious insurrection against the Portuguese took place among the Moslem States on the east coast; and as Pemba was prominently concerned in the matter, it may be referred to briefly here.

The revolt started at Mombasa in the following manner.

Yussuf, the son of Ahmed, the Sultan of Mombasa, had been sent when a lad to be educated at Goa, where he had been converted to Christianity. When his father died he succeeded to the rulership of Mombasa, at which place the Portuguese in 1594 had erected a powerful fortress. Friction arose between Yussuf and the Portuguese Governor, which resulted in an open quarrel, in which the former stabbed the latter to death, and a general rising of the native population ensued. The Portuguese who escaped fled for safety to the Convent, and after holding out for some days, agreed to submit, on the understanding that their lives would be safe and that they would be permitted to leave without molestation. Yussuf agreed, but no sooner did the unfortunate Christians leave the building than they were massacred without distinction of sex or age by the natives.

This massacre at Mombasa was the signal for a general rising on the coast, and Pemba was deeply involved. This we know for certain, for over the gateway of Mombasa Fort is a lengthy inscription in Portuguese, which, while recounting various episodes during the governorship of Francisco de Seixas and Cabreira, specifically mentions the punishments meted out to the rebels of Pemba.

The following is the translation of the inscription referred to. It is full of interest as being a contemporary record of the events of the period :

" In 1635 Captain Major Francisco de Seixas and Cabreira was commander of this fortress for four years, he being twenty-seven years of age : he rebuilt it, and constructed this Guard House. He again subdued to His Majesty [1] the coast of Malindi, which had rebelled in favour of the tyrant [1] : and he made the kings of Otondo, Mandra, Luziva, and Jaca tributary : he personally inflicted on Patta and Siu a punishment hitherto unknown in India, even to the razing of their walls : he punished the Muzungulos,[3] chastised Pemba and

---

[1] This King must have been Philip IV of Spain, who reigned from 1621 to 1665. Portugal was under the domination of Spain from 1580 to 1640.

[2] The " tyrant " no doubt was Yussuf-bin-Ahmed, who killed the Governor of Mombasa Fort and then massacred the Portuguese.

[3] A negro race dwelling in the vicinity of Mombasa. They were the terror of the Portuguese, who were continually apprehensive of these savages.

its rebellious people, putting to death on his own responsibility the rebel kings and all the principal chiefs : he caused to be paid the tribute which all had refused to His Majesty. For all these services, he was made Gentleman of the Royal Household, having already been rewarded for former services, by the decoration of the Order of Christ, with a pension of 50,000 reis, six years' government of Jafampatao, and four years of Biligao, with authority of being empowered to fill all the posts during his lifetime.

" Pedro da Silva was Viceroy, A.D. 1639."

The events enumerated in the above record fully explain the establishment of a Portuguese fort in Pemba, for it must be remembered that the people of that island, as being closely associated with Mombasa, were always hostile to the Portuguese.

With regard to this point, there is a very illuminating paragraph in the Letter of Instructions issued at Goa in 1598 by Francisco da Gama, Viceroy of India, to Ruy Soares de Mello, on the latter's appointment as Commandant of the fort at Mombasa.

The Viceroy instructs de Mello in the following terms :

" I order you to put down the insurrection in Pemba as it is from this island that all movements are made against the fortress (Mombasa). You must arrange that the new King is placed on the throne and supported in everything. This I expect from you."

Apart from the necessity of maintaining order among the disaffected people of Pemba, another reason which induced the Portuguese to build a fort there was that they seriously contemplated, at one time, the transfer of the seat of government from Mombasa to that island.

In 1635 a Portuguese named Barreto de Rezende, secretary to Count Linhares, the Viceroy of India, wrote an account of the Portuguese possessions in India and Africa, and from this work some idea of the condition of affairs in Zanzibar and Pemba at this particular time can be obtained.

Zanzibar, we learn, was at the above date independent, and had ceased to pay tribute to Portugal, but the Mahomedan ruler was on excellent terms with the Portuguese.

It is characteristic of Zanzibar to-day never to be bigoted

about anything. She took amicably to the Persians of the Middle Ages ; she was friendly with the Portuguese ; she tolerated the Indian ; she assimilated the Omân Arab ; and she welcomed the English. And we and the other aliens of past eras, who have invaded her shores and made ourselves at home within her gates, have become attracted by her charms, and like the lotus-eaters of old time turn back and seek her longingly. The sky is too blue, the scented airs of her gardens and groves are too fragrant and re-poseful, to quarrel about creeds and such-like matters. So Zanzibar welcomed all comers to her shores ; and while Pemba strove to drive the Christian out, Zanzibar sheltered him.

Rezende tells us that in his day there were several Portu-guese with their families living in the island, and cultivating their plantations in perfect security. There was actually a church, in which service was conducted by a brother of the Order of St. Augustine, and the Sultan actively protected those who were Christians.

The island was famed for its excellent timber, and no difficulties were ever placed in the way of the Portuguese obtaining all they required. The Governor of Mozambique had an agent at Zanzibar, who made all purchases required by the Portuguese.

It is evident from this rather meagre account by Rezende that the Portuguese were not deeply interested in Zanzibar, and had not exploited it to any extent. They maintained no garrison in the island, and had built no fort. The adminis-tration appears to have been entirely in the hands of the local Sultan, and no doubt the Portuguese were glad to know that there was at least one port on the East African coast whither their ships could resort in safety, and whence supplies of all kinds could be obtained.

With regard to Pemba, Rezende records that it was thickly populated, and could provide at least 5,000 fighting men. The island, he says, contained fourteen villages, inhabited by Moors and natives of Africa, the latter having been attracted to the island by the former—not by the Portuguese as is popularly supposed—for purposes of cultivation; and although the rigours of Portuguese rule had tended to diminish the number of its inhabitants, the island was forced to supply to the Portuguese 600 makandas [1] of rice annually.

This rice, Rezende mentions, was grown in great quantities, and was of better quality than that received from India. Besides rice, simsim and many varieties of fruit and vegetables were cultivated, and there were many large herds of cattle, and a quantity of butter was manufactured. Wild pig were plentiful, and Rezende attributes their presence in the island to the domestic pigs which the first Portuguese inhabitants had left behind them.

Rezende is probably correct in his surmise, for the wild pig of Pemba at the present day is distinct from the common bush-pig which inhabits Zanzibar and the mainland of Africa. Zanzibar no doubt received its contribution of pig from the African continent at the same period as its leopards, while Pemba, isolated as it is from Africa by sea-channels of vast depth, was safe from such intruders.

Rezende adds that both Mombasa and Mozambique were largely dependent on Pemba for their supplies of food.

To clearly understand the position of the Portuguese in Zanzibar, in Pemba, and on the east coast of Africa generally in the sixteenth and seventeenth centuries, it is desirable to reiterate what has already been said, that their occupation of these regions was not for the purpose of colonisation such as is understood at the present day. There is nothing to support the idea that either Zanzibar or Pemba or any other point along the coast was crowded with Portuguese colonists intent on opening up the country. In fact everything points to the contrary.

It must be remembered that their advent to East Africa was a means to an end, and that end was the acquisition of the wealth and produce, not of Africa, but of Asia and the Far East. Their occupancy of African ports was to ensure the safety of the sea-route between Lisbon and the Indies.

Primarily they did not come to Africa to colonise : that was the last thing they aspired to. Moreover, they were a small nation with tremendous imperial responsibilities, and

---

[1] *Kanda*, plur. *makanda*, a long narrow matting bag, broader at the bottom than at the mouth (Steere's *Handbook of the Swahili Language*). Makanda are still used in Zanzibar.

they could ill afford, even if their policy had so dictated, to garrison such an unproductive island as Zanzibar then was.

It required the acumen of an Arab to perceive the possibilities of Zanzibar, and to turn it into the chief spice island of the world !

It is true that the Portuguese founded settlements up the Zambesi, which exist to this day, but their object was not colonisation as we understand it, but the winning of gold. That was the lure which induced them to strain their national resources of man-power, and to embark in African enterprises in the interior of Africa. Their anticipations with respect to the extent of the Sofala gold trade had been disappointed, and so they endeavoured to find for themselves the sources of the gold which from time immemorial mankind had associated with some mysterious region of Africa. So the Portuguese, dominated by the gold tradition, pressed on into unknown Africa, and marked their course with the graves of some of their best men, and by the skeletons of thousands of natives who opposed their progress.

This being the case, there is little difficulty in understanding why it was that the Portuguese did so little to exploit or develop such places as Zanzibar during their sojourn on the coast of East Africa. Even if their policy had been one of colonisation and development, they could not have found the men to have made it effective.

They occupied and fortified certain places such as Mozambique and Mombasa, and even Pemba, for strategical reasons, in order to safeguard their road to India, and to prevent as far as possible the access of rivals, but it is certain that their occupancy and domination over Zanzibar was of the slightest.

III

Before passing on to consider the last phase of Portuguese domination on the Azanian coasts, it will be convenient at this point to refer briefly to certain episodes derived from Portuguese and other sources which refer to the local history and conditions of Zanzibar during the latter part of the seventeenth and the commencement of the eighteenth centuries.

These historical fragments are of no great importance in themselves, but they are of great interest as throwing some light on the local history of Zanzibar, and affording us some insight into the home politics of the island during the period in question.

It is desirable to bear in mind that up to the middle of the seventeenth century a dynasty of rulers from Omân did not exist in Zanzibar as at the present day, and the so-called " Kings " of Zanzibar were Sultans of African origin, born and bred in the island with possibly some strain of Persian or other Asiatic blood in their veins, derived from the ancient Persian colonists of the later Middle Ages.

Attention to this point will make it easier to understand much in the history of Zanzibar which at first sight appears incomprehensible. For instance, it is often asked how it comes about that there are no ruins of stone buildings at Unguja Kuu (Great Zanzibar), the site where it is believed the old capital of the island once stood. The ancient Persian settlers have left us mementoes of their sojourn in Zanzibar, in their ruined stone-built towns both at Tumbatu and at Kisimkazi, and at a score of places in Pemba, whereas the more recent " Kings of Zanzibar," to whom the Portuguese were always referring, have left no trace of their existence, and it may well be asked what is the reason of the deficiency. It appears to me that the reason must be sought for in the following considerations.

The rulers of Zanzibar Island during the period of Portuguese dominance were not Arabs such as we recognise as the ruling race in modern Zanzibar, although I do not doubt but that the old " Kings " claimed some kind of Arab or Persian descent. It may be conceived, then, that the old capital of the island at Unguja Kuu was not an Arab city or town of stone houses, but rather an extensive native town of native construction—more African than Asiatic. It was no doubt similar to the great native Swahili quarter of the modern city of Zanzibar at Ngambo, and composed mainly of perishable materials.

It was not until Arab influence began to assert itself in Zanzibar that buildings of permanence became the rule. Even in the case of modern Zanzibar town, we know for certain that until the arrival of Seyyid Said in 1828 the town consisted only of a very large conglomeration of native huts, interspersed with a few permanent buildings of masonry along the sea-front.

It has been recorded that the Portuguese were driven from Muscat by the Omân Arabs in 1650, and two years later, we learn, a large number of Arabs arrived in several vessels from Omân and attacked Zanzibar. They killed a large number of Portuguese and among them an Augustine priest. This attack by Arabs on Zanzibar fanned the flame of insurrection among the native races on the coast, and matters became so serious that Francisco de Seixas and Cabreira, who had been Governor of Mombasa fort in 1635, and who had left behind him an account of his doings during that period over the gateway of that fortress, was specially sent out from India to deal with the situation. In a report dated August 30th, 1653, Cabreira states that the rulers of Zanzibar, Pemba and Otondo had asked for help from Muscat, and that the coast was in an unsettled condition owing to the advent of the Arabs, and ready to rebel at any moment.

Attention must here be called to the name " Otondo " mentioned by Cabreira, because this place became very intimately associated with Zanzibar. Suffice it here to remark that Otondo is the modern village of Utondwe, now a place of no importance, situated on the main African coast twenty miles north of Bagamoyo, ten miles south of Saadani, and immediately due west of the modern city of Zanzibar.

Cabreira gathered together a force of 120 Portuguese, 40 Indian soldiers, and 120 men from the ever-faithful Malindi, and attacked Zanzibar. He tells his superiors in Goa that he drove out the " Queen " of the island and her son the " King " of Otondo, and destroyed the place.

Now these last statements are of very great importance to those interested in the history of Zanzibar.

In the first place we learn that in 1653 Zanzibar was governed by a woman, secondly that her son was the Sultan of Otondo or Utondwe, and thirdly that the town of Zanzibar (Unguja Kuu), the old capital, was destroyed.

The native tradition still current in Zanzibar with respect

to the first two items is thus fully confirmed by Cabreira's official report. With regard to the destruction of Old Zanzibar, it is significant that local tradition asserts that it was a few years subsequent to this period that natives first began to settle on the site where the modern city of Zanzibar now stands. The advent of the Arabs and the destruction of the old capital at Unguja Kuu accounts for the foundation of a new town on a more convenient site.

The association between Zanzibar and Utondwe was intimate, for at least two generations of the ruling families of these places intermarried on two occasions, and on a subsequent page of this book it will be found that during the seventeenth century there were two " Queens " of Zanzibar. Both these women were direct ancestors of that somewhat mysterious person the Mwenyi Kuu or Lord of Dunga, to whom reference has already been made. Fuller details with regard to the genealogy and offspring of these two Queens, who were known respectively as Mwana Mwema and Fatima, are given on a later page.

One result of the attack on Zanzibar in 1653 was the release, so Cabreira tells us, of 400 Christians (presumably natives) who had been constrained to become Moslems after the taking of Old Zanzibar by the Arabs during the previous year.

Cabreira's enterprise against Zanzibar did not do much to improve the position of the Portuguese on the coast, and in 1660 the Omân Arabs captured Mombasa after a lengthy siege, a blow from which the Portuguese never really recovered.

In the year 1697 we learn from official Portuguese sources that the " Queen of Zanzibar " addressed a letter dated March 30th of that year to the authorities at Goa. This Queen was named Fatima, the second female ruler of the island. It appears she had married Abdulla, the King of Otondo.

In 1710 we obtain another glimpse of Her Majesty and of Zanzibar town.

By this time it is clear that the old capital of the island at Unguja Kuu had declined, and the modern town of Zanzibar had at least been founded. Zanzibar at this period, like most of the other places on the coast, was under the control of the Omân Arabs, and it is evident that Queen Fatima had Portuguese sympathies, for we gather from Portuguese records that she was so closely guarded by the Arabs as not to be able to send letters to the Portuguese at Mozambique.

This pro-Portuguese Queen, it appears, when first captured by the Arabs, had been deported in company with her son Hasani to Muscat, but had been permitted to return in 1709. It is of interest to note that the current native tradition that Queen Fatima had a son called Hasani is fully corroborated by this Portuguese record of 1710.

This man Hasani eventually became Sultan of Zanzibar on the death of his mother, and we hear of him again in 1728—the year the Portuguese recaptured Mombasa—as being ordered by the Portuguese to report himself at that place on a certain date. He himself, it would seem, perhaps either from old age or infirmity, was excused from personally going to Mombasa, and he was permitted to send his son Moçu (Musa ?) in his stead. Local tradition asserts that Sultan Hasan's son was named Mahomed, and so it must be assumed that Moçu was either another son, or that Mahomed was known to the Portuguese by the name of Moçu. The point is only of importance because there is little doubt but that when Sultan Hasani slept with his fathers he was succeeded by a Sultan called Mahomed.

In this same year of 1710 we learn also that there was an Arab garrison of fifty men, under the command of an Omân Arab named Said, stationed in Zanzibar, and a garrison of thirty men in Pemba. The building which had been used as a church by the Portuguese in Zanzibar had been converted by the Arabs into a very feeble and insignificant fortification : which, it may be conjectured, was surrounded by some kind of stockade.

This block-house occupied the site of the existing Arab fort at Zanzibar. It had three doors or gateways, and at each was a small cannon. The first gateway opened towards the " fishing village of Shangani " : the second gave access to the well : while the third gateway was opposite " the house of the Queen." It is evident from this account of Zanzibar town in 1710 that the Bet-el-ajaib Palace occupies the site of Queen Fatima's residence. It is also clear that the Arab fort we know to-day was not then built, and as a matter of fact there is evidence to show that it was not built as recently as 1774, for in that year Dalrymple, in his *Collection of Charts, etc., in the Indian Navigation*, has a note on the map of Zanzibar to the effect that the fort at that place looked very like a ruined church. This finally disposes of the current belief that the fort at Zanzibar is of Portuguese construction. As a matter of fact it is almost certain that it only assumed its present form in 1828, when Seyyid Said determined to make the once insignificant Zanzibar his imperial capital. This subject, however, serves to remind me that I have somewhat outstripped the proper sequence of events and times, and it is necessary to consider in a fresh chapter the final disappearance of the Portuguese from Eastern Africa, and the rise to power of the Kingdom of Omân.

CHAPTER VII

HISTORICAL : THE SWORD OF OMÂN

*

It is a remarkable fact that the power which ousted the once all-dominant Portuguese from most of their East African possessions was not a European one, but an obscure and remote Arab principality situated on the Persian Gulf.

The Kingdom of Omân, for so this power was named, is so intimately associated with the past and present history of Zanzibar that it is essential to introduce it to the reader's notice, and to tell him something of its fierce tribesmen and their fights for liberty, so that he may understand how it comes about that a prince of Omân sits on the throne of Zanzibar to-day.

The domination of the northern portion of the east coast of Africa by the Portuguese did not last much longer than 200 years, for by A.D. 1698 they had lost every dependency north of Mozambique.

It must not be assumed that this collapse of Portugal, and her relegation to a subordinate position among the Powers of Europe, was entirely due to the prowess of the arms of Omân. Such was not, of course, the case ; but it is fairly evident that if the rulers of Omân had not taken offensive action against Portugal at the psychological moment, the Portuguese East African dominions would not be confined, as they are to-day, to the region south of the Rovuma River.

As a matter of fact the degeneration of the Portuguese as a nation was due to a variety of correlative causes which produced their results after a prolonged period of time.

It would be outside the scope of this book to go into this question with any fullness, so it will suffice to mention very briefly a few of the more apparent factors which contributed to the decline of the Portuguese sway, and incidentally to the rise of the Omân kingdom as the dominant power in East Africa.

In the first place, the very magnitude of the Portuguese conquests must be regarded as one of the prime causes which occasioned the final decline of their Empire. The country outran its strength, and interior dissensions contributed to its loss of supremacy in the councils of the world.

The glamour and glory which attached to the doings of the great Portuguese sea-captains of the fifteenth century had stirred the imagination and spirits of the younger generation, who freely volunteered to serve both as sailors and soldiers in the new Lands of Promise overseas, where fame, wealth, and adventure were to be acquired by all who dared.

Many families, at a later period, emigrated to Madeira and the Brazils, which sub-continent had been discovered by Pedro Cabral in 1500, when *en route* for the Indies : while the demand on the decreasing man-power of the nation for garrisons to hold the outposts in Asia—not to mention Africa—became more insistent as the extent of the domination and the number of rivals increased.

No one appeared to perceive at the time the inevitable results of the constant drain on the population of the mother country ; and its dire effects were masked by the increasing immigration into Portugal of coloured labourers and slaves, who for a time served to fill the vacancies caused by those sons of Portugal who, tempted by Fame, had gone forth to the distant regions of the world, to cement with their blood the great fabric of empire.

The introduction of the Inquisition into Portugal in the year 1536, by King John III,[1] had too a most dire effect on the diminished population of the country, and quickly destroyed what was left of the old Portuguese spirit.

Nearly half a century later a still more crushing blow fell upon Portugal, for in 1580 Philip II of Spain claimed the throne

---

[1] This is the king in whose reign the three large bronze guns now to be seen in Zanzibar were made.

of Portugal, and the country lost its independence and became a vassal of its powerful neighbour. This domination of Spain lasted from 1580 to 1640, and is known in the annals of Portugal as the " Sixty Years' Captivity." It was a period of disaster for the country, from which it never really recovered.

But besides these domestic afflictions the Portuguese had to cope with subtle and deadly menaces, which in due course —at any rate as regards their supremacy in East Africa— sapped their strength to breaking point.

The African enterprises in which they became involved in their search after gold drew upon them the hostility of the native races, and of the Arab colonists settled on the African coast ; while their penetration into the interior of the continent ever tended to cast upon them further burdens and responsibilities, which, as time went on, they became less and less able to bear. And above all, year by year, the deadly climate levied an increasing toll upon their weakening resources.

These, then, were some of the causes which led to the enervation and the decay of that marvellous empire with which the prowess of the early Portuguese explorers had endowed their mother land.

II

The Kingdom of Omân is situated at the extreme south-eastern corner of the Arabian Peninsula, and its chief coast town is Muscat.

It has for centuries been remarkable among the heterogeneous principalities of Arabia for maintaining its independence in spite of persecution and invasion.

Of its great antiquity there can be no doubt. It appears to have been populated by immigrants of the El-Azd tribes from Yemen and Southern Arabia ; and Yarub, a descendant of Kathan (the Joktan of Genesis) is alleged to have reigned over the whole of Yemen, including Omân, about 754 years before the Christian era.[1]

---

[1] Badger, *Imams and Seyyids of Omân.* (Hakluyt Society.)

During the reign of Cyrus the Great in about B.C. 536, Omân was under the domination of the Persians, who were eventually expelled, with the assistance of other Arab immigrants, from Southern Arabia. Pliny and Ptolemy both mention Omân, and the author of the *Periplus*, writing in about A.D. 60, alludes to it in the following terms:

" . . . To both of these market-towns (one of which is Ommana), large vessels are regularly sent from Barygaza (on the Gulf of Cambay) loaded with copper and sandalwood and ebony. To Ommana, frankincense is also brought from Cana, and from Ommana to Arabia boats sewn together after the fashion of the place: these are known as mandarata. From each of these ports there are exported to Barygaza and also to Arabia many pearls, but inferior to those of India; purple clothing after the fashion of the place, wine, a great quantity of dates, gold and slaves."

Omân may be regarded as the Wales of Asia, and indeed, apart from political similarities, the geographical contour of its coast-line bears some likeness to that of our own gallant little Wales. Its people share, with other sections of the Arab race, the reputation of being imbued with a fierce, untamable spirit of independence, and with a fanatical spirit with regard to religious matters, which has refused to accommodate itself to all that was strange, or savoured of new ideas.

They were hard fighters, and good haters, and it must be confessed that when judged by Western standards of morality, their conduct at times was grossly treacherous to their foes.

Nevertheless, Omân has maintained its identity as a separate principality with a definite status in the world, when far more pretentious and powerful kingdoms have lost their individuality, and have become merged into the insignificance of some local chieftainship.

This permanence which Omân has enjoyed is no doubt partly due to its geographical position, commanding as it did one of the ancient world's great trade routes; and its people have during the centuries been forced to mix and associate with other nations, and thus unconsciously, and probably unwillingly, have assimilated ideas which have had a broadening and beneficial effect on the national character.

7

Thus the invasion of Omân by Persia, and at a later date by the Portuguese, have undoubtedly given to the Omâni a wider field of view, a greater enterprise, and more ambitious aspirations, than have been vouchsafed to more secluded sections of the Arab race, living in less accessible regions.

The Omâni was a great trader, and a great sailor. At the beginning of history he saw the treasure-fleets from the East, *en route* for the ports which served Babylon and Nineveh, passing as it were his door. Ships from Cathay filled their water-jars at Muscat when the children of Israel were still bondmen in Egypt, and if, as some have conjectured, Ophir was situated on the Persian Gulf, then certainly King Solomon's Red Sea fleet, manned by King Hiram's Phœnician sailors, must at least have passed within view of the mountains of Omân.

Coming to much more recent times, the Arab traveller Masudi has told us how, during the tenth century of our era, Omân sailors went to Madagascar and to Sofala, and brought back to Omân African ivory, eventually destined for India and China.

This intercourse through the centuries must, as I have said, have had a stimulating effect on the Omâni, and, as we shall see, the principality produced " strong " men, who during national crises arose and saved their country from the toils of the invader.

While circumstances, derived from the prominent geographical position of Omân, may have influenced the people, and made them more enterprising than the average dweller in Arabia, the principal bond which has held the Omâni people together as a nation has been a religious rather than a political one. The Omânis are Moslems of the Ibathi sect, the tenets of which are considered unorthodox by the ordinary Mahomedan. Of course the followers of this heresy were persecuted, and Ibathism in consequence thrived.

It was in the year A.D. 744, about 110 years after the death of Mahomed, that an Arab named Abdulla-bin-Yahya-bin-Abaz (or Ibath) commenced to preach his particular tenets. These doctrines are not, except to a Moslem, of any particular interest, and I have no intention of wearying the reader by detailing the beliefs peculiar to this sect, except to say that.

the Ibathi Moslem is regarded by the orthodox follower of
the Prophet in much the same light as a Nonconformist is
looked upon by an " orthodox " High Churchman.   There
is nothing very peculiar, and certainly nothing terrible or
scandalous, in the Ibathi manner of viewing the Islamic
Revelation.

One cardinal point of the Ibathi belief has had, however,
such a profound effect in maintaining the unity and solidarity
of the Omân people, often against great odds, that it is
necessary to make a brief reference to it at this juncture.

The Ibathi Moslems maintain that when Hussein, the son
of Ali, who was the son-in-law to the Prophet Mahomed,
was murdered, the divinely appointed dynasty of the
Caliphate of Islam came to an end, and they assert that since
that event any suitable person is eligible to be elected by
the people as the Caliph or Supreme Pontiff of Islam : and
further that such a person may be deposed by the same
authority which appointed him.

Acting on this doctrine the people of Omân, in defiance
of the remainder of the Mahomedan world, have for certainly
a thousand years appointed, by public suffrage, their own
Imam,[1] or Pope-King.   The first record of such an election
dates from the year A.D. 751, when the Omânis proceeded to
elect a sovereign of their own in the person of Julanda-bin-
Masud, who was styled " the first of the rightful Imams of
Omân.[2]

Needless to remark, such an attitude of religious independence, when the Mahomedan world was burning with
zeal for their newly revealed faith, led to a series of persecutions and repressive measures against the upholders of
such a heresy.

But the Omân tribesmen, fierce and warlike, entrenched

---

[1] The word " Imam " means one whose leadership or example is to be followed ·
a pattern ; a model.   Moslems use the term in its fuller sense as :

    i. The Imam or Khalifa of the Moslem people.
    ii. The Imam or leader of any system of theology.
    iii. The Imam or leader of prayers in any mosque.

[2] It is to be regretted that the names of Omân and Imam are so similar, as
likely to lead to confusion.   For all practical purposes the expression " Imam
of Omân " may be taken to mean the King or Sultan of Omân.

by desert and high mountains on the west, and by the sea on the east, received the new doctrine with enthusiasm, and maintained their belief in spite of all opposition.

The persecution which followed simply confirmed and strengthened the Omân people in their belief in the doctrines of the Arab and martyr Ibath,[1] and more than this, it has welded the tribesmen into a homogeneous nation. It is true that the tribes which go to form the population of Omân are ever ready, as in other Arab States, to fight among themselves on the slightest provocation ; but once the national spirit is stirred, they forget their private quarrels, and league together to withstand any danger which may menace them from without.

This has happened again and again in the history of Omân, and during the twelve hundred odd years which have elapsed since the first Imam of Omân was elected, whenever the national existence has been endangered, the Principality has produced men of extraordinary power and resource, whose prowess has given to the country a prominence and influence which neither its size, wealth, nor the number of its people would seem to justify.

One cannot but admire these fiery Omân princes, who, while the remainder of Arabia was under the yoke of the Turk, maintained the independence of their kingdom, often in the face of great odds : for after all Omân was only a poor, remote, and mountainous country, without any particular natural advantages.

I have no desire to confuse and weary the reader by enumerating a number of dull and unfamiliar Arab names, but the history of Zanzibar and Pemba is so intermingled with that of Omân that some brief reference to past events in Omân during the last 250 years is absolutely necessary, if the events subsequent to the defeat of the Portuguese on the east coast of Africa at the close of the seventeenth century are to be rightly understood.

Apart from the above considerations, it is hoped that the details now about to be recorded will stimulate interest and

---

[1] The Ibathi belief is confined to Omân, and is not found elsewhere in the Mahomedan world, except a small community of the sect which resides in Morocco, and no doubt originated from emigrants from Omân.

sympathy in the little Arabian kingdom, which fought so pluckily for its national independence, and which in the course of time produced the founder and maker of modern Zanzibar.

III

As already related, the Portuguese captured Muscat, the principal coast town of Omân, in A.D. 1511, and the rich islands of Bahrein and Ormuz in the Persian Gulf also came eventually under their domination.

As in Africa, the Portuguese had little inclination to interfere with the interior economy or administration of the countries they conquered or occupied ; but the domination of an alien race of unbelievers over the coast towns must have been a bitter experience to the Omân people, and it was not until the year 1650 A.D. that a deliverer arose in the person of the Imam Sultan-bin-Seif.[1]

This remarkable man drove the Portuguese from Omân, and recovered Muscat from their clutches. This victory of Omân over the Portuguese at Muscat in 1650 marks a very important epoch in the history of Omân and Zanzibar.

The prestige of the Portuguese had already received a severe blow when in 1622 the world-renowned island of Ormuz had been taken from them by the Persians, and their reputation still further declined both in Asia and in Africa when Muscat was wrested from them. It was the beginning of the end of their domination in the East, and the Moslem colonies of East Africa realised that a new power had arisen in Omân, to which they could look for assistance in their endeavour to rid themselves of the hated yoke of the Portuguese.

In 1650 that close association of Omân and Zanzibar may be reckoned to have been renewed which culminated in the once despised island of Zanzibar becoming the Royal Capital of the Omân Empire ; although it must not be forgotten that long before Omân overcame Portugal in Western Asia, the

---

[1] This is a proper name and not a title. As explained, the ruler of Omân was known as the Imam. The royal family of the present Zanzibar dynasty is still always referred to as " Aulad Imam," or the " Family of the Imam."

Arabs possessed a traditional right of domination over the East African coast and its islands, a claim which had originated when, in the early days of the Christian era, Arab trading stations had been established on the Azanian coast, and this right had been in a measure ratified, by the widespread colonisation in East Africa, by the Arabs from the seventh century onwards.

In about the year 1660, upon the earnest supplication of the people of Mombasa, the Imam Sultan, who had created a navy, prepared an expedition, and presented himself with a powerful squadron before that city, which he captured from the Portuguese after a lengthy siege.

This victory of the Arabs seriously weakened the hold of the Portuguese over their African possessions, and led to a general slaughter of the Portuguese along the African coast. The ruler of Omân could not afford to follow up his success, with the consequence that after a time Mombasa again came under the sway of the Portuguese.

The Imam, however, attacked the Portuguese in another direction, and ravaged and destroyed the strong Portuguese possessions of Diu and Daman in India. These places he laid waste, and returned in triumph to Muscat, laden with booty of all kinds.

No inconsiderable record for a small and remote principality !

Sultan died in 1668, and after a time was succeeded by his son Seif, who displayed the same vigour and energy as his father had done.

He possessed a navy of twenty-eight vessels, and his largest ship is stated to have carried eighty guns, some of which measured as much as " three spans at the breech." [1]

In 1698 he attacked Mombasa, and like his father he drove the Portuguese out, and captured the citadel and town.

He then proceeded to consolidate the Omân power on the

[1] It is almost certain that three of these identical guns are at Zanzibar at the present time. They are fine bronze guns, evidently of Portuguese make. A Persian inscription on them records that they were captured from the Portuguese in A.D. 1622 The longest is 13 feet in length and 22 inches across the breech This would just be " three spans." A fuller description of these guns will be found in Chapter XIII.

east coast of Africa, and Pemba and Kilwa came directly under the domination of Omân.

It is said that he even laid siege to the great Portuguese fortress of Mozambique, and except for treachery would have captured it. This fort was no mere wattle-and-daub stockade, but a stone fortress planned and constructed on the most scientific lines.[1] It will be remembered that the Dutch—no mean adversaries—had in 1607, and subsequent years, thrice laid siege to the place, but had been forced to retire discomfited.

During his reign he effected the repair of the numerous water channels, upon which the fertility of Omân so largely depends, and he caused to be planted throughout his dominions tens of thousands of coco-nuts and date palms.

He died in 1711, and was succeeded by his son, but I have no intention of wearying the reader by detailing the events of each reign, unless they have some bearing upon the eventual history of Zanzibar and Pemba.

We can therefore pass on until we arrive at the reign of Seif's grandson, who, in accordance with the bewildering system of Arab family nomenclature, was also named Seif. In these pages we shall refer to him as Seif II.

Seif II was a boy when his father died, and, in consequence of this fact, civil war arose regarding the succession. Numerous claimants to the Imamate arose; some possessed sufficient influence among the tribesmen to be

[1] The architect, a nephew of the Bishop of Braga, and specially skilled in the construction of military works, had been sent out from Portugal to undertake the task. At the entrance of Mozambique Harbour the massive stone fortress was erected. It was quadrilateral in shape, with bastions at each corner, and was so large that a hundred guns could be mounted on the ramparts.

The walls were of great height and thickness, and the main entrance to the fort was so constructed as to be practically unapproachable and unassailable either from sea or land so long as any of the garrison remained alive.

The fort, which was not completed until the close of the sixteenth century, was named after Saint Sebastian. Its architect, after starting the work and settling the plans, was sent to Daman, in Portuguese India, to build another fort there. On his return to Portugal " he was favoured by Philip II, the husband of Queen Mary, and from his designs parts of the Escurial were constructed. Thus, in Fort St. Sebastian at Mozambique, there exists a specimen of the highest skill of the sixteenth century."

(*History and Ethnography of South Africa*, vol. i., by George McC. Theal. London, George Allen & Unwin, Ltd., 1910.)

elected as Imam ; but so many were the claimants, that the party which favoured the young Seif II were sufficiently powerful to keep the claim of that youth to the throne from being entirely invalidated. In 1728 Seif II came of age, and was duly proclaimed as the rightful Imam, but the rival claimants refused to recognise him as ruler, and civil war raged with greater bitterness than before.

The Portuguese in Africa, learning of the discord in Omân, seized the opportunity to wipe out the defeat which the victorious Imam Seif had inflicted upon them, and again captured and occupied Mombasa.

Seif II, driven to extremities, imprudently appealed to the Shah of Persia—the traditional enemy of Omân—for assistance, and the Persians, only too glad of an opportunity of invading Omân, willingly agreed to help the hard-pressed Imam. But their arrival in Omân resulted in the most terrible disaster. They seized town after town, and fortress after fortress, and the unhappy Seif discovered when too late that they were capturing the country, not for him, but for themselves. The Persian invaders were guilty of every excess. They killed the women and children, or sent them to be sold as slaves to Persia ; they ravaged and slaughtered all who opposed them.

The whole country was so disorganised that no effective resistance could be offered to the Persian invaders.

It appeared certain that Omân was doomed. The distracted Seif, hard pressed as he was, looked in vain for help. It seemed as if nothing but complete ruin and subjugation awaited him and his kingdom.

But when matters were at their worst, a strange thing happened.

A Man appeared, and saved Omân !

The name of " the Man " was Ahmed-bin-Said, and special interest attaches to him because he founded the dynasty of the Albusaid, which occupies the throne of Zanzibar to-day.

There is good deal of mystery about this remarkable person, who at a national crisis arose and hurled the invading armies into the sea.

He does not himself appear to have been of royal stock,

although descent is claimed for him from Kahtan (the Joktan of Genesis x), great-grandfather of Himyar, founder of the Southern Arabs, and brother to Saba, the builder of Marib in Sabæa.

There may be some doubt about his genealogy, but there is none whatever about what he did for his country.

What his exact occupation was before his call came is even doubtful ; some say he was a merchant, but whatever his vocation he appears to have had a high reputation for courage and administrative ability.

The first meeting of Ahmed with his sovereign was dramatic. The unhappy ruler of Omân was riding with his retinue from Muscat towards the royal city of Rastak, when in the distance the royal party espied a solitary figure approaching, mounted on a splendid camel. The solitary rider was Ahmed ! King and subject met thus in the desert : and Ahmed was in due course appointed Governor of the important fortress and town of Sohar.

Tales are also current as to prognostications which indicated the rise to the supreme power of Ahmed ; but the cynical will no doubt observe that these kind of stories generally only transpire after the event. One of these legends is to the effect that, when quite unknown to fame, Ahmed arrived at a certain place during a festival, where a great crowd of people was making merry, and amusing themselves with camel racing. Ahmed determined to compete in the races, and he was about to join the other competitors, when a strange woman seized his camel rein and restrained him from participating in the sport, saying : " Oh, Imam of Omân, it does not become your dignity to race with these people, who are your subjects ! "

" You are deriding me," he replied ; " I am not Imam of Omân."

" By Allah ! " cried the woman, " thou shalt be Imam ! "

On another occasion it is related, that in a dream he saw the sun rising from under his sleeve.

Again, once when travelling on his camel by night along a lonely track, his camel suddenly stopped, and Ahmed, peering forward, saw a mysterious figure of a man standing in the way. The shrouded figure greeted him as Imam of

Omân. Ahmed hastily dismounted from his camel, but failed to find a trace of any one.[1]

A pleasing story is told of him in the Arab records of his life.

It appears that Ahmed, before he attained to the supreme power, rested one day, overcome by the heat of the sun, in the shade of a large tree. Later on, when he was seated on the throne of Omân, he chanced to pass the same way, aecompanied by a large retinue of nobles and slaves. When he reached the spot where he had rested in the old days, he looked in vain for the tree which had sheltered him from the noon-day heat. At length he discovered only the parched roots of the tree. Much to the astonishment of his suite, he ordered carpets to be spread for him near the trunk of the withered tree, and also directed that all the horses and other animals comprising his caravan should be watered there.

When he arrived at his destination, one of the nobles of his suite asked him why he had rested by the dead tree during the day's journey. He related to his court how he had once taken shelter under its branches when it was green and flourishing.

" Do you," asked his courtiers, " respect that which is devoid of reason, and is dead ? "

"It does not become the generous," replied the Imam, " to forget benefits. The generous should recognise benefits received from the animate and the inanimate."

Another story which discloses the softer side of Ahmed's nature should be borne in mind when reference is made later to his treacherous acts of reprisals against his enemies. The tale goes that whenever he travelled between Rastak and Muscat he was always accompanied by camels laden with sweetmeats, which he used to distribute to the children of the poor, who were wont to gather round the great man ; and when he had given to each child a parcel of sweets, he would dismiss them saying, " Now go away, and may God bless you l "

Before he was elected Imam, he was, as already related, appointed to the command of Sohar. This important town

---

[1] The similarity of this legend from remote Arabia to the experience of Macbeth with the witches on the heath will no doubt occur to the reader.

was besieged for nine months by the Persians with an army numbering 60,000. Three thousand shots are said to have been fired into Sohar daily. The Persians soon discovered to their cost that the new Governor Ahmed was a terrible enemy, for he was wont to sally forth and slaughter them in a wholesale manner. At the end of nine months they were only too glad to come to terms, with the result that Sohar was saved, and most of the Persian forces withdrew to Persia.

Seif II, who in his extremity had sought the aid of Ahmed, died while the latter was besieged in Sohar : and when the Persians raised the siege, all Omân looked to Ahmed to assume the supreme power, and in A.D. 1741 he was elected to the throne as Imam of Omân.

He had not, however, quite finished with the enemies of his country. Although the force which had invested Sohar had fled back to their homes, Muscat, the chief seaport, still remained in their occupation ; but seeing what manner of man they now had to deal with, the Persian commanders offered to come to some friendly arrangement with the all-powerful Ahmed.

The Imam said nothing, but came to Muscat, and appearing to agree to their request for peace, prepared a magnificent feast for the Persian garrison, prior to their return home.

Great quantities of stores and food were requisitioned from the Omânis to provide the feast, and for days the preparations continued. At last all was ready, and Ahmed entertained the commander of the Persian Army and fifty of the chief officers in the castle, while the remainder of the force feasted outside.

As the banquet proceeded, the drum in the fort was sounded and a herald proclaimed · " Any one who has a grudge against the Persians may now take his revenge ! "

The Omânis straightway fell upon the defenceless Persians, and slaughtered them almost to a man, Ahmed's own guests being also put to the sword. Two hundred Persians who survived the massacre were placed on board ship, and informed that they would be sent back to their own country ; but when they had embarked, the ships containing them were set on fire, and the miserable Persians were either burnt to death or drowned.

It is not a nice story : such treachery cannot be extenu-
ated or excused except perhaps by the most depraved of
mankind.[1]

Having driven the Persian invader from his country,
Ahmed turned his attention to the administration of his
kingdom, and he displayed an administrative ability which
is unusual in Eastern princes. He drew up new rules for
the financial, judicial, and fiscal departments of the State,
and entirely reorganised the administrative system.

He strengthened his navy, and raised a small standing
army, so as to be more independent of the tribal levies.

Learning that his old enemies the Persians were in Basra,
he sailed with his fleet accompanied by an army of 10,000
men. Finding his entry to the Shatt-el-Arab and to Basra
barred by a chain, he drove his flagship *El Rahmany* against
it, and broke it He then fell upon the Persians and utterly
defeated and routed them. It is on record that the Sultan
of Turkey was so pleased at this assistance rendered by
Ahmed-bin-Said that he every year sent a present to the
Omân sovereign as a token of regard. This sum was paid
regularly to the ruler of Omân until the beginning of the
nineteenth century.

Another adventure of the Imam Ahmed was the extermina-
tion on the coast of India of a horde of pirates who had
intercepted food supplies intended for Omân. He proceeded
with his fleet to Mangalore to make inquiries as to this
stoppage of supplies, and was very courteously received
by Tippoo Sahib. He subsequently sought out and destroyed
the raiders who had ventured to interfere with Omân trade.
For this act Ahmed was laden with presents by the representatives of the Mogul Emperor, and a friendly treaty for
mutual defence was entered into between Haidar Ali and
the Imam.

The withdrawal of the Portuguese from the East African
coast, north of Mozambique, had led to the renewal of Arab
influence in that region.

---

[1] " It can only be said in extenuation that such treachery was regarded as
justifiable strategy by both parties, and that the atrocities perpetrated by the
Persians in Omân richly deserved retribution " (Note by G. P. Badger, translator of Salil-bin-Razik's *Imams and Seyyids of Omân*).

The civil wars in Omân which followed the accession of the youthful Seif II in A.D. 1719, and the subsequent invasion of that principality by the Persians, naturally weakened the hold of Omân on the African coast, with the result that in many cases the Arab governors, who had been entrusted with the administration of these outlying possessions of Omân, revolted against their master the Imam, and set themselves up as petty princes and sultans of the settlements to which they had been appointed.

This was especially the case with Mombasa. Here in 1739, prior to the accession of Ahmed, a governor of the turbulent Mazrui tribe had been appointed by the Imam. When troubles fell on the parent State, Mombasa, no longer fearing Portuguese intervention, declared itself independent of Omân ; and this example was followed by many other of the African coast towns, including Patta.

Zanzibar alone among these rebellious towns remained loyal to the Imam Ahmed, and for its protection against Mombasa it received in 1746 a garrison from Omân, and was placed under a governor named Abdulla-bin-Djad of the Albusaid clan.

With the exception of Kilwa, Zanzibar was one of the few dependencies which recognised the overlordship of Omân, and as the Imam Ahmed seemed little inclined to interfere in African affairs, the Mombasa Arabs determined to seize Zanzibar. With this end in view an expedition was prepared, and, using Pemba as a base, the Mombasa ruler presented himself before Zanzibar and occupied the town, but failed to enter the fort. The scheme to wrest Zanzibar from Omân failed, owing to dissensions breaking out between the commanders of the attacking forces ; and on the assassination of Ali-bin-Osman, the Arab ruler of Mombasa, the invaders took to their ships and returned to Mombasa. This attack on Zanzibar took place about 1753.

Pemba at this period was completely under the control of the Mazrui chief of Mombasa, and so remained until the Mazrui clan was totally defeated in 1822 by Mahomed-bin-Nasur, the Omân Governor of Zanzibar.

Enough has been said to indicate that Ahmed the Imam of Omân was no ordinary person ; and as the founder of the

Albusaid dynasty, as the grandfather of that remarkable man Seyyid Said (of whom more anon), and as the great-great-great-grandfather of the present Sultan of Zanzibar, it is appropriate that his memory should be rescued from entire oblivion.

It is sad to think that the close of his life was over-clouded by the revolt of his own sons against him. He died in January A.D. 1775, after a reign of thirty-four years.

IV

A short link remains to be forged in our narrative so as to connect ancient Omân with modern Zanzibar.

Of the seven sons and three daughters left by the Imam Ahmed, a brief reference to two of them only is necessary, to make intelligible the future development of Zanzibar as the capital of the Omân sovereigns.

The eldest son was of little account, and although he lived for many years, he was content to remain in retirement; but it must be recorded that during the brief period he exercised his functions of sovereignty an expedition was dispatched by him to East Africa in 1784, which resulted in the reassertion of the Omân influence in that region, and in the complete recovery of Zanzibar, which island, as already related, had been invaded by a force of rebellious Arabs from Mombasa and Pemba.

The fifth son was named Sultan, and this prince showed all the force of character and prowess of his father Ahmed, the great Imam. He soon assumed the supreme power as regent for his weaker brother above-mentioned. Sultan is only of interest to our narrative as being the father of that extraordinary man Seyyid [1] Said, who was destined to make

[1] The word " Seyyid " is an Arab title meaning " prince " or " ruler." It was assumed by the Imam Ahmed-bin-Said, and when used in connection with Omân and its princes it is always associated with the highest rank. Only those of the blood royal are entitled to the prefix. The title of " Sultan " as applied to the ruler of Omân was unknown, and the present Sultan of Zanzibar is always addressed and referred to as " Seyyid " by Arabs and his native subjects. The princes of the Zanzibar royal family prefix the word " Seyyid " to their names, and the princesses the word " Seyyida."

The combination of the title " Seyyid " and the name " Said " is somewhat the name of Zanzibar a household word throughout the civilised world, and who was incidentally instrumental in making the Omâni Arab a permanent feature of modern Zanzibar.

Seyyid Sultan-bin-Ahmed, ruler of Omân, was killed on November 20th, 1804, during a sea-fight against Arabs. Although the conflict in which he lost his life is of no couse- quence in itself, it is so typical of the kind of fighting indulged in by Arabs, and of the sporting spirit inherent in the Omâni Arab, that a brief reference may be made of it here.

Seyyid Sultan had been to Basra in one of his frigates, to receive the annual gift made to the rulers of Omân by the Sultan of Turkey in acknowledgment of the assistance rendered by Seyyid Sultan's father, the Imam Ahmed, when the latter had routed the Persians at Basra.

On Seyyid Sultan's return journey, he desired to proceed to Bundar Abbas on the Persian coast, so he quitted his frigate and embarked in one of his smaller vessels.

At midnight he was hailed by three ships belonging to certain hostile Arabs, who challenged the Seyyid to fight.

The challenge was, of course, at once accepted, and it was mutually agreed that the encounter should take place at dawn. It is said that the fight which ensued resulted in Seyyid Sultan's favour, but as his opponents were moving off discomfited, one of the enemy fired a musket at Seyyid Sultan and killed him on the spot.

So Sultan the son of Ahmed slept with his fathers, and Said his son reigned in his stead.

unfortunate, as likely to lead to confusion; for although there is no doubt about the words when spoken or written in Arabic, the transliteration and pronounce- ment of them in English is not distinctive. In other parts of Arabia, and in the Moslem world generally, the term " Seyyid," like that of " Sharif," is applied to the descendants of Mahomed through his daughter Fatima.

CHAPTER VIII

FORTUNATELY the modern history of Zanzibar is relieved from being prosaic by the participation, during the first half of the nineteenth century, of Seyyid Said, the son of the Imam Sultan, who, as described in the last chapter, was killed in a sea-fight in the Persian Gulf in 1804.

The kingdom of Omân could produce, as we have seen, rulers and men of more than average strength of will and force of character ; but Seyyid Said, the Imam of Muscat and the first Sultan of Zanzibar, with whom we now have to deal, stands out as one of the most remarkable and romantic figures in the history of Western Asia.

Although perhaps not one person in a million has even heard of this Arab prince, it is the author's hope that these pages may do something to preserve his memory. Some of his actions, it is true, may merit adverse criticism : but as a aithful friend of England for more than half a century ; as the founder and maker of Zanzibar ; as the zealous partici-pator with England in suppressing the slave trade ; as the initiator of an industry which supplies the world with cloves ; as a most princely host to hundreds of ships of the British Navy ; as a great soldier, and as a strong man, Seyyid Said-bin-Sultan-bin Ahmed at least deserves that his name should not be entirely forgotten.

Seyyid Said was born at Semail in Omân in A.D. 1791, so that when his father was slain in the sea-fight in 1804 he was only thirteen years of age.

He had an elder brother named Salim, but with this

prince we are not concerned, and he drops out of our narrative. He was a great many years older than Said, and, although nominally ruler of Omân, the greater energy and influence of his younger brother induced Salim to relinquish the direction of affairs to Said.

For two or three years after the death of Said's father, affairs in Omân were managed by the lad's cousin Seyyid Bedr ; but the real power appears to have lain with Said's aunt, the " Binti Imam." This woman evidently possessed great force of will, and had evidently inherited in full measure the dominant nature of her brother the late Imam.

Intrigue is a second nature in an Arab, and, as might have been expected, it was soon whispered that Bedr the Cousin-Regent had designs upon the throne of Omân. He had already treacherously intrigued and rebelled against his uncle the late sovereign.

The histories of most exalted Arab families are filled with stories of assassinations and " removals " of kinsmen, under circumstances which to the Western code of ethics can only be classified as treacherous. One cannot, of. course, alter our standard of right and wrong to condone or extenuate these crimes, but it is only fair to those responsible for them to remember that our own past history, and indeed the past history of every other European nation, is darkened with similar deeds of treachery.

It should be realised that in a comparatively primitive society, self-preservation often demands, and possibly justifies, the killing or execution of one person conspiring against another's life. In Omân there are no police-constables at every corner to whom the timorous householder can fly for assistance. A man in Omân has to look after himself : and this is precisely what the young princeling Seyyid Said did, for two years after his accession to power, when about fifteen years old, he killed his cousin the Regent Bedr with his own hand. He did the deed openly in broad daylight, during a reception. There were no hired assassins or poison connected with the affair. I do not doubt that Said himself, his family, his counsellors, and his people regarded the deed as a legal execution.

It is said that Seyyid Said was instigated to perform the

8

deed by his masterful aunt, the " Binti Imam." This may have been so, but judging by Said's character in after life, and remembering the fighting stock from which he came, it may be presumed that he required but little encouragement to act as he did in order to save his own life and throne.

There are one or two versions of the actual murder, which only differ in immaterial details. That held by the Albusaid family is as follows :

Seyyid Bedr was holding a reception or levee.[1] Near him was seated, in due order of precedence, his cousin the youthful Said, and the Arab nobles and members of the Court. A leading Arab named Khalfan-bin-Muhaisan had urged upon Said the necessity of Bedr being killed, if the former wished to save his own life. The boy had demurred, and had asked Khalfan to do the deed himself. Khalfan had refused, but promised that he would assist the young prince in the carrying out of the nefarious act.

It is customary for Arabs of any pretensions to wear a dagger in the sash encircling the waist. These weapons have curved blades shaped like the letter " J," and the handles and sheaths are often beautifully decorated with gold and silver filagree work. This decoration, however, is regarded as of secondary importance : the real value of the weapon lies in the age and temper of the blade. Seyyid Bedr appears to have been interested in the matter of war-like weapons, and specially prided himself on the value of the dagger he then wore.[2]

Khalfan remarked, during the course of the reception, that he had become possessed of a dagger of remarkable quality, which even surpassed that of Seyyid Bedr, and he asked to be permitted to test one blade against the other.

Bedr, unsuspicious of treachery, drew his dagger and handed it to Khalfan. The moment the wretched man was unarmed, Said leapt from his seat, and plunged his dagger into his cousin's body. Bedr, sorely wounded, jumped from

---

[1] Generally referred to in Zanzibar as " baraza." The function is akin to the Indian durbar.

[2] An Arab dagger of fine steel and ancient make is sometimes valued at Rs. 1,000 (£66).

a window into the courtyard below, where the horses were tethered. Mounting one bare-backed, he rode for his life, pursued by the adherents of the young Said, the latter being urged on, it is said, by the " Binti Imam."

The pursuit ended by Bedr falling from his horse, and being dispatched by his enemies.

From that time Seyyid Said remained firmly seated on the dual throne of Omân and Zanzibar for half a century.

Lest the reader should be unduly prejudiced against Seyyid Said for this act, perpetrated at the instigation of others when he was a mere boy, it is evident from unimpeachable sources that his nature was really a most humane one. For instance, we learn from official records that during his long and tempestuous life he could scarcely bare to utter a sentence of death even on a criminal. In later years, to escape the necessity of condemning criminals to death, he often paid from his own purse the blood-money, amounting to Rs. 1,700 (then valued at over £150), to the murdered person's relatives, who by Moslem law had the right to claim the murderer for purposes of vengeance. It is further recorded that, during the latter portion of his reign, at any rate, the mutilation of criminals by cutting off their hands for theft, which was only too frequent an occurrence in the Eastern code of justice, administered under autocratic auspices, was practically unknown in Zanzibar.

But to return to the story of Seyyid Said.

The first twenty years of his reign were fully occupied with quelling turbulent tribes, both within and beyond the borders of Omân. His most formidable enemies were the Wahabis, followers of that most fanatical and influential sectarian Muhammad-bin-Abdul Wahab, whose doctrine was the purification and regeneration of the Moslem religion. They were the Puritans of Islam, and their fanatical zeal shook the Mohamedan world to its foundations. One of the chief sources of this cult was amongst the desert tribes dwelling in the country to the north-westward of Omân ; and in consequence the Omân principality became exposed to the full force of the religious storm.

There is no need to refer to the matter in fuller detail except to remark that more than once during Seyyid Said's long reign, the Wahabi movement in Arabia threatened the security of Omân, and Seyyid Said was forced for the sake of peace to pay tribute to the fanatical leaders of the movement.

In A.D. 1809, and again in 1820, the Government of India assisted Seyyid Said in his military enterprises, by sending ships and Indian sepoys to co-operate with the Omâni forces against some turbulent tribesmen, who threatened not only the dominions of Seyyid Said, but also the *pax Britannica* of the northern sea-coasts of the Indian Empire.

It was not till 1828 that Seyyid Said was able to turn his undivided attention to his African possessions.

His first objective was the total subjection of Mombasa, and the uprooting of the Mazrui influence there, and with this end in view he set sail from Muscat with a squadron consisting of the *Liverpool* of seventy-four guns, carrying the flag of the Seyyid ; the *Shah Allum*, a frigate of sixty-four guns ; two heavily armed corvettes ; and some six sloops, and smaller vessels, armed with four or six guns apiece.

With this formidable force Seyyid Said arrived opposite Mombasa in January 1828, and after some fighting a treaty was entered into between the belligerents, by which the citadel was surrendered to Seyyid Said.

Leaving a garrison of 300 Baluchis in the fort, Seyyid Said sailed for Zanzibar, and for the first time beheld the beautiful island, which from 1832 became his home and the capital city of his dominions.

He was received with much pomp on landing at Zanzibar, and he commenced at once, with characteristic energy, to lay out the extensive clove plantations for which Zanzibar is, at the present day, famous throughout the world.

With this initial visit commenced the long and intimate association of Seyyid Said with Zanzibar.

He had, however, only been in Zanzibar for three months when he was recalled to Muscat to deal with a rebellion there, and no sooner had he started than the Mazrui Arabs of Mombasa, taking advantage of his absence, attacked the fort at that place and starved the garrison into submission.

During the course of the next few years Seyyid Said undertook three expeditions against the Mazrui of Mombasa but it was not till 1837 that the place finally came into his absolute possession, and the chiefs of the Mazrui clan, who had withstood him for so long, were captured by means of a ruse, and deported in chains to Omân, where they no doubt died miserably in prison.[1]

II

With the complete subjection of Mombasa, Seyyid Said found himself in undisputed possession of the east coast of Africa from Cape Guardafui to Mozambique.

With wonderful prescience this Arab prince, brought up as he had been since a child, amidst the clash of arms, and within the narrow circle of the Omân court, grasped the potential advantages which might arise from an exploitation of the hinterland of East Africa ; and he further clearly perceived, with the eye of a statesman and a soldier, the strategical position which the island of Zanzibar offered as a centre of operations.

Seyyid Said's choice of Zanzibar as his capital has been fully justified. A glance at the map will show its geographical advantages as a centre of trade and commerce. It is obviously the distributing centre, and the trade-focus for the whole of Eastern Africa. Apart from its geographical advantages, its natural features must quickly have impressed themselves upon the mind of such a man as Seyyid Said. It possesses deep harbours, wherein the largest modern vessels afloat can find

[1] Mombasa had been confined to the care of the Mazrui clan when the Imam Seif-bin-Sultan of Omân had captured the place from the Portuguese in 1698. The Mazrui were an Omâni tribe, a portion of which had been settled at Mombasa before the advent of the Portuguese. In course of time they threw off their allegiance to Omân, and claimed complete independence. The successive rulers of Omân, however, never recognised this claim, and always regarded this turbulent tribe as rebels. In 1823 the Mombasa Mazrui, fearing reprisals at the hands of Seyyid Said, sought British protection, but the treaty between them and Captain Owen, of H.M.S. *Leven*, was not ratified by the British and Indian Governments, owing to the strong protests by Seyyid Said.

The Mazrui Arabs governed Mombasa for about 139 years, partly as suzerains of Omân and partly as an independent Sultanate. The remnant of the clan who escaped the vengeance of Seyyid Said settled in what is known as German East Africa, and their descendants have, during the war, been generally hostile to the British.

safe anchorage. Its water-supply is the best between Alexandria and the Cape. To-day no steamer sailing in the Western Indian Ocean thinks of watering anywhere except at Zanzibar. It is the natural point whither sailing craft from India, from the Persian Gulf, and from the south direct their courses. Tactically considered its position with regard to the mainland is also unequalled. Its harbours are on the western or the sheltered side of the island. It is twenty-five miles from the main African coast, and while therefore conveniently close, it is safe and secure from unexpected attack or surprise. And lastly its soil is so fertile that hunger is unknown, and it is here alone, and in the neighbouring island of Pemba, that the clove tree flourishes.

No wonder that Seyyid Said, harassed by rebellious tribes in Omân, loved the beautiful island of the Indian Ocean, and determined to make it his home.

It was a momentous choice, and displayed the shrewdness of the Seyyid. The advantages of Zanzibar as a capital, while so obvious now, were then unappreciated, and it required a strong man to make a jungle-covered coral-islet, which had been despised as of no account for centuries, his Royal Capital. There was Mombasa Seyyid Said might have chosen; there was Kilwa, the capital for a thousand years of an Arab and Persian State. There were half a dozen more famous, more ancient towns on the coast such as Lamu, Mogdishu, all of which outrivalled Zanzibar in history and in wealth : but no ! Zanzibar was his choice, and in 1832 Seyyid Said and his court came permanently to reside there.

With him came hundreds of Omân Arabs, and with this incursion the real history of Zanzibar and East Africa commences. Unexampled prosperity followed the advent of Said and his Arabs. Trade flourished to an extent hitherto unknown. The Arabs pushed deep into the unknown regions of Africa, and from the Indian Ocean to the Atlantic the fame and influence of the Sultan of Zanzibar, as he became known, spread. It exists to the present day. The old saying is still apt :

> " When one pipes in Zanzibar,
> They dance on the Lakes."

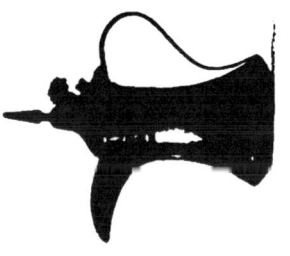

ARAB COFFEE POT.

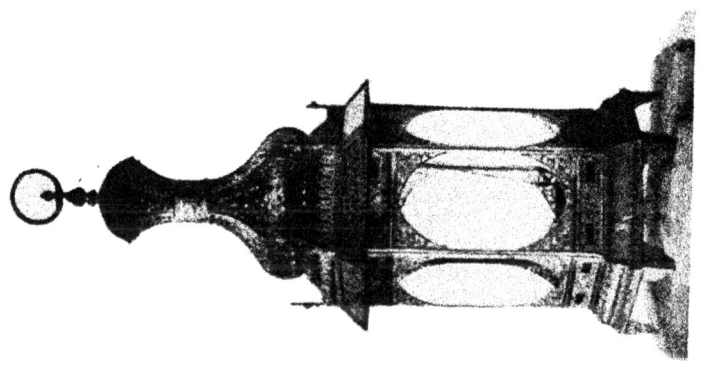

ANTIQUE ARAB LAMP.

PERSIAN COPPER VASE.

118

Zanzibar still remains to the African native of the far interior the Mecca and the Paris of his imaginings ; and the Sultan of Zanzibar is his Lord of the World.

In this connection an amusing instance may be quoted here, as showing how deep the influence of the Sultan of Zanzibar is in Central Africa to-day.

His Highness the present Sultan of Zanzibar, during the anxious months which followed the outbreak of war in 1914, very loyally exerted his influence to calm the susceptibilities of the Mahomedan Central African world, by distributing broadcast a letter of admonishment advising all to remain steadfastly loyal to the British cause, and not to be disturbed because the Turks had been dragged into the world-strife. The letter was circulated through the most distant and remote regions of Central Africa, and had an excellent effect. Among the many replies of loyal thanks received from native Mahomedan chiefs, was one which arrived months after the letter had gone forth. It was very badly written, and was in this strain

" We thank you for your letter. As regards the people called Turks we have never heard of them, and we know them not, and care nothing for them. But we do know our Sultan of Zanzibar, and we would wish to come to Zanzibar and lay presents at his feet. We are happy and at peace under English rule, but we have one complaint, that they stop us from shooting elephants : and therefore we cannot come as we would wish, to visit our Sultan of Zanzibar, for we are poor, and having no ivory, how can we come empty-handed ! "

Another chief wrote : " If the Germans are fire, let us pray to Almighty God that the English be made water, so that the fire may be quenched."

The Arabs who came from Omân with Seyyid Said were the pioneers of exploration in the Dark Continent, and the tales which they brought back of lakes and snow-clad mountains stimulated the interest of the Western world in Africa. Besides being merely traders, the Arabs settled in various parts of the interior, and, forming trading stations, became in time petty Sultans under the suzerainty of Zanzibar ; and thus within a few years of his arrival at Zanzibar, Seyyid Said's dream of an African Empire stretching from ocean to ocean began to materialise. The whole African coast from Cape Guardafui to Cape Delgado acknowledged his dominion, and it seemed as if Zanzibar might really become the imperial capital of this African Empire.

But Seyyid Said was born 500 years too late, for his aspirations and his ambitions of Empire were impossible of realisation in the humdrum nineteenth century, when European explorers and missionaries suddenly awoke to the fact that there was such a place as Africa, and that it was a continent worth possessing.

So it came to pass that instead of allowing Seyyid Said to possess the land, the nations of Europe divided it among themselves.

Seyyid Said was born out of due time !

III

Although Seyyid Said made Zanzibar the capital city of his African possessions, and chose to reside there rather than at Muscat, it must not be supposed that he in any way relinquished his domination over his kingdom in Arabia. He frequently travelled to and from Omân to Zanzibar, and when he was absent from one of his kingdoms he always appointed a governor to carry on the administration during his absence.   It must have been a most inconvenient arrangement, for as a rule he no sooner arrived in one of his possessions than troubles broke out in the other.

He maintained constant communication between Omân and Zanzibar, with India, and even with England, New York, and Pekin, by means of the very considerable squadron of ships he maintained.   This comprised three frigates, four corvettes, two sloops, seven brigs, and some armed merchant vessels of smaller size.   One of his largest frigates, the *Liverpool*, carrying seventy-four guns, he offered as a present to His Majesty King William IV.   The gift was accepted, and the *Imam*, as the vessel was renamed by the Admiralty, out of compliment to the donor, formed a unit of the British Navy of the period.

In Zanzibar he built himself two palaces, that in the city

being known as the " Bet-el-Sahil " or " the house on the coast," and forming the nucleus of a number of smaller palaces and mansions, occupied by his sons and the members of his Court ; and the second mansion at Mtoni, about five miles to the north of Zanzibar town. This latter was his favourite abode, and it is said that 1,000 dependents used to be accommodated, and fed daily within the palace precincts.

The Bet-el-Sahil was destroyed during the bombardment of Zanzibar by the British Fleet in the year 1896, but the ruins of the Mtoni palace still exist, and the steps on which Seyyid Said received and welcomed Captain Hart and the officers of His Majesty's ship *Imogene* in 1834 are still standing.

Burton writing of Mtoni as it existed in 1857 (that is, a year after Seyyid Said's death) says that it " has a quaint manner of Gothic look, pauperish and mouldy like the schloss of some duodecimo Teutonic Prince, or long-titled, short-pursed, placeless German Serenity. . . . We can distinguish upon its long rusty front a projecting balcony of dingy planking, with an extinguisher-shaped roof dwarfed by the luxuriant trees " in its vicinity.

The existing ruins show that it must have been an imposing pile in its prime, although from its low position at the end of a small bay it is not a very prominent feature from the sea.[1]

Owing to the encroachment of the sea, the old garden which stretched in front of the Palace has been covered with sand. It is said that at Mtoni were planted the first precious clove-seedlings, which were obtained from Mauritius in about 1828, and which formed the nucleus of an industry which has benefited the world.

One of the most remarkable characteristics of Seyyid Said was the rapidity with which he grasped the potential value of things.

---

[1] The whole place was falling into rapid decay, when circumstances in 1914 required that the ruins should be repaired and adapted for use as a Government storage go-down. While it is to be regretted that this old palace should thus be put to mean uses, the fact that the walls are now sound, and that it has been reroofed, will ensure that the old Arab arcade which formed the centre of the main block of buildings will be preserved from decay and total collapse.

In adapting it to its present uses, two upper stories were demolished and a large portion of the main building removed, so that the existing building gives but little idea of the magnitude of the original palace.

Here was a prince who till he was nearly forty years of age had scarcely left his remote and half-civilised kingdom of Omân. From his boyhood he had been engaged in quelling insurrections, and had lived amidst the clash of contending factions. He no sooner comes to Zanzibar than he at once determines to make it his capital. That in itself was a remarkable decision. Almost before his palaces are built in Zanzibar he foresees the possibilities of the clove industry, and immediately initiates, in spite of strong opposition, the systematic planting of the tree in his island dominions. Any ordinary man would have hesitated before undertaking such a task, the success of which was entirely problematical. Except for a few seedlings which had been planted at Mtoni, no one knew for certain whether this spice tree would really thrive, and if it did, whether the financial results would justify the enormous labour involved in such an enterprise.

Seyyid Said could have had only a very imperfect knowledge of agriculture of any kind, and yet, in opposition to the general opinion then prevalent, he persisted in his designs with the result that to-day Zanzibar and Pemba supply the world with seven-eighths of the cloves it consumes.[1]

Being an autocratic ruler of great determination, he carried out his intention of making Zanzibar and Pemba the great clove centre of the world, by issuing the ukase that unless every plantation-owner planted three clove trees for every coco-nut tree, he would confiscate the estate !

The labour of clearing such large islands as Zanzibar and Pemba was immense ; and the forming of nurseries for the young plants, and the actual planting out of the seedlings in their places, must have been equally arduous. That Seyyid Said's Arabs did their work well is evident from the splendidly laid out plantations, many now ninety years old, which we see to-day.

The magnitude of the work and the strength of will exercised to see it carried through are equally remarkable, for it must be remembered that there is no immediate return from the clove tree. Those planted in very favourable positions may bear after the fifth year, while others less

---

[1] About 10,000 tons of cloves are exported every year from Zanzibar. For further details concerning this spice see Chapter XX.

advantageously placed will not bear until the seventh year. Burton, who no doubt reflected the general opinions of other Europeans interested in the agricultural development of Zanzibar, deplored the extension of the clove plantations as likely to lead to certain ruin : and he advocated the cultivation of sugar as the only possible mainstay of Zanzibar's prosperity. But the Arab was right, and the European was wrong ! One thing is fairly clear that if there had been no Seyyid Said, there would be no clove trees to-day in Zanzibar.

The whole attitude of Seyyid Said with regard to the clove industry in Zanzibar and Pemba stamps him as a man of most unusual power and force of character, and the clove tree may well be regarded as the monument—and a very beautiful monument too—to perpetuate the memory of old Seyyid Said, the maker of Zanzibar.

Seyyid Said married several times. In 1827 he espoused a granddaughter of the Shah of Persia, Fath 'Ali Shah ; but the union did not prove a happy one, and the lady eventually left him. In 1833 he sent ambassadors to Madagascar, with the view of entering into a matrimonial alliance with the Queen of that island, but the latter would not countenance his proposals.

His next matrimonial venture turned out little better than his first. In this case the lady was a Persian, the daughter of Irich Mirza. She came to Zanzibar in 1849, with a large suite, including a private executioner, and appear to have scandalised the Omân Arabs by her behaviour.

Seyyid Said caused to be built for her the baths decorated in the Persian style at Kedichi, one of the highest points in Zanzibar Island, whence can be obtained magnificent views of the sea, and of Zanzibar gleaming white like a fairy city in a setting of lapis lazuli.

Seyyid Said possessed of course, in accordance with Eastern custom, a large harem of 70 concubines, and it is said that he was the father of 42 children, 21 being sons and 21 daughters. This number does not include those who died young. Tradition says that 112 children were born to him. At the time of his death 34 of his children were living.

In addition to the very considerable fleet, Seyyid Said also maintained a small army, and from time to time European sovereigns were wont to present him with gifts of artillery. The army was composed of various races, of which the Baluchi from Northern India and the Persian largely predominated.

Owing to the attention which was attracted in Europe by the growing influence of Arab power in East Africa, during the early years of Queen Victoria's reign, it was deemed expedient that British interests in Zanzibar should be entrusted to a properly qualified officer; and to meet this end, Captain Hamerton of the Indian army was appointed as Her Majesty's Consul and Agent of the East India Company at the Court of Zanzibar.

From this time British influence increased, and in time became the predominant feature in the politics of Zanzibar. There were many powerful rivals in the field, for the civilised world was just beginning to understand the political and commercial importance of Zanzibar as the dominating factor of Eastern Africa.

From correspondence written shortly after the arrival of Captain Hamerton, we gather some interesting facts concerning Zanzibar and its ruler.

The sanitary condition of the town must have been incredibly bad. Captain Hamerton wrote that in 1842 he counted no less than fifty corpses lying on the beach.

To turn to a less unsavoury subject, one garners some amusing insights into the perplexities which from time to time beset Seyyid Said.

It is related that in 1842 Her Majesty Queen Victoria graciously presented Seyyid Said with a valuable state carriage. The royal gift appears, however, to have considerably embarrassed the recipient. The first difficulty in connection therewith arose from the difficulty of finding competent carpenters and artisans to put it together. A Parsee was after a great deal of difficulty engaged, but he was assaulted by some Arabs, whom Seyyid Said punished so severely that one of the assailants died. Eight months dragged on, and still the coach remained in its original cases in the custom house, as no suitable place could be found in which to unpack it. After a year, a slight advance was made ; for a brake was constructed to exercise and train the horses destined to drag the coach.

Whenever Seyyid Said was approached as to whether any attempts should be made to unpack the coach, he replied " Inshallah ! " (" If God wills ! ").

He at length decided not to have the coach unpacked at all, because it dawned upon him and his courtiers that roads were a necessary corollary to a coach and horses, and as there were " no roads," it would be useless to put the coach together.

It is believed that the identical coach—still unpacked— was sent as a gift from himself to the Nizam of Hyderabad, in India, as an acknowledgment of an action the latter Prince had taken with regard to certain Zanzibar natives resident in his dominions.

Subsequently another royal gift was received from London. This time it consisted of a splendid silver-gilt tea service. This was duly unpacked, and highly admired, each piece being closely inspected by the Seyyid.

Just at this time, however, Omân was threatened by an invasion by the fanatical Wahabis, to whom Seyyid Said had paid large sums of money to desist from their intention of raiding his Omân possessions. In fixing the price thus paid for peace, he had urged his penury, and it is evident that he had no wish for it to be bruited abroad that he was the possessor of a magnificent set of " gold " plate ; so after inspecting the royal gift in the presence of the British Consul, he caused it to be repacked, and sent at dead of night back to the British Consulate for safe keeping. What eventually happened to this gift history does not record.

The Arab is particularly susceptible to a courtesy, or a gracious word or act from a superior. The gratification is largely due to the enhanced importance and distinction which will be attributed to himself and his family by his friends and the public. There is no word in English which quite describes this honorific status : *Heshma* is the Arabic word, and " reputation " or " prestige " the nearest English equivalent.

A typical illustration of how any increase in an Arab's

heshma affects him is told of an interview which took place at Zanzibar between the British representative and Seyyid Said.

As already mentioned, the Seyyid maintained a considerable squadron of warships, which flew the red flag of Zanzibar. These ships were sent periodically to be docked and refitted in Bombay. Shortly before the interview above mentioned, precedence had been given by the Indian Government to one of His Highness's war-brigs, which had been allowed to enter the dry-dock at Bombay before an English vessel.

This concession by the Indian Government deeply affected Seyyid Said, for it increased his *heshma*. At a full durbar which followed the reception of this news at Zanzibar, it is related that " His Highness made a most public demonstration of his joy." He informed the British Consul that he had never been more pleased. As he rose from his throne, and took the British Consul's hand, " tears ran down the old man's beard."

" Consul," he exclaimed, "you have always said that the Government of India was my friend, and by God Almighty you have told me the truth ! "

In acknowledgment of the courtesy thus extended to him, Seyyid Said sent four valuable Arab horses, two swords, and several other articles to the Governor-General of India.

The British flag was first flown over the British Consulate [1] at Zanzibar, at noon on September 29th, 1843.

The record of this event discloses the fact that Zanzibar had not yet attained that standard of enterprise which is so pronounced a feature to-day ; for it appears that the captain of H.M.S. *Cleopatra*, who arrived in Zanzibar, inquired of our Consul why he flew no flag on the Consulate. The reason adduced was the impossibility of obtaining carpenters at any price to make a flagstaff. The captain thereupon sent his six ships' carpenters ashore, who, starting work with a will, soon had a flagstaff rigged on the Consulate

---

[1] The British Consul at this period occupied the house now in possession of Messrs. Smith, Mackenzie & Co. The present European hospital at Shangani Point, for many years the residence of H.M.'s Agent and Consul-General, was not built till several years later.

THE " MNAZI MOJA   SPORTS GROUND, ZANZIBAR.

SEYYID SAID'S UNFINISHED
TOMB AT ZANZIBAR.

BASTION OF OLD ARAB FORT,
ZANZIBAR.

A PART OF THE OLD HAREM, ZANZIBAR.

[127

roof. The Union Jack was hoisted at the hour and date mentioned above, and the salute of twenty-one guns from His Highness's frigate *Shah Allum* was returned by the *Cleopatra*.

Seyyid Said died at sea on October 19th, 1856, at the age of sixty-five years, after a reign of fifty-two years. The event took place in the Indian Ocean, on board his frigate *Victoria*, while he was returning to Zanzibar from one of his periodical visits to Omân. He was buried at Zanzibar—the Spice Island of his choice !

His grave is situated in the burial-ground reserved for the members of the Albusaid family, which lies to the east of the Sultan's palace, and between the Government Gazette office and the house known as Bunder Abbas on the sea-front.

In the north-east corner of this cemetery, under a half-finished mausoleum, old Seyyid Said rests with his sons, Kaled, who predeceased his father, and the Sultans Barghash and Khalifa the First.

The unfinished tomb illustrates so forcibly one of the reasons why Zanzibar is deficient in beautiful buildings that a brief explanation may be given here how it comes about that the grave of the founder of Zanzibar is thus left desolate.

After Seyyid Said's death, his son Majid dutifully commenced the erection of what undoubtedly would have been a most beautiful and artistic mausoleum to receive the body of his father.

Architects, workmen, stone, and material were imported from India at great expense, and the work proceeded until the time came for the erection of the roof.

At this juncture the *mutawahs*, or puritans, of the Ibathi sect made a pronouncement that it was impious to cover a grave with a roof : and the further building of the tomb was in consequence abruptly stopped.

The unfinished tomb can be seen to-day, for a pathway runs through the ground and an inspection of the delicately fluted columns, and the rich and artistic embellishments of the walls of the uncompleted shrine, will indicate what a beautiful building has been lost to Zanzibar.

The dominions of Seyyid Said at the time of his death

included Omân, with certain islands in the Persian Gulf, and in Africa the continental littoral, with its islands, extending from Cape Guardafui to Cape Delgado. His claims to the African hinterland comprised the whole Central Region, as far as the Great Lakes, and indeed still farther westward.

How far these claims to the interior of Africa would be substantiated it is difficult to say : but the fact remains that at the time of his death, his influence, if not his government, certainly extended and was predominant in the regions mentioned : and he maintained at the more important centres regular garrisons of Arab, Baluchi, and Persian troops.

As already remarked in these pages, that sense of dominance has never been eradicated from the mind of the Central African negro, who still likes to think that there exists some indefinite bond of suzerainty between the Sultan of Zanzibar and himself. It should be pointed out, however, that this inclination is confined chiefly to those innumerable native communities who have during the last century absorbed some of the elements of the Mahomedan religion, and who regard themselves as pious Moslems. In the middle of the nineteenth century the trade routes across Africa were entirely under the control of those Omân Arabs who had followed Seyyid Said to Zanzibar ; and on these lines of communications were established Arab settlements, which were the distributing centres of the Islamic religion and the Zanzibar cult. The yearly or the biennial caravans passing through these outposts on their way to and from the coast helped to maintain and strengthen the influence and dominance of the Sultan of Zanzibar in these remote regions.

Of the permanence and extent of these Arab colonies in the central regions of Africa there can be no doubt. For instance, the Arab element in Nyasaland was only eradicated by force of arms as recently as 1895 ; whilst a vast number of other Arab settlements founded during the reign of Seyyid Said still exist in the Belgian Congo and in the territory hitherto known as " German " East Africa.

Had Seyyid Said possessed greater administrative ability, and had his Arab subjects better appreciated the significance of combined and united effort and of loyal subordination of self-interest to that of the State, he might have founded an African Empire on a more or less permanent basis. Destiny offered him the chance; but with all his foresight and strength of character, the means at his disposal were too unreliable to enable him to fully achieve his Dream of Empire.

No portrait of Seyyid Said exists, for, although he was for a Mahomedan the most unbigoted of men, he was old-fashioned enough to strongly object to his picture being painted or his photograph being taken.

Captain Hart of H.M.S. *Imogene*, who visited Zanzibar in 1834, when the Seyyid was about forty-three years old, describes him as a " tall, stout, noble-looking man with a benevolent countenance, clever, intelligent, sharp eyes, and a remarkably pleasant and agreeable manner."

Captain Guillain of the French Navy, and author of *L'Afrique Orientale*, visited Seyyid Said in 1846 and thus records his impression of him:

" It is rare," he writes, " to find combined in so high a degree as in the Sultan Said such majesty of figure, such nobleness of countenance, and such perfect grace of gesture."

Burton, writing a year after the Seyyid's death, thus describes him: " Shrewd and sensible, highly religious though untainted with fanaticism: affable and courteous, he was as dignified in sentiments, as distinguished in presence and demeanour. . . . An epitaph may be borrowed for him:

" First in war, first in peace, and first in the hearts of his fellow-countrymen. Peace be with his manes."

9

CHAPTER IX

1

SEYYID SAID was succeeded in Zanzibar by his second surviving son Seyyid Majid ; and in Omân by his eldest surviving son, Seyyid Thuwaini, the grandfather of the present Sultan of Zanzibar.

This arrangement marks the permanent political separation of Zanzibar from Omân. The administrative unification of these two principalities—so utterly unlike each other in topographical and other features—had only lasted for about seventy-two years, namely, from A.D. 1784, when Zanzibar formally accepted the supremacy of the ruler of Muscat, until the death of Seyyid Said in 1856 : but as we have seen in previous chapters the traditional rights of Southern Arabia and Omân over Azania and its archipelagoes had been established from the very earliest times ; and had been substantiated by force of arms, and by a long course of commercial activity and colonisation.

During the seventy-odd years in which the political entities of Omân and Zanzibar had been unified under one ruler, the relative importance of the two Sultanates had been much modified ; and with the exploitation of Zanzibar, and the awakening interest in African affairs, Zanzibar had suddenly blossomed forth into the metropolis and chief trade-emporium of the western portion of the Indian Ocean; and its capital soon grew to be the largest city, and the most important port, on the African coast between Alexandria and Cape Town.

Seyyid Thuwaini was Governor of Muscat when his father

died, and as the eldest son he not unnaturally looked upon Zanzibar as a portion of his rightful inheritance. Possession in this case, however, was nine-tenths of the law, for Seyyid Majid, who at the time was twenty-two years of age, gained the adherence of the chief Arabs and of the people of Zanzibar, and, ignoring the claims of his elder brother Thuwaini, duly succeeded his father as the second Sultan of Zanzibar.

After some parleying, and the inevitable series of intrigue between the brothers and their Arab partisans, Thuwaini assembled his tribesmen and forces in Muscat, and prepared to sail for Zanzibar and contest by force of arms his rights to the rich spice islands and the African dominions which he regarded as his heritage. Majid, backed by the whole of the people of Zanzibar, with whom he was popular, prepared to resist the threatened invasion by every means at his disposal.

What might have occurred had Seyyid Thuwaini been permitted to carry out his intentions to attack Zanzibar it is difficult to foresee, but fortunately for all concerned Her Britannic Majesty's Government intervened at the crisis, and forced Seyyid Thuwaini to discontinue his preparations against Zanzibar.

The rivals finally agreed to submit the question of the succession, and of their respective rights over Omân and Zanzibar, to the arbitration of Lord Canning, at that time the Governor-General of India; with the result that in 1861 the kingdom of Omân was awarded to Seyyid Thuwaini, and Seyyid Majid was confirmed in his position as Sultan of Zanzibar and of the African mainland dominions.

The death of Seyyid Said may be taken as marking the commencement of a new era in the history of Zanzibar and Eastern Africa. The British nation, deeply stirred as it had been by the work and exploration of Livingstone and other explorers in the Dark Continent, was just awakening to the potential value of tropical Africa. Hitherto the interior of the continent had remained a *terra incognita*, and a " No Man's Land " to Europe, although the Zanzibar Arab had, long before the advent of the modern European, penetrated into its innermost regions, and had indeed been the pioneer of subsequent European exploration. The great development which ensued, when Europe at length turned its attention and ambitions to East and Central Africa, obviously affected the position of Zanzibar, and while on the one hand its importance increased, the hitherto undisputed but rather vague claims of the Sultans of Zanzibar to the vast territories of the interior not unnaturally were laid open to inquisition.

The opening of the Suez Canal in 1869 also tended to draw attention to East Africa : so while the interest excited in Europe concerning Eastern Africa, and the attentions of European sovereigns, materialising as they not infrequently did in substantial and costly gifts to the Sultans of Zanzibar, were not unwelcomed, the undisputed and autocratic sway of the ruler tended to become circumscribed by treaties entered into with European Powers ; and the successors of Seyyid Said to the throne of Zanzibar must have frequently longed for the " good old days " prior to the development and exploration of the dark corners of Africa by Europeans.

The first treaty between a ruler of Omân and the British was that entered into between the Honourable East India Company and the Seyyid Sultan-bin-Said, the father of Seyyid Said, in 1798, to secure the co-operation of Omân against the designs of the French, and the Dutch in the Persian Gulf. The next treaty was dated January 18th, 1800, and provided that a representative of the East India Company should reside at Muscat, and act as the medium of intercourse between the Company and Omân.

In September 1822 a Convention which had for its aim " the perpetual abolition of the slave trade between the dominions of His Highness and all Christian nations " was entered into between His Britannic Majesty's Government and His Highness Seyyid Said. This agreement was followed by another materially restricting the zone within which vessels flying His Highness's flag could, with impunity, carry slaves without risk of capture. The zone was at a later date still further restricted, in order to facilitate the capture of slavers bound for British India. A further formal agreement was entered into in 1845, providing for the suppression of the export of slaves from His Highness's African dominions, and for the prohibition of the importation of slaves from Africa into Omân.

To all these measures Seyyid Said assented, but it may be presumed against his own inclination. He was indeed between the Devil and the deep sea. His concurrence with these treaties caused him heavy financial loss, and, more serious still from his point of view, it affected his prestige and popularity, and aroused the animosity of his own subjects, both in Asia and in Africa. On the other hand, he was shrewd enough to realise that it was essential to maintain good relations with the British and Indian Governments ; and in fairness to the Seyyid's memory, it must be recorded that however adversely his own interest may have been affected by these treaties which were thrust upon him, he invariably loyally adhered to the agreements to which he had set his hand. He moreover refused to accept from the British Government the somewhat inadequate monetary compensation which was offered to him to counterbalance the severe financial losses these treaties entailed on his resources.

As regards treaties with foreign countries, the first entered into by Seyyid Said was with the United States of America in 1833.

It may strike the reader as strange that of all nations the American Government should have been the first in the field to conclude a treaty with the ruler of so remote a principality as Omân, in the Persian Gulf. The explanation of this rests in the fact that American ships, engaged in the whaling industry, frequented the east coast of Africa and Zanzibar waters at that period.[1] These ships were of from 200 to 600 tons burden, and the chief whaling area was situated south of Mafia Island, but at certain seasons the whales were to be found much farther north.

American influence was predominant in Zanzibar during the years immediately following Seyyid Said's arrival there, and for many years the United States shared with the French the premier place in commercial interests on the east coast of Africa.

[1] The Arab traveller Masudi in the tenth century and Marco Polo writing in A.D. 1260 mention the quantity of ambergris and the number of whales in the East African seas.

The vertebræ and bones of a large whale which was stranded at Chwaka on the east coast of Zanzibar Island a few years ago are still to be seen in the garden of the Sultan's bungalow at that place.

To give an idea of the overwhelming predominance of American influence in Zanzibar during the latter half of the nineteenth century, it may be mentioned that in the year 1859 thirty-five American vessels entered Zanzibar and only one British.[1]

The American treaty with Seyyid Said was the prelude to others. Thus the treaty with France is dated November 17th, 1844 ; with the Hanseatic League (the towns of Lubeck, Bremen, and Hamburg), 1859. This latter Convention may be regarded as the first step in the development of German colonial enterprise in East Africa.

The treaty with Italy is dated May 1879, with Portugal, October of the same year ; with Germany, 1885 ; with Austria-Hungary, 1887 ; with Russia, 1896.

These treaties need not detain us, for they consisted in the usual formal clauses ensuring to the subjects of the signatories rights to trade and to reside without let or hindrance in Zanzibar. They further provide against taxation being imposed on Europeans, and mutually assure similar concessions to any Zanzibar natives who may happen to reside in the countries of the European signatories— a contingency not very likely to occur.

II

Seyyid Majid reigned in Zanzibar from 1856 to 1870. He was, it appears, an amiable and intelligent prince, and like his father a loyal friend of England. In appearance he was of fair complexion, and a full-length portrait in oils, now hanging in the Sultan's palace, depicts him as a tall man,

[1] The following table shows the shipping entering Zanzibar in the middle of the last century, and demonstrates clearly the prevailing influences at that particular period :

Nationality.	1852.	1853.	1854.	1855.	1856.	1857.	1858.
English	6	3	2	5	3	5	6
Hamburg	10	14	15	15	20	22	23
American	36	30	36	28	24	35	32
French .	14	18	18	13	23	26	21
Portuguese .	—	1	2		3	· 2	1
Spanish	3	1	2	2	2	2	1
Prussian	—	—	1		1	1	

of a pleasing and refined type of countenance. During his reign African exploration was at its height, for the dark years of the Crimean War and the Indian Mutiny were past, and the ensuing peace permitted the passion for adventure and exploration inherent in the British character unrestricted development. Fortunately for the peace of mind of this prince, the scramble for Africa by the Powers of Europe had not commenced before he died ; and he was thus spared much of the humiliation and bitterness of soul which afflicted his brother Seyyid Barghash who succeeded him, and arose from the seizure by the Germans of extensive portions of the African mainland which up till then had been regarded as the undisputed possessions of the Sultan of Zanzibar.

Leaving for a subsequent page the record of events in Sultan Majid's reign, it will be convenient here to trace briefly the events which resulted in the partition of Africa among the Powers of Europe, for, as may be conjectured, this event profoundly affected the territorial possessions and the political status of Zanzibar and its Sultans.

As mentioned already, the horrors of the slave trade in Africa resulted in the germination of an intense and growing interest in Africa, and numerous explorers of all nationalities penetrated to the innermost regions of the fascinating continent ; followed by a small army of missionaries of every persuasion, who settled in various parts of the newly discovered regions for the purpose of regenerating the pagan negro.

The Powers most interested in these exploratory and missionary enterprises were England and France ; and it was not until 1872 that Germany, flushed with her triumphant campaign against the latter country, turned her attention to the waste lands of Africa. At the time, and for a decade afterwards, it is strange to observe that no one amongst the statesmen of Europe seriously regarded the possibility of Germany ever aspiring to become a colonising Power. Her painstaking explorers, who systematically penetrated Africa, were regarded as mild and harmless professors, interested in abstract geographical questions and in the elucidation of problems mainly connected with botany and biology.

In about 1876 the King of the Belgians invited the leading nations of Europe to a Conference at Brussels, in order to discuss the whole question of the exploration and civilisation of Africa on purely international lines.

Christian Europe was in fact to combine and stretch forth the helping hand to the heathen, who " in his blindness bows down to wood and stone."

The Brussels Conference is a landmark in the history of Africa, for it was the first impulse which in a few years resulted in the parcelling out of the entire continent between the nations of Europe.

The International African Association, which was an off-shoot, or rather a consequence, of the Brussels Conference, was constituted, with its head-quarters at Brussels, to organise and direct the several explorations to be undertaken by the nations which had participated in the Conference. The philanthropic basis of these initial efforts were, it is not surprising to learn, soon modified into something more selfish, when the old delusions about the African climate and the impossibilities of European settlement in Africa had been largely dissipated by the investigations and experiences of explorers and missionaries.

Stanley had been commissioned by the King of the Belgians to undertake the exploration of the Congo Basin, and on the conclusion of his work in 1878 it was not very long before the Congo Free State materialised and came under the administration of Belgium. The discovery of the Congo as a waterway aroused the interest of other nations, and France, Germany, Belgium, and Portugal were all involved in dis-eussions and wrangles as to their respective rights to the region adjacent to the mouth of that river. Into these details we need not enter here, except to point out that the philanthropic interest exhibited by the Powers of Europe in Africa was rapidly obscured by a rising spirit of rivalry between themselves.

As regards East Africa up to the year 1884, British prestige both in Zanzibar and on the east coast was supreme, thanks to the influence of Sir John Kirk, who since 1868 had had the control and direction of affairs, not only in Zanzibar, but in East Africa as well. The domination of the Sultans of Zanzibar over the mainland regions, certainly as far west-ward as the Great Lakes, was undoubted, and an accepted fact. No one in Africa imagined that the right would ever be disputed ; and it may be assumed that Sultan Barghash would have been the last to believe that the British Government would ever sanction any interference with this portion of his dominions.

In 1884 the attitude of Germany in regard to Africa in general, and to East Africa in particular, was such as to cause Lord Granville, the Foreign Secretary to Mr. Glad-stone's administration, to inquire as to Germany's intentions, with the gratifying result that Prince Bismarck assured the British Ambassador in Berlin " that Germany was not endeavouring to obtain a protectorate over Zanzibar." So far so good : but Germany and her agents were otherwise employed, for the notorious Carl Peters had proceeded to East Africa, and on behalf of the Society of German Colonisa-tion had secretly entered into a number of " treaties " with natives in the region to the west of Bagamoyo—territory which was undoubtedly and indisputably under the domin-ance of the Sultan of Zanzibar. It is said, but with what truth I am unable to assert, that the signatures of the native chiefs to the so-called " treaties " were obtained by Peters by means of a ruse.

However this may be, Carl Peters hurried back to Germany, and there founded an association called the German East Africa Company, whose business it was to exploit and administer the territory which Carl Peters had become possessed of by means of his " treaties." To this Company the German Government gave its benediction and a Charter. This was in 1885. The whole transaction had been kept a profound secret until the Company had been duly con-stituted.

The Sultan of Zanzibar, directly he became acquainted with this usurpation of his right over the territories involved by the German action, protested vehemently ; as did Sir John Kirk, the British representative at Zanzibar ; but in spite of these remonstrances, on April 28th, 1885, the annexation of some 60,000 square miles of the Sultan's mainland terri-tories by the German Government was duly announced.

It was a shattering blow for the Sultan of Zanzibar, and, it must be admitted, for his chief adviser.

His Highness Seyyid Barghash, however, was not willing to accept this condition of affairs : and as his remonstrances had no effect, he dispatched troops to Usagara on the mainland, in the vain hope, it may be conjectured, of delaying the actual occupation of his possessions by German troops, and of gaining time, for the purpose of proceeding himself to Berlin, and laying his case personally before the Emperor. From this latter course he was dissuaded by Sir John Kirk.

General Lloyd Mathews, the Sultan's Commander-in-Chief, a man of great local influence, was dispatched by the Sultan to the Kilimanjaro district, in order to forestall the German " treaty-makers " in that region, which had always been regarded by the Sultans of Zanzibar as a portion of their dominions.

The Sultan remained obdurate to German advances, and refused to acknowledge their rights to the territory they had annexed, until a formidable German squadron appeared off Zanzibar on August 7th, 1885, and delivered an ultimatum to His Highness.   There was no course but for Seyyid Barghash to intimate his recognition of certain of the German territorial claims.   It must have been a bitter day of anguish to the Sultan of Zanzibar, and it cannot be supposed that our own prestige in the Eastern world was greatly enhanced by the action of Germany, although it must be remembered that at the time Zanzibar was an independent sovereignty and not under British protection.

With this initial success, German annexation proceeded apace.

At the commencement of November 1886, Great Britain, France, and Germany mutually agreed as to the extent of the dominions of the Sultan of Zanzibar.   These were to comprise a strip of coast ten miles in depth from the Rovuma River to the Tana River, a distance of about 600 miles ; the islands of Zanzibar, Pemba, Mafia, and Lamu ; and in addition the coast towns, not already included in the coast strip, of Kismayu, Brava, Merka, and Mogdishu, with territory of a ten-mile radius round each, and of Warsheikh with a radius of five miles round that place.

It will be noticed that the above arrangement left the Sultan of Zanzibar in full possession of the coast towns and ports between the Rovuma and the Tana rivers, but it was understood that the Sultan of Zanzibar would lease to the German Chartered Company the custom dues at the ports of Daresalaam and Pangani, both of which places still belonged to Zanzibar.

This agreement was of course but the prelude to the lease in 1888, by His Highness the Seyyid Khalifa I, who had succeeded his brother Barghash, of the entire ten-mile coast strip from the Rovuma to the Umba River to the German Company. This, as may be conjectured, was the beginning of the end ; for this lease not only gave the Germans free access to the coast, but placed in their control all the great caravan routes to the interior.

On August 16th, 1888, Germany took over the administration of the coast from the Sultan's Government, and, whether from indiscreet conduct, or from deliberate brutality on the part of the German officials towards the natives living within the area involved, the whole population, who regarded themselves as subjects of the Sultan of Zanzibar—Arabs and natives—rose as one man against their new masters.

The Germans termed this protest an " insurrection," and, knowing what we know to-day, there is no need to remark that it was eventually shattered with a " mailed fist."

This rising of the coast natives gave Germany the opportunity of assuming direct Imperial control of the whole region hitherto under the administration of the German Chartered Company ; and the Sultan's rights over the coast were purchased outright by Germany for 4,000,000 marks.[1]

Such was the genesis of " German " East Africa.

By the Anglo-German Agreement of July 1890, the respective boundaries between the British and German spheres of influence in East Africa were mutually decided upon, and the Sultan of Zanzibar's island dominions were saved from further disintegration by being declared under British protection on November 4th, 1890.

---

[1] The sum was lodged with the British Government on behalf of the Sultan of Zanzibar, and the interest on the sum in question (£200,000) is paid annually into the Zanzibar Treasury.

Germany agreed to recognise this British Protectorate over Zanzibar, and as *solatium* the island of Heligoland was given to her by Great Britain. The prevalent idea that Zanzibar was exchanged for Heligoland is, strictly speaking, not quite correct, for Zanzibar never belonged to Germany at any period of her history, nor was she at any time under German protection.

The remaining portion of the original ten-mile coast strip which is now comprised within the British East Africa Protectorate is leased from the Zanzibar Government for an annual rental of £11,000, and His Highness's flag still flies from the old Portuguese fort at Mombasa, to mark his territorial rights over that portion of the mainland.

This then is briefly the political history of East Africa from the advent to Zanzibar of Seyyid Said of Omân in 1828 until the close of the nineteenth century.

Mighty changes had taken place. Old Africa had been placed in the melting-pot, and the Great Powers of Europe had dipped their hands into the pot and grabbed as much of the contents as they could.

For a small native principality such as Zanzibar it was a critical period, and it might very well have happened that, amidst the struggle of the giants, the pigmy island-kingdom might have been obliterated. But although old Seyyid Said's dream of a great African Empire, stretching from ocean to ocean, and dominated by the Sultans of Zanzibar, has faded for ever, his island kingdom still survives as a British Protected State, under its own Sultan and its own Flag !

PART II

CHAPTER X

No one can approach the island of Zanzibar without expressing admiration for its verdant beauty. It is true that there are no mountain peaks, but the combination of softly undulating hills, covered with masses of waving palms and scented clove plantations, of white sandy beaches, washed by a clear sea of every imaginable shade of blue, gives an impression of a soft, luxuriant, and seductive beauty which can never be forgotten.

If the traveller approaches during the months of March or November, rain clouds may for a time dim and obscure the hill-tops, but Zanzibar is one of those places where it is "always afternoon," and normally a mellow sunshine illuminates the landscape with radiance, and creates a wonderful contrast between the sun-lit foliage and the cool rich shadows beneath the denser vegetation.

Scattered off the coast are small coral islets, which are especially numerous near the island of Pemba. These emerald-tinted islands, rising from the vivid blue of the sea, give a charming variety to the approaches of Zanzibar; while the lanteen sails of the fishing fleets, and the larger sails of the romantic-looking native craft hailing from India and the Persian Gulf, impart to the scene a vivacity and sense of life which unadulterated Nature often lacks.

When the voyager comes within the range of the land-breeze, he may, during the clove harvest, scent the spice-laden air, and he will thereupon realise, possibly for the first time, that he is approaching the main sources of the world's clove supply. Hitherto cloves may not have entered very prominently into the purview of his existence, but even casual visitors to Zanzibar when they depart on their several ways cannot fail to regard the clove for the rest of their lives from a more intimate and enthusiastic standpoint.

It will be noticed that the shore of the island is fringed by a low cliff of coral, which is always much undermined by the action of the waves beating against its base. This coralline formation when exposed to the action of the sea is often worn into the most distorted and fanciful shapes, and innumerable caves, which might serve very well for the abodes of mermaids, are to be found beneath these overhanging cliffs. On the top of the low cliffs, there springs the exuberant tropical vegetation, which covers the entire island, and which led the ancient Arab navigators to bestow the name of the " Green Island " on Pemba.

There is nothing sinister or morose in the vegetation which decks Zanzibar. No dark or gloomy forests, with their atmosphere of reeking vegetation, overwhelm or depress the spirits of the traveller in these Isles of the Sun ; all is brilliant with wholesome sunshine, and free to the open sky. Most of the vegetation is indeed reassuringly the result of human enterprise and occupation. Nearly every acre is owned and cultivated in the fertile zones, and in its most favoured aspect Zanzibar presents the appearance of a great garden, wherein every form of tropical plant and fruit and flower contends for its share of air and light. Every hamlet and country village is embowered in its scented orange groves, or shaded by fragrant clove trees and rustling palms.

The channel by which vessels approach Zanzibar from the north runs close to this lush shore, which is dotted at intervals by ruined palaces of former Sultans. The first prominent features which the traveller arriving from the north will see are the two lighthouses which mark the northern extremities of the island. The nearest, named Mwana Mwana, is situated on a small coral islet.

Immediately after this lighthouse is passed, the island of Tumbatu is reached. On this islet are extensive ruins, the identity or age of which has not yet been definitely determined.[1]

The inhabitants of Tumbatu, who claim to be of Persian descent, have a reputation for aloofness and individuality,

[1] For an account of these ruins see Part III of this book.

coupled with an addiction to witchcraft and the black arts. The Admiralty sailing directions for these waters refer to these islanders as being the most skilful pilots and sailors in the Zanzibar seas.

Through the narrow channel which separates Tumbatu from the main island, a pretty glimpse of the Government administrative station of Mkokotoni backed with palm-clad hills is obtained.

A mile or two farther on, another lighthouse is passed, situated on the very edge of the low coral cliff. Opposite this beacon, the sea, which is generally of a rich sapphire blue, is deep up to the very shore.

This locality in the old slaving days was a favourite point for shipping slaves in dhows for Muscat and the Persian Gulf. Many Arabs possessed large estates in the immediate vicinity, and the local name Manga-pwani (" the Arab shore ") is derived from this fact.

A mile to the south of the lighthouse, close to the shore, but invisible from the sea, is a relic of the slave traffic, in the form of a subterranean chamber in which slaves were concealed prior to embarkation.

Half a mile southwards of the slave chamber, an attractively situated Government bungalow is passed, and in its vicinity is a remarkable cave-well, from which the population obtain their water. The cavern is of considerable size, and is entered from the ground level by a flight of masonry steps. A subterranean passage, over a mile in length, runs from the bottom of this cavern to the sea-beach. A few years ago, some adventurous Europeans explored this passage, and nearly reached the sea-shore, but their experiences on that occasion have not induced any one else to follow their example.

A ruined but not ancient mansion situated on the seashore is next passed. This is Chuini (" the leopard's lair ") Palace, which was built by Sultan Barghash in 1872, and accidentally destroyed by fire in 1914. Close to this ruin is a disused sugar factory, a memento of the period in the nineteenth century when Zanzibar produced some of the finest sugar in the world.

Now straight ahead the traveller will see the shipping

10

lying at anchor in Zanzibar harbour, and behind it, apparently rising from the waves like a tropical Venice, the white city of Zanzibar comes in view.

At a distance its appearance is somewhat imposing, and indeed if the religious tenets and artistic perceptions of its inhabitants permitted, it might be one of the most beautiful cities in the world.

Built as it is on a low promontory, jutting out into the bluest of seas, it has every advantage of site. But alas! one looks in vain for the domes and minarets and clustered pinnacles which an Eastern city should possess.

This lack of embellishment may be briefly explained by the fact that the tenets of the particular Mahomedan sect to which the Zanzibar Arab belongs does not aspire to ornate places of worship. The consequence is that every mosque in Zanzibar is constructed on the simplest and plainest lines, not unlike the " Bethels " and meeting-houses of our own chapel folk. In spite of this architectural handicap, which causes Zanzibar to suffer from an æsthetic point of view, the first view of the town is not unworthy the metropolis of Eastern Africa.

Before the actual anchorage is reached, the small town of Bububu, nestling amidst dense groves or palm trees, is passed, while farther inland the hills rise to a considerable altitude, and are covered with clove plantations and every form of tropical growth.

On these verdant ridges, which run parallel to the sea-coast, are some of the finest clove plantations in the world.

Bububu is possibly chiefly remarkable for its somewhat extraordinary name ; it is also the terminus of a diminutive railway which plies six or seven times a day to Zanzibar town. The service is most popular and useful, and is largely used by the native population. A special first-class coach is run for the benefit of those passengers from steamers who wish to obtain a glimpse of the island. The railway traverses some of the narrowest streets of the city, and it is a constant source of wonderment how passers-by escape being run over. Europeans resident in Zanzibar regard the railway with an amused tolerance.

ZANZIBAR CITY FROM THE SEA.

As the harbour and town are approached by sea, the houses and mansions on the shore become more frequent. The newly built palace of the present Sultan, recognisable by the red-tiled roof and the square tower, is passed after leaving Bububu. It is splendidly situated on the very edge of the sea. The original mansion which stood on the site was supposed to have been haunted.

Another ruined palace, conspicuously situated on a small promontory, is next passed. This is the palace known as Bet-el-Ras, and was built during the reign of Seyyid Said, the founder of Zanzibar, but it was never finished owing to his death.

A few hundred yards beyond the Bet-el-Ras ruin, which apart from its ideal position is of no historical interest, is situated a far more interesting relic of past days. This is the ruined Palace of Mtoni, the first palace built by Seyyid Said in Zanzibar when he left Muscat to make Zanzibar his chief capital. It was in the grounds of this mansion that the first clove trees were planted in Zanzibar in about 1828.

The ruins, which are inconspicuous, although they stand on the very edge of the sea, comprise a boldly designed arched courtyard, the women's quarters, and the baths. Rumour asserts that the vast treasure accumulated by Seyyid Said, the builder of this palace, still lies buried and hidden somewhere within the precincts of the ruined buildings. No one has yet located the spot, but, on the strength of a statement by an ancient Arab soothsayer, a treasure hunt was authorised some years ago. The Arab stated that he had miraculously been informed of the exact place where the treasure lay concealed, and he bargained that when it was found he should receive half as his share. The digging was continued under the supervision of Sheikh Saleh-bin-Ali, Arabic interpreter on the staff of the late British Consul-General, for three days to an accompaniment of incantations, and much reading from the Koran by the informer, but unfortunately the quest proved entirely unsuccessful. A secret chamber skilfully constructed under the main staircase was disclosed at a later date, but it contained neither valuables nor treasure of any kind.

When Seyyid Said held Court at Mtoni Palace, it is said that a thousand dependents, comprising the royal household and slaves, were fed daily within the Palace precincts. Now all is desolation.

In the roadstead opposite the palace, the once famous fleet of Seyyid Said was wont to ride at anchor. This squadron consisted of some twenty-eight vessels of all sizes, and previously included the *Liverpool*, a 74-gun frigate, which as stated previously was presented to King William IV by Seyyid Said.

It was on the steps of the palace of Mtoni that Seyyid Said, the Imam of Muscat and Sultan of Zanzibar, received and entertained the officers of H.M.S. *Imogene* during their visit to Zanzibar in 1834.

The first recorded visit of an English man-of-war, if we except the advent of the *Edward Bonaventure* in 1591 in Queen Elizabeth's reign, was in 1799 when H.M.S. *Leopard* and *Orestes* arrived at Zanzibar.

The reception accorded to these vessels by the inhabitants of Zanzibar was on the whole favourable, and they obtained without difficulty the " refreshment " they needed.

Lieutenant Bissel of the *Leopard* in his report of the visit states : " Here we got wood, water, bullocks, and every kind of refreshment . . . but the Governor or Chief [1] made a monopoly of the sale of all kinds of articles we paid exorbitantly for them. The inhabitants sell their things much cheaper. We got very fine bullocks, goats, poultry, rice, dholl, coco-nut oil, etc. Their fruits are very delicious and they are of all kinds."

The beauty of the island struck these English sailors, and any one who has seen Zanzibar can well understand how pleasant and refreshing the green slopes of the land must have appeared to them. Lieutenant Bissel writes : " This island has a most beautiful appearance in sailing along it, and everywhere very woody."

He also affords us an interesting glimpse of Zanzibar trade methods. " In their mode of trade they [the Zanzibaris]

---

[1] At this period Zanzibar was administered by a Governor appointed by the Imam of Omân. It will be remembered that Zanzibar did not become the residence of the Imam until Seyyid Said's reign in 1828.

are singular. A guinea is of no value : but an anchor button, or a button of any kind, is a gem in the eyes of the lower class of people. An instance occurred on board the *Leopard*, where they refused a guinea, which was offered in exchange for some fowls ; and a marine's button put an end to the bargain."

It must be assumed that this predilection by the natives of Zanzibar for buttons arose from the belief that they were made of gold. Burton [1] refers to a similar belief and appears to connect it with the practice of the old buccaneers, who infested these eastern seas during the sixteenth and seventeenth centuries, of wearing buttons of real gold made from the treasure obtained from their prizes and subsequently melted down.

The same writer (Burton) also refers to pots containing gold nuggets hidden by pirates having been found by natives in Zanzibar. What the source of Burton's information was will probably never be ascertained. Inquiries at the present day about such treasure-trove having been found in the past elicits no definite information. This, however, must not be taken as entirely discrediting Burton's story, for a native is naturally secretive, and disinclined to give information on such a subject to European inquirers. That pirates, both European and Asiatic, haunted the coast and seas of Zanzibar and the adjacent islands is a matter of history.[2]

Just beyond Mtoni lies another ruined palace known by the name of Marahubi. It is not of ancient date and was burnt down in 1889. There are some decorative water-tanks in the grounds containing beautiful purple water-lilies. The grounds of this palace are pretty and planted thickly with mango trees, imported direct from India. The remains of the Harem baths are also worthy of note, although the marble flooring and other embellishments have been removed.

The traveller is now close to Zanzibar. Four coral islets will be seen facing the town. That nearest to the mainland

---

[1] *Zanzibar, City, Island, and Coast*, by R. Burton. London.
[2] For further remarks concerning pirates and treasure-trove, see the chapter on Pemba Island.

is known as Grave Island. It was reserved by a former Sultan for the burial of Christians. The graves are chiefly those of officers and men of the Royal Navy who have died in these waters.

Twenty-four men of H.M.S. *Pegasus*, who were killed in the action with the German cruiser *Königsberg* on the fateful morning of September 20th, 1914, lie buried here.[1] This island was formerly known as French Island, at the time when the French influence was predominant in Zanzibar.

The next islet is uninhabited, except by bats and pythons, and is little more than a coral rock. The third island is the chief quarantine station for Zanzibar. It is, however, always known as Prison Island, from the fact that it was originally destined to be the site of the Central Prison. Neither of these names—Prison or Quarantine—sounds very cheerful, but as a matter of fact the island forms one of the favourite resorts of the European residents in Zanzibar. The best of bathing can be obtained from the shore; the air is comparatively fresh and invigorating; and well-built, comfortably furnished houses also exist.

The fourth island which faces Zanzibar city is named Bawé. Although uninhabited it is of importance, as it is here that the main cables of the Eastern Telegraph Company which connect Zanzibar directly with Aden, the Seychelles, Durban, and London come ashore. The operating station is situated in the town of Zanzibar. A mile south of Bawé Island the wreck of the Eastern Telegraph Company's cable ship the *Great Northern* will be noticed perched high on a treacherous reef, upon which she ran at night some twenty years ago. Eight miles to the south of Zanzibar town, and three from the coast, Chumbe Island, with its lofty lighthouse, guards the southern approaches to Zanzibar Harbour. A few years ago, some piratically inclined Arabs attacked the lighthouse keepers and severely wounded them. The keepers, being without arms, were totally at the mercy of the raiders, who unfortunately escaped in their dhow without being captured.

The traveller to Zanzibar having passed these encircling

[1] Two officers and thirty-six men were killed or succumbed to their wounds. Four officers, two warrant officers, and fifty-two men survived their wounds.

islets finds himself within the roadstead known as Zanzibar Harbour. Immediately opposite the anchorage, on the very edge of the sea, lies the crowded city of Zanzibar, the chief features of which will be described in another chapter.

The country to the south of the town is wilder and less thickly inhabited than the northern portion of the island we have already seen from the sea. The natural features, however, continue, except that the low coral cliffs give place, for a time, to higher cliffs of red earth and grey sandy loam. The soil is also less rich, and outcrops of infertile coral rock appear, while the eternal fringe of coco-nut palms, so prominent a feature in other parts of the island, thin out, and dense thickets where an occasional leopard still lurks take their place. These wild stretches of country alternate with small coco-nut plantations and peaceful fishing hamlets.

Sometimes the low coral cliff merges into a sweep of sand dunes, blown up into ridges by the trade winds. The limits of the land and sea are here defined by fringes of casuarina trees, screw pines, and coarse grass, backed by dense " bush " country. On the south-western coast of the island, the shore line is often broken by creeks and shallow lagoons, thickly filled with mangrove trees. Some of these trees attain quite a large size, and it is curious to see full-sized isolated trees springing straight from the sea. This unusual condition of growth explains the old traveller's yarn about the country where oysters are picked off trees. Although the name of mangrove is somewhat redolent and reminiscent of swamps and oozy mud, the wood forms a most useful product, and in Zanzibar is largely used for fuel and roofing timber. A large quantity is exported to Muscat for building purposes, and an extensive coast-trade is carried on by a fleet of native sailing craft, which transport the cut poles and logs to Zanzibar town from the eastern side of Zanzibar Island.

When once the southern extremity of the island is rounded, the curious formation of the " boat channel " commences and continues almost without intermission along the whole length of the island.

This formation, which is not uncommon in coral islands, is

no doubt due to the cutting-down by wave action of the original coral cliff, and the resultant submerged " flat " is in process of time worn and scooped out into a trough by the constant wear of rolling rocks and sand set in motion by the tides. At low tide this channel or canal which runs parallel to the coast is nearly dry, but when the tide comes in, the water is sufficiently deep to allow boats of considerable size to sail along it.

On the western side of Zanzibar Island the sea is always calm, and of every imaginable tint of pellucid blue ; on the east coast the aspect of the sea is liable to change: The water in the aforesaid " boat channel " is calm enough, and being very shallow the yellow of the submerged sand mingles with the natural blue of the sea above it, and creates an unsurpassed variety of vivid greens, quite impossible to describe or to depict in colour. Outside the reef, surges and swells the Indian Ocean, stretching unbroken in its strength to Sumatra and Australia. Close to the shore the sea is 150 fathoms in depth, and this quickly increases to abysmal profundities. Hence the eastern coast of Zanzibar is fringed with a turbulent ocean of a most wonderful dark-violet hue —a contrast to the sapphire seas which wash the western side of the island.

Villages and hamlets are to be found dotted along the entire coasts at frequent intervals. These fishing villages are always picturesque, embowered as they are in verdant coco-nut palm groves ; and if sometimes the odour of fish is a little too pronounced, the people appear happy and contented. Many never leave their villages except to put to sea for fishing, and they live their little lives of peaceful ease, unmindful and careless of the throes of the great world which lies beyond their limited horizon.

The palms rustling in the trade wind, the white stretch of sandy beach, the blue sea, a canoe, and their family life are all they want.

The men are expert fishers and sailors, and on every village strand will be seen the boats hauled up, and the nets and fish baskets spread out to dry and for repair.

These fish baskets, it will be remembered, are similar, it is believed, to those mentioned by the unknown author of the

Periplus of the Erythraean Sea in A.D. 60 as being peculiar to the isle of Menouthias, generally accepted by the learned as identical with modern Zanzibar.

In addition to fish, great quantities of shell-fish and clams are consumed by the native population. A very favourite item of the Zanzibar menu is the cuttle fish or squid. These are caught in large numbers, and most unappetising and repulsive they look, hung up on frames to dry, in every village street. When caught, they are kneaded thoroughly, while alive but inert, by the women, who by this process eliminate the acrid and poisonous juices secreted by these molluscs.

A large trade is done in locally manufactured rope. Not only is the whole of the local native shipping supplied, but large exports of the finished product is made to East Africa. The process of preparation is tedious and primitive, but the resulting rope is of a high quality, and, except in the case of the largest hawsers and ropes, all the work is carried on by the village women.

The children of these fisher folk appear to lead a happy life, and one constantly sees them, naked as when born, sailing their model canoes in the shallow pools left by the ebbing tide, with as much pleasure and zest as the London boy sails his model yacht on the Round Pond in Kensington Gardens.

One would naturally expect to find the shores of a coral island in a tropical sea strewn with beautiful shells and molluscs. As a matter of fact, except for a few cowries, the number of marine shells to be found on the shore at Zanzibar is scarce and their appearance disappointing. Even on the most promising-looking reefs, which are only uncovered at the lowest tides, the display of marine life and corals is uninteresting. Crabs and other crustaceae, sea slugs (*bêche de mer*), and the less showy forms of coral organisms abound, but it is rare that those brilliant-coloured molluscs which one associates with a tepid tropical sea, and which are so plenti-fully found near Mozambique, reward the seeker in Zanzibar.

CHAPTER XI

I

HAVING given a general impression of the aspect of Zanzibar as seen from the sea, we will now make a hasty tour through the island, so as to afford some idea as to its interior.

Leaving the description of Zanzibar City for a subsequent chapter, let the reader imagine himself seated in one of the many motor cars which are always available for hire in the town, and ready to start to explore the island.

There are two main roads which leave the town and are available for wheeled traffic. It should be remembered that the town of Zanzibar is built on what was almost an island at high tide, the only connecting link being a narrow thread of land, which at the present time, by means of reclamation, has developed into a broad and pleasant recreation ground.

For the purposes of our motor trip, we will select the southern exit from the town, as offering a greater variety of scenery and diversion. Once outside the town, Zanzibar offers a choice of no less than five excellent macadamised roads, which penetrate into the interior of the island in different directions, the two longest and most frequented being the north road which runs to Mkokotoni, twenty-three miles distant, and that leading to Chwaka (twenty miles) on the eastern coast of the island, where further progress is barred by the Indian Ocean. This latter road is an extremely pleasant one, and passes through many of the best clove and coco-nut plantations in the island, besides traversing some of the less fertile zones, so it is this road we will select for our imaginary trip.

On leaving the landing-place, our car threads some extraordinarily narrow streets, and negotiates some equally startling corners. At one or two points the houses on opposite sides of the road are connected by a bridge, and at one point the road passes through a kind of tunnel, formed by the adjacent houses having been built over the street. The broad rich shadows cast by the surrounding houses on to these tortuous and quaint streets will tempt the traveller armed with a camera to stop the motor for the purpose of making records of these very Eastern features. The town roads are never of constant breadth for very long : each house has been built without very much concern as to the position of the neighbouring ones, and the result is that sometimes the roadway is reasonably broad, while at other times it dwindles down so that a wheeled vehicle has difficulty in getting past. Some streets are so narrow as to preclude the passage of anything more bulky than a donkey.

Just beyond the Post Office, a narrow stretch of the main-road has to be negotiated, and it is all our car can do to squeeze through. It was at this very place that the 4-inch guns salved from the sunken *Pegasus* stuck fast when, after being mounted on field carriages, they were dragged from the Government workshops to their positions : and a generous portion of the two obstructing houses on both sides of the road had to be sacrificed to allow them to continue their way.

The English Club, the Law Courts, recognised by the clock and domed roof, the British Residency, with the Union Jack flying from the tower, the Victoria gardens exactly opposite to the last-named house, are passed in rapid succession, and we begin to shake off the town. The road broadens, and is pleasantly shaded by lofty casuarina trees, which make a soft whispering noise in the wind, reminiscent of a pine forest.

A crenellated white building on the right, with an assortment of cannon parked in front, was formerly the barracks of the Zanzibar army, maintained in former times by the several Sultans. The force was largely composed of Baluchis from India. There was also a body of cavalry, and a body-guard of Arab horsemen—wild-looking gentry—who clattered after the Sultan when the latter took the air. This partially disciplined force was disbanded about ten years ago, and Imperial troops in the shape of a detachment of King's African Rifles took its place. The old barracks are now used partly as an oil go-down, and partly as a temporary lunatic asylum.

Opposite to this building is a picturesque Arab cemetery. Burial places, whether in Africa or Europe, are not particularly cheerful places, but I think it will be admitted that if all were similar to that opposite the old barracks at Zanzibar, they would be free from offence. The tombs are not really very old, and only date from about seventy years ago, but they have acquired a picturesque aspect of antiquity and a mellowness of tone which blends pleasantly with the green undergrowth between the graves. These latter lie scattered indiscriminately in this wooded place, dappled with sunshine glancing through the trees above.

The whole area has been permitted to assume and retain a certain air of ordered wildness, and at certain seasons of the year the ground is covered with masses of white and red lilies, and at other times with wild flowers of other vivid hues.

In former times, it was the custom to bury the dead without much regard for the living. The noble Arab families resident in Zanzibar each possessed their own family burial-ground, and it required considerable diplomacy on the part of the Public Health Officer to close these private cemeteries, many of which were situated in the most crowded districts of the city. Those families without a private burial-ground were interred in what was then the outskirts of the town, with the result that the whole of the modern quarter, where Europeans now reside, is built on the site of ancient graveyards. There are old Arab tombs in nearly every garden attached to the European houses, and no excavation work can take place close to the town without ancient human remains of past generations being turned up. In one case an ancient Arab tomb has been imbedded, as it were, in the fabric of one of the houses occupied by a senior official of the Zanzibar Government service, but the fact that the corner of the house is thus superimposed upon the grave does not appear to disconcert the Arab who periodically tends and prays over the grave. Both Arabs and Swahilis venerate any form of grave, and when any improvement in the laying out of the town is contemplated, the existence of ancient tombs in awkward positions is apt to prove disconcerting to the zealous town reformer.

Immediately after passing the old barracks, and this pleasant old Arab burying-ground, the road traverses an attractive-looking open space. That on the right is the well-known " Mnazi Moja " (One Coco-nut Tree), until recently the only recreation ground for the dwellers of Zanzibar to disport themselves upon. Burton, when writing of Zanzibar as it was in the year 1857, mentions the Mnazi Moja, and is not complimentary to it. At that period it was not traversed as it is to-day by the main road, but was merely the edge of the creek which runs at the back of the town. Burton's criticism was to the effect that if the " Mnazi Moja " was where the people of Zanzibar amused themselves, he was not surprised at them preferring to stay at home !

To-day it is one of the most attractive recreation grounds in Africa. It is laid out with tennis courts, and a nine-hole golf course, with grass greens not unworthy of Europe.

On the opposite side of the road is the new Recreation Park, dedicated to the use of the public, and largely patronised by the Goan, Indian, and native communities for football and cricket. Prior to 1914, this splendid extent of grass land was a dismal and malodorous stretch of sand, covered periodically at high tides by the sea. A causeway now shuts off the sea, and the new " lung " for Zanzibar has been laid out and developed by Government for the benefit of hundreds of young people. Adjoining the Mnazi Moja golf links lies the Cooper Institute and Naval Recreation Ground. This area was given by Seyyid Barghash, Sultan of Zanzibar between 1870 and 1888, to Her Majesty's Navy to commemorate the death of Lieutenant Cooper, R.N., who was killed in Zanzibar waters during a fight with slave-dealing Arabs. The relatives of Lieutenant Cooper erected the Institute Room and Canteen to his memory. In those far-distant times of peace, the institute and ground were seldom used more than once or twice in the year during the annual visit of the Cape squadron, but since 1914 they are in constant demand, and form a most welcome and excellent resort for the bluejacket ashore.

A turn in the road conceals the town from view, and the car is soon running along typical avenues, shaded by high trees which shut out the blue sky overhead. Orange gardens, small residences embowered in a mass of foliage, some Indian club-houses all flash past as we approach the country districts. Ziwani, the head-quarters of the King's African Rifles, with its castellated buildings most picturesquely situated on the summit of a grassy slope amidst park-like surroundings, will be seen on the right as we leave the last vestige of the town behind us.

All sorts of strange people and vehicles will be met on the roads. Zanzibar is the coloured man's paradise. I know of no place where West and East meet on more friendly and intimate terms, or where there is less colour snobbism than in Zanzibar. The fact that Zanzibar is an Arab State, and Europeans and Indians alike are strangers within its gates, possibly tends to this mutual good feeling and absence of race prejudice.

In addition to the carriages and motors of the wealthier Indians, vehicles of every design will be often seen conveying Arabs, Indians, and Swahili women. Motor cycles and pedal bicycles ridden by Indians and Swahilis are numerous, for Zanzibar prides herself on her excellent roads which radiate from the town in several directions. At times very antique and quaint vehicles drawn by equally prehistoric animals are encountered. These equipages must be closely related to the famous cabriolet which conveyed Mr. and Mrs. Raddle to the house of Mrs. Bardell !

The vehicle most frequently seen on the roads is the two-wheeled bullock or donkey cart, generally driven by the ubiquitous Indian. These unobtrusive little carts carry all the inland produce, destined for local consumption and for export, from the plantations to Zanzibar town. The roads are never free from them, and they ply unceasingly night and day through the island. The carts are manufactured locally, and their number has so increased during the last decade, that it is difficult to understand how, before their introduction, the produce grown in such profusion in the island was transported to its destination.

At intervals along the road-side will be noticed little stalls or tables, upon which is displayed a variety of bottles and glasses containing a pink liquid. This is sherbet for the refreshment of the passer-by. Sometimes in addition to sherbet, cigarettes, betel leaf, and sliced areca nut are on sale. These last-mentioned articles are of course the items which go to make up the chewing " quid " which is so indispensable throughout the Eastern world. The betel leaf is from the betel pepper-plant (*Piper betle*), a creeper which is most carefully tended and guarded by the natives living on the eastern coast of Zanzibar Island. These leaves are sold by tens of thousands in every market and bazaar. The areca nut (*Areca catechu*), which is about the size of a filbert, grows on a graceful palm, and is easily recognised by its extremely straight stem. The nut is sliced, and rolled up in the aforesaid betel leaf, with a little slaked lime, a small piece of red colouring matter (*katu*), and sometimes a piece of tobacco. The " quid " is then ready for chewing.

After skirting the northern edge of the Swahili quarter of the town along a beautifully shaded avenue, the road swings sharply towards the east, and it is soon evident that we are really in the country. It will be noticed that nearly every acre is cultivated. There are no hedges, or open fields, but the whole earth is covered with a profusion of vegetation. The most prominent feature is of course the graceful coco-nut palm. It occurs singly, in masses, in copses and in forests. The whole road is fringed by them, and their interwoven fronds obscure the landscape, and sometimes even the sky itself. Where thousands of these palms grow together, the perpendicular, bare stems without branch give an odd but not unpleasing aspect to the scene. Although these palms appear to be planted promiscuously, every one of them has an owner, who jealously guards his property. Wealth in Zanzibar is often reckoned, especially among the poorer classes, by coco-nut or clove trees. The value of an estate, or of land in general, is not reckoned by the price per acre, but by the number of trees growing thereon. The Zanzibari does not yet fully appreciate the value of land ownership. He cares little about who owns the land he lives on, all his concern is for the coco-nut or clove trees which are his. He knows every one of them, even although they may be mixed up with those of his fellow villagers. If he borrows money from the Indian moneylender, his coco-nut palms or his clove trees are his security, and not the land on which they thrive.

The price of a coco-nut palm varies considerably according to the kind of soil in which it grows. On fertile ground a tree will be valued at 15s. to £1 ; on poorer soil at 6s. to 12s. Coco-nut palms are very prolific, and a tree will bear a crop every three months, giving about fifty nuts each time.[1]

Unfortunately for the owner, a coco-nut plantation is a difficult one to guard from marauders, and a large number of nuts is invariably stolen. An owner considers himself fortunate if he harvests two-thirds of the total number of nuts on his estate. Very often he has to be contented with a still smaller proportion of the total harvest. The chief product obtained from coco-nuts is of course " copra," or the dried meat or kernel of the nut. There is always an immense demand in Europe for copra, for the manufacture of margarine, soap, candles, and all kinds of fats and oils. In fact the civilised world could not get on without copra. Most of the Zanzibar copra is shipped to Marseilles.

The process of obtaining copra is very simple, and admirably suited to the temperament of the Zanzibar native.

The nuts are generally picked by a professional picker, or, if only a few trees are involved, by any casual native. To a European the task of climbing a single tree, which may be anything from 40 to 60 feet in height, would appear almost hopeless, but a professional native picker will climb a score of trees, and pick the nuts in a very short time, without thinking he has done anything very extraordinary. As a matter of fact the climbing of coco-nut palms is an extraordinary feat of human activity and endurance, and to be appreciated must be seen. All that the Zanzibar climber requires is a loop of coir cord about eighteen inches long. This loop he slips over his insteps, and having seized the trunk of the palm with his hands stretched as far as possible

---

[1] The present price of coco-nuts in Zanzibar is from £2 10s. to £3 10s. per thousand nuts (1918).

FANTASTIC CORALLINE ROCKS ON THE ZANZIBAR COAST.

Gomes.

A COCO-NUT PLANTATION, ZANZIBAR.

above his head, he lifts up his legs and grips the sides of the stem with the soles of his feet, which are kept in position by the connecting cord loop. With incredible power he straightens himself out against the stem, and seizes the stem above his head. Then up go his legs again to a fresh purchase. So he pursues his way up the tree with extraordinary swiftness. When he has reached the nuts, he slashes off the ripe ones, and in a minute or two is descending the tree in a similar manner to which he ascended it.

The climbing of a single tree would exhaust a European, but the native will continue climbing tree after tree, apparently without exertion. A picker is paid one pice (a farthing) for each tree he climbs, or sometimes he receives a proportion of the nuts he picks.

Having collected the nuts, the next process is to take off the husk which surrounds it. This is effected by jabbing (this word exactly describes the action), the coco-nut on to a sharpened stake of hard wood, fixed firmly in the ground at an angle. The husk is in reality a most valuable commercial product, but in Zanzibar it is generally discarded, except on the coast, where, as already described, it is manufactured into rope. This unfortunate waste of valuable material is due to the lack of efficient and cheap transport of the husk to the factory.

The nut after being rid of its enveloping husk is then divided into two parts by a few sharp taps with a heavy knife, and the milk is allowed to run to waste. The white meat is then scooped out whole, and when dried in the sun becomes known as " copra." Unfortunately Zanzibar copra is often insufficiently dried, partly because the producer desires to make it as heavy as possible by the retention of the natural moisture, and partly because the humid nature of the climate prevents complete desiccation.

Although the prime reason for the cultivation of the coco-nut is to benefit the soap and candle manufacturers of Europe, the native grower himself utilises the tree and nuts for his own domestic needs.

The meat of the nut is grated, and its oil is expressed and used as a cooking medium in his household. The oil too may serve him as an illuminant, in place of candles and paraffin lamps. The shell is used as fuel or manufactured into ladles for drinking purposes, while, as already explained, the husk after maceration in the sea is frayed out and made into rope. The branches or fronds when split down the central rib are plaited together, and utilised as thatch for the roof and fencing for the back-yard.

There are two varieties of coco-nut palms grown in Zanzibar. The first is the ordinary species, while the second is a diminutive variety known as the Pemba coco-nut. This latter palm is very much smaller than the ordinary species, and with its clusters of gold-coloured nuts has a most pleasing and graceful appearance. It is planted to mark boundaries, and its milk is esteemed for drinking.

The offering of a freshly picked Pemba coco-nut, with its top sliced off, and brimming over with the so-called milk, is a little courtesy the Zanzibar native, however poor he may be, will always confer upon a European visitor to his village. The clear liquid thus presented looks tempting and cool, but in reality it is somewhat insipid, and does little to assuage one's thirst.

Mingled with the coco-nut palms will be seen a great variety of other growths, some of economic value, others of less value : but whatever their nature, all contribute, with the assistance of the sun, to render an impression of rich luxuriance and of entrancing and ever-changing beauty to the Zanzibar landscape.

Stately mango trees with their dark-coloured foliage often overshadow the road, and their very massiveness and size make a striking contrast to the more attenuated and mobile-fronded palms. Zanzibar is famous for its mangoes. Enormous numbers are brought into the town markets, and consumed throughout the islands. There are a great number of varieties, for although they are readily grown from the seed, there is no certainty that the resulting tree will be of the same species as the parent tree. Hence the only certain method of ensuring the propagation of any particular variety is by grafting, a science the native neither practises nor understands. Therefore many of the mangoes sold are of indifferent quality.

Areca-nut palms, one of the most graceful of tropical

growths, exist in large numbers round every native settlement. Their beautiful straight stems, surmounted by clusters of rich green feathered fronds and embellished with bunches of red and yellow fruit, are to be seen at every turn. Orange trees cluster around every native village, although the most favoured areas for orange cultivation are at some distance from the main roads of the island. In the localities where this fruit thrives best, the trees are often weighted down with the oranges. Many varieties are grown, including the Tangerine and Mandarin, and, although a number of inferior kinds find their way into the markets, the finest kinds grown in Zanzibar have few rivals in the world. It appears probable that the orange was brought to Zanzibar by Indian merchants long prior to the advent of the Portuguese to East Africa in the fifteenth century. The reader will no doubt recollect that when in A.D. 1498 the Portuguese ship *St. Raphael* lay stranded on a reef not far from Zanzibar, two canoes approached, laden with oranges, which the Portuguese declared to be superior to those of Portugal.

Amidst all these trees will be seen every variety of banana, from the delicate " lady's finger " to the gigantic species nearly a foot in length. Most of the beautiful golden bunches of this fruit which one meets being carried to the town are ripened artificially, by being placed in a hole in the ground previously heated with charcoal.

Trees which bear the less-known varieties of fruit thrive in Zanzibar wherever planted. The dorian or jack fruit is exceedingly common, and will be found growing alongside the road and in every native village. They attain to a great size. A peculiar feature of this tree is that the fruit, which often attains so great a size and weight as to be a man's load, grows directly from the tree trunk and not from the branches.

The bread-fruit tree is also common. This fruit when cut into slices and toasted is somewhat reminiscent of the household loaf. The similarity is increased if the slices are served in a toast rack, and eaten with butter, a little pepper, salt, and imagination.

Of course in addition to all the above-mentioned fruit and other trees to be seen from the road at every turn, there are scores of other varieties such as shaddocks, pomelows, guavas, limes, lemons, pineapples, custard apples, papayas, cashew nuts, lichis nutmegs, all growing in wild profusion, and bursting from the soil in exuberance of life.

Such then is the typical vegetation which covers much of the inhabited areas of Zanzibar Island. There may be indeed a riot of growth, but each participant of the riot is highly respectable and useful.

No one could starve in Zanzibar ; Nature and the fertile soil would not permit it.

In enumerating some of the trees and growths which give such beauty and luxuriance to the landscape of Zanzibar, I have purposely omitted to mention the most important of all.

I refer to the clove tree, the pride, the gem, the particular speciality of these Isles of the Sun. This is the spice which gives distinction to Zanzibar, and lifts the little island above the level of the ordinary " tropical possession " and places it upon a pedestal by itself. For Zanzibar and Pemba supply the world with cloves.

Until one has been to Zanzibar and seen something of the clove industry, and with what eagerness the civilised world strives to purchase its fragrant harvest, no one can realise the importance of this spice in the world's domestic economy. This being the case, I have devoted a special chapter to the description of the clove tree, rather than class it with such ordinary growths as the orange and the coco-nut.

II

Lest the reader begin to weary of the trees and fruits of Zanzibar, we must continue our imaginary trip across the island. It will be remembered that we have left Zanzibar city far behind, and are running due east along a beautifully graded road, bordered by a wonderful green landscape filled with verdant trees and waving palms, illuminated with a brilliant sunshine and sweet with the intoxicating scent of flowers and spices.

For the first two or three miles the road runs on fairly level ground, until suddenly it mounts a sharp incline which brings us to the summit of the main line of hills that run longitudinally, like a spine, through the island from north to south. There are three such ridges, which run parallel to each other at a distance of about two miles. The valleys between these ridges are shallow ones, so that the " hills " of Zanzibar are not very terrifying, in fact most visitors would refer to the island as being flat. Nevertheless even the humble hills of Zanzibar, the highest of which does not exceed 450 feet in height, and the corresponding declivities afford a pleasantly undulating scenery well in keeping with the rich luxuriance of its vegetation and its soft and scented breezes.

From the summit of the first ridge pleasing views of Zanzibar city, shimmering white in the sunshine, and backed by the blue sea studded with islands of emerald green, can be obtained through the trees. Leaving the summit, the road dips down and continues with gentle undulations and bends, amidst an ever-changing variety of vegetation.

Dotted amidst the palm groves will be seen the huts and hamlets of the country folk, and occasionally through a short vista a more pretentious residence of some Arab.

The native houses are of fair size, and well fashioned on a framework of timber filled in with red clay and limestone rock. They are really more elaborate and commodious than one would at first suppose. Nearly all have a small verandah or *baraza*, where the master sits and chats with his friends ; many have windows, and still more have some kind of carved or ornamented door. Sometimes the appearance of the house is enhanced by being painted white.

In every cluster of huts, the ubiquitous Indian shopkeeper will be found. The native of Zanzibar is rich compared with his wilder cousin of the mainland, and the variety of articles to be found in a village store in the centre of Zanzibar Island is surprising, and significant of the general prosperity of the inhabitants. Here is an incomplete list of articles offered for sale in a small Indian shop situated some twenty miles from Zanzibar town—coloured printed cloths of all kinds, oil lamps, matches, paraffin, candles, coloured oleographs of all subjects (mostly German I regret to say!) tea, sugar (both done up in farthing packets), salt, pepper, rice and a variety of food grains, bread, sweet biscuits of European manufacture, sweets, coloured paper for decorations, soap, washing blue, soda, reels of sewing cotton, needles, crockery, cups and saucers, knives, beads, mace, nutmegs, salad oil, ginger, turmeric, dyes for colouring mats, incense, a variety of perfumery, both European and native made.

The Indian shopkeeper is of course the buyer of local produce and the village money-lender. Piles of coco-nuts, copra, and areca nuts will be seen lying outside his premises at all seasons of the year, awaiting transport to " Town," which term is universally used throughout the island to signify Zanzibar city.

Nearly every village possesses its little mosque, always recognisable by the projection from the northern wall. This projection is the *kibla*, which is so built as to always lie in the direction of the Holy City of Mecca. Another inevitable feature of a mosque, of whatever size or pretensions, is the well, tank, or, in the case of very small mosques, large jars of water, which afford to the worshippers the means of making the prescribed ablutions before prayer. Unfortunately the mosques of Zanzibar are entirely without beauty or architectural merit.

At about six miles from Zanzibar, a small bungalow belonging to His Highness the Sultan is passed. This house may be taken as marking roughly the commencement of the clove zone. To the north clove plantations extend for twenty miles, but it is as well to remember that the island of Pemba, and not Zanzibar, is the great clove-producing centre of the world. However, the area under cloves in Zanzibar is large, and it is the Zanzibar clove, as distinct from that of Pemba, which always fetches the higher price.

Whenever the road runs through a clove plantation, the air is deliciously scented with a spicy aroma, which is more marked when the clove is on the tree. At about nine miles from Zanzibar there are some extensive clove *shambas* (plantations), and there are few prettier walks than those which lead through forests of clove trees. One especially charming ramble can be taken by leaving the main road and following the path along the top of the ridge towards the Government clove plantation known as " Marseilles."

This name, so reminiscent of France, is historically interesting, as recalling a period in the recent history of Zanzibar, when the French were the predominant influence in the island.

The fact is that Zanzibar was " discovered " by the French and the Americans long before England awoke to the importance of this key of the Western Indian Ocean, or the commercial potentialities of the east coast of Africa.

We have already remarked on the fact that in the middle of the last century America held the chief trade monopoly for a time, and an interesting light is thrown on our own position during the early fifties, by an official application from the British Consul to his superiors to be supplied with a Union Jack for his Consulate. He explains that hitherto he has made up the flags locally, and had had to purchase the material for them from the American stores in Zanzibar.

But to return to the " Marseilles " clove plantation. This property belonged originally to Seyyid Said, the first Omân Sultan of Zanzibar. On his decease in 1856 his property was divided among his numerous progeny, and this plantation fell to the share of one of his daughters. Her brother, the Seyyid Barghash, was of an ambitious nature, and on several occasions he intrigued against his elder brother Majid, who had succeeded Seyyid Said on the throne of Zanzibar. The Sultan Majid favoured the English, while Barghash looked to the French for assistance in his designs against his brother. Out of compliment to his French friends he named this clove plantation " Marseilles," after having received some gifts of value from the Emperor of the French.

Barghash previously to 1859 had attempted to assassinate his brother, and when he failed in this enterprise he sought the protection of the French Consul at Zanzibar to escape punishment. Shortly afterwards he fled to the interior of the island, and began to place the " Marseilles " palace in a state of defence, by loopholing the walls, making breastworks of sandbags, and mounting guns. He gathered around him a large number of Arabs of the Harthi tribe, and this force was supplemented by large numbers of mercenaries and armed slaves. On October 14th, 1859, the Sultan Majid moved out to attack the position with about 5,000 Arabs, Baluchis, and Comoros.

The Sultan was accompanied in his enterprise against his rebellious brother, by Lieutenant Berkeley, R.N., and a party of officers from Her Majesty's steam-frigate *Assaye*, and from the steam-sloop *Lynx*. After reaching the neighbourhood of "Marseilles," the British officers rode forward to reconnoitre, and were received with discharges of cannon and musketry. After much trouble the British officers managed to get two guns into position, and remained for several hours exposed to a heavy fire from the insurgents. Finally these guns blew in the palace gates, but even then the troops of the Sultan remained supine and refused to advance against the rebels. Darkness led to a cessation of hostilities, and the Sultan's force spent the night at the sugar factory of Kinuni-Moshi. Sultan Majid now applied for further British aid, and the next morning Lieutenant Berkeley with one hundred British seamen and marines from the *Assaye* and *Lynx*, and a 12-pounder howitzer and rockets, marched to Marseilles to again attack the rebels. On arrival at that place they found it evacuated, and so it only remained for Lieutenant Berkeley and his force to blow up the buildings, the remains of which can still be seen.

It appeared that the heavy punishment inflicted by Lieutenant Berkeley and his companions with their guns on the first day, when some fifty or sixty of the rebels were killed, had so demoralising an effect on Seyyid Barghash and his forces that the rebels determined to surrender, and their leader escaped from his battered position on the first night and surrendered himself to a party from H.M.S. *Assaye*.

Sultan Majid, who was greatly loved by his subjects, on his return to Zanzibar, accompanied by Lieutenant Berkeley, was acclaimed by the whole population, and thus a revolution which threatened bloodshed and ruin was quelled by a few British officers. Prince Barghash was banished to India, and while French pretensions received a shattering blow, on the other hand British prestige was increased to a marked degree, not only in Zanzibar, but throughout the whole region of East Africa and in Arabia.

The ruins of Marseilles palace left by Lieutenant Berkeley

have been further disintegrated by the storms and sunshine of half a century, but some vestiges of walls still stand to mark the spot where a handful of British naval officers so pluckily tackled the rebels. The ruins are now surrounded by splendid specimens of clove trees, and by a grove of nutmeg trees.

As we approach the centre of the island, a change in the scenery becomes apparent. The dense groves of coco-nuts become more attenuated, and the rich vegetation is obviously scantier. The road too becomes more deserted, and the hamlets are smaller and more isolated. Carts are seldom seen, and on the road only a few country folk are encountered. Occasionally, however, one obtains a glimpse of most picturesque figures of Arabs riding their white Muscat donkeys.[1] These Arabs, with their flowing beards, their white draperies, and sandalled feet, are living materialisations from the Old Testament, and seem a little out of place even in romantic Zanzibar ; while they are possibly the only specimens of humanity who can ride donkeys without loss of dignity. Their beasts of burden are as picturesque as themselves, for the donkeys' milk-white coats will be set off and caparisoned with a brilliantly coloured and tasselled pad in place of a saddle. No stirrups or bit are used, the rider most deftly guides his animal by lightly tapping it on the head with a small switch.

Roughly the island of Zanzibar may be divided into two distinct zones—the fertile and comparatively hilly western area, and the infertile and comparatively level eastern half. The reasons for this orographical variation has already been alluded to, so it will suffice to repeat here that the super-imposed earth cap, which covers the basic coral formation, is thicker on the western half of the island than on the eastern, and hence as we approach the latter side of the island we see evident manifestations of the hard coralline limestone upon which the island of Zanzibar is founded, projecting through the thin layer of fertile soil.

[1] These fine white donkeys are generally referred to by Europeans as " Muscat," although known to the Arabs as " Bahrein " (on the Persian Gulf). The true " Muscat " donkey is a small dark-coloured animal. The white donkeys often cost more than a horse and are much prized.

It will be clear, then, to the traveller who crosses the island from west to east, as we are supposed to be now doing in our imaginary trip, how it is that the scenery suddenly changes, and the dense vegetation of the western portion gives place to the scantier growths and open bush-country in the eastern half.

This open moorland, or *wanda* country, comes as a pleasant change to the soft luxuriousness of the inhabited and cultivated areas. Instead of the view being restricted by dense masses of palms and clove trees, the eye can range far ahead to distant ridges, and the fresh breeze from the open sea which meets us is in marked contrast to the tepid atmosphere of the western coast.

The open coral-country is carpeted with green grass, and covered with scattered bushes and thickets, while masses of bracken fern fringe the roadside. This home-like growth seems strangely out of place in such a tropical country, but it is all the more appreciated for that reason. The *wanda* moorland looks inviting for walking purposes, but the grassy covering conceals a surface of sharp knife-like edged rocks, which makes progression almost impossible. Sometimes a native footpath strikes across the *wanda*, but even on such a track walking is a labour, as the pedestrian's eyes must be constantly earth-bound in order to avoid the iron-hard pinnacles of coralline rock which project from the sparse layer of soil.

In some parts of this coral country cattle thrive, and there are many small oases, where natives grow good crops, excellent tobacco, and chillies, while nearly the whole east coast is bordered with an interminable fringe of coco-nut palms.

At a distance of about ten miles from Zanzibar town, a broad stretch of typical *wanda* country is traversed. Directly ahead the traveller will see a low ridge, topped with groves of coco-nut palms, a sure sign in Zanzibar of human settlement. We are now approaching the ruined and reputedly haunted palace of Dunga, and as the grounds are utilised as an experimental station by the Government Agricultural Department, it will be of interest to break our journey to the east coast at this point for a few minutes and inspect the old gardens of this dismantled mansion.

RUINS OF THE HAUNTED PALACE OF DUNGA.

A SWAHILI'S HOME.

CHAPTER XII

A CERTAIN degree of mystery and romance is associated with the name of Dunga.

It stands on the crest of a well-defined ridge, which rises steeply from the open *manda* country, and the road approaches the ruins through an avenue of some of the finest clove trees to be found, I suppose, in the world.

Dunga palace is situated very nearly in the centre of the island, and is eleven miles from Zanzibar town.

It was built about the year 1845 by a somewhat mysterious personage named Ahmed-bin-Mahomed-bin-Hasan el Alawi, known throughout Zanzibar as the " Mwenyi Mkuu " or " The Great Lord."

To appreciate the sinister repute which attaches to the name of Dunga and its lord, it must be explained that this Arab was practically the last of a long dynasty of rulers who governed the inhabitants of Zanzibar Island long before the permanent settlement of the Omân Arabs in the island. The Mwenyi Mkuu was in fact the descendant of the old " kings " of Zanzibar referred to by the Portuguese and by Sir James Lancaster when he came to Zanzibar in the year 1591.

The last Mwenyi Mkuu, the Lord of Dunga, is believed to have been of Persian descent, and his existence as a ruler of the Wahadimu, some of whom claim to be derived from Persian stock, raises all those fascinating historical problems connected with the identification of the early settlers in Zanzibar, and of the builders of the ancient ruins which are described in the latter portion of this book.

Not very much is known about the Mwenyi Mkuu, but it

seems certain that he was born in 1785 and died in 1865. As already stated, prior to the advent of Seyyid Said and his Omân Arabs, the Mwenyi Mkuu was in fact the Sultan of Zanzibar, and governed the Wahadimu, who now inhabit the eastern portion of the island. When Seyyid Said of Omân made Zanzibar his capital, a curious system of dual control between him and the Lord of Dunga ensued.

The wealthy Arab Sultan lived in state in Zanzibar town, and controlled therefrom his dominions, which at that period (1832) included the kingdom of Omân, some of the rich islands in the Persian Gulf, and the East African coast from Cape Guardafui to Cape Delgado, while the Lord of Dunga still retained jurisdiction over his own subjects in Zanzibar Island. The Arab Sultan in Zanzibar town was wise enough not to interfere with the local jurisdiction and powers of his rival of Dunga. The two rulers lived therefore in amicable relationship at their respective capitals, which were only eleven miles apart. It appears that the Mwenyi Mkuu collected the hut-tax from his subjects, and divided the proceeds equally with the Arab Sultan at Zanzibar.

The builder of Dunga Mansion is credited with having exercised the most extraordinary influence over his people, who formed a large proportion of the total population of the island. His will and word were law, and he held absolute power of life and death over his own people. Strange tales are still current as to his supernatural powers. It is related that on one occasion he quarrelled with Seyyid Said, who dared to confine him in the fort at Zanzibar. The same night, however, the Mwenyi Mkuu miraculously disappeared from the prison, and was next heard of on the mainland. During his absence from Zanzibar Island, no rain fell for three years, and ruin and famine stared both the Arabs and the native population in the face. The people petitioned Seyyid Said to pardon the Mwenyi Mkuu and permit him to return to Zanzibar. On his doing so the rain fell in abnnd-ance, and the quarrel between the two rulers was amicably settled.

The whole native population regarded both the Mwenyi Mkuu and his abode with superstitious dread. No native would dream of approaching the vicinity of the palace at Dunga after dark, and none of his subjects ventured into his presence except on their knees with uncovered heads.

If the Great Lord went out, any person who happened to be in a tree, picking cloves or coco-nuts for instance, was obliged to descend at once on pain of death or torture, as it was considered sacrilegious for any one to be higher than he. A large pit is said to have existed near the palace into which were cast those unfortunate persons who were executed by the orders of the Mwenyi Mkuu, and when the well near the ruins was cleaned out in 1914 several human remains were discovered therein.

The fear and dread inspired by the Lord of Dunga increased as he grew older, and the belief in his supernatural powers deepened. There can be no doubt but that the Mwenyi Mkuu was a remarkable man in many respects, and it is possible that towards the close of his life his seclusion due to the infirmities of age, at his lonely mansion at Dunga, added to his sinister reputation among the simple country folk.

Strange rumours began to be current regarding sights and sounds seen and heard at the palace, and after the old man's death both Arabs and natives declared the house to be haunted.

Tales are still told of treasure lying concealed at Dunga, and when the place was demolished a few years ago it was hoped that some trace of it would be discovered. That such treasure might exist in these old Arab mansions seems possible, for even to-day Zanzibar Arabs are not sufficiently up-to-date to confide their money to any bank ; and although much of their wealth is in the form of immovable property, such as plantations and houses, it may reasonably be presumed that a good deal of hoarding of jewels still goes on. In former days when conditions of life were less settled and secure, the inducement to hide valuables was naturally greater. The occupant of Dunga Palace, from its remote and lonely position in the country, would most certainly have hidden his surplus wealth in some secret chamber in his house. When the Mwenyi Mkuu died in 1865, at the age of eighty years, no doubt the chief valuables were appro-

priated and spent by his successor, who is described as a
common-looking person, of a distinctly negro type of countenance [1] ; but there is of course always the possibility of some
treasure having eluded discovery.

Only the shell of the palace walls now exists, but the hollow
sound emitted when the basement floors are struck evidently
indicate that the ground is not solid beneath them.

One of the main causes of the sinister reputation attached
to the house of the Mwenyi Mkuu was the tradition that
when the mansion was built many slaves were sacrificed,
and immured alive within the foundations.

It is difficult to ascertain whether such a custom of human
sacrifice really existed in Zanzibar. The general opinion
favours such a belief, and the native is convinced of its truth.
On the other hand, so many houses are built on old graveyards that the finding of human remains beneath a demolished
house must not be accepted as absolute proof of the existence
of such a practice.   I have been assured that·even to-day
no house is built without some sacrifice, such as a cock, being
offered by the builder.

When Seyyid Barghash built the Bet-el-Ajaib, or the
House of Wonders, in Zanzibar, it is said that the greatest
difficulty was experienced in obtaining labour to dig the
foundations, as it was the current belief that human sacrifices would be required, and that the workers would be seized
for the purpose.   I understand that the palace in question
is built on the site of an old grave-yard, and when in the
course of years the time comes to pull it down, human
remains will be found beneath its walls, and our successors
will see in these remains confirmation of the tradition that
slaves were sacrificed when the building was erected.

When the Arab mansion situated in Zanzibar town and
occupied by the Eastern Telegraph Company was pulled
down in 1914, several human remains were discovered beneath the walls.   Mr. Court, the European Clerk of Works
who superintended the demolition, has informed me that
he is convinced, from the relative position of the skeletons
and the foundations, that the latter must have been deliberately built over the bodies, and that it is impossible to think

[1] See the portrait of the Mwenyi Mkuu and his son.

Gomes.

SULTAN BARGHASH.

THE "MWENYI MKU" THE LAST OF THE OLD KINGS
OF ZANZIBAR.

that the bones were not connected in some way with the building of the foundations.

A point urged against the prevalence of such a custom is that slaves represented monetary value to their masters, and that it was not in the interests of the latter to permit the immolation of their serfs, on the principle that a live donkey is better·than a dead lion. Moreover it is notorious that Arabs who owned slaves treated them considerately, and in fact allowed them such licence that they became a nuisance to the peaceful inhabitants of Zanzibar.

On the other hand, the very essence of a sacrifice or a dedicatory offering is the surrendering of something of value, and the tradition is so definite that sacrifices were perpetrated when commencing the erection of an important building, and the practice is one of so universal an application throughout the world that it must be assumed that at least in some instances such immolations were practised in Zanzibar. Certainly if such acts did take place at all, it is highly probable that they were employed at the building of Dunga mansion, because the Wahadimu, the subjects of the Mwenyi Mkuu, were descended from the pagan tribes of the African continent, and it is more than likely that they brought with them, and perpetuated, some of the savage customs of their country of origin.

II

Whatever happened at Dunga with respect to human sacrifices, one thing is certain, that the Mwenyi Mkuu was looked upon with the utmost awe and veneration by the entire population.

Associated with Dunga are the carved drums and horns, which were regarded by the Wahadimu with superstitious reverence. The sacred horn is stated to have been sounded only on special occasions, and to have been kept hidden in some secret place, known only to one man, who passed on the information at his death.

When occasion arose for the blowing of the horn, the effect on the people was instantaneous and far-reaching. It is stated that the last time it was blown was three days

after the death of the Mwenyi Mkuu in 1865. There were in
fact two horns and two war-drums. All are of wood, the
drums being of mango wood elaborately carved in Arabic
characters. The smaller of the two horns is evidently
much older than its fellow, and their decayed appearance
certainly tends to confirm the idea that they were buried
until some occasion of national importance required their
use.[1]

The Mwenyi Mkuu, who, as related, died in 1865, was
succeeded by his son, a man of no influence or character. He
in due course died in 1873, and with him terminated the
dynasty of the ancient " kings " of Zanzibar. The Dunga
estate passed into the possession of an Arab named Mahomed-
bin-Seif, but so sinister was the reputation attached to the
palace that no Arab or native would sleep in it, and the new
owner is said to have been obliged to build for himself a
residence away from the old pile of buildings.

The Arab and native story of the uncanny manifestations
at Dunga generally related to the apparition of an Arab lady
who " walked " the long corridors at dead of night followed
by a black dog. Occasionally ghostly sounds, as of chains
or heavy articles being dragged about, were said to have
been heard.

The Dunga ghost is raised from the ordinary level of
psychic manifestations by having been seen in December
1895 by one whose credibility is above suspicion, and who
is well known to every one who has resided in Eastern Africa.
I refer to Dr. A. H. Spurrier, C.M.G., O.B.E., who has kindly
permitted me to use the subjoined account of his experiences.

" I would not sleep in either of the partitioned-off rooms
at the end of the long room, but I had a bed brought out into
the central part of the room which was furnished as a sitting-
room. I slept in the eastern third of this part, with a wall
bracket lamp behind me. There were three round tables
in the length of the room, one opposite my bed, which was
against the wall.

" Between three and four o'clock in the morning, I was
awakened very suddenly, and sat up in bed, and saw standing

---

[1] The wooden horns and the drums are now kept in the main hall of the British
Residency at Zanzibar.

at the table opposite me a tall man in a whitey-brown
burnoose with hood up concealing his face, which was looking
eastward.

" I must confess I was unable to speak or move. The
apparition appeared slowly to give place to nothing : but
looking down the room, there it was again, standing in the
same way looking to the east.

" In a similar way it gradually vanished, and then—but
only then—did I seem to be able to move.

" I unfastened the door and went out into the corridor,
and aroused the ' boys,' and insisted that two must go off
at once to Zanzibar with a message to F. of the Mission—now
the Archdeacon of C——, who was coming in a day or two to
stay with me at Chwaka. I asked him to come out at once,
and go with me, for I would not stay there another night at
Dunga.

" The interest lay in what I saw being entirely unlike anything hitherto described, so that I was not expecting or
dreaming anything of the kind. I never previously or since
experienced the feeling of the tongue cleaving, and all action
paralysed, as in the on-coming of a nightmare's crisis, as I
did when I saw the Dunga ghost, or rather a ghost at Dunga.

" It is a fact that the old well at the back of the enclosure
wall contained a large number of human bones, and that
when the old gateway at the entrance was pulled down, it
was necessary to obtain the labour of Christian mission
natives from the mainland, as the tradition at Dunga was
that the blood of many slaves had been used in the foundations, and all around dreaded to disturb the stonework."

So much for the Dunga ghost !

To-day an inner entrance-archway, one of the staircases,
and some of the basement rooms can be inspected. Around
the ruined pile, which was much larger than the existing
remains would lead one to suppose, lies a small but beautiful
garden, encircled by a mellowed and picturesque old wall.
There is a wonderful display at certain seasons of the year
of richly coloured vegetation, and in the immediate vicinity
of the old house is a variety of economic growths, which
include nutmegs, cocoa, kola, vanilla, oranges of the best
varieties, pine-apples, and of course clove trees in perfection.

Through the trees of the garden, quite extensive views—for Zanzibar—of the surrounding country towards the west can be obtained, and the palm-feathered ridge upon which " Marseilles " is situated can be clearly defined.

Leaving Dunga and its ghost behind us, we continue our journey eastward.

We at once see that the country to the eastward of Dunga is more open and wilder than on the western side ; and the freshness of the breeze too blowing straight off the Indian Ocean is soon apparent. The road, pleasantly diversified by turns and dips, sweeps on through the open country-side. Thick scrub and jungle take the place of the luxuriant coconut palm groves and scented clove plantations.

This " bush " land is broken at intervals by tempting-looking green grass glades and open moorland, but, as already explained, this open country is difficult of access owing to the rough and jagged surface of the coralline rock, while the bush itself is quite impenetrable.

In this jungle dwell the wild fauna of Zanzibar. The list is not a very extensive one, but includes leopards, serval cats, mongoose, various kinds of ferrets and weasels, monkeys, and the " paa " or diminutive gazelle of Zanzibar.

Wild pig exist in enormous and ever-increasing numbers and are a burden to the native cultivator, who utilises the walled enclosures which some past generation was energetic enough to construct to protect his crops from the ravages of these pests. All over the eastern part of the island these substantial stone walls will be seen. They are built of rough blocks of coralline rock, and skilfully constructed without mortar. In some instances the blocks used are of great size, and the extent of the walls makes it evident that the former population must have been a large and an enter-prising one. Who the ancient builders exactly were is unknown, but it is obvious that many of these stone enclosures are of considerable age.

Verdant and luxuriant as Zanzibar is, the bareness of the fields enclosed within these stone walls on the eastern side of the island is indescribable. One has to look twice to realise that it is a " field " intended for the cultivation of food crops, and then one has to make a third and closer inspection to see where the soil is. The first impression is that there is none at all, and that an area of rock—and very hopeless-looking rock too—has been enclosed for some incomprehensible purpose. After careful search one sees a few patches of brown soil between the crevices of the rough and irregular surface. A more hopeless-looking " field " cannot be found the world over, but nevertheless the natives manage to grow maize, millet, beans, cassava, and chillies on this unpromising soil, and the pigs know it too, and do their best to come at night and rob the husbandman of his harvest.

As we approach Chwaka, many of these walled fields will be observed on each side of the road. The twentieth mile-post from Zanzibar stands at the entrance of Chwaka, and the road runs through the village to the sea-front. The village is beautifully situated in dense palm groves, and the houses and the people have an aspect of cheerfulness and prosperity. Many of the inhabitants live by fishing, and a market on the sea-beach is the resort of the villagers when the boats come in with their catches. There is a considerable dhow traffic with Zanzibar round the south end of the island, in the transport of fuel and poles, which are extensively cut in the creeks immediately to the south of Chwaka village.

Chwaka is a Government administrative station, and the chief buildings consist of a jail, a police station, some Government offices and magistrate's courthouse, a dispensary, three bungalows and a small house belonging to the Universities' Mission.

There is a pleasant air of repose and charm about Chwaka, which is soothing to the overwrought European fresh from the heat and turmoil of Zanzibar town.

On the land side the bush creeps close up to the settlement, and makes exploration inland, except by the main road, difficult. The chief line of communication northwards is along the sea-beach, and at varying intervals fishing villages are dotted along the shore, right up to the northern point of Zanzibar Island.

Southwards of Chwaka extends a sparsely inhabited country composed of coralline limestone. As in the northern portion of the island, a fringe of coco-nut palms marks the limits of sea and land, and every few miles small villages are found. At one of the largest on the east coast named Bweju, an ancient mosque probably of Persian origin still is in use. At the south-east corner of the island, the population thickens, and it is in this region that cattle thrive exceedingly, growing fat and sleek in the excellent pasturage which covers the underlying coral rag. Large quantities of tobacco are grown in this district, and after being cured is plaited into rolls and sent to Zanzibar, Pemba, and even to the continental mainland for sale. Many vines of the betel-pepper are also cultivated, and the leaves sent into Zanzibar. This south-eastern portion of the island is also the chief seat of the coir industry, and large quantities of rope are manufactured and shipped by sea to Zanzibar town.

With all these local trades, it is not surprising that the inhabitants are well-to-do and prosperous.

Although this portion of the Sultanate is only about twenty-five miles from Zanzibar town, it seems almost as remote as if it lay ten times that distance away. This is due to the difficulty of travelling over the rough and jagged surface of the intervening country. Narrow paths traverse this portion of the island, but, owing to the rocky outcrops, progress is always slow and laborious, and the most convenient way of visiting the southern portion of the island is by sea.

In due time a road will no doubt be made to link up these outlying areas of Zanzibar Island.

CHAPTER XIII

THE CITY OF ZANZIBAR

I

It is certain that the city of Zanzibar is of no great antiquity, and its rise into prominence as the metropolis of the East African coast was subsequent to the withdrawal of the Portuguese in the eighteenth century from that region.

Enough has been said in previous chapters to indicate that the island of Zanzibar was not accounted of very great importance in the past, and it was not until the advent of the Omân Arabs to the island in the early years of the nineteenth century, and the subsequent exploitation of Central Africa by them, and later by the Great Powers of Europe, that the modern town of Zanzibar may be said to have become famous.

' The chief factors which led to its rise have already been alluded to, and it is only necessary here to remind the reader that its predominant geographical position on the east coast gave it control of the great trans-continental routes of the interior from the Indian to the Atlantic Ocean. It became, as Ormuz before it, a great commercial depot and clearing port for the exchange of all kinds of merchandise from Asia, Europe, and America, and its name became familiar with the world at large, owing largely to its association with the East African slave trade.

A good deal of uncertainty exists as to the identity of the several towns called " Zanzibar " mentioned in ancient records, and it has certainly been unfortunate from a historical point of view that the name of the island and its capital has been identical. The doubt as to the old capitals obviously increases when it is asserted that the modern city is scarcely 200 years old, and the question not unnaturally arises as to where the " Zanzibars " of past ages are to be found.

The difficulty is somewhat lessened when it is realised that each incursion of new-comers—whether ancient Greeks, Arabs, Persians, or Pagans—who during the centuries have inhabited Zanzibar Island has led to the founding of a new capital. Where the capital of classic Menouthias was situated no man can tell, but it can be asserted with some confidence that it was almost assuredly built on one of the small islets which fringe the coast of Zanzibar. Coming to a later period we tread on firmer ground, and there is scarcely any doubt but that the capital of the island during the Shirazian or ancient Persian occupation from the tenth century onwards was situated on Tumbatu Island, where the ruins of a substantial stone-built town still exist, while less extensive ruins of a similar character are also to be found in the extreme south of Zanzibar Island at Kisimkazi. The reader will not need to be reminded that the town of Tumbatu or " Tombat " was mentioned by the Arab geographer Yakut in the twelfth century, and it is evident from the existing ruins that it must have been one of the largest and most important settlements on the Azanian coasts. Hence it is probable that the " Zanzibar " mentioned in the early Kilwa chronicles was the ancient Persian town on Tumbatu Island.

Long before the Portuguese arrived on the east coast of Africa, the old Shirazian colonists had disappeared, and their towns, like themselves, had mostly crumbled to dust. By the close of the fifteenth century when Vasco da Gama sailed past Zanzibar, the island was inhabited by people of African origin who had embraced Islam, and the " town of Zanzibar "¹—the capital of the " kings " of Zanzibar to whom the Portuguese so frequently refer—was undoubtedly to be found at the place known to-day as " Unguja Kuu " or " Great Zanzibar." Considering the fact that coins at least 600 years old have been found at this ancient site, it appears probable that the Shirazian city on Tumbatu Islet, and—perhaps the smaller settlement at Kisimkazi, may have existed contemporaneously with the indigenous capital of Zanzibar Island. The prefix " Great " which is now applied to the old capital of the island of Zanzibar is somewhat misleading, as implying that it was a mightier and more extensive city than the modern town of Zanzibar, and this perplexity is increased when the fact is revealed that there is scarcely a vestige of a ruin to be found at the old site of Unguja Kuu. But the explanation is quite simple. The adjective " Great " is, it would seem, of recent adoption, and probably was not in use until the modern settlement of Zanzibar on Shangani Point began to materialise in about the year 1660. For instance, in none of the Portuguese or other records is mention ever made of such a town as " Great Zanzibar " : it is invariably plain " Zanzibar " : and therefore it seems evident that the term " Great " was simply used in a relative sense to distinguish the old town of Zanzibar at Unguja Kuu from the small new settlement on the site of the modern town.

If the word " big " is used instead of " great," the matter is rendered clearer. Old Zanzibar town was only " big " in comparison with the new town of Zanzibar which sprang into existence during the last years of the Portuguese domination of the coast north of Mozambique. But, as has been remarked, the new town did not become of great importance until the Omân Arabs seriously asserted their rights over the Azanian coasts about the middle of the eighteenth century, and it was not until the year 1828 when Seyyid Said of Omân came to Zanzibar, and determined to make the town his capital, that modern Zanzibar blossomed forth into the handsome and beautiful city we see to-day.

Unguja Kuu had then been dead for some years, and the people inhabiting the south of the island chose to reoccupy the site of the old Persian settlement of Kisimkazi. Here to-day we find vestiges of a ruined stone-built fort with a few graves near the sea-shore, and a restored Shirazian mosque, within which is a lengthy inscription in Cufic character, which alone shows that the foundation of this place of worship must be at least 700 or 800 years old.[1] Another inscription in this mosque in ordinary Arabic script states that the building was repaired in A.D. 1773.

Enough has now been said concerning the ancient capitals of the island of Zanzibar, and it is time to turn our attention to the history of the modern city of Zanzibar.

For a town of so recent an origin, there is a strange lack

[1] The deciphering of this inscription has yet to be undertaken.

of information concerning its foundation, but it appears certain that prior to the middle of the seventeenth century the site was only occupied by a few fishermen's huts on the sandy point known as Shangani, which to-day is covered with the substantial mansions and houses of the European and wealthy Arab inhabitants.

Native tradition asserts that the name Shangani is derived from the name Shangaya, a district on the mainland coast westward of Zanzibar, whence the fisherfolk who favoured the locality came.[1]

.At the beginning of the seventeenth century the descendants of the three races or communities which at various periods had laid claim to the island of Zanzibar had become merged by intermarriage into a more or less united people. There is no need to confuse or weary the reader with a recital of these domestic politics, although those interested in the matter will find some further reference to the subject in a subsequent chapter,[2] and it will suffice to remark here that the remnants of the ancient Shirazian communities, the descendants of whom resided at Tumbatu Island and at Kisimkazi, had become affiliated by marriage with the ruling stock of African origin, which during the Portuguese occupation had brought forth the so-called " kings " and " queens " of Zanzibar, and this racial fusion was further accentuated by the mutual mingling of the people and ruling families of Zanzibar, with immigrants from Utondwe and Shangaya, and possibly from other places, such as Mafia and Kilwa, on the mainland coast. That this was indeed the case we know from the fact that when in 1828 the Omân Arabs poured into Zanzibar in the train of Seyyid Said, the ancient races of the island were united under the rulership of the Mwenyi Mkuu, the last of the " kings " of Zanzibar.

In 1710 we find a similar condition of things, and we learn from native tradition that a " king " of Zanzibar

---

[1] It is, however, just as easy to derive the name " Shangani " from the Swahili word " Mchangani," which means literally " at the sand," or " at the sandy place or beach." The name " Mchangani " is common along the Zanzibar coasts to denote a sandy beach.

[2] Chapter XVI, " The Swahili."

named Yussuf, as representing in his person the amalgamated tribal and racial interests aforesaid, divided the island when he died into two portions. The southern portion of the island with Kisimkazi as its capital he allotted to his son Bakiri, while the northern part of his island kingdom, inclusive of the site of the modern town of Zanzibar, he gave to his daughter Fatima. This lady must have lived from about 1650 to about 1715, and she is well known by local tradition and in the Portuguese records as " Queen of Zanzibar." It is during the life of this woman in the year 1710 that we gain our first glimpse of the modern town of Zanzibar from Portuguese sources.

At the above period the place consisted of a fishing village on Shangani Point, and a ruined building which had been used successively as a church and residential quarters by the Portuguese. This building occupied the site of the existing Arab Fort. Adjacent to this ruined church was the house of Queen Fatima.

This, then, was the extent of modern Zanzibar town in 1710, although it may be assumed that there were, in addition, native huts scattered along the sea-shore.

The town was occupied by a garrison of fifty Omân Arabs, and it is stated that they had converted the ruined Portuguese church, which was probably the only masonry building in the place, into a very primitive fort. As already stated, this extemporised fort occupied the site of the picturesque Arab-built fort of the present day. We are told that there were three doors or gateways to this defensive work, and at each gate there was a small cannon.

Although Dalrymple, who published a collection of charts and plans of the Indian Ocean, records that in 1774 the fort at Zanzibar looked very like a ruined church, it is reasonable to suppose that between the years 1710 and 1774 some extensions must have been undertaken, for during that period we know that it received a permanent Arab garrison in 1746, and was unsuccessfully attacked by the Mazrui Arabs from Mombasa in 1753.

In 1784 Zanzibar definitely came under the immediate jurisdiction of Omân, and it may be conjectured that it was during this and subsequent years that the fort began to assume the appearance which it presents to-day. It will be noticed that the common belief among Europeans in Zanzibar that the existing fort was built by the Portuguese is entirely without foundation, and indeed it is easy to see from its architectural features that the work is of Arab construction. The only places within the dominions of the Sultan of Zanzibar where the Portuguese built a fort were in Pemba and at Mombasa.

Queen Fatima had a son named Hasan, and it was this man who must be regarded as the founder of the city of Zanzibar, for when Queen Fatima died he succeeded her as Sultan, and he began energetically to make unto himself a capital.

He cleared the surrounding bushland, and started to extend the little settlement where the modern city of Zanzibar now stands. He agreed to leave the mainland fishing-folk settled at Shangani in possession, and native tradition states that these people raised no objection to the extension of their village on condition that they were con-sulted in important affairs affecting the place, and that their names were mentioned in all public proclamations. Subsequently some Mafazi Arabs came from Patta and settled at the new site, and Sultan Hasan assigned to them the Mwavi quarter, so named from a large Mkumavi tree which is stated to have existed at that period near the site of the present Ismailia Khoja Jamat-Khana.[1]

At a later date came Shatri Arabs from Mafia, and the new town of Zanzibar, finding favour with the new-comers, grew in size and importance. Traders from Arabia and India must soon have appreciated the new port and its conveniences, for there was a good harbour which enabled ships of any size to anchor close to the shore, the port was easy to approach and easy to sail away from, it was within a short distance of many mainland towns, and the country in the vicinity of the new town was infinitely richer and

---

[1] The identification of places by the names of trees is a common feature of Zanzibarian nomenclature. Thus the well-known Sports Ground is known as " Mnazi Moja," or one coco-nut tree ; Mkunazini, " the place where the Mkunazi tree grows " (the leaves of which are used as a soap) ; Mbuyuni, " at the place of the Baobab tree " ; at the Mzambarau tree, etc.

more fertile than the arid coral soil which encircles the old towns of Unguja Kuu and Kisimkazi.

By the close of the eighteenth century the importance of the new town of Zanzibar was beyond question, and when an Arab governor was appointed from Omân the fishing village of 1710 had blossomed forth into a large native town, throughout which were dotted the stone-built houses of the wealthier Arabs and Indian merchants.

The first intelligible record of modern Zanzibar at present known, is that by Lieutenant Bissel of H.M.S. *Leopard*, from which extracts have already been quoted in a previous chapter.

We are informed that when the *Orestes* and *Leopard* entered Zanzibar Harbour the fort fired a salute of three guns, so it is evident that a fort of some kind existed in 1799.

Of the town Bissel remarks that it was composed of " some few houses, and the rest are huts of straw mat which are very neat. The island," he adds, " is tributary to the Imam of Muscat and the Governor or Chief is appointed by him. They have a great deal of trade with the French for slaves and coffee, and many of them talk that language in consequence."

Twelve years later, in February 1811, two more British ships visited Zanzibar. These were the East India Company's cruisers *Ternate* and *Sylph* under Captain Smee, who has recorded his impressions at some length.

The town of Zanzibar, he observes, " is large and populous and is composed chiefly of cajan (plaited coco-nut leaves) huts, all neatly constructed with sloping roofs.

" There are, however, a good number of stone buildings in it belonging to the Arabs and merchants ; and in the centre close to the beach stands a fort, seemingly partly of Arab, partly of Portuguese construction. It is square, with a tower at each corner, and a battery or outwork towards the sea, in which I observed four or five guns of French manufacture, remarkable for their length. In the middle of the town, we observed a tree of uncommon size ; its height was about 8 or 10 feet, and from a rude measurement which we took, its circumference could not I think be less than 36 or 40.[1] . . . The number of the inhabitants of the island may be estimated at 200,000, three-fourths of whom at least are slaves. . . . The trade of this coast is chiefly in the hands of the Arabs from Muscat, Maculla, etc., and a few adventurers from Cutch and the coast of Scinde."

Up till about the year 1822, the harbour was often the resort of Spanish and Portuguese slavers and pirates, who carried on their nefarious trade with every accompaniment of cruelty. The arrival of Seyyid Said and his Arabs in 1828 led at least to some form of law and order, although from all accounts the town continued to be inconceivably filthy and insanitary, and it was not till 1875, after Sultan Barghash's visit to England, that any serious attempt appears to have been made to cope with the scandalous condition of affairs.

Dr. Ruschenberger, writing on Zanzibar in 1835, concluded that " the town of Zanzibar possesses as few attractions for a Christian stranger as any place or people in the wide world "; and as will be seen later, he but voiced the opinion of every visitor to Zanzibar for the succeeding forty years.

In 1841 Captain Hamerton, of the Indian Army, was appointed as Her Majesty's Consul and Representative of the Honourable East India Company at the Court of His Highness Seyyid Said, Sultan of Zanzibar and Imam of Muscat.

House accommodation suitable for the British representative was difficult to find in those early days, but finally Captain Hamerton obtained accommodation for his consulate in the house now occupied by Messrs. Smith Mackenzie and Co., while the American Consul resided close by. The large Arab mansion at Shangani Point which eventually became the British Consulate-General, and is now used as the European Hospital, was only built between the years 1847 and 1850.

During this period the condition of the town still remained

---

[1] The baobab tree grows to enormous sizes in Zanzibar and Pemba. The author measured one with the assistance of Mr. J. Gilbert at Mtangani on the east coast of Pemba, and found its circumference to be 70 feet and 8 inches at five feet from the ground. A measuring tape was used. The tree was about 100 feet in height. In the south of Zanzibar Island there are some which may exceed these measurements.

THE OLD BARRACKS, ZANZIBAR

A PORTUGUESE BRONZE GUN, ZANZIBAR, CIRCA A.D. 1550.

Gomes.

"AT THE GATES OF THE SULTAN'S PALACE."

incredibly insanitary. Captain Hamerton, writing in 1842, mentions that he had seen no less than fifty corpses of slaves rotting on the sea-beach. When a slave died, it was no one's business to bury him, so the body was thrown on the beach to be either washed away by a high tide or eaten by the pariah dogs.

This practice of disposing of dead slaves continued more or less till as late as 1857 ; and indeed until the great cholera outbreak of 1869, when 15,000 of the population died, no adequate method of disposing of the dead was adopted. Captain Smee in 1811 had remarked on the casual method of burying the dead in Zanzibar town, and stated that the graves were so shallow that the bodies were hardly covered, the limbs of the corpse being constantly exposed.

This callousness was no doubt partly due to laziness, but it may be pointed out that the covering of soil over the hard, underlying coral rock anywhere near the town is so thin that it is a difficult matter to dig any kind of hole. This geological formation greatly hindered the digging of trenches during the early stages of the war in 1914, and it was found necessary in many places to build up defences with sandbags, rather than attempt to dig downwards.

Between 1846 and 1850 a map and sketch of Zanzibar became available, thanks to the energy of Captain Guillain of the French Navy, who subsequently published his well-known book *Documents sur l'histoire et la geographie de l'Afrique orientale.*

With regard to Guillain's view of the town, the fort is easily recognised, with the battery in front. The arcade immediately behind the large flagstaff was the old palace of Seyyid Said, a site now occupied by Bet-el-Ajaib. The house to the left of the flagstaff is the Bet-el-Sahil, the chief palace of the Seyyid.

The next two buildings were occupied by the dependents of the palace, the larger one being, at the present day, the palace of His Highness Seyyid Khalifa. The house with the pent roof next to this was occupied by Seyyid Majid, the favourite son of Seyyid Said. The French Consulate lies just behind this mansion.

To the right of the fort, the building with a very high

flagstaff appearing above a cluster of coco-nut palms was the British Consulate, now the business premises of Messrs. Smith Mackenzie & Co. The next flagstaff marks the American Consulate, and the last house visible is the present European Hospital. At the time of the sketch it had only just been completed, and the owner, Sheikh Salim-bin-Bushir-bin-Salim el-Harthi resided there. His Highness Seyyid Said visited the Sheikh in his house. It was afterwards occupied for a time by the Universities' Mission to Central Africa, and subsequently became the residence of a long succession of British Consul-Generals.

When His Highness Seyyid Said died in 1856, the estimated population of Zanzibar was 25,000, rising to 40,000 during the north-east monsoon, when the town became full of piratical Arabs from the Persian Gulf.

The outrages perpetrated by these Arabs during their periodical visits to Zanzibar were a constant ground of complaint by the inhabitants of the town during the middle of the nineteenth century, and it was only the presence of some of Her Majesty's ships on the east coast of Africa which restrained these ruffians from committing worse crimes than they did. Old documents of the period contain frequent allusions to the intolerable condition of affairs in Zanzibar when the north-east monsoon brought these unwelcomed visitors to the Sultan's dominions.

The British Consul, writing from Zanzibar in 1859, remarks that during the northern monsoon (January and February) the town was full of many thousands of these piratical Arabs from the Persian Gulf, Soor, and Hadramaut. " They come," he says, " solely for the purpose of kidnapping slaves and children, which they convey for sale to the coasts of Arabia and Persia."

" These pirates," he adds, " are the terror of these coasts. They commit murders and thefts with impunity, for the Sultan's soldiers are afraid of them." On March 9th, 1861, they severely wounded four servants of the American Consulate ; they then locked the American Consul in his house, and blockaded it the whole day, posting themselves at all the windows which commanded the interior of the Consulate, and calling out that they were determined to take the life of the American Consul.   Others went about the town all day, brandishing their swords, and calling out that they would have the blood of a white man.

The cause of their attack upon the American Consulate was that the Consul had placed one of his servants in front of the house, to desire the pirates not to commit nuisances just in front, as a lady was staying in the house.   During the day they sent parties with drawn swords, who concealed themselves around the British Consulate, and one of them committed a nuisance at the entrance of the Consulate, with the obvious intention of provoking the sepoys on guard to interfere with him.   Remonstrances were of course made to the Sultan, who, no doubt terrified nearly out of his life, did nothing.   At 9 p.m. the same evening, the pirates were observed to be collecting round the American Consulate again, using the most threatening and insulting language.

By this time no European resident dared quit his house after dark.   Further urgent remonstrances were made by the two Consuls, and eventually His Highness sent an Arab to the rioters, and actually bribed them to disperse by a gift of a thousand rupees !

During this period, even the Sultan was constrained to discontinue his daily levee, and kept in the upper story of his palace to avoid insolent and importunate demands.

Fortunately for the peace of Zanzibar, when these ruffians thought they had the town completely at their mercy, a British cruiser—H.M.S. *Lyra*, commanded by Captain Old- field—arrived.   The situation was soon in hand, and Captain Oldfield gave the slavers forty-eight hours to leave Zanzibar.

H.M.S. *Lyra* was well known on the coast, owing to the energy of her commander and crew in suppressing the slave trade, and Oldfield's proceedings inspired such fear that his ship was known along the whole length of the East African coast as " El Shaitan," or " The Devil."

To give but one more example of the condition of affairs in Zanzibar during the early years of Seyyid Majid's reign.

At the town of Chake Chake, the capital of Pemba, at the beginning of 1860, fifteen large vessels arrived crammed with pirates from the Persian Gulf, who terrorised the district, and plundered the whole country ; and they were only deterred from looting the town itself by the timely arrival of one of the Sultan's ships of war.

The whole object of the visit of these men to Zanzibar was to obtain slaves by sale or kidnapping. Their vessels used to bring no cargo, and, except kidnapped children, carried none away. During the time these northern Arabs were in the town, Zanzibar resembled a city with a hostile army encamped in its neighbourhood, and every person who was able to do so sent his children into the interior of the island for safety. People were afraid to stir out of their houses after dark, and reports were daily made of children and slaves being kidnapped. Sometimes these pirates would enter houses, and take away the children by force. On several occasions, it is recorded that kidnapped children with their mouths tightly gagged were carried through the public streets in large baskets. The Sultan's so-called soldiers were worse than useless. First of all they were afraid to interfere, and secondly they assisted in these outrages. A case is related of a confidential Turkish jemadar in the service of the Sultan, who was placed in charge of a body of " soldiers " to patrol the beach at night, in order to prevent slaves being shipped under cover of darkness. When so employed this man is stated to have actually sold sixty-two children to the very people he was supposed to arrest !

However willing the Sultan himself may have been to assist the British Consul in repressing the slave trade, he was practically helpless, and the Consul himself found his efforts thwarted and defied at every turn. What made his task so difficult was the fact that the slave trade was actually encouraged and participated in by the representatives of certain European Powers in Zanzibar. And yet the good work of emancipation and repression slowly progressed, and it was largely to the entiring devotion of Her Majesty's Navy that the vile trade was finally suppressed.

In 1859 no less than 19,000 slaves were openly imported into Zanzibar, about half of whom were subsequently shipped to Cuba, to Arabia, and the Persian Gulf. About this year, slavers flying European colours used to make Chwaka their haunt, and reference is officially made of a large slaver being anchored off the bay, full of chains and irons ready to receive a cargo of humanity.

In the subjoined list, taken from an old document showing the current prices in the markets in 1859, the inclusion of slaves as marketable commodities reads strangely.

PRICES OF ARTICLES [*sic*] IN MARKETS OF ZANZIBAR

	s.	d.	s.	d.
Bullocks	54	0 to	90	0
Sheep	20	0 ,,	44	6
Goats	18	0 ,,	36	0
Arabian Donkeys	90	0 ,,	225	0
Fowls, per dozen	6	9 ,,	9	0
Ducks, per pair	4	6 ,,	6	9
Geese, each . . .	9	0 ,,	13	6
Slaves, adult (male or female)	45	0 ,,	135	0
Slaves (boy or girl) . . .	25	0 ,,	50	0
Hides, each	5	6 ,,	6	9

(All the above prices in English shillings.)

It was during the year 1859 that Zanzibar town was visited by one of those dreadful outbreaks of cholera, which periodically wrought havoc among the people of the Swahili Coast. On this occasion, it is estimated that 20,000 people in Zanzibar died from the disease. Another such outbreak occurred ten years later, to which further reference will be made. It should be stated that these outbreaks did not originate in Zanzibar Island, but were invariably brought from the mainland, nevertheless so deficient was Zanzibar in the most elementary principles of sanitation, and the town was in such a filthy condition, that it is not surprising that disease and death found a happy hunting-ground. Indeed, it is remarkable that the ravages were not far more serious and of greater frequency.

II

At this period (1858) the locality to the east of the creek known as Ngambo, which to-day forms the great Swahili quarter of Zanzibar city, was still unbuilt upon, and was

13

covered by coco-nut plantations and bushland, wherein the pariah dogs of Zanzibar laired.

The creek which runs at the back of the main town and divides it from the Ngambo quarter was almost invariably referred to by the travellers in the middle of the nineteenth century as the " fetid lagoon," while the adjacent open ground known as Mnazi Moja—at the present time (1918) the most cherished and delightful spot in modern Zanzibar, constituting as it does one of the prettiest and greenest golf links, football grounds, cricket pitches, croquet lawns, and several excellent tennis courts under the management of the European Sports Club—was wont to be mentioned by Europeans with a shudder.

Here is Burton's description of it in 1857. " This bit of open ground is the Bois de Boulogne of Zanzibar, the single place of exercise, and we did not wonder that so many prefer to stay at home."

But worse is to come. Dr. Christie,[1] writing in 1869, refers to " Nazemodya "[2] as being used as a common burial-ground, and states that several Europeans are buried there.

" The part next to the sea is covered with bush," he tells us, " and is the place usually selected by the negroes for exposing their dead. . . . Nazemodya, however, is a place of many horrors, and those who have explored that narrow neck of land seldom think of it without a shudder. It is rather a trouble to dispose of the dead body of a large animal, so that dying dromedaries, aged and infirm horses and donkeys, and hopelessly diseased cattle of all sorts are led out to Nazemodya in the evening to shuffle off the mortal coil, and there become food for the wild dogs before morning.

" When the supply is greater than the dogs can dispose of, portions of the putrid carcases defile the atmosphere, and Europeans are scared away for a time. Few natives and fewer Europeans, however, visit the precincts of the sea-beach in the neighbourhood, although it is but a few

[1] *Cholera Epidemics in East Africa*, by James Christie.

[2] Dr. Christie here of course refers to the modern recreation area of Zanzibar known as " Mnazi Moja." The system of orthography adopted by travellers and others in the middle of the last century is essentially different to that now in use. Burton, for instance, spells the very common African name " Mwera " as " Mohayra."

yards distant, for sights may be seen there sufficient to shock even those who have been familiar with the dissecting-room. I have seen on many occasions human remains lying there in the bush, *membra disjecta*, the fragments of the last night's meal of the shamba dogs.

" When the death-rate is low among the negroes the wild dogs become ravenous and dangerous after sunset, and they have frequently attacked human beings trespassing on their haunts. At such times it is dangerous to be in the streets at night, as they parade the town in troops in search of garbage : but without their excellent services as public scavengers the town would scarcely be habitable."

Can it be wondered at that plague and pestilence were a common feature of Zanzibar life in the early sixties of the last century ?

The condition of the Mnazi Moja suburb was bad, but the state of the streets and the beach was worse. Dr. Christie makes further reference to this matter and states :

" Countless millions of ants and beetles, millions of rats, and armies of wild dogs, aid in removing the garbage of the town and suburbs, and the rain sweeps away to the ocean much of the filth of the place." When there was no con-venient place to deposit rubbish, it was carried to the shore and " thus the beach all around the town is made, at every available part, the site of a dung-heap, and the lanes leading to the shore become impassable to any but natives, from deposits of filth and rubbish. These dung-heaps fringe the entire shore in the native quarters of the town, and in many cases a solid, permanent deposit has been formed, upon which native huts are erected.

" When such deposits become inconvenient or offensive beyond endurance in the European quarter of the town, it is necessary to employ 'a gang of negroes to remove them ; but a fresh accumulation begins immediately. . . There are few points of the shore, even at high tide, where a European can get into a boat without crossing one of these dung-heaps, and no one would ever think of doing so except from urgent necessity.

" No stranger ever lands at Zanzibar without expressing extreme disgust at the odious state of the sea-beach, even in the best-kept part of the town. To some it occasions nausea and vomiting, and both olfactories and optics are most painfully affected. Except at high tide no one ever thinks of boat exercise, and it is only at that time that European ladies can approach the shore."

Lest it may be thought that Dr. Christie is exaggerating the condition of affairs, we find that Dr. Livingstone, who was in Zanzibar during 1866,[1] fully corroborates him with regard to the sea-beach, and the old Scotchman actually makes a joke !

" The stench," writes Livingstone,[2] " from a mile and a half to two square miles of exposed sea-beach, which is the general depository of the filth of the town, is quite horrible. At night it is so gross or crass, one might cut out a slice and manure a garden with it : it might be called ' Stinkibar ' rather than ' Zanzibar.' "

One more extract and I will lead the reader into pleasanter paths.

Speaking of the outbreak of cholera in 1869, Dr. Christie says :

" When the plague was at its very height, raging in every quarter of the city like a devouring element, threatening all with destruction, praying parties and Koranic chanters were organised, and they perambulated the streets by night invoking God to stay the pestilence and spare the living. . . . The only sounds that broke the stillness of the night were the footsteps of the negroes passing along the bridge [3] bearing a dead body to be thrown into the tide below ; but from no great distance much more disagreeable sounds greeted the ear, and sent a shudder through the frame, proceeding from the wild dogs at Nazemodya, growling and fighting over the bodies of the dead. The stench from the dead bodies penetrated the outskirts of the town ; and this combined with the horrid effluvia from the sea-beach and lagoon, before the morning breeze has set in motion the stagnant air, was often overpowering and causes nausea. . . .

" The ground set apart for burial was soon filled up, and

[1] The house he occupied is still standing.
[2] *Last Journals.*
[3] Darajani Bridge.

fresh fields had to be opened in the suburbs. When the violence of the epidemic was somewhat abated, I had leisure on one occasion to walk over part of the suburbs devoted to interments at Nazemodya, and the entire space was red like a newly ploughed field. Thousands must have been buried there within the preceding two months ; fresh bones and skulls were scattered about on the surface of the ground ; and in the vicinity of the sea-beach, headless and limbless trunks were lying in the bush, emitting a dreadful odour. It was about this time that the negroes commenced to throw the dead bodies over the bridge,[1] and to expose them on the sea-shore within reach of the tide. . . . The town and suburbs at this time was a reeking mass of abomination."

[1] Darajani Bridge.

CHAPTER XIV

ZANZIBAR might have been one of the most beautiful cities in the world.

Built as it is on a spit of land jutting out into a sea of lapis lazuli, studded with green islets, and backed by verdant hills covered with waving palms, it should have no rival. Nature has done her best, but man has failed to take advantage of his opportunities. Even as it is, Zanzibar seen from the sea is attractive in appearance, but one looks in vain for the pinnacled mosques and the glistening domes of an Eastern city. The existing mosques of Zanzibar are very unpretentious, and it is no exaggeration to say that if one sees a particularly plain, single-storied, whitewashed building, devoid of ornament or artistic beauty, it may safely be put down as a mosque. Not a few of the older palaces and mansions, which were built by the Arabs who followed Seyyid Said to Zanzibar, disclose a kind of massive strength, which well suits their plain exteriors, but none of them enhance the beauty of the town.

And yet, while the individual buildings lack grace, Zanzibar possesses characteristics of its own which are possibly unique.

In the first place the horrors of the last century, referred to in the preceding chapter, exist no longer, and Zanzibar is one of the cleanest and most inoffensive cities in the world ; and yet it has retained many of those features which make an Eastern town so fascinating. The town is a maze of tortuous, narrow streets, so narrow, many of them, that no sort of wheeled vehicle can pass through them.

It is a city of brilliant sunshine and purple shadows ; of dark entries and latticed windows ; of mysterious stairways, and massive doors in grey walls which conceal one does not know what ; of sun-streaked courtyards and glimpses of green gardens ; of barred windows and ruined walls on which peacocks preen. It is a town of rich merchants and busy streets ; of thronged market-places and clustered mansions.

Over all there is the din of barter, of shouts from the harbour ; the glamour of the sun, the magic of the sea, and the rich savour of Eastern spice.

This is Zanzibar !

It is quite instructive to stay for a time at some busy spot in the city and watch the varied crowd go by. There are few places of the same size where one can study the races of mankind with greater facility and ease. One will see none of the ordered pomp of India ; no jewel-bedecked rajah will pass by, and no bespectacled B.A. of Calcutta University will obtrude the view, but the spectator will be able to rub shoulders with some of the wilder and less-known people of Africa and of Asia ; and the lack of display is compensated for by the genuineness of the whole scene. Zanzibar is an epitome of the ancient Bagdad of Haroun-el-Raschid, rather than of the Europeanised India of to-day.

It must be confessed that Zanzibar possesses no building of interest.

The first building which arrests the visitors' attention on arrival in Zanzibar Harbour is the Bet-el-Ajaib or House of Wonders, conspicuous by its many verandahs and central clock tower. It is situated on the edge of the sea, and overlooks the harbour. It was built by one of the most famous Sultans of Zanzibar—Seyyid Barghash—in 1883 ; not as a residence, but for ceremonial purposes. It communicated with the older range of palaces adjoining by covered ways and passages. Architecturally it has no merit, but it evidently startled the Arab population, who gave it the name it bears. Two succeeding Sultans dwelt in it, but in 1911 it was taken over by the Zanzibar Government, and now houses within its capacious salons the offices of the Zanzibar Government Departments. The visitor to Zanzibar should make a point of inspecting the interior of the building.

When the two adjoining palaces were utterly destroyed by the guns of the British Fleet during the bombardment of 1896, the Bet-el-Ajaib was spared, and it escaped with a few shells through its walls.

Two very ancient Portuguese bronze guns stand on plinths before the main entrance of the building. They are worthy of close inspection, not only on account of their historical interest, but as fine specimens of bronze casting. They were probably made during the reign of King John III of Portugal, who reigned between 1521 and A.D. 1557. On the larger of these guns the embossed mouldings are elaborately worked, and comprise the royal arms of Portugal, the cipher and standard of King John III, and the planisphere of the world, a proud badge worthy of the nation which included among its intrepid sailors and explorers Prince Henry the Navigator—whose mother, by-the-by, was an English princess—Diogo Cam, Bartholomew Diaz, Vasco da Gama, and a score of others equally famous in the annals of Portugal and the world.

The royal arms above referred to display seven castles representing the seven provinces of Portugal, and on the inner escutcheons, which are emblematic of the five wounds of Our Lord, are shown the twenty-five golden coins traditionally paid as tribute by the Kings of Portugal to the Pope.

The royal standard, which bears the crown and five escutcheons, as described above, is supported by a heraldic lion, while the royal cipher is an ornate initial letter " J " or " I."

The size of the guns is remarkable, and in their day they must have been considered masterpieces. The larger outside the Bet-el-Ajaib measures 11 feet 9¼ inches in length, 7¼ inches bore, and 21 inches in diameter across the breech; the second is 10 feet in length, 7 inches bore, and 17 inches across the breech.

A third gun of similar make stands in the garden of the Residency. This one is 13 feet long, 7⅝ inches bore, and 22 inches across the breech, and is thus the largest of the three Portuguese guns in Zanzibar.

A fourth gun is said to have existed, but its whereabouts are at present unknown.[1]

That one at least of these guns has been in action is evident from the deep impress of a cannon ball 4⅞ inches in diameter in the breech, and the fact that the line of impact is slightly upwards makes it appear probable that the hit was made during a sea-fight; for it is evident that to make so deep an impress, the shot must have been fired at close quarters from the flank, and nearly on a level with the gun itself. This would have been unlikely if this gun had been mounted in a fortress. If this supposition is correct, there is every reason to believe the Arab chronicler who states that when Seif-bin-Sultan, the ruler of Omân, attacked Mozambique in A.D. 1711 he had in his fleet guns measuring three spans at the breech; and it appears probable that the guns now outside the Bet-el-Ajaib in Zanzibar are two of the identical weapons.

It is clear from a Persian inscription upon these three guns that they were captured from the Portuguese in the year A.D. 1622 by the Persians.

The inscription translated into English reads as follows ·

IN THE NAME OF GOD AND BY THE GRACE OF MAHOMED AND ALI CONVEY TO THE TRUE BELIEVERS WHO HAVE ASSEMBLED TOGETHER FOR FIGHTING THE GOOD TIDINGS OF SUCCESS AND VICTORY, IN THE YEAR 1031 HEGIRA [A.D. 1622]. DURING THE REIGN OF SHAH ABBAS, SAFAWI, KING OF THE EARTH AND OF TIME, WHOSE POWER IS EVER INCREASING, IMAM KULI KHAN BY THE GRACE OF THE SHAH, THE DEFENDER OF THE FAITH, CONQUERED FARS, LAR, MOUNTAIN KAIWAN, BAHREIN AND FORT ORMUZ AND CAPTURED IBN AYYUB.

This Persian inscription upon these ancient Portuguese cannon is distinctly interesting, for it epitomises the history

[1] The arms on the guns are evidently those of Portugal, and this being so, it is safe to conclude that the royal cipher is that of João III. Portugal became subject to Spain in 1580, and remained so until 1640, a period known as " the sixty years' captivity," and it is therefore certain that the cipher is not that of João IV, who was crowned in 1640. Apart from this consideration, it is improbable that such magnificent pieces could have been spared for the defence of Ormuz during the troublous period of the Spanish domination of Portugal; moreover it must be remembered that the Portuguese had captured Ormuz in 1507, and the guns in question came into the possession of the Persians in 1622.

The three guns may therefore be regarded as having been made not later than the middle of the sixteenth century, and two of them at least are very fine specimens of elaborate bronze casting.

of Persia during the reign of the most famous sovereign who ever ruled over the Land of the Lion and the Sun.

Abbas " the Great," Shah of Persia (of the Sufi or Safawi Dynasty which lasted from 1499 to 1736), was a contemporary of Queen Elizabeth of England, and ascended the throne in 1586. During his reign of forty-two years he raised the Persian Empire to a pre-eminent position among the great powers of Asia, and he successfully waged war against the Ottoman Sultan, and against the Great Moghul of Hindustan. At his court were ambassadors from England, Russia, Spain, Portugal, Holland, and India, and to his Christian subjects he displayed a tolerance and kindness which were truly remarkable.

Imam Kuli Khan mentioned in the inscription was one of his most famous generals, founder of a college at Shiraz, and a man of the highest character and attainments. The conquest of Fars took place shortly after the accession of Abbas to the throne : and after concluding a peace with the Ottoman Sultan, he deputed Imam Kuli Khan to consolidate and extend his power along the sea-board of the Persian Gulf. Bahrein and the city of Lar surrendered to the victorious general about the year 1597. In 1621 Shah Abbas determined to drive the Portuguese from the rich island of Ormuz, which they had seized in 1507. A large Persian force under the command of Imam Kuli Khan was collected and, assisted by troops of the East India Company, laid siege to Ormuz, which finally surrendered to the Persian commander. There can be little doubt 'but that the bronze Portuguese guns now resting peacefully at Zanzibar were a part of the booty taken by the Persians at the fall of Ormuz.

Hence the pæan of victory inscribed on the captured guns.

Shah Abbas died in 1628, and it is sad to have to relate that the aged Imam Kuli Khan, who had served his master so faithfully, was put to death by the debauched youth who succeeded the great Abbas on the throne of Persia. The new Shah, whose name was Sufi, was the grandson of Abbas, and among his many infamies he is credited with having murdered his mother, his sister, and his wife.

A CARVED DOOR IN ZANZIBAR.

203

It may be asked how, if the guns were captured by the Persians in 1622, do they come to be in Zanzibar. There are two explanations. The first is, that in the early years of the nineteenth century, Seyyid Said, the ruler of Omân and Sultan of Zanzibar, leased the island of Ormuz, to which Omân considered it had at least a traditional right, from the Shah of Persia, and appointed his eldest son, Seyyid Thuwaini, as governor. The lease eventually fell through, and it is stated that Seyyid Thuwaini, when he sailed from Ormuz for Muscat in the sailing ship *Sultani*, took these old Portuguese guns with him.[1]

The more probable explanation is that they were captured by the Omân Arabs from the Persians, and that when Seyyid Said transferred his capital from Muscat, the guns were brought to Zanzibar. From the time the Portuguese were expelled from the Persian Gulf by the Omân Arabs, there was constant warfare between the Omânis and the Persians, who hated each other, so there were plenty of opportunities for the guns, originally captured by the Persians from the Portuguese, to change hands.

Zanzibar town is famous for its carved doors, and the finest examples are to be found in the Bet-el-Ajaib. It will be noticed that the great entrance doors of this palace are studded with ornamental brass spikes and bosses. These decorative excrescences are a modification of the ancient Indian practice of studding the doors of medieval castles and strongholds with sharp steel and iron spikes, to prevent their being battered in by war-elephants.

On the upper floors of the Bet-el-Ajaib are some beautiful doors. The frames and lintels are richly carved and gilt, and the entire doors are covered with texts from the Koran in relief, gilded on a green ground. The effect is particularly rich and effective.

The marble pavements of the Bet-el-Ajaib were all imported from Europe, as were the massive silver decorations on the staircases.

---

[1] It seems unlikely, however, that Seyyid Thuwaini ever had the opportunity to take the guns away, as his father the Seyyid Said does not appear to have been in a position owing to financial reasons to accept the terms of the lease.

In the office of the British Resident, formerly used as the private sitting-room of His Highness the ex-Sultan,[1] is some fretted cedar and teak panelling, and a good example of antique Persian brass work in the form of two massive lions. They are considerably heavier than they look, and can only just be lifted by a strong man. Extensive views of the old fort, of the city, and of Zanzibar can be obtained from the clock tower.

His Highness the Sultan Khalifa II now occupies the palace to the north of the House of Wonders, and the Zanzibar standard—a plain red flag—flies from a lofty flagstaff in the palace garden. This garden is the site of the old palace of Seyyid Said, the first Sultan of Zanzibar, which was destroyed with an adjoining palace known as 'the Bet-el-Hukm (Government House) by the guns of the British Fleet on August 27th, 1896.

Why did a squadron of British warships bombard Zanzibar? it may be asked. The story has been told so often, and the event is of so comparatively recent a date, that only the briefest account is necessary.

On August 25th, 1896, the Sultan Hamed-bin-Thuwaini died, and a young prince of the royal house, Seyyid Khaled, son of the famous Sultan Barghash, attempted to usurp the throne in defiance of the orders of the British representative in Zanzibar. Seyyid Khaled-bin-Barghash was an ambitious man, and he was undoubtedly encouraged in his schemes by the Germans, who have always regarded Zanzibar with a jealous eye. It is true that in 1890 they had, in consideration of receiving Heligoland from Great Britain, formally agreed to a British Protectorate being declared over Zanzibar; but Zanzibar is an important place in the politics of Eastern Africa and of Arabia, and the loss of British prestige there would influence millions of people both in Africa and Asia.

Sultan Hamed had himself exhibited an inclination to defy the protecting power to whom he owed his throne, and his subjects, quick to follow the example of their ruler, began to show open disrespect to the English in Zanzibar.

[1] Seyyid-Ali-bin-Hamoud, who abdicated the throne in 1911, and died in Paris in 1918.

Whatever underhand intrigue was at work, the fact remains that the moment Sultan Hamed was dead, Seyyid Khaled-bin-Barghash, accompanied by hundreds of armed Arabs, broke into the palace and proclaimed himself Sultan. He only reigned for a few hours !

In that short space of time, however, he augmented his force by many thousands, and the palace bristled with artillery of all kinds.

Fortunately at this crisis in the affairs of Zanzibar, the British Fleet suddenly appeared upon the scene and settled matters. A squadron under the command of Admiral Sir Harry Rawson assembled in Zanzibar Harbour, and anchored off the palace within point-blank range.

An ultimatum requiring complete submission and disarmament of the usurper and his forces before 9 a.m. on the following day was delivered to Seyyid Khaled, who defiantly ignored it.

Although the inhabitants of Zanzibar had frequently seen British and German men-of-war, they had little idea of the power of modern artillery, or what a bombardment meant, and up to the last moment the Arabs had no conception of what their truculency would lead to. Their soothsayers proclaimed that the English guns would be innocuous and would only spout out water.

At nine o'clock on the morning of August 27th, 1896, the Zanzibar Arab and Swahili learnt his lesson, and he has never forgotten it. A hail of shell from Her Majesty's ships made the town rock, and the two adjoining palaces, crammed with the adherents of the usurper, crumbled visibly away, while the defenders with their guns and muskets were swept away in one bleeding and distorted mass of wreckage.

After twenty-five minutes the rebels hauled down their flag, and Seyyid Khaled, horrified at the destruction he had caused, fled to the German Consulate—a very significant fact. He eventually embarked on a German gunboat, and was taken to Daresalaam, where, until his capture in " German " East Africa by the British forces in 1917, he lived as a pensioner of the German Government, using his influence with both Arab and native alike to injure British interests in East Africa and Zanzibar. He has now been deported to a salubrious and remote corner of the British Empire, where, for the sake of the peace of Eastern Africa and Zanzibar, it is to be hoped he will remain permanently.

On the south side of the House of Wonders lies the old Arab fort, or rather the remains of it. Fortunately its walls and most picturesque towers still remain intact, but the great gateway which faced the sea has been demolished, and against the whole of this side a series of unsightly and mean buildings have been erected. The other three sides remain much as they were originally, and offer to the artist and photographer some picturesque subjects for record. The old place of execution where culprits were beheaded with a sword was situated outside the east wall of the fort.

In addition to serving the purposes of defence, the fort was also used as the state prison, and whenever the soil is disturbed human remains are discovered. The interior is now utilised partly for Customs purposes, and partly as a Government railway workshop. It is to be regretted that the old gateway was not preserved, and although the present uses to which the fort is turned are sufficiently unromantic, it ensures that the walls and bastions are preserved instead of being allowed to fall into ruin. It is to be hoped that some day the interior may be cleared and laid out as a public garden and museum, to remain as a permanent memorial of the past history of Zanzibar.

It will be noticed that at many street corners stand-pipes exist which give to the population the inestimable boon of a good water supply. The water is brought into the town from a spring, situated about four miles distant, and the credit of this accomplishment must be given to His Highness Seyyid Barghash, who reigned between 1870 and 1888. For a considerable portion of the way the original Arab conduit is still being used. To add to this supply a scheme has been approved for bringing in water from another source, distant about six miles from the town.

It may be mentioned at this point that the whole of the city is lit by electricity generated by the very latest patterns of Diesel engines worked as a Government undertaking. The entire island is linked up with telephones, and it is possible to speak to nearly all the villages and police stations in the island. The Government also maintains a wireless installation for the purpose of maintaining prompt communication with Pemba Island and Mafia Island.

To return to the description of the main features of the town. The large white mansion on the extreme southern point of the harbour is the European Hospital. It is a good specimen of old Arab mansion. It was for many years the residence of the British Political Agents and Consul-Generals, and it was here that many of the great African explorers, such as Livingstone, Burton, Speke, Cameron, Baker, and Stanley, found accommodation while organising and completing arrangements for their great enterprises on the mainland. It is said that when in course of construction slaves were immured alive according to custom within the foundations. This sinister rumour is applied to nearly every old house, and it is difficult to entirely discredit it. I have referred to this matter in another chapter,[1] so there is no need to reiterate the arguments for and against the probability of the practice; but it may be remarked that a number of houses in Zanzibar town have the reputation of being haunted, or at least of possessing something uncanny about them. This belief rises from the above-mentioned idea that slaves have been immolated within the foundations, and no doubt in many of these old houses dark deeds have been perpetrated in the past.

The houses rather lend themselves to the generation of superstitious fears. They have the appearance of being very old, and many of them possess dark gloomy staircases, strange recesses and blind passages which seem to lead to nowhere, and dark corners where shadows lurk. It is not always the Europeans who imagine these things, but more frequently Arabs and natives. In some of these old houses the servants affirm that as they ascend the stairs or pass some empty room, " something " clutches at their garments, or even catches them by the arm, attempting to hold them back.

Beyond the European hospital referred to above, lies, facing the sea, the newly erected quarters of the Eastern Telegraph Company, occupying the site of an older building

[1] See Chapter XII.

erected for the company by Seyyid Barghash. It was under the foundations of this house that about twenty human skeletons were discovered. Zanzibar is an important cable station, in fact the most important on the east coast of Africa, for here come ashore the direct cables from Aden, South Africa, the Seychelles, and subsidiary lines from British and " German " East Africa.

We now enter upon the European residential quarter, in which are situated the houses of the chief Government officials, the Law Courts, some of the foreign consulates, the English Club and the banks, the General Post Office, and the most important shops. Prominent amidst other pleasantly situated houses is the British Residency, easily distinguished by the Union Jack flying from the tower. Opposite are the Victoria Gardens, originally laid out by His Highness Seyyid Barghash as a place of recreation and rest when returning to Zanzibar from his palace at Chukwani. It serves now as a shady public garden, in the midst of which stands the Victoria Hall, containing a swimming bath and a small up-to-date stage.

Adjoining this part of the town lie the famous Mnazi Moja Sports Ground and the new public recreation park. The horrors for which this area was infamous during the last century, and concerning which so much has been said in this book, have all been swept away ; and it is hard to believe, as one looks at the waving trees, the green turf putting-greens, and the crowds of golfers and cricketers who disport themselves every afternoon, that the nightmare tales of the past can be true.

Zanzibar possesses two cathedrals, one belonging to the Catholic Mission of the Holy Ghost, and the other that of the famous Universities' Mission to Central Africa.

The former fane, conspicuous by its twin spires, is situated in the middle of the city near the European quarter ; while the latter with one spire is built facing the creek in the native quarter on the site of the old slave market. The main activities of these missions are centred among the native populations of the mainland, but both communities find plenty of useful work to do in Zanzibar. The Universities' Mission, besides the purely clerical duties inseparable

Gomes.

NARROW STREETS, ZANZIBAR CITY.

Gomes.

THE ENGLISH CATHEDRAL ON SITE OF OLD SLAVE
MARKET.

from its ministrations to both European and native congregations, maintains in Zanzibar a theological training college for native students, a large school in the town, a girls' school, numerous village schools in the suburbs, and a most excellent hospital for native patients. In Pemba they support a religious and educational establishment at Weti.

And what can be said of the real Arab city of Zanzibar? To attempt to portray its details would be like describing the maze at Hampton Court, except that Zanzibar is a thousand times more picturesque and interesting. It is almost hopeless for a stranger to find his way to any particular spot without a guide through the tortuous and narrow lanes which serve as streets, for if he attempted to do so, it is highly probable that instead of reaching his destination, he would, after some aimless wanderings, either find himself back at the point from which he started or at some locality far removed from his intended goal.

But let not this difficulty of finding his way deter any interested in Eastern life, and, with an hour to spare, from boldly plunging into the city maze. He will see much to interest him, and he may be assured that wherever fortune leads him he will be safer from molestation and annoyance than if he walked in London. There is only one thing the visitor must not do, and that is, enter a mosque : he may peep discreetly in from a distance, but this must be the limit of his inquisitiveness. As Zanzibar is practically an island, the extent of a visitor's peregrinations will in any case be limited in any one direction, and if he loses his bearings altogether he may be certain that every passer-by will smilingly and courteously indicate the direction he should take.

The outstanding features of the Arab city—as distinct from those of the European quarter—are, as already stated, few in number. They are the old Arab fort, the Bet-el-Ajaib, and the Sultan's palace on the west, the Roman Catholic Cathedral in the centre, and the English Cathedral on the east. The extreme northern portion of the city is given up to the poor tenements of seafaring and fishing folk, and around a lengthy "rope-walk" cluster the houses of the rope makers. Near this area is the Malindi quarter,

14

favoured by Persian Gulf and Somali Arab seamen who visit Zanzibar when the favouring north-east trade-wind blows. In the numerous Arab coffee-houses and restaurants here, very interesting and romantic types of humanity may be seen at the proper season of the year.

The houses adjoining these poorer quarters to the southward become more imposing and substantial, and in them reside wealthy Arabs, scions of the nobility, ex-Sultans, and Indian merchants. As a rule, each race, whether European, Asiatic, or African, favours a particular part of the city. The European quarter has already been alluded to, and of the numerous Asiatic communities it may be noted that the Baluchis from Mekran have their residential colony just outside the northern boundary of the town : the Shihiri Arabs from the Hadramaut nearly all reside in the Malindi quarter, and carry on an extensive trade in the manufacture of mats, baskets, and reed bags used for the packing of cloves. Each particular sect of Indian Moslems clusters round its own special mosques, religious houses, and dispensaries, and makes these establishments the centres of its religious and social life. Similarly, the Hindus keep apart, while the French Comorians, the British Cingalese, and the Portuguese Goans cling to the outskirts of the European zone. In every quarter, no matter by whom inhabited, the ubiquitous British-Indian shopkeeper will be found, and a very enterprising man of business he is. It is traditionally supposed that everything or anything can be purchased in Zanzibar l

The Government Markets, which lie between Darajani Bridge and the English Cathedral, merit a visit at about 10 o'clock in the morning, for at about this hour the produce brought in from the country is auctioned, and as a rule a varied collection of fruit and other produce can be seen. At the fish market near by, the visitor may see some fine varieties of fish, often including those species not frequently met with, such as, for instance, hammer-headed sharks, which are esteemed by the Swahili a great luxury. All such produce has to be brought straight to the markets to be auctioned, in order to ensure that the fisherman or husbandman obtains the current market price of the day, and also to afford the opportunity for all foodstuffs intended for human consumption to be examined by the Government inspectors.

The visitor will have many opportunities while wandering through the city to watch the native and Indian craftsmen at work. These men labour in full view of the street, but often in so ill-lighted premises as to cause the mere European to marvel at the efficiency of their optics, and in the case of the jewellers at the skill and dexterity with which they handle their gems and gold in most uncomfortable-looking surroundings.

Distinct from the Arab city and the European zone is the great conglomeration of wattle and daub houses on the eastern side of the creek where the bulk of the Swahili population dwell. This area is known as Ng'ambo, and it forms in fact a separate town of some 15,000 inhabitants. The houses composing this town are by no means mere "kafir huts," but substantial rectangular buildings of several rooms, which have windows, and ornamented and carved doors. Some of course are more elaborate and better finished than others, but the whole quarter is kept scrupulously swept and garnished, and gives the impression of general prosperity. The European may wander through the midst of this purely native town with impunity, and if he happens to be interested in things African he will be able to gauge to a nicety the difference between the Zanzibar Swahili and the " Shenzi " of the mainland.

Zanzibar town is being improved every year. Until quite recently clusters of insanitary native huts surged up to the very walls of the houses occupied by Europeans. Such areas are being cleared, and open spaces so obtained are laid out as gardens. The whole of the refuse of the town—and in a native city of some 36,000 souls a large amount is collected daily—is burnt in a special and most efficient incinerator. Nothing comes amiss to this destructor—carcases of camels and oxen are all consumed by its ever-burning furnaces.

Zanzibar, with its excellent water supply, is one of the healthiest native cities in the world, although to look at its dark and tortuous streets and lanes, and its dense population, one would scarcely venture to think so. The Health Department, which is charged with the maintenance of public health, is ever on the alert for danger. Its work is never-ending. Thousands of rats are killed, dissected, and examined monthly ; organised brigades to hunt down and eliminate mosquitoes are at work day and night, and research work and analytical examinations of all kinds of a highly specialised nature are matters of daily routine.

Progress may appear slow, but it is far from easy in a crowded native city to rectify the results of the haphazard methods of building of the past, when every builder was free to erect his house exactly where and how he pleased, without the slightest consideration for either his neighbour or the common weal. That there are any streets at all is only due to the unwritten law that a builder was required to plant his scaffolding poles in his own plot of land.

Matters are improving year by year, and it is hoped that Zanzibar, once the City of Dreadful Night, may in course of time become the City Perfect.

CHAPTER XV

THE INHABITANTS OF ZANZIBAR : THE ARAB

I

ZANZIBAR is the meeting-place of the people of three continents, and it is therefore scarcely surprising that it possesses a very mixed and heterogeneous population. The island is a small one, and the number of its inhabitants trivial, in comparison with the great commercial cities of the world, but its insignificant size causes the several species of the human race which throng its narrow streets to be all the more conspicuous and remarkable.

The Englishman, during his hour's stroll in Zanzibar, will probably encounter, in addition to representatives of every European country; cannibals from the Congo, China-men, Nubians, and Abyssinians, Somalis and Cape " boys," specimens of humanity from every part of Africa, the deep-chested coast negro, and the sturdy Yao ; the Baluch and the Egyptian ; the Persian and the Chinaman ; the exclu-sive Hindu and the native from the Comoros and Mada-gascar ; the Indian trader of every caste and persuasion are there in hundreds ; the Cingalee and the Turk ; the Goan and the Japanese ; the would-be pirate from the Persian Gulf and the Syrian Jew ; and, in addition, the visitor will most certainly see the stately Arab, looking almost as strange and out of place in the promiscuous throng as the Englishman, for the Arab and the European are both foreigners in Zanzibar.

The total population of the Zanzibar Protectorate is about 197,199, of which Zanzibar supports 117,000 souls, and the sister island of Pemba about 80,000. The inhabi-tants of Zanzibar Town are reckoned to number about 36,000.

The European population is very small, and further reference to it may be obviated by recording at once the numbers of the more important communities.

British, 140, including women and children ; French, 9 ;
Portuguese, 8 ; American, 1 ; Norwegian, 2 ; Greek, 7 ;
Italian, 1 ; Roumanian, 2 ; German, 1.

Apart from the European communities the remainder of
the population may be classified in the following groups :

1. The Arab.
2. The Swahili.
3. The Indian communities.

As already mentioned, there are representatives of other
races and nationalities in Zanzibar, but the above groups
comprise the bulk of the permanent population, apart from
the European elements, and a brief review of their histories
and characteristics will enable the reader to obtain a fair
idea of the inhabitants of the Sultan of Zanzibar's island
kingdom.

II

The most interesting and in some respects the most important community in Zanzibar is that of the Arab.

The term " Arab," like the word " British," is a wide
and comprehensive one, so it will be as well at the outset
to specify that the Arab now to be described is the true
Arab of unmixed descent.

Thousands of Zanzibar natives claim to be " Arabs," but
what they really mean is that they are of Arab descent or
at least possess a modicum of Arab blood in their veins.   This
generic use of the word " Arab " has not improbably done
a good deal to besmirch the reputation of the true Arab,
especially with reference to the now extinct slave trade.

There are plenty of natives in Zanzibar to-day, who proudly
claim to be Shirazis, or of ancient Persian descent, and who
look down upon the walrus-nosed negro ; and yet one seeks
among them in vain for any trace of a greater refinement
of feature, or in mode of life.   A drop of the blue blood of
some ancient Persian " Vere de Vere " may run in their

veins, but it is not apparent ; and similarly the Zanzibar negro, whose great-great-grandmother may have had some connection with an Arab harem, cannot fairly be classed at the present day as an Arab, as the term is understood in Zanzibar.

This preliminary warning is the more necessary because names and races are often miscalled in Africa.   For instance, the inhabitant of Cape Town refers to the Malay settlers in that colony as " Arabs " ; and the Natalian invariably calls a native of British India a " coolie," irrespective of race, caste, religion, or occupation.

The Arabs of the Zanzibar Protectorate number about 10,000 souls, and may be classified into the following groups :

1. The Mshihiri Arabs from the Hadramaut.
2. Comorian Arabs from the Comoro Islands.
3. Shatri, Mafazi, and Coast Arabs.
4. Omân Arabs.

The first-named Arabs, who come from the southern coast of Arabia, form an important section of the Arab population of Zanzibar.   In physical appearance, pursuits, and mode of life they differ somewhat from the Omân Arab. The Mshihiri is a thin, spare man of medium height, without an ounce of superfluous flesh on his body.   His face is long and thin and generally hairless ; and those of them who have not resided sufficiently long in Zanzibar to become enervated by its softening climate and surroundings possess a marked glitter of the eye, indicative of hidden fires within, which might burst forth on little provocation.

Under the normal conditions of life in Zanzibar they are hard and willing workers, keeping much to themselves, and living together in a special quarter of the town.

While some of the more influential and wealthier Mshihiris have made Zanzibar their permanent home, the majority come to the Sultanate for a period in order to earn money, and they then return to their own homes in Arabia.   When in Zanzibar they work in the port, loading and unloading ships, and they are in great demand as stevedores up and down the coast.   The lighter forms of labour sought for by the Mshihiri is water carrying from house to house, and they perform this work with the same assiduity and tirelessness as in the heavier labour connected with shipping. They also make all the matting bags, baskets, and coverings required for the packing of cloves.

The Mshihiri community possesses its own mosque and burial ground in Zanzibar. In religious views they differ from the Omân Arab by adherence to the Sunni belief.

Arabs from the Comoro Islands are few in number. They possess a similar cast of countenance to the Omân Arab, and are generally of fair complexion. From what part of Arabia the Comorian Arab originally came cannot be specified with any certitude, but it is held by some ethnologists that they are descended from Idumean Semites from the Red Sea littoral, who colonised the Comoro Islands during the reign of King Solomon. However this may be, the original Arab stock has been in some cases modified by Persian and possibly by Chinese and Malay interbreeding.

The Arabs known as Shatri and Mafazi are interesting, because they represent the Arab communities which were already settled in Zanzibar and on the east coast of Africa long before Seyyid Said, the Imam of Muscat, came to Zanzibar with his following of Omân Arabs.

They are indeed the descendants of those Arabs who from time to time during the last two thousand years have found their way to the Azanian coast as colonists. The Mafazi Arabs are derived locally from Patta, an old Arab settlement near Lamu, to the north of Mombasa. Patta, or as it is sometimes called, Paza, or Faza, was one of those petty sultanates formed during the last thousand years by Arab colonists from Asia.

III

The way is now clear to devote a few pages to the description of the most numerous and important section of the Arab race in the Sultanate. I refer to the Omân Arabs, now permanently settled in Zanzibar and Pemba.

The head of the community is of course His Highness the Sultan, Sir Khalifa-bin-Harub-bin-Thuwaini-bin-Said, K.C.M.G., K.B.E. This most amiable and enlightened prince

A ZANZIBAR ARAB.

ascended the throne in 1911, succeeding his cousin Seyyid Ali-bin-Hamoud, who abdicated.

The Omân Arabs within the Sultanate constitute the chief land-owning class and the aristocracy, and a very dignified aristocracy they are too, for the Zanzibar Arab is as a rule a tall, spare, handsome man, with clean-cut features and of a dignified presence, and possessed of a calm which is never ruffled, at any rate in the presence of subordinates.

His complexion is only a little swarthier than that of a European, and indeed, judged by this standard, he is often fairer in hue than the inhabitants of the southern countries of Europe.

There is a general consensus of opinion that whatever the shortcomings of the Arab may be, he is, above all things, a perfect gentleman. His manners in intercourse are charming and courteous to a high degree, and his rigid adherence to the dictates of etiquette is sometimes embarrassing.

The hospitality of the Arab race is proverbial, and to entertain his guests gives the host keen pleasure. The European visitor will be regaled with coffee *à la Turc*, sherbet —not the effervescent kind known to schoolboys, but a pink or white *eau-sucrée* mixed with iced soda-water—his handkerchief will be impregnated with scents of varying quality and pungency, and if the call has been made in the country, he will be lucky to escape without being presented with a goat or some other equally embarrassing gift. This extension of hospitality to the stranger dominates in full measure the poorer and lower orders of the Arab people. Thus, for instance, if a visit be made to a dhow, hailing perhaps from some remote port in Arabia or the Persian Gulf, the European will be received with every courtesy ; and coffee, hot from the earth-filled fire-box on deck, will be poured from some antique looking coffee-pot, and handed to the honoured guest in cone-shaped cups innocent of handles. A rug or blanket will be spread as a seat of honour on the poop, and the rather wild-looking hosts will squabble among themselves as to who among them shall hold the improvised awning to shield their guest from the sun.

The Arabs of Zanzibar are of course Moslems, and it is only when residing in a cosmopolitan place of moderate dimensions like Zanzibar that one realises how divided Islam really is.

The prevalent idea in Europe, that the Mahomedan religion comprises an unbroken brotherhood with one common enemy—the Christian—is erroneous. There are far more diverse and numerous sects and followings comprised under the term " Moslem " than are to be found among the followers of Christ ; and if a non-Mahomedan may offer an opinion, the points of variance between the sects of Islam are as little likely—less likely, it appears to me—to be reconciled as those which prevent the amalgamation of the various Christian beliefs into one supreme and indivisible Church.

The Zanzibar Arab is not a fanatic in religious matters. He has associated for too many centuries with people of every conceivable creed to be a bigot. The majority of the Arabs in Zanzibar are of the Ibathi persuasion, which is considered by the ordinary Sunni and Shiah Moslem as unorthodox.

As already stated, when Seyyid Said, the Imam of Muscat, transferred his capital to Zanzibar in 1828, the Arabs who followed in his train brought Ibathism with them, so that members of this sect are now to be found in Omân, where the cult originated, in Zanzibar, and in Morocco.

Many of the Zanzibar Arabs are wealthy men, and they own some of the finest clove plantations in the two islands. But many, alas ! are involved in debt, with their estates heavily mortgaged to the Indian moneylenders.

With a few exceptions they are not good business men, and they fall an easy prey to those who are ready to accommodate them in times of financial stress. This lack of business acumen and the perennial financial embarrassment of the Arab reflects adversely on the prosperity of the Sultanate, for the clove plantations are year by year becoming more neglected, and little is being done to replace those clove trees which are now long past their prime. The abolition of slavery seriously affected the welfare of the Arab, and his temperament scarcely permits him to adapt himself voluntarily to new ideas.

The system of government he understands, and likes, is that of the old Sultans like Seyyid Said, who fostered the clove industry, not by wasting his time in pointing out to his subjects how beneficial it would be if they would be so kind as to plant their estates up with clove trees, but by ordering them to do so, on pain of having their property confiscated if they failed to promptly carry out his orders.

It must be confessed that the temperament of the modern Arab of Zanzibar is not inclined to energy or sport of any kind. His immediate ancestors must have been men full of energy and resource, but the soft balmy climate of these Isles of the Sun has evidently done its insidious work and sapped to a great extent the pristine vigour for which his forefathers were remarkable. The name " Arab " is ever associated with horses and horsemanship, but here in Zanzibar horses will not thrive,[1] and hence one of the most invigorating means of exercise and amusement is denied the Arab. The days have become prosaic, and the period when men went armed, and a dispute was settled with a dagger thrust, is departed. Milder methods prevail, and as a natural consequence milder natures have been evolved.

Possibly the advice of Abu Tammam, the Arab poet, how to deal with one's enemy still lies dormant within the hearts of the Arabs of Zanzibar, but the end is attained by different methods to those anticipated by the author of *Hamasa*, who says :

" Humble him who humbles thee, close tho' your kinship be,
  If thou canst not humble him, wait until he is in thy grip :
  Friend him whilst thou must : strike hard when thou hast him on the hip."

The law court has taken the place of the dagger.

This want of energy not only afflicts those of mature years, but unfortunately extends to the younger generations of Arabs in Zanzibar. Many of these young men possess considerable wealth, but largely owing to the lack of appreciation by their parents of the need of discipline, and of education on modern lines, these young men drift aimlessly through life,

---

[1] Ponies can live in Zanzibar, as the existence of the Zanzibar Polo Club testifies, but the animals have to be kept in the town, and the general use of horses in the country districts is not possible, owing to horse sickness and other disease. There is no tsetse fly in Zanzibar or Pemba.

often ruining themselves and their fortunes by excesses of
every kind.

If these youths have prospects, as many of them have,
the moneylender finds a ready victim who will sign literally
any bond, without reading it, so that the money required at
the moment is forthcoming. Arabs are by their religion
and by law forbidden to drink alcohol in any form, but a
young Arab brought up in idleness and without an object
in life, secure in the knowledge that British " freedom " will
safeguard him from timely interference which might save
him, finds little difficulty in obtaining vile European spirits
through the agency of his Comorian servant. These latter
people, scarcely to be distinguished in appearance or mode
of life from negroes, are entitled, being French subjects, to
purchase liquor in any quantity with the same freedom as a
European. So it comes about that the servant may buy
liquor, but the master may not do so !

We English are so fond of thrusting our own ideas and
institutions upon other people, without inquiry as to whether
they are suited for the conditions of life of those we are
so anxious to benefit, that I fear our unfortunate *protégés*
sometimes live to curse instead of to bless our gift of complete personal liberty, which entitles a young man, no
longer a minor, to waste his substance in riotous living, and
to dissipate his fortune on the most futile objects.

The law of Islam is wiser in this respect than our own,
for the former ordains, if it be shown a person of any age
is wasting his substance and fortune in riotous living, to
the detriment of himself and the State, that his estate shall
be managed for him, and that he be granted an allowance
until such time as it shall be apparent that he has mended
his ways. The Arab system of governance was that of a
Royal Patriarchal Magistracy, autocratic in a measure, but
strictly limited by custom and Koranic law. The Arabs
still appreciate this system, and the lack of a controlling
discipline in their lives often leads to many difficulties and
abuses and the ruin of many young men.

The Sultan in former times was the father of his people
to admonish, to direct, to discipline ; and to-day, if the
Arab race in Zanzibar is to be saved from itself, some such

control, exercised under the restraint of the Sultan's principal European adviser, might well be given a trial.

Precisely similar effects have been experienced in Africa,
when the powers of the old chiefs were abrogated, and
English "liberty" substituted. The people, free from the
strict and wholesome discipline of the old days, lapsed into
a condition of slothful licence. The villages remained un-
swept, the huts fell into disrepair, concubinage took the
place of marriage ties, the fields remained unhoed, men left
their villages without restraint or permission, and without
making any provision for their wretched wives and children
they left behind. They might remain absent for years,
perhaps for ever, and the wives, in order to support themselves and their families, often took the line of least resistance and fell.

Such was the effect of unrestrained British freedom on
the negro. And the remedy for the abuses engendered was
the re-establishment of the old system of tribal discipline
modified to suit modern requirements.

IV

The Zanzibar Arab of any pretension dwells in a massive,
many-storied mansion built of coralline limestone. The
outside appearance of such a house is of the plainest character, and entirely without embellishments, except perhaps
an elaborately carved, brass-studded front door. The entry
appears dark and uninviting, but sometimes a glimpse of
an inner courtyard is obtained by the passer-by, and this
often looks bright and cool with growing palms. The lower
windows are always heavily barred, and this custom even
extends to modern houses inhabited by Europeans. This
precaution is of course a hindrance to would-be burglars,
but it is probably an echo of the old days, when an unruly
slave population, or an incursion of pirates and slavers
from the Persian Gulf, used to put terror into the hearts of
the inhabitants of Zanzibar.

Previous writers on Zanzibar often refer to the depredations of the slave population. Thus Burton, writing of

Zanzibar in 1857, says : " Such is their [the slaves'] habit of walking into any open dwelling, and carrying off whatever is handy, that no questions are asked about a negro shot, or cut down in the act of simple trespass. At night they employ themselves in robbing and smuggling, and at times in firing a house, when they join the crowd, and spread the flames for the purpose of plunder. They are armed burglars, and not a few murders are laid at their door."

As regards the incursion of pirates from the Persian Gulf enough has already been said in a previous chapter to demonstrate that iron-barred windows were a real necessity in Zanzibar town during the middle of the last century.

The interior of an Arab's house is sparsely furnished, judged by the European standard. The rooms are long and narrow, and some mats and Persian carpets, with a few chairs, is all there is to relieve the bareness ; pictures are rigorously excluded.

Around each room are lofty shelved recesses which break the continuity of the walls. These recesses serve the purposes of tables, and on each shelf are displayed articles and pottery of more or less value. Clocks are a favourite ornament, and it is said that some of the older Sultans were in the habit of ordering massive silver-mounted timepieces, which played tunes on every possible occasion by the score. All were from the best London makers, and although many must be fifty years or more old, they still exist to this day, and perform their striking and musical functions in a regular manner.

Thanks to the " Pax Britannica " the Arab of Zanzibar is no longer required to be a fighting man, and so he spends much of his time extending hospitality to his friends and seeking entertainment within the privacy of his family circle. The targe and silver-mounted matchlock of his ancestors are either lost or kept as relics of the glorious past, while his sword and daggers are only carried for display on public occasions.

The Arab rises daily at 4 a.m. to recite the prescribed prayers, and after a cup of coffee he retires again to rest until the sun is risen. He partakes of food at irregular hours of the day, but at all times he keeps open house, and

there are few meals at which relatives or friends do not
share his food. He seldom eats alone, and the quantity
of food prepared is always much in excess of his own needs.
His Highness the Sultan, for instance, daily sends the dishes
from his table to friends or dependents. After rising in the
morning the Arab gentleman generally breaks his fast at
about eight o'clock. The meal is ample, and consists of
three or four kinds of dishes, various assortments of bread,
with Arab cakes, sweetmeats, and fruits, together with tea
and milk.

Breakfast finished, he prepares to receive his friends in his
reception-room. Here for two or three hours during the
morning he sits, and welcomes and chats with a constant
stream of visitors. To every batch of visitors, dishes of
halwa—a kind of Turkish delight composed of ghee, honey,
eggs, arrowroot, and spice—and dates are offered, to be followed by the inevitable coffee.[1] No matter how numerous
the guests may be, the host invariably sees that each visitor
is served, and he himself will partake with his friends of the
sweetmeats and coffee.

The midday meal is partaken of at no specified hour, but
generally between two and three o'clock. This is the chief
meal of the day, and consists of a large platter of rice with
three dishes of meat and fish, together with sweets, dates
and various kinds of fruit. His wife does not eat with her
husband, but she has her own table in the women's part of
the house. The Arab is a hearty eater, and the food is
heavy and substantial rather than light.

When an Arab invites a friend to look in and partake of
" a cup of coffee," the guest had better be prepared, for he
will probably find a feast sufficient for twenty or thirty
persons spread before him. This lavish style of showing
hospitality is universal, and is in no way confined to the

---

[1] Coffee in an Arab's household is an important item, and most Arabs keep a
servant specially to prepare it. The coffee bean is roasted on iron pans : it is
then pounded fine in an iron mortar. After boiling the water, the used coffee of
the previous day is put into the boiling water, and some fresh coffee is added.
The whole is then boiled together for some time, being thoroughly stirred during
the process. The sediment is then allowed to settle, and the liquid is poured off
into a copper or silver coffee pot, and served, very hot, and of course without
milk or sugar. Sometimes a few drops of rose-water are added.

wealthy Arab, for the poor man will similarly load his table with ten times the amount of food required for his guests.

After the midday meal the Arab takes a siesta.

The Ibathi Arab, especially those of the old school, looks askance at music, and neither plays an instrument himself, nor encourages others to do so. There exist, however, reciters of poetry, very often blind men, who frequent the houses of the wealthy, and regale the master and his guests with recitations of Arab verse.

The Arab has not many recreations. In former times he would attend the war-dance or race his horses, but these amusements have been unfortunately entirely given up. His reading is confined to the Koran, the Commentary on the Koran, and The Traditions of the Prophet, and some other books dealing with Moslem jurisprudence and religious topics.

A few read the Arab newspapers from Cairo, and still fewer, books on history and geography. In a modern sense the older Arab is entirely uneducated, and his knowledge of the world, and of the latest developments of modern science or art, is practically *nil*.

The Arab does not smoke in public, but most of them, with the exception of the very strict Ibathis, indulge in a cigarette in the privacy of their own homes.

It will be apparent, then, that except for the entertainment of their friends the Arab has not many recreations, and he not unnaturally has recourse to the society offered him in his harem. According to Mahomedan law, a Moslem may marry four wives, and keep as many concubines as he wishes or can afford. In the old days the Arabs, following the example of the reigning Sultan, maintained extensive harems, but now these establishments are everywhere very much reduced.

Arab ladies of the higher ranks of society keep very closely to the house, and never go out during the daytime. Her Highness the Sultana sets an excellent example in this respect, by frequently driving out, closely veiled, during the afternoon, but other Arab ladies, though generally anxious, as in other climes, to copy the doings of royalty, do not

Gomes.

AN ARAB LADY, WEARING THE "BARAKOA" OR FACE MASK.

appear to have summoned up courage to adopt this beneficial practice.

An Arab lady in her harem commences the day by super-
intending the duties of her household, and issues her orders
to her servants for the day's work. She invariably has
in her employ a confidential maid, who is chosen from among
her other female servants for her good looks and her fluent
tongue. This *mpambe*, as the servitor in question is
called, has very important functions, which, while they are
somewhat onerous, must afford her a great deal of satisfaction and some mild excitement.

After the morning fast is broken, the mistress summons
her mpambe and instructs her to visit her mistress's
female friends at their several residences, and to deliver
various complimentary messages regarding the health of
the lady visited and of her children. The mpambe will
make several such visits during the course of the morning,
and by long practice will deliver the messages word for
word as given her by her mistress. At each house visited,
replies to the inquiries and other messages will be entrusted
to the mpambe to carry back to her mistress, and by
noon, when the round of calls by deputy is completed,
the girl will return home and will recount in detail her
doings, and repeat exactly word for word the replies and
messages which have been entrusted to her. She will also
give a full report of all the things she has seen during her
peregrinations, and describe for her mistress's edification
the latest fashions in jewels, trinkets, and clothes she has
noticed.

This recitation will occupy a long time, and helps to pass
the hours of the day. After dark the lady herself may
venture forth, attended by a numerous suite of female
attendants and eunuchs carrying lanterns, to pay personal
visits to her relatives and friends. These nightly expeditions are invariably made on foot, as the streets in Zanzibar
are generally too narrow for wheeled traffic.

In former days these evening excursions of Arab ladies
to the houses of their friends were quite an institution,
and the closely veiled and perfumed groups with their
swinging lanterns presented a perfect picture of Eastern

15

life as they wended their way through the narrow streets of the city.

Since 1897 this custom of paying visits by night has nearly died out.

The Orient is conservative, and much of the wisdom and many of the conveniences offered by the West find no place in the domestic economy of the Arab of Zanzibar.

For instance, he does not believe in banks. If he has spare cash—which nowadays is not often—he prefers to keep it in strong wooden chests [1] in his house, where he knows that it will be guarded by his trusty ancestral blade. The influence of the planets and stars on human affairs is still believed by many Arabs and their households. On the birth of a child, the astrologer is called in to cast the horoscope. In the case of a marriage, the geomancer or seer is invariably engaged to ascertain a propitious day for the ceremony to take place. These geomancers, or, as they are called locally, *Mpigabau*, or board-strikers, from the method of utilising for their divination a board covered with sand, which when tapped tends to shape the sand into various patterns, have a very large *clientle*, especially among women. Arab ladies patronise these people if in trouble or doubt as to their husband's constancy, and indeed

---

[1] These boxes, known to Europeans as " Zanzibar chests," are of two kinds— the large undecorated species, and those of smaller size, coloured red and profusely studded with brass nails. Both kinds originate from Surat in India, and are called "Surat chests" by the Arabs. They have evidently been an item of importation into Omân for a very long period—possibly for centuries—and they were introduced into East Africa when the Omân Arabs came to Zanzibar in the early years of the nineteenth century. The first-mentioned chests are the older, but they are of such an enormous size and so plain in appearance that they are seldom sought for as curios. The more ornamental and smaller kind, on the other hand, are favourite purchases by those seeking a useful and distinctive memento of Zanzibar. Both kinds are still used by Arabs in their houses, and the smaller, brass-studded chests are favoured by Arab ladies for the safe keeping of their treasures and jewels. Some of these boxes possess a secret compartment.

In purchasing a chest, the following points are worthy of attention. The lid' should be without join, viz. one piece of wood ; the sheet-brass should be thick, and the devices cut thereon should be well-defined patterns : in most genuine chests, the remains of a gold-coloured tinsel will be seen underlying the brass decorations. More brass bosses there are the better ; the lock-hasp should be as elaborate as possible, and the perforations thereon should form a definite pattern.

there is scarcely a subject upon which these wizards are not consulted. Palmistry is not practised by the Arabs, and is confined in Zanzibar to the Indian communities.

A good many of the older Arabs still prefer to use the pounded leaves of a certain tree (*Rhamnus nabeca* [1]) instead of modern soap. The name of the tree is *sidr* [2] in Arabic, and *Mkunâzi* in Swahili, and it grows freely in Zanzibar; in fact, the quarter of the city occupied by the English Cathedral and the Universities' Mission is known as "Mkunâzini," or "the place where the mkunâzi grows." The mkunâzi tree is frequently found in graveyards; for according to Mahomedan belief, it will be under this tree that the human race will assemble from their graves on the Last Day. For this reason, I presume, arises the idea that it is unlucky to cut the tree down.[3]

The effect of washing with "sidr" is not unpleasant. No proper lather is obtained, but besides cleansing properties the leaves impart to the skin a soft and satiny feel, highly appreciated by the lady of the harem. Arab ladies invariably wash their hair with sidr leaves. The best leaves come from Muscat, whence they are imported into Zanzibar. The leaf is small and almost circular; the branches are protected with curved thorns, and, owing to this protection, weaver birds often choose it to build their beautiful nests at the extremities of the branches, where they are safe from snakes and other marauders of nests. The tree itself is about 25 feet in height.

The Arab is scrupulously clean in his person, and the bathrooms in his house are considered a most important

---

[1] The *Rhamnus nabeca spina christi* of Linnæus.

[2] Pronounced as if rhyming with the English word "bidder."

[3] This tree is referred to more than once in the Koran. One of the joys of the Moslem Paradise is the existence therein of thornless sidr trees. In Mahomed's vision of Heaven a sidr tree is also mentioned, and a further reference is made in describing the desolation which followed the bursting of the reservoir at Marib or Sheba, when all the luxuriant gardens of the locality were destroyed, and nothing was left except trees giving bitter fruit, tamarisks, and "a few sidr trees."

The fruit of the sidr tree is called Nabbuk, and is a berry about the size of a cherry. It is a great favourite with the Bedawin Arabs, but cannot be compared with the luscious fruit of Europe or the tropics. It is sold in the bazaars in Zanzibar.

and indispensable detail. He does not go in for what Europeans call Turkish baths, but every Arab house of any pretension has a system of copper water cisterns for flushing drains, and for obtaining hot and cold baths. While even the wealthiest Arab takes little heed of stained or discoloured walls, broken plaster, or similar trifling defects in a house, which mean so much to a European, the sanitary condition of his residence will leave little to be desired.

Like most Moslems, the Zanzibar Arab wears a beard : it is regarded as an honourable and dignified appendage. Sometimes middle-aged men dye their beards such an intense black as to leave no doubt to the casual observer that it is dyed. Fortunately the more aged men do not attempt to hide the grizzled and white hairs of old age, and this adds very greatly to their handsome and picturesque appearance. The more old-fashioned ones keep their heads shaved, but the younger generation compromise matters by having their hair closely cropped.

There is a tradition that any person who shaves on a Wednesday is destined to become a Sultan's Minister of State, so it is possible that those superstitiously inclined generally shave on the day in question.

The Zanzibar Arab clothes himself when in public in a dark blue *joho*, or open robe, decorated along the edges with gold, red, or black braid. In the old days of Seyyid Said, when the puritanism of the Ibathi sect was rife, the decoration of the men's clothes was very scant, and it was not until Seyyid Barghash's reign that the braiding became broader and the patterns more elaborate.

Beneath the joho or bushti is worn a *kanzu* of fine white cotton, which reaches from the neck to the ankles. It is reminiscent of the nightgown of the Victorian era, but is nevertheless admirably suited for the climate of Zanzibar, looking always clean and cool, and its snowy whiteness sets off the flowing joho or the gold-embroidered bushti. The only ornament permitted on the kanzu is some fine needlework in red silk at the neck opening. The finer the texture of the material used for the kanzu, the more expensive it is. On high days and festivals the Arab winds an expensive gold sash round his waist, into which he sticks his *jambia*, or curved dagger, shaped like a letter " J." The sheath and handle are generally covered with finely chased silver, and in some cases gold. His other weapon is the sword, which is always carried in the hand. The sheath, like that of the dagger, is handsomely decorated with gold or silver.

These swords are sometimes of great age, and are regarded as heirlooms. Not infrequently the blades are of old Portuguese or Spanish manufacture, as is evident from the arms of these nations stamped thereon. They are romantically reminiscent of the period during the sixteenth century when Portugal attacked and captured Muscat, and of the seventeenth century when the tables were turned and the fiery princes of Omân drove out the invaders from their possessions on the Persian Gulf.

There are three kinds of swords used by the Arabs of Omân. The first, called *sef franji* or *felegi*, is a straight, broad, two-edged, weapon, without a guard. It is about 4 feet 3 inches long and can be used with both hands. The handle is bound with plaits of black leather and real gold and silver ribbon, forming a check pattern. These are the swords, the blades of which may be of European manufacture, as the name Franji (Franks) [1] implies. The second kind is the *hittareh*, a sabre with a curved blade, and generally of Persian or Indian workmanship; while the third pattern is called *yemeni*. This is a cross-hilted, short-bladed weapon, which is comparatively rare in Zanzibar. As the name implies, it is manufactured in Arabia, although it is possible that some of the blades may have been brought to the East by the Crusaders.

Under the kanzu is worn the *kikoi*, or waistcloth of fine cotton with a fringe of many colours. When wearing European boots or shoes, a pair of white trousers is substituted for the kikoi.

As regards footwear, a pair of openwork leather sandals is worn, and retained on the feet by means of a strap passing over the instep and another between the big and second toes.

The head is always covered in public by a *kilemba*, or

---

[1] All western Christians were called Franji (Franks) by the Saracens from a very early date—certainly as early as the thirteenth century.

turban, of mingled red, yellow, and blue stripes, and less often by a plain white one. These white turbans are only worn by certain Arabs,[1] who may be noted for piety or learning. The Sultan and the members of the royal house wear the ordinary coloured kilemba, but with the distinction of having the front over the forehead raised in a peak.

In his own house the Arab doffs the heavy joho or bushti, and substitutes for the turban a white embroidered cap. These linen caps, always spotlessly white, are most becoming, and are beautifully made with very fine patterns done in needlework. They are always sewn in Zanzibar by men, and a great deal of the spare time of many natives is usefully occupied by this needlework. It is a common sight to see the servants of Europeans, when waiting for their masters, industriously stitching at these caps.

Strictly speaking, a Mahomedan is forbidden to wear jewels and especially gold, but the strict Ibathi gets over the difficulty by having his finger ring made of silver, and this enables him to wear on his finger a fine diamond or emerald.

V

The Zanzibar Arab shows little aptitude for business, although there are some of the race who are shrewd enough at a bargain. The ordinary Arab, however, I fancy considers business to be beneath his dignity, and that accounts and receipts and haggling about money are well confined to such strange persons as Europeans and Indians. The Arab prefers open-handed largesse as long as the money lasts, and when that is gone it is time to find some accommodating Indian who will advance him more.

---

[1] Those Arabs of the Ibathi persuasion who wear the white turban are known as *mutawah*. This distinctive head-dress is worn by those who are noted for piety and for the strict adherence to the tenets of their faith; but inasmuch as this emblem is donned entirely at the wearer's discretion, it loses somewhat of its significance as a mark of special sanctity. It may also be regarded in Omân as having a certain political significance, as indicating those who side with the pretensions and claims of the Imam or religious party, as distinct from those who favour the secular government of the Sultan of Muscat.

In the case of the Sunnis, a white turban simply implies that the wearer is a learned and good Moslem.

The repayment does not worry him at all : " sufficient for the day, etc.," is his motto. He is an indulgent master and he would consider it mean and derogatory to his personal honour to charge rent to the tenants on his estate, even though they do steal half his coco-nuts and rob him of a large proportion of his cloves. What an Arab likes is to live in a kind of feudal state, with as many dependents and underlings around him as possible. The more he can display, the greater his importance. This weakness is largely responsible for the poor condition of many Arab estates, for, if a landlord insisted on his tenants paying rent or working for him, they would move off and be welcomed by some other proprietor, who would thus gain added prestige by an increase in the number of his retainers.

The racial, social, and family systems of Arab life are founded upon the organisation of the tribe. The tribe is divided into clans, and the clans subdivided into families, in much the same way as in former days the Scottish and Irish nationalities were organised. In the primitive stages of tribal life the individual was of little account, save as a tribal unit, and his identity was sufficiently marked by a single name. The individual simply existed for the tribe or clan, and the sole justification for his existence was that he should contribute his services for the maintenance, supremacy, and safety of his clan. When the tribal instinct, with the advance of civilising influences, weakened, and became merged into the higher and broader conception of a national life, the tribal cipher was enabled to assert his individuality, and the family, rather than the tribe or clan, became the unit upon which national organisation was based.

At present the tribal instinct is the dominant factor of Arab life, with the result that the identification of individuals is often a difficult matter to a stranger. Thus an Arab is content with a single name, and is identified by that name coupled with the name—not the family name—of his father.

So we have to deal and associate with a community composed of individuals who are only designated by names which, for the sake of clarity, I may term " Christian " names.

It is a confusing system. We have, for instance, an Arab known as Ali-bin-Mahomed; that is, Ali the son of Mahomed. If Ali has a son, the latter is almost certain to be called Mahomed after his grandfather. So the son will be known as Mahomed-bin-Ali, or Mahomed the son of Ali. There are, of course, tens of thousands Ali-bin-Mahomeds.

It is as if we discarded our surnames, and wandered through life endeavouring to identify our relatives and friends by such designations as John the son of George, or William the son of Henry. If we wished to be more explicit as to a person's identity, we should have to go back a generation, and refer to the individual as William the son of Henry the son of Charles, or whatever the name of the grandfather might have been. If identification was still dubious, the last resource would be to refer to the person's tribe or clan or the district or city whence the family originally came from, as for instance, William the son of Henry the son of Charles, the Yorkshireman, or of the Smith clan.

Regarded from a tribal or family point of view this system of nomenclature may be feasible, and even advantageous, inasmuch as it preserves the generations of the family, unit, but from a national and social aspect the system is confusing and imperfect.

In referring to the Arab community in Zanzibar, a brief mention must be made of the formal and ceremonious receptions or durbars it delights to indulge in. These receptions are known as *barazas*.[1]

Former Sultans used to hold these barazas on a very large scale, at which both Europeans and Arabs attended in full dress. Seyyid Barghash sat in baraza four times every day. His Highness Seyyid Khalifa II, the present Sultan, holds one reception weekly for Arabs, and additional ones on occasion of religious and public festivals. The British Resident holds one for Arabs monthly at the Residency.

Coffee and sherbet are generally dispensed, but at impor-

---

[1] "*Baraza*, stone seat or bench table, either outside the house or in the hall, or both, where the master sits in public and receives his friends: hence the durbar or public audience held by the Sultan. . . ." (from Bishop Steere's *Handbook of the Swahili Language* (S.P.C.K.).

tant functions held on special occasions a more picturesque
and elaborate ceremonial is followed, as described in the
subjoined account written by Sheikh Saleh-bin-Ali, the
Arabic interpreter on the staff of the British Resident at
Zanzibar.

The occasion referred to is one of the great Mahomedan
annual festivals.

" At daybreak the Arabs, both Seyyids of the Aulad-el-
Imam and the principal Arab Sheikhs in gorgeous robes,
from all parts of the town and from the country districts,
began to assemble in and around the mosque known as
El-Hadith.

" Here they remained and awaited the arrival of His
Highness the Sultan. At 7 a.m. the Sultan entered the
mosque through a private door, which opens from the
palace to the mosque. Sheikh Seif-bin-Nassur el Kharusi
then stepped forward and led the service, and then Sheikh
Mahomed-bin-Said el Kindi recited the exhortation of Eid.
This done, the Malindi battery fired a salute of twenty-one
guns, announcing His Highness's departure from the mosque
to the palace. Here tables were spread with a sumptuous
feast, and the Sultan and all the Arabs, having seated themselves, proceeded to help themselves to the luxuries so
abundantly provided.

" After the repast His Highness proceeded to the Baraza
Hall, and the Arabs in turn stepped forward and shook
hands with His Highness, each repeating congratulatory
phrases referring to the festival of the Eid. When all were
seated coffee was handed round. This was followed by a
party of the royal servants carrying silver receptacles containing aloe and rose otto. They passed before each guest
and applied a drop from each bottle to the palm of each
person's hand. The receiver rubs his hands together, so as
to properly mix the two scents, and then, according to taste,
wipes his robe, his turban, his beard, or his handkerchief
with the scent. After this, other servitors entered carrying
in one hand silver censers with perforated lids containing
a burning mixture of aloe, musk, and ambergris, and in the
other rose-water sprinklers of silver. Each guest held out
both his hands with the palms upwards to collect the drops

of rose-water and the smoke from the censers, thrusting his face downwards into the fumes, and uttering at the same time a short prayer. Others held their beards over the censers for a moment, so as to allow the smoke to penetrate.[1]

" When these ceremonies were ended His Highness left his throne, and standing at the head of the grand staircase, bade his guests farewell."

[1] This censing at a reception is a very picturesque ceremony. What the origin of this Arab custom is not known, but the Arabs themselves assert that it is of very great antiquity, and was brought by their ancestors from Omân.

In former times the censers were placed between the feet of the guests, so that the fumes might penetrate every fold of his garments. Incense forms no part of the religious customs of Islam. It is, however, used as an offering at shrines of Moslem saints, and is extensively employed in the so-called science of magic (Da'wah).

CHAPTER XVI

THE INHABITANTS OF ZANZIBAR : THE SWAHILI

I

THE bulk of the inhabitants of the Zanzibar Protectorate are a mixed race of negro stock, known generically as Swahilis. The word " Swahili " is derived from the Arabic *sawahil* (the plural form of the word *sahil*) meaning " coast " · and so the full significance of the name Swahili is " coast people." [1]

The designation " Swahili " is not confined to the inhabitants of the islands of Zanzibar and Pemba, but is applied to the native populations inhabiting the East African littoral between the Juba River, which marks the southern boundary of Italian Somaliland, and the Rovuma River in the south, which divides the " German " and Portuguese territories. The neighbours of the Swahilis on the north are the Somalis, and on the south the Makua negroes.

There are three essentials to be fulfilled before a person can be regarded as a Swahili : first of all he must be of African descent ; secondly, he must speak the Swahili language ; and thirdly, he must have originated from the East African littoral, between the Juba River on the north and the Rovuma River on the south, or the islands contiguous thereto.

It is obvious that the governing condition of this definition is a geographical one, and it is for this reason that it appears to me impracticable to attempt to define more closely the term " Swahili."

---

[1] Bishop Steere, of the U.M.C.A., writing in 1870 with regard to the derivation of the name Swahili, says, " The natives themselves jestingly derive it from *Sawa hila*, which a Zanzibar interpreter would explain as ' All same cheat ! ' "

The word " Swahili "—a coast man—is itself indefinite, and its application can only be general.

To attempt to confine the appellation " Swahili " to any particular section of the very mixed population living within the coast region is an impossibility. The term itself is too general to permit of any such application.

The Swahilis cannot be regarded as a nation, and scarcely as a distinct race, but rather as a breed of Africans, generally of Bantu stock, whose negroid characteristics, both physical and temperamental, have been slightly modified by a strain of Asiatic blood. They are, then, a mixed race, essentially African in appearance and habit, with a mentality quickened partly by inherited qualities and partly by the influences under which they and their forbears have existed for centuries.

One of the chief characteristics of the Bantu negro is his adaptability and his imitativity. These attributes have powerfully influenced the negro in his development from his initial savagery. No matter who his mentors may be, whether European or Asiatic, he will be content to adapt himself to their peculiarities, and to their conventions, social or otherwise.

He will wear the trousers and starched collar of the West, or the turban and sandals of the East ; he will sing Christian hymns in perfect tune, or he will recite in sing-song monotone the Koran of Mahomed. He will get drunk on European gin, or will observe most scrupulously the great Fast of Ramadan.

So the Swahili has found no difficulty in assimilating himself to the varied conditions of life which have influenced the east coast of Africa during the last two thousand years. He has rubbed shoulders with all kinds of people and nations ; has absorbed some of their virtues and some of their vices in proportion to the extent and length of association, and we find him to-day a full-blown Moslem, with his mosques in every village, and taking as his pattern in life his superior the Arab.

However heterogeneous the component items of the Swahili breed may be, there is no escaping the fact that the Swahili people possess a mother-tongue of their own, which is the *lingua franca* of Central Africa, and will carry a man from the Indian to the Atlantic Ocean. It is the polite tongue of nearly every native race of the equatorial regions, and its acquisition by the Central Africa negro is the first step, in his own estimation, along the road of progress.

The Ki-swahili language is, of course, thoroughly well accredited by philologists, and is classified as belonging to the middle branch of the Bantu languages, which are characterised by carrying on the work of grammatical inflexion by means of changes at the beginning of the word, a most confusing arrangement at first to the student of the language.

The formation of the Swahili race has been in progress from the commencement of the Christian era, and probably prior to that epoch. There is no need at this juncture to reiterate the facts connected with the association of the people of Arabia with the east coast of Africa. The intercourse is as substantiated as any historical fact is ever likely to be, but it may be permissible to refer the reader once more to what the author of the *Periplus of the Erythraean Sea* tells us with regard to the settlement of Arabs during the first century among the aboriginal natives residing on the mainland, in the vicinity of Zanzibar.

" Along this coast [the East African coast in the neighbourhood of Zanzibar] live men of piratical habits, very great in stature, under separate chiefs for each place. The Mapharitic chief [1] governs it under some ancient right, which subjects it to the sovereignty of that State, which is become first in Arabia.

" And the people of Muza [2] now hold it under his authority, and send thither many large ships : using Arab captains and agents, who are familiar with the natives, and intermarry with them, and who know the whole coast and understand the language."

From the above extract it is clearly demonstrated that at this early date Arab blood was being infused into the native populations indigenous to the Zinj or Azanian coast ; and in order to realise the conditions existing at that period,

---

[1] The chief or sheikh of Ma'afir, a district in south-western Arabia, to the north of Aden.

[2] The modern Mocha.

it is as well to remember that Claudius Ptolemy in A.D. 140 gives the names of at least six trading stations on the coast between Cape Guardafui and Zanzibar. To all these Arab vessels must have plied and carried away the cargoes of local produce which the agents of the merchants of Muza had bartered from the natives.

Subsequent to the rise of Islam, when the Arabs swarmed into Africa, the intercourse with the native populations must have been greatly extended, and the establishment of numerous Arab and Persian sultanates between Cape Delgado and Mogdishu, during the Middle Ages, still further stamped upon the coast people the characteristics of these alien colonists.

So much for the Swahili people of the continental littoral, but we are more concerned with the inhabitants of the Zanzibar Sultanate, and so will confine our attentions to the Swahili as found in the islands of Zanzibar and Pemba.

That which has been written with regard to the origin and genesis of the coast Swahili applies equally to the Zanzibari, and indeed one would expect to find in the island a purer and a more distinctive type of half-caste than on the mainland, owing to the probability that the blood of the inhabitants of an island—as being more remote and therefore exclusive—would be less likely to be contaminated or affected by extraneous influences.

This supposition receives some corroboration from the fact that there are sections of the population both in Zanzibar Island and Pemba which, although it must be confessed they present no very marked variation to the common Swahili, are very insistent, at any rate in two instances, in claiming descent from uncontaminated sources.

I refer to the Wahadimu and Tumbatu communities in Zanzibar Island, and to some of the inhabitants of Pemba. The two first claim descent from the Persians or Shirazian colonists of the Azanian coast during the later Middle Ages, while the latter may be derived from similar lineage, possibly obscured by contact with the Makua, a native race belonging to the south-east coast and hinterland of Africa.

A factor which has enhanced the difficulty of placing the Swahili of Zanzibar as a distinctive type has been the

A SWAHILI OF ZANZIBAR.

influx for nearly a century of hundreds of thousands of slaves, both male and female, drawn from nearly every region of the continent. This influx must have in course of time greatly modified any definite characteristics of the older Swahili type, except in the case of the Wahadimu and Tumbatu people who lived removed from contact with this immigration. From the time when Seyyid Said, the Imam and founder of Zanzibar, made the latter city his capital, the importation of slaves became a regular feature of the island trade; and although all those imported did not remain, nevertheless, as the prosperity of the Zanzibar Arabs increased, the number of their slaves augmented, and these extensive additions of pure negro stock to the original Swahili population must have tended to obscure the effect of any previous infusion into the aboriginal population.

In 1835 it was estimated that the population of Zanzibar town was 12,000, of whom two-thirds were slaves. The slave has always been stated to have been unproductive, but at the same time many of the poorer Arabs took unto themselves negro wives and concubines, and thus to some degree maintained the mixed Swahili breed.

In appearance the Zanzibar Swahili (or, as I propose to call him, the " Zanzibari ") is essentially African. He has the curly " wool " of the negro, and almost invariably possesses in full measure the facial characteristics of the African.

The prominent forehead, the inexpressive eye, the small, well-placed ear, the broad, flattened nose, and the prognathous jaw are all his. His colour is chocolate, but this feature, like others, naturally depends upon his descent and the amount of alien blood in his veins.

Marco Polo, the Venetian traveller, who wrote in about A.D. 1260, describes the appearance of the inhabitants of the east coast of Africa as follows :

"   . their mouths are so large, their noses so turned up, their lips so thick, their eyes so big and bloodshot, that they look like devils : they are, in fact, so hideously ugly that the world has nothing to show more horrible."

The association of the coast man with the Arab has not therefore done much to modify him physically, and it seems the chief distinction between a Zanzibari and the pure Bantu is a slight mental elevation and an increase in enterprise. For instance, the mainland Swahili and the Zanzibari are skilful fishermen and bold sailors. *The African Pilot*, the Admiralty compilation dealing with the navigation of the Azanian Seas, mentions that the island of Tumbatu supplies the best sailors and pilots to be obtained in these waters. The antipathy of the true negro for the sea is characteristic, and it is clear that the strain of Arab or Persian blood has markedly modified him in this respect.

Association with civilising influences has also sobered the Swahili. He still loves his dance and his music, and the future and the past have for him as little significance or meaning as they had during the epoch when the horizon of life was limited by the village grain-fields somewhere in Central Africa ; but the pleasures of life in a large centre like Zanzibar have to be paid for, and the burden of debt to the Indian shopkeeper tends to check the exuberance of his pristine existence.

The Zanzibari is, of course, a Mahomedan, and although the extent of his belief may be open to question, there is little doubt but that his profession of Islam has disciplined him and raised his self-respect.

Many, however, still retain in their natures the old pagan beliefs of their unregenerate days, and fall back on their " medicine " and black magic when things go wrong.

An eclipse of the moon is still in the opinion of the Swahili caused by a snake devouring that orb, and he considers the most efficacious method of preventing its total annihilation is to shout and beat drums to scare the uncanny reptile away. He finds after a few hours that his efforts are successful !

The Zanzibari clothes himself as a decent Moslem should, in a spotlessly white kanzu and a white cotton cap. Whatever custom or tradition has influenced him to adopt this most suitable and simple costume deserves commendation, for such garments befit him far better than the outrageous European trousers and coats affected by so many Christian and pagan Africans on the mainland.

The house of a Swahili would not suit a European at all,

for it is deficient in every feature which the latter considers essential for a habitation, especially in the tropics. It is composed of a framework of poles, which are tied together with coir cord, and the walls are then constructed with red clay and lumps of coralline limestone. There is a door, but seldom any windows, and the interior is pitch dark. The house is no mere negro hut, but a rectangular structure of quite imposing dimensions. The interior is partitioned off into several chambers, and a mat or reed fencing at the back forms a little courtyard, where the women of the establishment can carry on their domestic duties.

The roof is of dried fronds of the coco-nut palm, plaited together. This is the simplest form of residence. In accordance with the means of the owner, the size and structure of the house improve. Limestone takes the place of clay, the house floor, instead of being flush with the ground, is raised on a platform, windows are inserted in the walls, and a door, often embellished with carving, gives access to the interior. A baraza, or outside seat, affords accommodation for visitors, and a coat of whitewash makes the place look quite smart and cheerful. In the matter of house accommodation, the Swahili shows his superiority over his pagan cousin the negro.

The food of the Swahili is simple, and consists of rice, porridge made from the flour of the mubogo, or manioc root, yams, beans, pulse, dates, cooked banana, curry, and a relish in the form of a small piece of meat or fowl, or more frequently some fish or dried shark's flesh. This last item is preferred to anything else, and large quantities are imported annually from the Somali coast. The shark-market in Zanzibar has an overpowering stench, and is situated in a remote area of the town, but nevertheless the wind occasionally diffuses the odour through the more aristocratic quarters.

Fresh shark is always on sale in the town markets, and owing to the great demand for it, it is relatively more expensive than the better kinds of fish. The coco-nut enters largely into the domestic economy of the Zanzibari : the shell is used as a fire-kindler, and the meat of the nut is grated, mixed with water and pressed by hand, the resulting liquid

16

being used for mixing with rice and curry. Bread baked in small loaves is also regularly eaten, and an enormous trade is done in such commodities as tea and sugar.

Cigarettes are in great demand, and nearly every native shop and roadside stall sells them, while the betel leaf and areca nut for chewing purposes are universal.

The Zanzibari lives in considerable affluence, for wages are high, and a not very strenuous standard of industry is either expected or obtained from him. His womenfolk are well dressed, and if he was only a little less prone to waste his money on perfectly useless articles, he might be considered comfortably off. As it is he is generally deep in debt to the accommodating Indian shopkeeper, who permits this indebtedness to continue so as to retain his customer as a permanent patron.

The Zanzibari obtains his livelihood in a variety of ways. He may be a cultivator on his own little *shamba*, or plantation, or he may grow produce for the town markets. A large number of the population are of course fishermen, while many more earn a living as a sailor, either in native craft or employed as " seedi-boys " in His Majesty's Navy. Then there are of course numerous forms of manual labour which absorb a large proportion of the adult males, such as dock labour, clove-picking, road-making. Many are artisans, and engaged in such trades as village carpenters, boat-builders, masons, tailors, rope-makers. The Imperial military services, local police, marine, agricultural, public works, and other Government Departments employ a large number of the younger men, while not a few are absorbed in the callings of mosque attendants, private servants, messengers, and the innumerable forms of employment which a population concentrated in a large town creates.

There are four kinds of vessels used by the Zanzibari—the canoe fitted with outriggers on both sides, called *ngalawa* ; a slightly larger canoe without outriggers called *mtumbwi* ; a *betela*, which is considerably larger than either of the above, with a curved prow and ordinary boat-stern of European pattern ; and lastly the typical Zanzibar craft known as *dau*, or dhow, which is characterised by a very sharply projecting prow and a pointed stern.

There are other native vessels which frequent Zanzibar waters, but they are foreign craft, and come from India, the Persian Gulf, the Hadramaut, from Socotra, from Hafun, and from other ports of the African coast.

These large deep-water vessels of foreign make are generally referred to by Europeans as dhows, but the ship a Zanzibari knows as a dhow is the typical locally built craft referred to above.[1]

The ngalawa canoe when at anchor looks exactly like those aquatic insects known in England as "water-boat-men." It is fashioned out of a single log of mango wood, and is, in fact, a "dug-out." The stability of these craft, however, is ensured by a powerful outrigger projecting from each side. They are fitted with a mast and an abnormally large sail, and although they are "wet" craft, their pace is amazing. Considering their fragile appearance, they are good sea-boats, and the Zanzibari will take them out in any weather. A large proportion of the fishing is done from these small craft.

The true Zanzibar dhow is sharp at the stern, and with a sharp, projecting prow, which gives to the vessel a smart appearance. They are generally undecked, but they have a thatched roof placed amidships, which serves as a cabin. They possess one mast raking forward and a large lateen sail. All these craft are speedy before the wind, but poor sailers when close-hauled—in fact, the native sailor scarcely attempts to sail close to the wind. His lateen sail is not cut to sit flat, but on the contrary to belly out, so that to sail close-hauled is an impossibility. He cannot, moreover, tack with facility, as the lateen sail has to be shifted from one side of the mast to the other on each separate tack[2] Long before this manœuvre is carried out, the craft has lost

---

[1] Each of these foreign craft has its distinctive name. Thus the *bagla* (the dhow of the European) has a very high, square stern, and tall poop, and low, projecting bows. The *bedeni* from Omàn is distinguished by a very high rudder head, a sharp stern, a clipper bow, and a mast which does not rake forward. The *mtepe*, with a large mat sail, pegged or sewn planks, and a sharp prow, was until quite recent years a common sight, but is not often seen now in Zanzibar waters, being confined to Lamu.

[2] The sail is not lowered, but is swung round from one side of the mast to the other. To enable this to be done the mast is raked forward.

all her way, and has drifted far astern and to leeward. Matters could be improved by fitting lee-boards, and deepening her draught aft, but the Swahili prefers to stick to his bellying sack of a sail. Fortunately the elements are very kind to him, and the diurnal and seasonal changes of the wind are so regular that the native sailor knows that during some part of the twenty-four hours the wind will blow in the direction he requires. For instance, the wind blows from the south for six consecutive months, and from the north during five of the remaining months of the year. During the first-mentioned period, the local daily changes are remarkable for their regularity. Daily the wind blows fresh from the south-west during the early morning and forenoon, gradually veering round to the south. By sunset the wind is blowing from the south-east, a change during the day of 90°. During the night it returns to the south-west.

The Swahili is physically well-fitted for rough manual labour, and he is freely employed in loading and unloading ships, and in the transport of heavy goods to and from the Custom House and business premises in the town. He works better at tasks requiring extreme bodily exertion than at less violent forms of labour. He understands it better, it requires less mental effort, he is cheered and encouraged by working in unison with others, and he is partly hypnotised into continued and unconscious effort by the rhythmical chanties of himself and his fellow-workers. Tell the same man to weed a lawn by himself, and he not only will idle, but will do the work badly.

A great deal is written about the laziness of the African by those who do not understand him, but often injustice is done to him in this respect.

Normally he is not energetic, and he does not care as a rule to apply himself indefinitely to one task, as a European does. For instance, no one would expect a negro to spend the whole of his working life on an office stool. Give him work that will interest him, under a master who understands him and treats him justly, and the negro will work well and faithfully. He is blamed because he will not work for Europeans in Africa, but it must be remembered that

much of the work, such as mining, may be highly distasteful
to him.   By nature and training he is an agriculturist, and
he naturally hesitates, as I should assuredly do myself, if I
were expected to walk a hundred miles or so and work at the
bottom of a coal mine.

There is another much more important factor which
should be considered before cursing the " nigger " (hateful
word !) for his reluctance to work for the white man.   The
prevalent idea that the African native spends his life sprawling about his village doing nothing is erroneous : as a
matter of fact he has a busy time with his own affairs.

In the first place he has to provide himself and his family
with food, and in the African village there are no convenient
baker and butcher shops.   If a man wants food he must
grow it, and I often wonder how many Europeans who pride
themselves on their wonderful energy, and talk glibly about
the " Dignity of Labour " to the black man, would care to
betake themselves to their grain-fields every year in October,
to hoe and prepare the land for their next year's food supply
for themselves and their families.

The hoeing and the sowing are only the beginning of
things.   When once the crops begin to sprout, there is the
weary night watching to scare off the pig and the game.   I
have known the crops of a whole village totally destroyed
in a night by a herd of elephants ; I have known rice fields
completely ruined in an hour or two by marauding hippo-
potami.   Such occurrences are everyday events in Africa,
so the women and children watch the fields by day, and the
men by night.   There is not much " sprawling about the
village " during the weary months the next year's food is
growing !   When a native harvests his crop, there is still
plenty for him to do.   Native huts do not last for ever,
and if he wants a new one he is the one to go out and collect
the material, and he is the one to build it.   The same
remark applies to his canoe, his fishing gear, and to all the
paraphernalia required for the upkeep of his home.

Besides feeding, he has to clothe himself, his wife, and
his children.   Formerly most of the weaving was done in
the village, and this implied the growing of the cotton as
well, but now he purchases his calico from the Indian mer-

chant. For this and for the hut-tax due to Government he has to find money. To do so he will think nothing of walking a hundred miles or even more. He leaves his home and his family with just as much regret as a white man does ; and soon the Pleiades—known in Africa as the hoeing stars—will be seen rising in the east, telling him that it is time to turn homewards and once more prepare his grain-field for the next year's crop.

One more point in extenuation of the black man's " laziness." His life is much shorter than that of a European. The majority do not reach fifty years, and at forty or forty-five he is much in the same condition as a white man of sixty. At the latter age a European begins to think that it is about time to knock-off work and enjoy the fruits of his toil. The black man is worn out long before arriving at such a climacteric.

To return to Zanzibar and the Swahili.

As a cultivator the Zanzibari grows much of his own food, and trades in a small way by selling his coco-nuts or his cloves to the Indian middleman. His eggs, his goats, his oranges he sells at the town markets. His life is quiet and uneventful, and he is free from many of the anxieties of his mainland cousin. Except for wild pig he is not worried by wild beasts. The rains never fail him ; the fertile soil requires a minimum of cultivation—he never has to spend two months clearing virgin forest with a home-made axe of diminutive dimensions in order to break fresh ground to replace the worn-out soil of his old grain-fields ; he pays no tax, and he knows no one can starve in the Isles of the Sun !

A brief mention must be made of the Swahili woman. To European tastes she is undoubtedly ugly, and indeed in some cases hideous would not be too strong an epithet to employ, but this latter term is in some measure due to the fantastic and bizarre embellishments which the Swahili lady employs to enhance her attractiveness in the eyes of her lord and master.

Her ears, for instance, are so distorted by the insertion of large coloured discs cunningly made of tightly rolled paper as to leave that organ practically unrecognisable ; her

A S AI BI WOMAN.

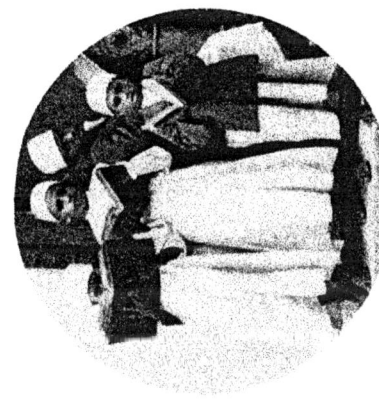
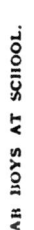

ARAB BOYS AT SCHOOL.

A ZANZIBAR POLICEMAN.

face, too, on high festivals is ornamented with geometrical patterns painted thereon, while a good-sized gold or tinsel jewel is inserted through the nostril of her broad nose. Her hair, which Nature has decreed shall be of the scantiest, is " done " in a number of ways, but the usual coiffure affected is the plaiting of her sparse locks into a series of ridges disposed at regular intervals over her head, which ridges are separated from one another by shallow valleys of bare scalp.

Her gala costume consists of a head-dress of coloured silk made up into a kind of extravagant turban or mob-cap, while her legs are encased in tight-fitting trousers, terminating with large frills which fall over and cover her feet.[1] Her body is decorously and elaborately clothed in patterned and coloured fabrics of varying qualities.

The Zanzibar woman not of the working classes, and who aspires to follow the Arab conventions, moves about closely veiled and swathed in a black cotton or silk wrapper which covers her from head to foot, and conceals all but the upper portion of her face. The clothes of the poorer Swahili woman or of the peasant are of course of a less elaborate character, but it can be said that whatever her station the Swahili woman is always decently if somewhat fantastically attired.

But, after all, the foibles of the Swahili woman with regard to dress, although they may appear uncouth to Europeans, are no more strange than the fashions of our own people, and in any case they may be condoned, for beneath the gaudy finery of the Zanzibar female is a merry, careless —too careless, perhaps—kindly soul, who enjoys her short life, and spends the sunny days of youth without much thought for the morrow.

[1] This odd fashion is said to have been introduced into Zanzibar by the Circassian concubines of Sultan Barghash.

II

There are two sections of the population of Zanzibar which merit a brief reference. These are known as the Wahadimu and the Watumbatu. There is a good deal of mystery as to their origin, and while physically they appear in many respects similar to the ordinary mixed breed known as Swahili or Zanzibari, they hold themselves aloof from the rest of the population, and reside in their own villages in remote parts of the island.

They are probably the oldest inhabitants of Zanzibar, although it would be going too far to assert that they are the aborigines.

From the very earliest times it is probable that fisher-folk, with the "men of piratical habits, very great in stature," from the mainland visited the islands, and they may have established temporary settlements on the beaches. The fact that leopards still exist after all these centuries in a comparatively small place like Zanzibar tends to show that the island could never have been very extensively or permanently occupied. It is fairly established that the Wahadimu came from the mainland just opposite Zanzibar, and it is a significant fact that many of their villages in the island bear similar names to those on the mainland coast.

They themselves claim connection with the early Persian settlers in Zanzibar, and it is possible that like the Arabs of later times the old Persian colonists took into their harems the young women of the local natives, whom they may have brought into the island for agricultural and other industrial work.

The name Wahadimu is generally accepted as signifying "servants" or "slaves," from the Arab word *hadim*, which means a "slave," but this does not help us to arrive at any definite conclusion as to how or when they came to settle in Zanzibar.

When the ruler of Omân, the redoubtable Seyyid Said, transferred his capital and his court from Omân to Zanzibar, there were two Sultans in the island—Seyyid Said, who lived in Zanzibar town, and the Sultan of the Wahadimu, who resided at Dunga.   The subjects of the latter entirely ignored the Arab Sultan, and continued their allegiance to their own ruler, and they withdrew from the western region of the island and settled as far away as possible from the Omân strangers, in the south and eastern portions of Zanzibar Island, where they still thrive.

It is therefore fairly evident that the Wahadimu were not affected ethnologically by the incursion into Zanzibar of the numerous slave populations during the nineteenth century.   In this respect at least the Wahadimu differ in some degree from the Zanzibar Swahili, and they may be regarded as types of the inhabitants of the island prior to the advent of the Omân Arab.

There exists between the Wahadimu and the people of Tumbatu Island some not very clearly defined historical and racial affinity.   Tumbatu is, as already explained, a small islet lying close to the north-western coast of Zanzibar Island, and although it is of little interest in itself, there are some interesting points connected with its population and its past history.

In the first place, it is one of the few islands off the East African coast, which are mentioned specifically by name in the writings of medieval writers.   Allusion has already been made to the reference to be found in the writings of the Arab geographer Yakut, who records that the people of " Tombat " were Moslems in the thirteenth century.   That the modern island of Tumbatu is referred to by Yakut is clear owing to the statement of the same writer that the people of Languja, or Lendguja (which is undoubtedly iden- tical with the modern name Unguja, the Swahili name for Zanzibar) fled for safety to Tombat.

The Tumbatu islanders of the present time, like their kinsmen the Wahadimu, show but little variation from the ordinary Swahili type, but nevertheless they strongly main- tain that they are distinct from the negro " coast man," and that they are directly descended from the kings of Shiraz.

In some respects they do seem to differ from the Zanzi- bari.   They hold themselves more aloof than even the Wahadimu, and they allow no settlers on their island.   They will not even tolerate the ubiquitous Indian shopkeeper to open a store among them, and they. seldom marry outside their own community.

The characteristic which struck me most in my dealings with them was the genuine interest they took in their ancient descent, and in the ruins in their island. This trait is unusual in the negro, who generally refers to ancient ruins as *ukuta* (walls), and appears to think that no more need be said about them.

The Tumbatu headmen, on the other hand, waxed quite enthusiastic about their ruins, and not only cleared the more important ones of jungle growth, but were full of stories as to what the various buildings may have represented, and of the people who built them. One of my informants produced his genealogical " tree," which showed a list of no less than fifty-seven generations !

The following is the information given me by the gentleman with the fifty-seven ancestors, regarding the foundation of the city in Tumbatu Island.

The first man to settle in Tumbatu was named Yusuf-bin-Sultan-bin-Ibrahim el Alawi. He was a prince of Shiraz and came from Bushire. On his journey from the Persian Gulf he first of all stayed at Merka,[1] and built a mosque there. He left some of his people there under a governor named Mahomed Khan, and he and the bulk of his following eventually came and settled on Tumbatu Island. It was then uninhabited. The buildings we now see in ruins were constructed by Yusuf, who built for himself a very large palace.[2]

Yusuf sent his son Ismail to Kilwa, and there he founded a city, which became very important and wealthy, so much so that the glory and fame of Ismail eclipsed that of his father Yusuf. Yusuf when he died was buried on Tumbatu at Kichangani, as were his wife and a daughter. The old mosque near where he lies buried no longer exists, as it was replaced by the present mosque, which was built on the site of the old one.

[1] One of the smaller ancient settlements on the east coast, south of Mogdishu. The Admiralty sailing directions refer to Merka as " a large walled town of far more imposing appearance than either Brawa or Mogdishu " (*African Pilot*, Part III).

[2] The ruins of the alleged palace still exist.

Unfortunately my informant could give no dates of any kind, so it is impossible to verify any of his statements, or to know whether he was not unwittingly mixing up the ancient tradition of Yusuf, which undoubtedly is very prevalent, with some other Yusuf of more recent date.

At the present day the number of Watumbatu living on the island does not exceed one thousand. They live principally in the villages of Jongoe in the extreme southern end of Tumbatu Island, and at Kichangani on the east coast.

At the first-named place the visitor is shown a block of masonry which is stated to be the remnant of the ancient mosque, and scattered among the existing mud huts are remains of stone buildings. At Kichangani, which is four miles from Jongoe, are three small modern mosques. Between these two settlements lie the bulk of the ruins of the medieval city referred to by Yakut in the thirteenth century. As to its extent there is no doubt, and it is equally evident that it was never built by African negroes.[1]

From what has been said above it is clear that the Wahadimu and the people of Tumbatu Island may be regarded as representatives of the older inhabitants of Zanzibar. The former community has undoubtedly been augmented at intervals by immigrants from the continental littoral, and the consequent intermarriage must have modified to some extent the original type of the so-called Wahadimu—a designation which in itself is without ethnological significance.

With respect to the islanders of Tumbatu it would seem that they are the most unaltered representatives of the original island stock, for there is no record that they ever associated or intermarried with any native races from the mainland, since at least the advent of the Portuguese to East Africa, and the fact that they live on an island, and are of a characteristically suspicious and retiring disposition, points to the probability of their having maintained their racial individuality to a greater degree than was possible in the case of the Wahadimu.

They are, however, essentially African in type, and they

[1] Further information concerning these ruins on Tumbatu Island will be found in Chapter XXVII of this book.

must be included in that comprehensive term " Swahili " or coast people ; but their greater mental alertness, their interest in the past, their pride of lineage—matters about which the pure-blooded African cares little—confirm their own claim that in their blood runs some strain of civilised ancestors, which marks them as superior to the ordinary Swahili of the African coast.

CHAPTER XVII

HINDUSTAN has had a very lengthy association with the east coast of Africa. We know that as early as the first century of the Christian era, Indian ships brought merchandise from the ports of Gujerat to the trade emporia on the shores of the Gulf of Arabia.

The cargoes of these ships savoured of India—wheat, rice, ghi, sesame oil, cotton goods, and sugar—in fact, the same commodities which every British-Indian steamer sailing from Bombay carries to Zanzibar and East African ports at the present time ; and it is hard to believe that at the ancient trading stations on the Azanian coast, and in the island of Menouthias, the middleman was not the Indian merchant who is such a familiar figure in modern Zanzibar.

Fourteen hundred years later, we find Vasco da Gama and his chroniclers making frequent allusions to the Hindu traders they found established at every port along the east coast of Africa. Curiously enough the Portuguese mistook them for Christians, and they were confirmed in this belief by the attitude of certain Banyans who visited da Gama's flagship, and who, according to the Portuguese, made reverence to the statue of the Madonna and the Infant Jesus on the poop.

No doubt the Hindus were as mystified as to who the Portuguese were as the latter were concerning the Hindus.

Moslems the Portuguese had good cause for knowing, for when da Gama sailed for the Indies, the Ottoman Power was threatening the very integrity of Christian Europe, and a Moslem was regarded as a potential enemy by every true

Christian. But of Hinduism, the Portuguese in Vasco da Gama's squadron had apparently never heard, and so it was but natural that they regarded civilised folk who were not Mahomedans as fellow-religionists, especially as every Portuguese had been brought up from childhood to believe that somewhere in Africa was the great Christian kingdom presided over by that half-fabulous personage known as Prester John.

It will be remembered that it was a native of Gujerat named Cana who piloted Vasco da Gama from Malindi, across the Indian Ocean to Calicut.

Writing in 1512 Barbosa tells us that the Moors of Zanzibar, Pemba, and Mafia used to purchase silks and cottons from the merchants of Cambay resident in Mombasa, and in 1591 Captain Lancaster noticed during his stay in Zanzibar harbour that vessels arrived from Indian ports.

In Zanzibar at the present time (1919) the Indian communities, which are composed of British subjects, number about 10,000 souls, and comprise both Moslems and Hindus.

Many of these Indians are wealthy, and practically the whole of the local trade of the Protectorate is in their hands. Nearly all come from Cutch and Cambay, and few speak or understand Hindustani.

The community with the largest number of members is the Ismailia Khojas, whose spiritual leader is that well-known personage the Aga Khan, or, to give him his full style and address, His Highness Sir Sultan Mahomed Shah Aga Khan, G.C.S.I.

Thanks largely to the influence of their leader, the Ismailia Khojas of Zanzibar make loyalty to the British Raj a special cult, and take every opportunity to inculcate this sentiment into the minds of their young. They are a hospitable people, and their fine club premises, situated just outside the town, are not infrequently the scene of receptions given in honour of Europeans, while they evidently entertain among themselves on a generous and lavish scale.

As a race they are prolific and have large families. Many of them, indeed, I believe the majority, regard Zanzibar as their permanent home, and their young men speak Swahili rather than Cutchi. The Khoja women are generally good-looking and take an active part in their husbands' business.

Except for the head-covering, which takes the form of a made-up turban-cap of gold brocade, the everyday costume of the Khoja men is not very distinctive. It consists of a coat and trousers of white cotton material, the garments being cut on European lines. At a function, however, the heads of the community blossom forth into a handsome kind of uniform, consisting of a richly embroidered cloth-of-gold turban and a robe composed of a very beautiful material of Persian manufacture, heavily embellished with gold lace.

The dress affected by the young Indian in Zanzibar is distinctly ugly, and comprises a small black " polo cap " as a head-covering, a white or black cotton jacket reaching to below the knees, similar in shape to the now prehistoric European frock-coat, and a pair of rather tight white trousers.

The Ismailia Khojas are Moslems converted from Hinduism ; and they still retain somewhat curious customs, reminiscent of their former faith. For instance, in most cases of the names borne by their children, one is of Hindu and the other of Mahomedan origin ; they do not attend a mosque for religious purposes or prayer, but assemble in their *Jamat-khana*, or Community House, for their devotions and for observing festivals. They do not consider it incumbent to perform the pilgrimage to Mecca, nor do they depend greatly on the Koran for spiritual illumination.

The tenets of the Ismailia Khojas are supposed to be somewhat peculiar, and centre round the belief that Ismail was the seventh true Caliph of Islam, after the death of the Prophet ; and they further hold that since the death of the son of Ismail, the Imams or Caliphs of Islam, although alive, remain concealed or unrevealed until the last days of the existence of the world. This latter doctrine as to the final appearance of the " Mahdi," or " Director," during the last days, is similar to that held by the Shia Moslems.

The Ismailia Khoja community in Zanzibar hold enlightened views on most modern subjects, and it is to be remembered to their credit that when the plague threatened

Zanzibar, and while others held back, the Ismailia Khojas set a good example and came forward voluntarily and permitted themselves to be inoculated with the preventive serum.

The local head of the community is Waras Mahomed Remtulla Hemani, a highly respected resident of Zanzibar.

The Khoja population in Zanzibar is divided into two distinct sects. One is that of the Ismailias already referred to, and the other is known as that of the Ithnasheri Khojas. The Ismailias number about 2,000, while the Ithnasheris comprise about 1,500 members, and socially and racially are similar to the Ismailias. They differ, however, on religious grounds, the latter sect adhering strictly to the teaching of the Koran and performing their devotions in the ordinary Moslem mosques.

The Boboras are another important community of British Indians, numbering about 700 persons, settled in Zanzibar. Many of them are influential and wealthy merchants, and have been established in Zanzibar for a very long time. Prior to becoming permanent settlers in the island, their vessels, like those of the Khojas, traded regularly between Cambay and the ports of East Africa. One of the prizes taken by Captain Kidd, the famous pirate who roved the Indian Ocean at the close of the seventeenth century, was a ship belonging to a Cambay Khoja merchant.

The early Bohora traders came from Surat, while the first of that sect to live in Zanzibar originated from Cutch and at a later date from Kathiawar. Among the goods usually dealt in in the early days were cotton goods made in Cutch, hardware, copper and brass wire, silver ware, beads, and precious stones. Most of these goods were bartered for ivory.

The attire of the Boboras is plain and unassuming, consisting of a long white coat and loose white cotton trousers. The usual head-dress is a small round cap, but the more affluent members of the community wear a cloth-of-gold turban-cap somewhat similar to that worn by the Khojas. The Bohora women keep closely veiled, and do not participate in business like those of the Ismailia Khojas. The community holds a deservedly high reputation in Zanzibar.

Among the less numerous British-Indian communities in Zanzibar may be mentioned the Memons and Sindhis.

The Hindus are represented by the Battias and others of lower castes. They form an influential and important section of the population, and inasmuch as they regard themselves as a single community, irrespective of the several castes, they outnumber any particular section of the Moslem population.

They are by nature of their beliefs of a retiring disposition, and hold themselves much aloof. The Battias are extremely shrewd men of business, and their main *motif* in life appears to be the making of money. Although affluent, they are quiet and law-abiding. Their diet consists solely of pulse and grain, and it is scarcely necessary to mention that the taking of life under any circumstances is a forbidden thing. The tenets of their religion preventtheir participation in any social amenities with others than of their own persuasion. Dr. Christie, author of an interesting work dealing incidentally with Zanzibar, mentions that during the many years he was a medical practitioner in Zanzibar during the late sixties and early seventies of the last century, and during the great cholera outbreak, when 15,000 inhabitants of Zanzibar town died, he never saw a Hindu in the act of eating or drinking, even although he attended many scores in a professional capacity.

The Battia Hindus of Zanzibar are distinguished by their costume, which comprises an ample loin-cloth, a white or tweed coat, and a closely fitting red and gold-embellished cap, while girt over the shoulder is the *chudda*, or scarf. Many of them are tall, spare, good-looking men. They take their exercise by walking in company with each other ; beyond this they appear to take no recreation, nor are they seen driving either in carriages or motor-cars.

Generally they do not bring their women-folk with them to Zanzibar, but return periodically to their families in India.

Mention must also be made of the colony of Cingalese settled in Zanzibar. They are all connected with the manufacture and sale of precious stones, of gold and silver jewellery, and of fancy articles of tortoiseshell, ebony, and

17

ivory. These people do an enormous trade with the passengers of passing steamers, and the chief firms have branch
establishments at Mombasa and Daresalaam.

Last, but not least, are the Parsis. They are of very
recent advent to Zanzibar. In 1861, the official archives
show that there was only one Parsi in the Sultanate. Since
that time they have slowly increased, and now number about
sixty-four. Thoroughly well educated on modern lines,
broad-minded, affable, enlightened, and highly civilised,
they are respected by all and much liked by the European
communities.

With respect to Asiatics other than British subjects, there
are about 450 Goanese resident in Zanzibar. These people
are of course Portuguese citizens, and nearly all of them
are Roman Catholics. They are largely employed in the
subordinate ranks of the Government service, while not a
few are engaged in trade, as store-keepers, boot-makers, and
tailors. Most of them write and speak excellent English,
and as a race they are law-abiding, clever, and many of
them are proficient musicians.

To complete the tale of Asiatics in Zanzibar, there are a
few hundred Baluchis and about fifty Persians. These are
the remnants and the descendants of the Zanzibar Army
maintained by Seyyid Said and succeeding Sultans.

A few Syrians engaged in trade, a dozen Japanese, and
some Chinamen employed in collecting that most unappe-
tising-looking luxury, the *bêche-de-mer*, or sea-slug, complete
the list of alien Asiatics living in Zanzibar.

CHAPTER XVIII

I

ALTHOUGH in the hierarchy of eastern princes the Sultans of Zanzibar may not be able to claim pre-eminence with respect to the magnificence of their Court, or to the extent of their dominions, they are probably better known by name and reputation than many a potentate whose revenue and subjects are reckoned by millions. There pertains to Zanzibar a certain romantic interest; and deep as the ignorance of the man-in-the-street is concerning the British Empire, it seems that there are not a few stay-at-homes in England who have actually heard of the island and its Sultans.

Apart from the mere question of wealth, there is a reason for the comparative simplicity of life and lack of display of the rulers of Zanzibar.

The system of governance as constituted in Omân was a somewhat peculiar one for an Eastern State ; for the office of ruler or Imam was not, strictly speaking, of a hereditary character, but elective. The Imam—that is, the Sovereign-Pontiff, or King-Priest, for the status, primarily religious, was endowed with temporal power—was for centuries elected by the suffrages of the whole people, and it was a fundamental principle of the constitution that the people who made could at their will unmake, and dispossess the ruler of his sovereign powers.

The Imam was an autocrat in so far as he was the guardian of the State and the maintainer of order among his subjects, but in other respects, the system of government from about the eighth century was based on purely democratic principles.

It went farther than this, for the rulers were not necessarily elected from a royal caste ; any worthy person could aspire to the throne, and thus become royal. There was a possible crown in the cradle of every Omâni infant.

That this system of filling the throne of Omân was a reality, and not a specious political formula, is clear—to cite but one case—from the events which placed Ahmed-bin-Said upon the throne of Omân in 1741. As the reader will no doubt recollect, Ahmed, an obscure merchant whose very occupation prior to his elevation is not known with certainty, arose when his country was being crushed by the Persian invaders, and became its deliverer. He was elected Imam, and founded the Albusaid dynasty, of which the present enlightened ruler of Zanzibar is a member.

The people of Omân, though brave and fierce fighting men, were of simple habits and tastes, and their elected Imam was expected to conform strictly to this national trait. Although all the wealth of the State passed through his hands or under his control, he was permitted only to retain sufficient for his own needs, and it was expected that the remainder would be expended for the benefit of the people and of the State. Thus it came about, through the course of the centuries, that the rule of life of the kings of Omân was one of great simplicity. No doubt they could have ridden on gorgeously apparelled elephants like the great princes of India, but all such display would have been contrary to the first principles under which they held their sovereign rights, and would scarcely have been tolerated by their subjects. Such display would have laid them open to ridicule, if to nothing worse.

When Seyyid Said came to Zanzibar, the old conventions of his ancestors still influenced him, and his own mode of life, even to his very costume, was of the most simple character. He often walked from the town of Zanzibar to his country palace at Mtoni, although his stables were filled with splendid Arab horses. On one occasion, it is related, when news was brought to him that his favourite son was ill, he sought a means to quickly reach him. Although he owned a fleet of war vessels, he leapt into a fisherman's canoe in order to save time, and with his own hands helped to paddle it to the palace where his son lay sick. Even the braid which decorated his robe was of a most unostentatious pattern, his sword hilt was only silver, and in all that he did the same economy and simplicity were apparent. And yet he was not parsimonious as regards his friends. An open-handed liberality distinguished him, and the reader who has perused the chapter of this book devoted to his life will realise that his simplicity of life was but the corollary of his royal state.

I once asked a prominent Arab why Seyyid Said had hidden the silver-gilt tea service presented to him by Her Majesty Queen Victoria. The reply was that had he used it, he would have been ridiculed by his subjects.

Enough has been said to explain the comparative simplicity of the royal regime in Zanzibar. Of course the Sultans are not now elected like their forerunners the Imams of Omân, nor are they dependent upon the popular vote for their thrones; but the old style of simplicity is still sometimes evident, and those who may be inclined to criticise what may appear undue economy will find in the above remarks some explanation for its existence.

If we reckon Seyyid Said as the first Sultan of Zanzibar, we find that nine Sultans, inclusive of His Highness Seyyid Khalifa-bin-Harub, have occupied the throne of Zanzibar since 1828; and although no very striking events have marked the reigns of these princes, it is desirable, if only for purposes of record, to briefly refer to each of them.

The chief political events of far-reaching importance which have affected Zanzibar since the death of Seyyid Said in 1856 have been referred to in another chapter, so it will suffice to merely mention them at this juncture.

The first was the separation of Zanzibar from Omân; the second was the suppression of the slave trade; the third was the partition of Africa among the Powers of Europe, and the consequent reduction in extent of the dominions claimed by the Sultans of Zanzibar; the fourth the proclamation of a British Protectorate over Zanzibar; and the fifth the emancipation of the slaves in Zanzibar.

When Seyyid Said died in 1856 he was succeeded at Zanzibar by his second surviving son Seyyid Majid.

SEYYID MAJID (1856–1870)

This prince, who was in his twenty-second year, was highly popular in Zanzibar, and he was unanimously elected by the Arabs and the natives of East Africa as the indisputable successor to his father.

There were, however, powerful influences at work in Zanzibar, which sought to dispossess Majid of his kingdom, and for the first years of his reign he was occupied in dealing with these intrigues against his throne and person. His brother, Thuwaini, was no doubt the *deus ex machinâ*, and he found an all-too-ready accomplice in his ambitious younger brother Seyyid Barghash. The numerous members of the powerful Harthi tribe, who were settled in Zanzibar, favoured the cause of Seyyid Thuwaini; and a series of conspiracies were fomented by these hostile factions against the young Sultan.

These intrigues are too intricate and trivial to follow in detail, and it will suffice to observe that these internal dissensions only ceased when the chiefs of the Harthi tribe were arrested and imprisoned and Seyyid Barghash was exiled to India.

Seyyid Majid was of a mild and charitable disposition, and like his father a firm friend of the English.

In 1866 the Government of India invited him to pay a State visit to Bombay. For this great event he equipped three of his warships, the *Victoria*, a frigate of fifty guns, the *Iskander-Shah*, and the *Nadir-Shah*.

The Sultan, his two young brothers, Khalifa [1] aged eleven years, and Nasur, nine years old, with most of the important Arabs holding high positions in the Government, embarked in the *Victoria*.

The other two vessels carried the Governor-General of East Africa and his two nephews Nasur-bin-Said and Salim-bin-Said, together with Ali-bin-Saud, and the Minister of War, Hamed-bin-Suleiman.

It was Seyyid Majid who instituted the Order of the Brilliant Star of Zanzibar in four classes, and a number of princes of the ruling families in Europe are members of the Order.

[1] Afterwards Sultan Khalifa I (1888–1890).

Seyyid Majid, who was a voluptuous prince, died in 870 at the early age of thirty-six years. He left one daughter, who eventually by her marriage with Seyyid Hamoud became the mother of Matuka, the wife of Seyyid Khalifa II, the reigning Sultan of Zanzibar.

BARGHASH-BIN-SAID (1870–1888)

Seyyid Barghash-bin-Said succeeded his brother Majid on the throne of Zanzibar. It was a memorable reign, for during it Zanzibar passed through troublous times, and it is likely that had it not been for the protection afforded by Great Britain and the steadying influence of. Her Majesty's representative at Zanzibar, in the person of Sir John Kirk, the Sultanate, as an independent State, might have been engulfed and destroyed in the turmoil and stress resulting from the scramble for Africa by the Great Powers of Europe.

Seyyid Barghash was a remarkable man, and possessed many of the striking qualities of his father the old Seyyid Said, the founder of the Sultanate of Zanzibar. He was an ambitious man, and certainly twice, if not more frequently, plotted against his brother's throne with a view to usurpation. At the same time he was an honourable man, and when once his word and bond was given, no self-interest or other inducement could prevail upon him to break his faith.

Of a sanguine and energetic nature, he had had advantages which neither his father nor his brother possessed. He had lived in Bombay, and there had acquired a knowledge of the world and of modern ideas which were quite beyond the attainment of previous rulers of Zanzibar. On his accession the strait-laced simplicity of the old regime gave place to a more luxurious and up-to-date existence. Gold took the place of silver, and silk and modern jewels from London, Paris, and Bombay replaced the barbaric ornaments indigenous to Muscat.

Money was lavishly spent, and indeed Seyyid Barghash appears to have been afflicted with the mania for building palaces.

The palaces at Chukwani, Marahubi, Migombani, and

Chuini were all erected by him, but of course his supreme effort in this line was the erection of the Bet-el-Ajaib or the House of Wonders, which now houses the offices of the various departments of Government. He also laid out the Victoria Gardens, at that time surrounded with a high wall, as a place of rest and refreshment on his journeys to and from Chukwani.

For one great work of public utility the memory of Seyyid Barghash must always be respected both by European and native alike. This was the introduction into Zanzibar of a pure water supply. Hitherto the inhabitants had been dependent on the water from shallow wells, and the mortality from drinking this water was enormous ; while periodically, fearful outbreaks of dysentery and other diseases occurred which can be traced to this befouled water supply.

In the late sixties of the nineteenth century, the American Consul had sent samples of Zanzibar water to America for analysis, and the report thereon can scarcely be read without a shudder.

Seyyid Barghash did the work well, for the Arab water conduit from the spring to the city is still used to-day. The task was not an easy one, for the difference in level between the spring and the town is so slight that the building of the conduit must have been a very difficult matter.

Thanks to this beneficent public work, Zanzibar now possesses the best water supply on the east coast of Africa, and no ship touches at Zanzibar without filling up her tanks with this pure spring-water ; in fact, steamers from neighbouring ports visit Zanzibar for this purpose.

The memory of this prince is still cherished in Zanzibar, for his generosity in giving free passages in one of his ships once a year to all who wished to perform the pilgrimage to Mecca, and the sumptuous entertainment of his Arab subjects on the occasion of the chief Mahomedan festivals is also recalled with fervour at the present day.

On the other hand, the force of his character, his strength of will, and his autocratic manner caused considerable resentment in those who came under his displeasure. It is said that if he coveted a particular plantation, he would force the unfortunate owner to dispose of it at the price he (the Sultan) offered. If the offer was refused, the estate was simply confiscated. He never hesitated at once to seize any article or jewel which took his fancy, often making the owner hand over the article on the spot. None dared to refuse him

In 1875 the British Government having officially invited Seyyid Barghash to visit England, he departed from Zanzibar attended by a numerous suite, and accompanied by Sir John Kirk. Everywhere he was received with royal honours. While *en route* for England, he paid an official visit to the King of Portugal at Lisbon, where the British Fleet had been assembled to salute his arrival.

When the time came for his landing to visit the King, he became much incensed at the smallness of his retinue which was to accompany him ashore, and thereupon he caused every available servant and lacquey of his following to be arrayed in gala costume to swell his train. This novel procedure is said to have caused a good deal of embarrassment to the Portuguese court functionaries.

In England he was the guest of the nation, and he was entertained right royally. Visits to the Queen and the Prince and Princess of Wales were made, and one of his deepest impressions appears to have been on the occasion of his visit to the Prince of Wales, when their two eldest sons —Prince Albert Victor and Prince George—were introduced to him. They were dressed in sailor suits, and this fact Seyyid Barghash could not get over for a long time.

He visited every sight worth seeing, including the chief manufacturing towns. At the Crystal Palace a special firework display was given in his honour, and included a set piece showing his monogram in Arabic letters. He attended Ascot and Doncaster races, and a most amusing illustration of the latter event culled from some illustrated paper of the period, is reproduced in the Arabic account of his visit to England, which he caused to be prepared in book form. The drawing in question—for it was before the kodak-epoch —depicts Seyyid Barghash with another Arab standing in an open carriage, with the conventional race-glasses in his hand, watching the finish of a race. Around his carriage is clustered the cream of London society, including apparently royalty. The men wear high top-hats and long whiskers, while the ladies wear the strange fashions of the period. One feature of his visit to England which must have caused him considerable embarrassment was the dead-set made at him by numerous missionary societies, who sought interviews with His Highness on the subject of slavery. At these interviews he must have felt very like Daniel in the lions' den !

After his visit to England was concluded, he proceeded to Paris, and thence to Berlin.

The prevalent idea that an autocratic ruler of an Eastern kingdom, such as Seyyid Barghash was, spends his days in slothful ease, toying with his concubines, is not always in accordance with facts. On the contrary, the daily routine of Seyyid Barghash entailed an amount of work which might well astonish the most assiduous European. The following brief account of how Seyyid Barghash was wont to spend his day will cause the reader to congratulate himself that he was not " born in the purple."

Daily at 4 a.m.—that is, two hours before daylight—Seyyid Barghash was accustomed to enter the throne-room, carrying a Koran in one hand and a lamp in the other. He took his seat in his chair of state, and proceeded to recite various passages from his book. At 4.30 a.m. twelve Arabs noted for piety were wont to approach him, and each in turn read some passage from the Koran. At about a quarter-past five, the Seyyid would rise, and in company with twelve Mutawahs—or persons of blameless life—perform the early morning prayers. These concluded, further extracts from the Koran were recited. At 6 a.m. as the sun rose, trays containing tea, milk, and light cakes were brought and the Seyyid and the Mutawahs broke their fast. This done, further supplications known as the rising-sun prayers were recited by all present. These being finished, the Mutawahs took their leave, and the business of the day commenced. At 6.30 Seyyid Barghash's confidential agents would enter and make their reports as to the occurrences of the night, and of any other events of importance. By 7 a.m. other important functionaries such as the treasurer and custom officers would attend to submit

their reports and receive instructions from the Sultan. A
stream of other officials and merchants followed, all seeking
interviews until at 8 a.m. the Seyyid rose, and for the first
time since his entry at 4 left the throne-room.

He retired for a short respite into his private apartments,
and then partook of the first meal. He always ate alone,
seated at a large table covered with all kinds of comestibles.
Around the room stood a dozen eunuchs of all ages with
their hands folded across their breasts, and these servitors
were dispatched with dishes from the royal table to those
ladies of the harem who were in favour at the time.

Before 9 o'clock, Seyyid Barghash would again be
seated in the throne-room for the transaction of business of
every kind. A swarm of suitors would by now have assembled in the precincts of the presence chamber, each
with his own particular petition or business. Besides these
private claimants on the time of the Seyyid, there would
be a host of palace officials to be seen and instructed.
Abdulla Salim el-Kheimri, Seyyid Burghash's agent in
Egypt, Constantinople, and other Eastern capitals would be
summoned to receive instructions as to the purchases to be
made on his next journey. These might include carpets,
jewels, batteries of artillery, watches, slaves, ammunition,
ships, clothing, and every kind of article big and small.
Every detail would be gone into by the Seyyid himself,
and indeed this was the universal rule of his life. The purchase and sale of clove plantations, the building of palaces,
of bridges, importations from Bombay, the settlement of
disputes, were all dealt with personally by the Seyyid.

At 11 o'clock he would again retire to the harem palace,
and took a siesta till 1 o'clock, when he re-entered the
Audience Hall, and the midday prayers were then recited
by the Mutawahs. When the prayers were finished, trays
of sweets and fruits were handed round, and a few Arabs,
favoured by the friendship of the Seyyid, would usually be
present, and partake of the refreshments. Discussions on
religious matters used then to ensue until about 3.30 p.m.,
when the afternoon prayers were recited. After these were
finished, the Seyyid retired to his apartments and partook
of food. On returning to the Audience Hall, he would very

often turn his attention to the proceeding of the native judges, who were wont to dispense justice in the Palace Square. Here all manner of cases were heard and adjudged upon, and it was fortunate for a convicted person if, before he was dragged off to imprisonment in the fort, he could attract the attention of the Seyyid by his cries of " *Mawlana Mathlun* ! " (My Lord, I am wrongly convicted !). About this time of the afternoon Seyyid Barghash would very often be looking out from his palace windows, and he sometimes ordered the convicted party to be brought before him to hear his grievance. Not infrequently he caused the culprit to be released.

At 6 p.m. one of the great functions of the day took place. This was the picturesque ceremony of the Sultan announcing the end of the day and the commencement of the next, for the Arab day is reckoned from sunset to sunset. The function was accompanied with some display. The Sultan used to stand in the verandah of the palace overlooking the sea, surrounded by his courtiers. As the sun disappeared beneath the horizon, the Sultan raised his hand, and immediately the guns fired a salute, the royal band played the Zanzibar National Anthem,[1] and the Red Ensign of Zanzibar fluttered down from the lofty flagstaff in the palace square.[2]

Immediately after this ceremony evening prayers were recited, and the Sultan held another reception in the throne-room to receive visitors. Between sunset and 7.30 p.m.

---

[1] The score of the Zanzibar National Anthem was arranged by Lieutenant Dan Godfrey, of Her Majesty's Grenadier Guards, for a full band, and it is on record that the anthem was played at the guard mounting at St. James's Palace on May 2nd, 1879.

[2] The Arab method of reckoning the hours of the day is still kept in Zanzibar, and all the public clocks are set to show that time. The day commences at sunset, which throughout the year varies little from 6 o'clock. Thus 7 o'clock according to Western system of chronology is 1 o'clock by the Arab method of reckoning, 9 a.m. is 3 o'clock, and noon is always 6 o'clock. The system is at first a little confusing, and it is as well in making an appointment with an Arab or native to make certain whether the Western hour is meant or the Arab time.

According to the Arab reckoning, the night of a day precedes the daylight portion of it. Thus Friday evening, for instance, according to Arab usage would really be our Thursday evening. Our Friday would not commence of course till midnight, the Arab Friday commenced six hours previously.

the proceedings were sometimes enlivened by a recitation of poetry on the subject of war, and valour, and similar subjects. In due course, the time for the recitation of the night-prayers came round, after which the baraza would disperse, and His Highness would seek rest within the palace, after, it must be confessed, a long and busy day.

It will be seen from the above that the position of Sultan was no sinecure, and the ever-recurring religious devotions which as an upright Ibathi he was bound to observe, coupled with the transaction of public and private business, gave but little time for relaxation so long as he remained in his capital.

To obtain some remission from his public duties, Seyyid Barghash was wont to spend a week or ten days every month at one of his country palaces, where no doubt the strict regime demanded of him in Zanzibar was somewhat relaxed.

Seyyid Barghash caused to be minted a gold five-dollar (about Rs. 15) piece stamped with his name and super-scription, but these coins only had a limited circulation.

He had only one wife. This lady, known as Bibi Moza-binti-Hamed-bin-Salim, died in 1918. She resided in Zanzibar town, engaged during the last years of her life in constant warfare with the medical officer of health, who strongly objected to the lady keeping a large number of cows in the basement of her house ! She is said to have amassed great wealth.

The last years of Seyyid Barghash's life were embittered by the humiliations imposed upon him by the political changes which deprived him of the vast possessions on the mainland of Africa which had hitherto been regarded as being under the domination of the Sultans of Zanzibar.

That his death was hastened by the mental anguish and humiliations of these bitter years there is nothing to show, although the course of events must have aggravated the maladies—consumption and elephantiasis—from which he suffered.

He died at Zanzibar in 1888, aged fifty-five, after a reign of eighteen years, and was succeeded by his brother.

KHALIFA-BIN-SAID (1888–1890)

We will refer to him as Khalifa I, to distinguish him from the present reigning Sultan, Seyyid Khalifa-bin-Harub, or Khalifa II.

Khalifa I had been imprisoned in a chamber beneath the Bet-el-Hukm Palace by his brother for six years, for having intrigued against him. What the actual facts of the conspiracy were which brought Seyyid Khalifa to trouble are not worth the trouble of ascertaining; but there is no doubt that the treatment he received adversely affected him mentally; and during his brief reign of two years he lived a most retired life in company with his two friends Salim-bin-Khalfan and Selim-bin-Khamis. He sent a deputation of Arabs to England, Berlin, Paris, and Vienna. The envoys were honoured, it is said, with an interview with Queen Victoria, the Kaiser, and the President of the French Republic; but the chief tradition of their journey which has survived in Zanzibar relates to the pinchbeck watches presented to them by the German Kaiser. These timepieces, evidently " made in Germany," were engraved with eagles and the imperial monogram, but were found, so report goes, to be made of some base metal, covered with a very thin plating of gold.

It was during this reign that the last public executions took place in Zanzibar by decapitation. Seyyid Barghash had been exceedingly loath to allow capital sentences to be carried out, and as a consequence, after his lengthy reign of eighteen years, there were several convicted murderers lying in the fort. Seyyid Khalifa was induced to have all these malefactors executed, and accordingly on two successive days eight of them in two batches of four were decapitated in the vegetable market outside the eastern wall of the fort. The executioner was a Baluchi sepoy, who wielded a curved Arab sword. The decapitated bodies remained lying on the ground for many hours before they were removed.

There is little doubt there would have been more executions on the following day, but for the fact that there was a British-Indian detained in the fort on the charge of manslaughter, and the Indian communities, apprehensive that their fellow-countryman might be led out to execution, made representation to the British Consul, Colonel (afterwards Sir) Charles Euan-Smith, who prevailed upon the Sultan to give instructions that no further executions were to take place.

He died in 1890 aged thirty-six years, after a brief reign of two years. He left one son named Mahomed, who did not long survive his unfortunate father.

ALI-BIN-SAID (1890–1893)

He succeeded his brother, Khalifa I, as Sultan. His reign was short and without incident, save for one important political event—the proclamation of the British Protectorate over the islands of Zanzibar and Pemba, on November 4th, 1890.

During his last illness he was advised by Her Majesty's representative in Zanzibar to make a will, and leave to his family some portion of the wealth he had at his disposal, but, probably regarding such an act as unlucky, he refused, with the consequence that his children were left in anything but affluent circumstances.

He died on March 5th, 1893.

Ali was the last of the sons of old Seyyid Said to sit on the throne of Zanzibar, the succession at his death passing to the younger generation and grandchildren of the founder of the modern Zanzibar.

HAMED-BIN-THUWAINI-BIN-SAID (1893–1896)

The next Sultan was the son of Seyyid Said's eldest son Seyyid Thuwaini, the first Sultan of Muscat. Seyyid Thuwaini had hotly contested the right of his younger brother Seyyid Majid to the throne of Zanzibar; but as the result of the arbitration of Lord Canning, the Governor-General of India, the principalities of Omân and Zanzibar had become separate political entities, Thuwaini being confirmed as ruler of Omân, and Majid as Sultan of Zanzibar.

Thuwaini was murdered whilst asleep by his son Salim (in 1866), who was obliged to flee from Omân and take refuge in India. He was succeeded on the throne of Omân by a cousin, Azzan-bin-Kais, who in turn was killed by one of Thuwaini's brothers named Turki. This prince had a daughter named Turkiyyeh, married to Seyyid Hamed.

Turki, after killing Azzan-bin-Kais, became Sultan of Muscat, but his son-in-law Hamed conspired to murder him.

In consequence of this conspiracy, Hamed was forced to divorce his wife, Turkiyyeh, and was banished to India by his father-in-law, Turki. From India he came to Zanzibar, and on the death of the Sultan Ali-bin-Said ascended the throne.

The lady Turkiyyeh later married the Seyyid Harub, a son of Seyyid Thuwaini. This marriage resulted in the birth of a son, Khalifa, the present Sultan of Zanzibar.

The above little fragment of family history is given, not only to explain the close relationship which exists between the reigning families of Zanzibar and Muscat, but to serve as an example of the intrigue, conspiracy, and feuds which are—or rather, were—a common feature of Arab life.

In 1896 the Sultan was struck down with illness, and while he lay dying in his palace his Persian bodyguard was conspiring to assist Seyyid Khaled, a son of the Sultan Barghash, to usurp the throne. No sooner was Seyyid Hamed dead, and before he was buried, than Seyyid Khaled with the armed forces of the dead Sultan broke into and seized the palace, in spite of the protests of Her Britannic Majesty's representative. The result of this usurpation has been referred to in another portion of this book, so it will suffice to remark here that the timely arrival of a squadron of British war-vessels frustrated the plans of the usurper, who, after some of the royal palaces had been destroyed by the guns of the British Fleet, fled for safety to German East Africa, where he resided until 1917, when he surrendered himself unconditionally to a British force.

HAMOUD-BIN-MAHOMED (1896–1902)

Hamoud was a grandson of old Seyyid Said, and his father Mahomed was a brother of Seyyid Thuwaini. It is reckoned in Zanzibar among the Arabs that from Seyyid Hamoud's accession Zanzibar changed from an Oriental State, governed purely on Eastern lines, to its present condition.

Seyyid Hamoud was a very intelligent ruler, and intensely English in his sympathies. He insisted upon his son, Seyyid Ali, being educated at an English public school, and in every way he advocated by his example the adoption of English ideas. Of a generous nature, as befits a royal ruler, he maintained his court on a lavish scale, although he did not possess great wealth.

Before his death he made his will in English, appointing as executors well-to-do Englishmen.

His daughter, Bibi Matuka, married Seyyid Khalifa-bin-Harub.

Sultan Hamoud was a man of fine physique, and of a most courtly and charming presence. His brother, Seyyid Khaled-bin-Mahomed, now advanced in years and in poor health, still lives in Zanzibar, highly respected and honoured by all who have the privilege of his acquaintance.

ALI-BIN-HAMOUD (1902–1911),

the son of Sultan Hamoud, was, as a boy, sent to England and educated at Harrow. It is said that on his return to Zanzibar he had forgotten the Swahili language, and the intervention of an interpreter was necessary before he could speak to his father or relations. It is also asserted that he failed to recognise his mother and sisters, but these are but native stories, and there is no foundation for them, except that perhaps his female relations had some difficulty in at first recognising him in his European garb.

He represented his father at the coronation of King Edward VII, and while absent on this mission his father

18

died at Zanzibar from a stroke of paralysis at the age of fifty-five.

At this time Seyyid Ali was still a minor, and the affairs of State were transacted by Mr. Rogers, formerly Vice-Consul in the East Africa Protectorate, who was appointed Regent of Zanzibar on July 18th, 1902.

It was Mr. Rogers who built the mansion in Zanzibar now known as the British Residency.

Seyyid Ali, who of course spoke English fluently, attained his majority in June 1905, and immediately took an active part in the government of his dominions. The administration of his household and his mode of life were organised generally on the lines of a royal court in Europe, and, as he was fond of travelling, he frequently left Zanzibar and spent some part of the year in Europe. On one occasion he performed the pilgrimage to Mecca and the holy places, in company with his cousin, Seyyid Khalifa-bin-Harub. On another occasion he paid a visit to the Sultan of Turkey at Constantinople.

In 1911 he left Zanzibar to attend the Coronation of His Majesty King George, and while in Europe decided to abdicate. He had two sons, Saud and Ferid, at the present time (1919) at school in Cairo.

His sister, a most intelligent and clever lady, is, as already stated, the wife of Seyyid Khalifa II, the present Sultan of Zanzibar.

Seyyid Ali died in Paris in December 1918.

II

Before bringing this chapter to a close, it will be but a measure of justice to make a brief mention of those representatives of Great Britain in Zanzibar who during the last century, in fair weather and foul, upheld the prestige and honour of their country, and by their advice contributed so materially to the welfare and prosperity of the Sultanate.

Zanzibar during the last century was not the health resort it is to-day, and enough has been said in these pages

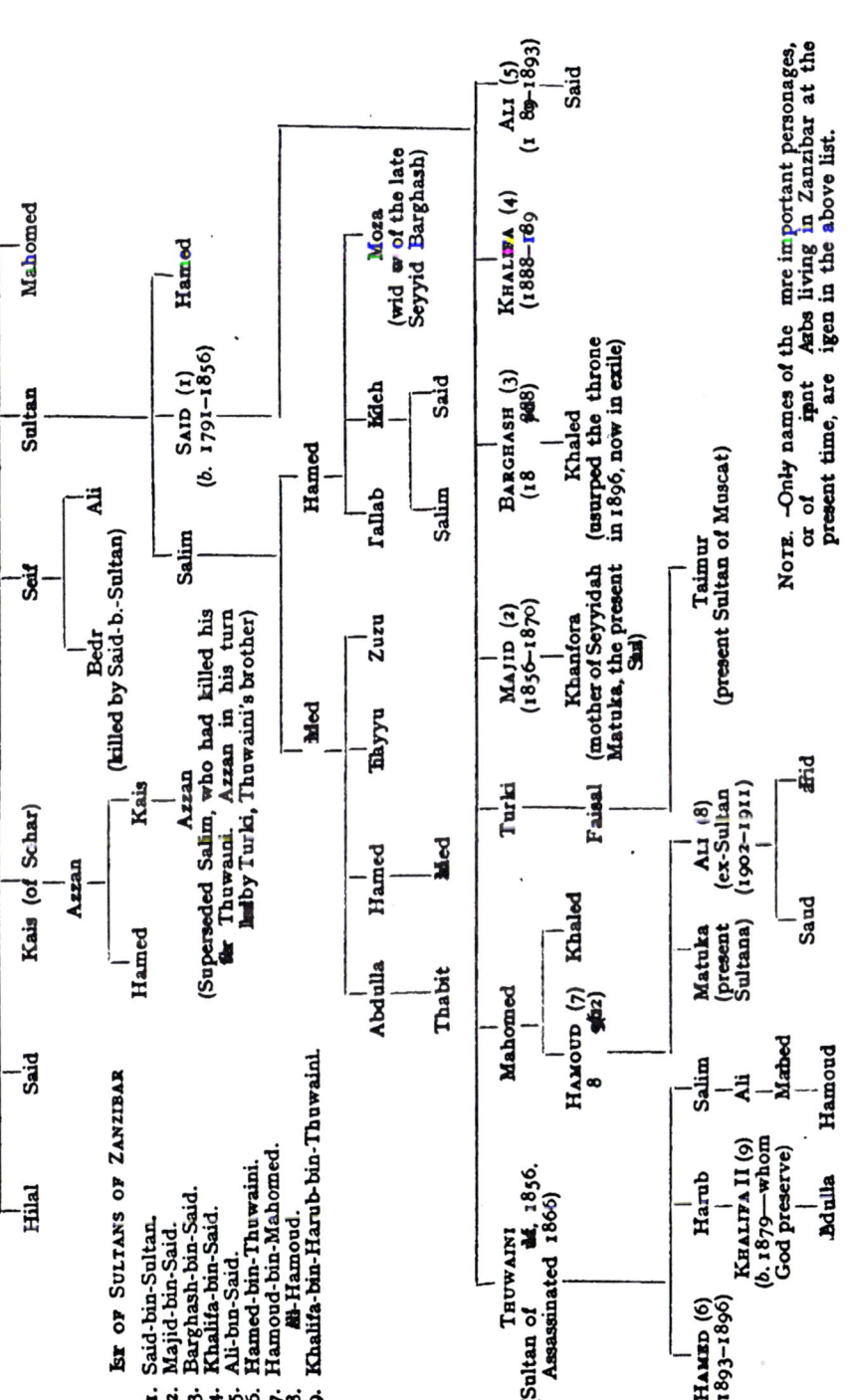

LIST OF SULTANS OF ZANZIBAR

1. Said-bin-Sultan.
2. Majid-bin-Said.
3. Barghash-bin-Said.
4. Khalifa-bin-Said.
5. Ali-bin-Said.
6. Hamed-bin-Thuwaini.
7. Hamoud-bin-Mahomed.
8. Ali-Hamoud.
9. Khalifa-bin-Harub-bin-Thuwaini.

Hilal   Said   Kais (of Schar)   Saif   Sultan   Mahomed

Azzan
Hamed   Kais
Bedr (killed by Said-b.-Sultan)
Ali
Azzan
(Superseded Salim, who had killed his brother Thuwaini. Azzan in his turn killed by Turki, Thuwaini's brother)

Salim   SAID (1) (b. 1791–1856)   Hamed

Med   Hamed

Abdulla   Hamed   Med   Turki   Thuyu   Zuzu   Jallab   Kdeh   Moza (widow of the late Seyyid Barghash)
Thabit   Faisal   MAJID (2) (1856–1870)   Salim   Said   KHALIFA (4) (1888–1869)   ALI (5) (1890–1893)
Khanfora (mother of Seyyidah Matuka, the present Sultana)   BARGHASH (3) (1870–1888)   Said
Mahomed   Khaled   Khaled (usurped the throne in 1896, now in exile)
HAMOUD (7) 1902   Matuka (present Sultana)   Ali (8) (ex-Sultan) (1902–1911)   Taimur (present Sultan of Muscat)
Saud   Said

THUWAINI (Sultan of Muscat, 1856. Assassinated 1866)
Harub   Salim   Ali   Mahed   Hamoud
KHALIFA II (9) (b. 1879—whom God preserve)
Adulla
HAMED (6) (1893–1896)

NOTE.—Only names of the more important personages, or of Arabs living in Zanzibar at the present time, are given in the above list.

275

to indicate that the surroundings and circumstances of existence in Zanzibar were well calculated to undermine the strongest constitution. But the trials of these upholders of British prestige in Zanzibar were not confined to physical discomforts, for they had to cope with and counteract, often on their own responsibility, subtle and mischievous schemings and misrepresentations of a political nature, set on foot by interested rivals with the object of belittling British influence.

The names of those who served their sovereign in Zanzibar during the nineteenth century are no mean ones, and it is pleasant to realise that many of them have attained a world-wide reputation in the highest ranks of His Majesty's Diplomatic Service.

The following is a fairly comprehensive record of those who have represented Great Britain in Zanzibar.

I. Under the Foreign and India Offices

i. Lieut.-Colonel Hamerton, 1841–1857.
ii. Lieut.-Colonel (afterwards General) P. Rigby, 1858–1861.
iii. Sir Lewis Pelly, 1861–1866.
iv. Colonel Playfair, 1866.
v. Mr. Churchill.

II. Under the Foreign Office

vi. Sir John Kirk, 1873–1887.
vii. Sir Claude McDonald, 1887–1888.
viii. Colonel Sir Charles Euan-Smith, 1889–1891.
ix. Sir Gerald Portal, 1892–1894.
x. Sir Rennell Rodd, 1893.
xi. Sir Arthur Hardinge, 1894–1900.
xii. Sir Charles Eliot, 1901–1904.
xiii. Mr. Basil S. Cave, 1904–1908.
xiv. Mr. Edward Clarke, 1909–1913.[1]

[1] In 1914 the Zanzibar Protectorate came under the control of the Colonial Office, and the author of this book was appointed British Resident in Zanzibar, the old consular regime coming to an end.

The first representative of Great Britain appointed to Zanzibar was Captain (afterwards Colonel) Hamerton. He was an officer in the Honourable East India Company's service, and had formerly resided at Muscat. In 1841 he was appointed as Her Majesty's Consul and Agent of the East India Company at Zanzibar.

He remained in Zanzibar, with occasional absences on leave of absence to England, until 1857, when his constitution, worn out by the rigours of the climate, failed and he died in Zanzibar, and was buried on Grave Island.

Thirteen months elapsed before a successor was appointed, owing no doubt to the disorganisation caused to the Indian Government service by the Mutiny.

Lieutenant-Colonel P. Rigby was appointed as Her Majesty's Consul and British Agent in 1858, and was succeeded in October 1861 by Colonel L. Pelly, who subsequently was appointed Political Resident in the Persian Gulf, and at a later date joined Sir Bartle Frere's Mission to Zanzibar in 1873. He was awarded the G.S.C.I. and the G.C.B.

Sir Lewis Pelly was relieved by Colonel Playfair in 1866, and the same year was succeeded by Mr. Churchill as Her Majesty's Consul and Agent.

Sir John Kirk needs no introduction, for his name is so associated with Zanzibar as to be even now a household word. It was during his tenure of office as Her Majesty's Diplomatic Agent and Consul-General that the affairs appertaining to the Zanzibar Sultanate came directly under the supervision of the Foreign Office. During the absence of Sir John in Europe, whither he accompanied His Highness Seyyid Barghash on his state visit to England, his duties were transacted by Colonel Euan-Smith.

Colonel Samuel Miles and Mr. Frederick Homewood also officiated as Acting Agents and Consul-Generals for varying periods.

On the resignation of Sir John Kirk, the Right Honourable Sir Claude McDonald, G.C.M.G., C.V.O.K., C.B., famous for his defence of the Legations at Pekin, while British Minister to the Emperor of China, and subsequently promoted to be Ambassador at Tokio, acted as Diplomatic Agent and Consul-

General in the Dominions of the Sultan of Zanzibar from July 1887 to March 1888, until the permanent appointment of Colonel Sir Charles Euan-Smith to Zanzibar.

Sir Charles held the posts of Agent and Consul-General from 1889 to 1891, and his name is still remembered from the school known as the " Euan-Smith Madressa," which under his auspices was founded in Zanzibar.

It will be remembered that among the eminent posts held by Sir Charles in subsequent years was that of Her Majesty's Representative in Morocco.

Sir Gerald Portal is well known in the history of Eastern Africa, for while Diplomatic Agent and Consul-General in Zanzibar he was deputed by Her Majesty's Government to proceed to Uganda, to report upon the advisability of retaining that country under British influence. Thanks to his report and recommendations, the country was not relinquished to rivals, and definitely came under British protection. The hardships of the journey, however, so undermined his constitution that Sir Gerald died shortly after his return to England.

It was Sir Gerald who initiated in Zanzibar a settled and organised system of administration on modern lines.

Up to the time of his advent there had been no regular control over the machinery of Government, except such as the Sultan had felt inclined to exercise. No accounts were kept, and the Customs Revenue was farmed out to the highest and most accommodating bidder, who was generally an Indian, often resident in India.

Peculation throughout the Government service was of course rife, and not a rope for one of the warships, or a horse, or a watch was purchased by the Sultan but half a dozen persons obtained some pickings from the transaction.

Sir Gerald Portal put a stop to all this ; a Civil List was instituted, Government Departments were formed under responsible officers, and the old abuses gradually died a natural death.

In this cleansing of the Augean stables, Sir Gerald was ably seconded by Sir Lloyd Mathews, who was the first appointed European Prime Minister to the Sultan of Zanzibar. Mathews was a well-known character in Zanzibar, and for nine years he ruled the country with a rod of iron, much to the country's benefit. Both Arabs and natives respected and feared him, and nothing was done without reference being made to Sir Lloyd. He was born at Madeira in 1850, the son of Welsh parents. He entered the Royal Navy in 1864, and served in the Ashanti war of 1873. He was afterwards appointed to H.M.S. *London*, and during that ship's tour of service in Zanzibar waters, Lieutenant Mathews, as he then was, was seconded and joined the Sultan's Administrative Service. He was made a K.C.M.G. in 1894, and died in Zanzibar on October 11th, 1901. He is buried in the English Cemetery, and a monument erected to his memory stands at the cross-roads near the Golf Links.

The Right Honourable Sir James Rennell Rodd, His Majesty's Ambassador at Rome, is one of those distinguished diplomats who served for a time as Acting Agent and Consul-General at Zanzibar, during the period Sir Gerald Portal was absent on his mission to Uganda in 1893.

On the death of Sir Gerald Portal in England, Sir Arthur Hardinge was appointed Agent and Consul-General for the Dominions of the Sultan of Zanzibar, and Consul-General for German East Africa in February 1894. In addition to his consular duties he was also appointed H.M.'s Commissioner and Consul-General in British East Africa. He remained at Zanzibar till 1900, when he was promoted to be Envoy Extraordinary and Minister Plenipotentiary to the Shah of Persia. After filling many important posts he became British Minister in Belgium, and at a later date held a similar post in Portugal, being promoted in 1913 as Ambassador to Madrid.

Sir Charles Eliot, who succeeded Sir Arthur Hardinge as Agent and Consul-General in Zanzibar, is of course well known as the distinguished author of many interesting books, among them being *Turkey in Europe*, and *Letters from the Far East*.

Mr. Edward Clarke, who, to the regret of all, died suddenly in Zanzibar on February 13th, 1913, was the last of a long succession of distinguished Political Agents and Consul-Generals in the Sultanate of Zanzibar. After his death Zanzibar was transferred from the Foreign Office to the

Colonial Office, and the somewhat confusing system of dual control by a Consul-General as representing the British Government, and by a First Minister as representing the Government of His Highness the Sultan, was done away with, and the functions of both posts became merged in the post of " The British Resident in Zanzibar."

CHAPTER XIX

1

SEYYID KHALIFA, the amiable and enlightened prince who to-day occupies the throne of Zanzibar, was born at Muscat in Omân on August 26th, 1879.

His father was Seyyid Harub-bin-Thuwaini-bin-Said, a member of the royal clan of the Albusaid, a dynasty founded by the redoubtable Ahmed, the Imam and ruler of Omân, in the middle of the eighteenth century. The romantic story of how Ahmed the Imam ascended the throne of Omân is related in another portion of this book, so it is not necessary to reiterate that history here, but it will be realised that with such a redoubtable great-great-great-grandfather as Ahmed, and with such a great-grandfather as Seyyid Said, the present Sultan of Zanzibar comes from a royal and fighting stock of ancestors.

His Highness informs me that he does not remember his father the Seyyid Harub, for this prince died young, when Prince Khalifa was still a child.

The fatherless boy was first taken care of by his grandfather Seyyid Turki-bin-Said, and it was as playmates during the years of childhood that the friendship sprang up between Seyyid Khalifa and Seyyid Taimur, another grandson of Seyyid Turki ; an association which causes the cousins still to regard themselves as " brothers."

Both the children were destined to sit on thrones, although in those early years there appeared no probability, except that they were of royal stock, that either of them would ever be called upon to fill such eminent positions. .

But the fates weaving the web of destiny brought it about that the Seyyid Khalifa is to-day the Sultan of Zanzibar, and his former playmate the Seyyid Taimur is the Sultan of Muscat.

The times during the early boyhood of the future Sultan of Zanzibar were turbulent ones, as indeed is so often the case in Omân. The aspirations and quarrels of contending factions made the position of the reigning family a difficult and often a precarious one, and young Khalifa was brought up in no atmosphere of domestic calm.

It would be unprofitable to detail specifically the claims of the rival factions in Omân at the period with which we are now dealing, but the conditions under which the Seyyid Khalifa spent his childhood will be appreciated if it is explained that when Seyyid Thuwaini was murdered Seyyid Azzan-bin-Kais superseded the patricide Salim, who fled to India. Azzan was in due course driven from his throne by Seyyid Turki, a brother of the murdered Thuwaini. Both of these princes had their respective followings, and the local politics in Omân were further complicated, as indeed they had been for centuries past, by the fact that many of the more fanatical tribesmen favoured the view that the only acceptable ruler for Omân was the one who had been elected by the suffrages of the population, irrespective of lineage or descent.

This contention is indeed, as already explained, the basic principle of the Omân constitution, and, while it has often been disregarded during the last thousand years, it has proved a source of constant civil discord ; and is, in fact, the cause of strife at the present day. Such a system of governance is obviously pregnant with possibilities of discord, especially among a warlike and turbulent people; and whatever advantages such a constitution may theoretically possess, in practice it has proved a source of bloodshed and discord to Omân.

To return, however, to Seyyid Khalifa. It will be clear that the young prince was brought up amid " alarums and excursions," and it cannot be doubted that he benefited both physically and in character by the strenuousness of the times in which his early life was spent. For instance, His Highness became an expert horseman at an age before most children have left the nursery.

When Seyyid Khalifa was thirteen years of age a great change took place in his life. One of his uncles, Seyyid Hamed-bin-Thuwaini, succeeded to the throne of Zanzibar, and in 1893 summoned his young kinsman to come to him. This move was a tremendous event in the boy's life, and, although the journey to Zanzibar in the Sultan's steamship *Aboukir* was a pleasant distraction, the more restricted and formal life of the Zanzibar court made the young prince regret, at any rate at first, the freer and more strenuous life of his native Muscat.

He soon, however, made many friends in his new home, and, young as he was, he associated with many nobles and important personages attending his uncle's court, and the latter insisted that his young nephew should always attend the official receptions and levees, which are such a feature in Arab life.

The year 1896 was a memorable one for Seyyid Khalifa, for his uncle the Sultan Hamed, at whose instance young Khalifa had come to Zanzibar, only reigned three years, and it was on his decease that the inevitable trouble as regards succession occurred, for, as already related elsewhere in this book, Seyyid-Khaled-bin-Barghash, a son of a former Sultan, attempted to seize the throne.

Fortunately the scheme of Khaled and his German friends failed, owing to the unexpected arrival of a British squadron at the most critical stage of affairs.

What occurred is well known, and it is only necessary here to repeat that Seyyid Khaled having failed to submit to the British ultimatum, the British squadron opened fire on the group of palaces occupied by the usurper.

In this bombardment Prince Khalifa was an interested but most unwilling participant !

He found himself, when the firing commenced, alone in his house, which stands considerably closer to the sea and to the menacing guns of the fleet than that portion of the palace in which the usurper had entrenched himself. His position caused him considerable anxiety, for the basement of the mansion in which he resided at this period had always been used by former Sultans as a factory for making gunpowder, and large quantities were actually stored beneath his apartments. Moreover, in another portion of the basement a large quantity of paraffin oil, used for lighting purposes, was kept; so when the British shells began to whistle past, it may be imagined that he was not in an enviable position. Seyyid Khalifa thereupon very sensibly took the earliest opportunity to quit his own house with its powder magazine, and seek shelter in a less-exposed position.

To show that the risk was not an imaginary one, His Highness relates that on leaving his house he found the native soldier on guard outside lying before the gate disembowelled by a fragment of shell.

The next important event in Prince Khalifa's life was his marriage in the year 1900. His bride was Seyyida Matuka, daughter of the Sultan Hamoud, whom the British had placed on the throne after the futile usurpation of Khaled. The mother of the Lady Matuka was Seyyida Khanfora, daughter of the Sultan Majid-bin-Said, so it will be seen that Seyyid Khalifa and his bride were distant cousins, and in both ran the royal blood of the great Seyyid Said of famous memory.

II

Two of the photographs facing this page, representing Seyyid Khalifa at various ages, were supplied by His Highness, and are now published with his permission.

The first shows Seyyid Khalifa, wearing the Muscat Arab head-dress, with his bicycle. This photograph was taken at Zanzibar about two years after the arrival of the young prince from Muscat, when he was about fifteen years of age. At that period European costume was worn more frequently by the younger members of the royal clan in Zanzibar than is the case at present, and it is gratifying to realise that the tendency for Arabs to adopt European fashion in clothes has almost entirely disappeared. It will be admitted by all that the plain, graceful, flowing Arab costume is far better

Gomes.

SULTAN KHALIFA AT HOME

SULTAN KHALIFA, AGED 14 YEARS, WEARING
THE ARAB HEAD-DRESS.

SULTAN KHALIFA, AGED
32 YEARS.

284)

suited for the Oriental than the awkward and unsightly
style of garments Europeans are required to wear. Fortunately, no one realises this fact better than His Highness
the Sultan himself.

The second photograph was taken while Prince Khalifa
was *en route* with his cousin, the then reigning Sultan Ali, to
attend the coronation of His Majesty King George V.

Seyyid Hamoud, who, it will be remembered, succeeded to
the throne immediately after the bombardment, died in
1902, and was succeeded by his son the Seyyid Ali, brother
to Seyyida Matuka.

One of the first acts of Sultan Ali was to perform the pilgrimage to Mecca, and he took with him as his companion
his brother-in-law, Seyyid Khalifa.

The event, apart from its religious significance, was one
of great interest to Seyyid Khalifa, who since his arrival
when a lad from Muscat had never left Zanzibar Island.

Landing at Jeddah, the prescribed pilgrimage to the
holy places was duly and scrupulously performed by the
two princes without any special incident.

The next great event of Prince Khalifa's life was his
visit to England in 1911, to attend the coronation of His
Majesty King George. At this time he had not ascended
the Zanzibar throne, but, as during the Mecca pilgrimage,
he merely accompanied his brother-in-law, Seyyid Ali, as a
friend.

It is needless to emphasise the deep and indelible impressions created on Seyyid Khalifa by the long journey to the
very centre of the world's civilisation, culminating as it did
in the magnificence of the coronation ceremonial in West-
minster Abbey.

To a certain degree one can gauge the excitement of these
Arab princes at this sudden plunge into the vortex of London
life. The languid calm of Zanzibar was for the nonce left
behind, and for four glorious weeks Seyyid Khalifa experienced, in the heart of the empire, the marvels and wonders
of the West. Could any magic carpet of Eastern tales have
effected so sudden and varied a change? This short visit
to London was a story worthy of Eastern tradition, and
redolent of the *Arabian Nights* and the fables of Haroun-

el-Raschid and of Sindbad's Valley of Diamonds ! And
indeed the similarity is still more striking, for Seyyid Khalifa
left Zanzibar for Europe merely a prince of the royal house,
without any immediate prospect of advancement, and he
returned from his flying visit to find a vacant throne awaiting him.

But of this more anon.

To advert to the "great adventure" of the journey to
England.

Seyyid Ali and his brother-in-law Seyyid Khalifa left Zanzibar on May 7th, 1911, for England. At Naples, Seyyid
Ali left the steamer and proceeded to Paris, where shortly
afterwards he announced his intention to abdicate. Seyyid
Khalifa proceeded on to Marseilles, and landed at Dover on
May 29th. London at that time of high festival was filled
with royalties of every degree, and so the flowing Arab robes
and the jewelled dagger of Seyyid Khalifa caused but little
remark or curiosity in the crowded streets of the capital.

Owing to the absence of the reigning Sultan of Zanzibar,
Seyyid Khalifa was obliged to assume the position of the
chief representative of the Sultanate during the weeks of
ceremonials and festivities which preceded and followed the
actual coronation. To any one brought up as Prince Khalifa
had been, within the confines of the Island of Zanzibar,
where the spice-laden breezes and the languorous climate
little befit a man for the rush and roar of London life, the
position in which he found himself must often have been a
trying and anxious one, however pleasurable it may have
been ; but whatever embarrassments may have presented
themselves to the young Arab prince, one thing is certain,
that the graceful demeanour, the calm serenity, and smiling
courtesy of the perfect Arab gentleman were never missing
in all that he was called upon to do.

Besides attending the actual coronation ceremony in the
Abbey, he enjoyed to the full the round of gaieties and functions which London afforded at that auspicious season. He
attended one of the State banquets at Buckingham Palace,
and he is always proud to recall that seated at the same
table as himself was the famous Japanese General Nogi and
the equally renowned Admiral Togo. The garden party at

Windsor Castle has also left delightful and imperishable memories in His Highness's mind. He, of course, like every other visitor to London, did the usual " sights," including the Tower, the Zoo, the Crystal Palace, the theatres, the Horse Show, Olympia, the shops, and a number of other novel and remarkable objects of interest.

The state performance at the Opera, and the visit to Portsmouth to attend the great Naval Review, are two items that His Highness is never tired of recalling; and above all, there stands out pre-eminent in his memory the gracious amiability of their Majesties the King and Queen.

On June 29th Seyyid Khalifa left England for Zanzibar. Shortly after his arrival in Zanzibar the abdication of the Sultan Ali-bin-Hamoud was definitely announced, and after the vacant' throne had been offered to Seyyid Khaled-bin-Mahomed,[1] brother of the Sultan Hamoud, who, owing to impaired health and advancing years, felt constrained to decline the honour, Seyyid Khalifa was approached by the British Government, and on December 9th, 1911, duly ascended the throne of Zanzibar.

The Sultan is, of course, a strict Mahomedan of the Ibathi sect, and, it is needless to remark, a total abstainer from every form of alcohol. His Highness writes and speaks English fluently, and while he adheres strictly to every convention of his religion and nation, he is the first to extend his cordial support to every kind of charitable enterprise, whether such affects Christians, Hindus, or his own subjects. His attitude in this respect is indeed typical of the Omân Arabs of Zanzibar, who are remarkable for their tolerance of other religions and people.

To every kind of sport His Highness lends his generous patronage : a splendid horseman himself, he was largely instrumental in introducing the game of polo into Zanzibar by obtaining from Abyssinia a number of suitable ponies. It is to be regretted that recently he has given up actually playing polo, although his interest in the sport is just as keen as ever.

[1] This Arab prince must not be confused with Khaled-bin-Burghash who was responsible for the bombardment of Zanzibar in 1896.

His absolute and whole-hearted loyalty to Great Britain is too well known to require comment here; but it may safely be affirmed that his steadying influence, not only over his own subjects within his dominions, but over the Moslem populations of East and Central Africa, largely contributed to the maintenance of peace among the Mahomedans of mid-Africa during the critical periods of the Great War in those regions.

Seyyid Khalifa's chief residence is, of course, situated in the city of Zanzibar. The palace in which he resides, while pleasantly built near the sea, is a plain and unpretentious building with a small garden attached. In this garden the great flagstaff, from which flies the Red Flag of Zanzibar, is planted, and a small chalet or summer-house is also built within the same enclosure.

Within the palace, which is of Arab design, are some interesting portraits. Among these are two painted by Kiss of Vienna, representing the late Emperor of Austria and his Consort the Empress Elizabeth. These life-sized pictures were the gift of the late Austrian Emperor to Seyyid Barghash, who reigned between 1870 and 1888. The gift actually arrived in Zanzibar after the death of the above-named Sultan. The portrait of the Empress must have caused considerable embarrassment to the recipient and his somewhat strait-laced court. It depicts Her Imperial Majesty in an extremely *décolleté* ball-dress of the Victorian era, and the magnificent diamond and ruby jewels which decorate her arms and throat do little to conceal the beautiful bare shoulders and bust of the Empress. His Highness smilingly admitted that the picture probably shocked the pious Omân Arabs of Zanzibar, and hinted that on receipt it was promptly consigned to oblivion in some lumber-room, until more enlightened views of Western art became the vogue in Zanzibar.

The pictures arrived from Vienna accompanied by two elaborately carved gilt frames, the tops bearing respectively the Imperial initials " F. J." and " E." By that as yet obscure law which demands that if two alternatives present themselves, erring humanity shall select the incorrect one, the pictures have been fixed in the wrong frames, so that to-day the Emperor's portrait is surmounted with the royal initial "E.," and that of Her Majesty by " F. J."

Among other royal gifts presented from time to time by European monarchs to former Sultans of Zanzibar is the beautiful state barge given to Seyyid Ali-bin-Said by Queen Victoria in 1892. Unlike the unsuitable gift from the Emperor of Austria referred to above, this barge, in addition to being a handsome specimen of British workmanship, is of real use, and adds much to the spectacular effect when a visit is made by His Highness to a British or foreign man-of-war. The barge is propelled by a double bank of sixteen rowers, and in the stern there is an ornamental roofed pavilion richly chased and embellished with gold, capable of accommodating some twenty-five persons.

A state coach presented by the late King of Italy is another gift which is often usefully employed by His Highness the Sultan. This carriage, arriving as it did when Zanzibar possessed roads, proved a more acceptable present than did the state coach presented to a former Sultan by Queen Victoria in 1837.

On various occasions during the last century, gifts of artillery have been made to the several Sultans by European sovereigns, but many of these pieces have now disappeared. Among those remaining may be mentioned a presentation field-piece (probably one of a battery) from the King of Prussia, dated 1866, and marked " Spandau." As related on another page, the silver-gilt tea service presented by Queen Victoria to Seyyid Said in 1845 has disappeared.

The other portraits in the palace worthy of note include one of Seyyid Majid, who reigned from 1856 to 1870. This picture is the work of a French artist. A portrait of Seyyid Barghash also hangs in the gallery, and was painted while that Sultan was on a visit to Europe in 1875. A somewhat striking full-length portrait of the present Sultan's father-in-law, Seyyid Hamoud, was painted by an Austrian named Strauch.

Seyyid Khalifa has a small but interesting collection of swords, many of them being of considerable antiquity. The majority of these weapons were brought to Zanzibar by former Sultans, and are of Persian and Indian manufacture.

19

A few of the older blades are evidently of European origin, and one of the latter is remarkable for its elaborate and profuse engraving. It appears to be of German medieval make, but how it came to find its way to Omân is not known. Some of the Persian swords, characterised by the almost semicircular sweep of the blade, are inscribed with the cipher of Shah Abbas, who reigned during the close of the sixteenth century. It may be noted that the swords affected by the Omân Arabs were those with straight blades without any cross hilt. The grip of this class of sword is always decorated with a chequered pattern of gold or silver, formed by an interlacing of black leather with strips of gold or silver. In the finest blades, a disc of pure gold, about the size of a threepenny piece, is inserted near the point.

One of the most interesting weapons possessed by His Highness is a sword supposed to have belonged to Seyyid Said-bin-Sultan, the founder of the kingdom of Zanzibar.

The country residence of His Highness the Sultan is situated close to the village of Bububu on the sea-coast, about six miles to the north of Zanzibar town. This small palace was completed in 1915. It is pleasantly built on the very edge of the sea, and a charming view of the city of Zanzibar —white and glistening in the sun—can be obtained from it.

It is here that His Highness delights to spend his hours of ease with his family, removed from the turmoil and heat of the town. Here he is enabled to live the quiet family life he most enjoys. His Highness has one son, Prince Abdulla, born in 1909, and among their Highnesses' first interests in life is the care of this only surviving child. Young as the little prince is, he has all the innate courtesy and good breeding of his race, coupled with a pretty deference.

He likes lessons no more than any other right-minded boy, and I once found him in tears over his arithmetic. A very human touch !

The palace is generally filled with children's voices and sounds of childish games, and a pleasing glimpse of the homely life led by His Highness was vouchsafed to the author one evening when, in company with the Sultan, he arrived at the country palace by the sea, and little Abdulla and his playmates ran out with glee to meet his royal father

Gomes.

PRINCE ABDULLA, THE SULTAN'S ONLY SON.

290]

CHAPTER XX

THE CLOVE

I

The clove tree is of such paramount importance to Zanzibar that it must have a chapter to itself.

No one who comes to Zanzibar can fail to become interested in this spice, for the scent of it is in the air, the landing places and the city street are redolent with it, and the beautiful clove tree borders many of the country roads, and covers the rolling hills of Zanzibar and Pemba.

Those who come prejudiced against the clove depart with an admiration for it, and no one who has seen and scented the clove in the Isles of the Sun can fail for the remainder of his life to retain a favourable memory of it. The clove does not enter largely into the economy of the untravelled European's existence, and he is only dimly aware from an occasional encounter—very often undesired—that such things as cloves are grown. Where they come from, who grows them, how they grow, what form of plant produces them, who requires them, and why they are cultivated are matters beyond his ken.

Zanzibar is " the place where the cloves come from," and the two little islands of Zanzibar and Pemba practically supply the world with this particular spice.

It is often asked " What is a clove ? "

The answer is, that the clove of commerce is the dried unexpanded bud of the flower of the *Eugenia caryophyllata*, or clove tree, which belongs to the natural order *Myrtaceae*.

The fact that the spice is really a flower-bud, and not the fruit, places the clove in an almost unique position amidst the products of the world. If this valuable bud is permitted to develop into the flower, the clove of commerce vanishes : so it is evident that the harvesting of the buds is a critical period in clove production.

The name " clove " is derived from the Portuguese *clavo* or *cravo*, and from the French *clou*, owing to the resemblance of the dried spice to a nail.[1]

The clove tree can only be cultivated in a few favoured spots in the world, and the soil and climate which are congenial to it are found in perfection in the islands of Zanzibar and Pemba. It is still cultivated on a small scale in the Molucca Islands in Sumatra, Penang, Malacca, Madagascar, and the West Indies, but these places only produce a small fraction of the world's supply. This limited range of growth is striking, and it is also remarkable that its extended cultivation in Zanzibar and Pemba was due to the foresight and enterprise of the Omân Arabs at the commencement of the nineteenth century.

The original home of the clove tree was in the Molucca Islands—not of course to be confused with Malacca in the Malay Peninsula. The Moluccas lie much farther towards the east, midway between the Celebes and New Guinea, and about 800 miles to the north of Australia.

The clove is not mentioned in the Bible by name, although it was probably one of the most prized spices of the ancient world, and early records show that the spice came from the islands of the Far East. In about A.D. 500, Cosmas Indicopleustes, speaking of the trade of Ceylon, mentions that cloves, silk, and sandalwood were brought to that island from the Farther East. Marco Polo, the Venetian traveller, writing in about A.D. 1260, when describing the trade of Malabar says, " The ships which come from the East bring coffee in ballast : they also bring gold and silver and cloves and spikenard and other fine spices."

The Arabian geographer, Ibn Batuta of Tangiers, who

---

[1] The origin of the French and Portuguese names is obviously the Latin *clavus*, a nail. The Portuguese *cravo*, besides being applied to the clove, is specially used to signify a horse-shoe nail, and the nails used at the Crucifixion on Calvary.

The Arabic word *karanful*, and the Swahili *karufu*, both denoting the " clove," are probably derived from the Portuguese *cravo*, rather than, as has been suggested, from the French word *girofle*.

flourished about A.D. 1325 mentions cloves when referring
to Java. He says:

"As to the clove, it is a thick and high tree. It is found
in greater numbers in the countries of the infidels than of
the Moslems. It is not claimed as property on account of
its great abundance. . . What is called the flower of the
cloves in our countries is that which drops from the blossom
and is like the blossom of the orange."

It is not quite clear to what Batuta is referring, but if he
means that the clove of commerce " drops from the blossom,"
he is of course wrong.

Duarte Barbosa, the Portuguese who wrote a description
of the coasts of East Africa and India and the Far East in
about 1512, thus describes the Molucca Islands :

"The islands of Maluca are five. . . . There are five
islands, one before the other, which are called the islands
of Maluca in which all the cloves grow, and the islands
belong to the Gentiles [pagans] and Moors. Their kings are
Moors, and the first of the islands is called Bachan, the
second Maquian   the third is called Motil, the fourth
Tidory, the fifth Ternaty.

" The hills of these five islands are all of cloves, which grow
on trees like laurels, which have their leaves like those of the
arbutus, and they grow like the orange flower,[1] which in the
beginning is green and then turns white, and when it is
ripe it turns coloured, and then they gather it by hand, the
people going among the trees, and they put it to dry in the
sun, where it turns brown, and if there is no sun, they dry it
with the smoke, and after it is very dry, they sprinkle it
with salt water for it not to crumble, and that it may preserve its virtue.

" And there are such quantities of cloves that they never
can finish gathering them, so that they let much of it be
lost. And the trees from which they do not gather it for
three years, after that become wild, so that their cloves are
worth nothing. . . . The cloves are worth very little in
these islands, so as to be had almost for nothing.

" This king of Maluca is a Moor, and almost a Gentile.

---

[1] As a matter of fact, there is no particular resemblance between the clove
and the orange blossom.

. . He is served by humpbacked women, whom he orders to have their spines bent from childhood, for state and show : and he may have eighty or a hundred of these who always go with him, and serve him as pages : some give him betel, others carry his sword, and they render all other services."

Barbosa falls into the same inaccuracy as Batuta in supposing that the clove is the fruit or seed, and not the bud : and indeed it is a mistake which a casual observer might very well make.

In an account of a voyage made by Juan Serano, and certain others, who fled from Malacca in the year 1512 it is recorded :

"We departed . . . as for the islands of Malut. In them grow much cloves ; they are five in all, the largest of them is smaller than Bandan. The Maluquese people are very wretched and worth little, they are very beastly, and of a brutal mode of living, they do not differ from animals in their customs, but only in possessing the human face. . . . The cloves grow in another island which is smaller and is called Tidory : the tree on which it grows is like the box or buxo. When the cloves are ripe on the trees, they stretch cloaks and sheets on the ground, and sweep the trees, and the inhabitants gather the most they can."

The price of cloves at this period (sixteenth century) at Calicut appears to have been about 6$\frac{3}{4}$d. per lb.

In Reinel's map dated about 1517, the Molucca Islands are shown definitely as five large islands and some of smaller size. The group is marked " Ilhas de Maluco, domde do clavo " (the isles of Maluco, whence the cloves). In an anonymous map of Munich dated 1520, the same islands are labelled " ilhas de maluqua domde vem ho cravo " (the isles . . . whence come the cloves).

The spice trade of the Indies was one of the chief incentives which induced the nations of Europe towards the close of the fifteenth century to seek out a sea-route to India and the Far East. Thanks to the prowess of Vasco da Gama, the Portuguese were first in the field, but, as related in a previous chapter of this book, their monopoly of the clove and spice trade was quickly invalidated by the appearance of rivals who followed them round the Cape of Good Hope. The Dutch were their most formidable and dangerous trade competitors, and in 1605 they finally expelled the Portuguese from the Moluccas and the clove trade became a Dutch monopoly.

It is evident that the new owners of the Clove Islands were determined to maintain the clove trade in their own hands, for they proceeded to destroy the whole of the clove forests, except in Amboyna, an island in the Dutch East Indies.

Here they cultivated the clove, and supplied the world with it at a profit which must have been enormous, if the price paid by Mr. Pepys in the middle of the seventeenth century may be taken as representing the current price in Europe at the time.

Pepys's entry in his Diary concerning his purchase of cloves is characteristic:

" 24th September 1665 (Lord's Day).—Waked, and up, and drank : and then being about Greyes and a very calm, curious morning, we took our wherry, and to the fishermen, and bought a great deal of fine fish, and to Gravesend to White's, and had part of it dressed : and in the meantime we to walk about a mile from the town, and so back again ; and there one of our watermen told us he had heard of a bargain of cloves for us, and we went to a blind ale-house at the further end of the town, to a couple of wretched dirty seamen, who, poor wretches ! had got together about 37 lbs. of cloves, and 10 lbs. of nutmeggs, and we bought them of them—the first at 5s. 6d. per lb. and the latter at 4s., and paid them in gold : but Lord ! to see how silly these men are in the selling of it, and easy to be persuaded almost to anything. But it would never have been allowed by my conscience to have wronged the poor wretches, who told us how dangerously they had got some, and dearly paid for the rest of these goods." [1]

In 1770 the French introduced the clove tree into Mauritius and into French Guiana, but the experiment nearly failed, owing to the death of all but a few seedlings. As already

[1] Lord Braybrooke's note on this transaction is to the effect that the cloves had been stolen from the Dutch prizes taken by our Fleet.

remarked, the geographical distribution of the clove is most restricted, and attempts which have been made to introduce this spice into apparently suitable regions of the globe have' generally proved abortive. In some cases the seed refuses to germinate or the seedling to grow; in other cases the tree will grow for a few years, and then suddenly withers away or refuses to flower.

This exigeant nature of the clove tree appears likely to be due largely to soil, and not to climate, for attempts made by the Germans to propagate the clove in the island of Mafia, which is but 150 miles from Zanzibar have hitherto proved fruitless.

Even in Zanzibar and the still more favoured island of Pemba, the clove will only flourish in certain well-defined localities, where the soil, altitude, and general surroundings are congenial to its growth.

The most suitable soil appears to be a well-drained reddish or orange-coloured loam, although any predominance of sand immediately affects the trees adversely. The gently undulating hills of Zanzibar and Pemba, composed as they are of a rich loam, with a porous substratum of argillaceous sandy soil, based on honeycombed coralline rock, ensures the perfect drainage which the clove tree demands, and the finest plantations are in consequence always to be found on the slopes or summits of the ridges which traverse both islands.

Although so capricious as to its habitat, the clove tree is fortunately a hardy and long-lived tree and appears to suffer less from the innumerable insect pests and diseases than other exotic growths in Africa.

Guillain [1] mentions that we have to thank a certain M. Sausse, a creole of either Réunion or Mauritius, for having endowed Zanzibar with the clove tree. This is said to have occurred either at the close of the eighteenth century or during the early years of the nineteenth century.

On the other hand it is recorded [2] that at the end of the eighteenth century a certain Arab named Harameli-

---

[1] *Documents sur l'histoire, la géographie, et le commerce de l'Afrique Orientale.* (Paris, 1857.)
[2] *Travels in East Africa,* by Fitzgerald. (London.)

THE FAMOUS CLOVE-TREE AVENUE AT DUNGA ZANZIBAR

Gomes.

297

bin-Saleh accompanied a French officer from Zanzibar to Réunion, and obtained permission to take back with him a few seeds and plants.

I am informed on good authority that an Arab had been exiled from Zanzibar by Seyyid Said, and on his return he brought back with him some clove seedlings to Zanzibar. This so pleased the Sultan that the exile was pardoned.

Burton mentions that the person who introduced cloves into Zanzibar died a beggar.

Possibly there is a substratum of truth in all the above versions, for M. Sausse may have been the person who gave permission to Harameli to take back the clove seedlings to Zanzibar, while the latter may have been the exile who was pardoned by Seyyid Said. In any case it was the last-named personage who by his influence and example caused the cultivation of the spice to be undertaken in a regular manner and on a wholesale scale.

Every tradition among the Arabs in Zanzibar regarding the introduction of the clove tree into the island points to the fact that it was brought from Mauritius about the year 1829[1] at the instance of His Highness Seyyid Said, who, with remarkable prescience as to its potential value, caused its cultivation to be undertaken on an extended and systematic scale in Zanzibar, and subsequently in Pemba. Attempts were also made at the time to grow the spice at Bagamoyo on the mainland, but without success.

The first seedlings are said to have been planted in Zanzibar at Mtoni Palace four miles to the north of Zanzibar city, and the first clove plantation of any size was situated at Kisimbani, one of Seyyid Said's estates, where he had a mansion, the ruins of which still exist.

II

The clove tree is a most pleasing object to gaze upon, with its dense masses of aromatic and glossy leaves, which effectively conceal the branches and the trunk of the main

[1] This tradition and date are confirmed to some extent by official documents at Zanzibar.

growth : in fact, the term " tree " is somewhat misleading from a purely descriptive point of view, for seldom more than four or five feet of the trunk or stem can be seen, at which height from the ground the heavily leaved branches commence to grow, thus giving to the " tree " rather the appearance of an enormous shrub or bush.

Nevertheless the clove " tree " attains a height of 30 or 40 feet, and in this particular, at any rate, justifies the term " tree " being applied to it. The leaves, which are highly aromatic, are about 3 or 4 inches in length, and are of a rich green hue. They sprout from a mass of small branches and entirely envelop the main structure of the plant.

Clove trees are raised either direct from seed or from the seedlings which germinate by themselves under the shelter of the parent tree. While they grow with such luxuriance in Zanzibar and Pemba, the young plants for the first year or two of their existence require constant care, especially in the matter of being watered with regularity, and it is this close supervision during a lengthy period which deters many estate owners from extending their clove acreage.

When planted in very favourable soil, a clove tree will commence to bear during the fifth year, but more generally a tree has to be seven years old before it gives any return.

In its original home—the Molucca Islands—the clove only bears in the seventh or eighth year, while in Amboyna, which was planted with cloves by the Dutch during the seventeenth century, it is stated that ten or eleven years are required before the tree flowers.

The life of a clove tree is not at present definitely known, but in the Dutch East Indies about seventy-five years is regarded as the average duration, although there are said to be trees which are 135 years old. The period of life is largely dependent upon the soil, climate, and other considerations which affect the bearing and productivity of the plant.

The trees in Pemba Island are considerably older than those in Zanzibar, owing to the fact that the track of the great cyclone, which devastated the plantations of the latter island in 1872, passed clear of Pemba.

The majority of the clove plantations in Zanzibar had to be replanted in 1872 and subsequent years, and consequently most of the trees in this island are not above forty years old, while in Pemba some are stated to be double that age.

In Zanzibar and Pemba the clove trees are systematically planted in rows at intervals of 30 feet, and there are few more beautiful sights than a well-managed clove plantation. So symmetrical are the trees, in their dense covering of glistening leaves, and so fragrant the air with the aromatic scent of the spice !

In the Dutch East Indies the trees are topped and kept within a height of 8 to 10 feet for the greater convenience of picking, but in Zanzibar this procedure is not practised, and they are allowed to grow to their full height, which often exceeds 30 feet. This of course makes picking the cloves a very difficult task.

The buds—the most important items of the growth— appear in small clusters upon branched peduncles at the extremity of the boughs, and after about four months' growth they are sufficiently matured to be picked as the clove of commerce.

They are at this period of development of a delicate pinkish hue, and there are few more delicately beautiful things than a clove tree in full bud. All the buds on a tree do not ripen at once, and thus on a tree will be found clusters of buds varying in colour from a delicate green tinged with rose, to the over-mature bud about to burst into blossom. At this latter stage, its colour is a magnificent crimson-lake hue. On the same tree will probably also be found buds which have flowered ; and the calyx then assumes a still richer and deeper crimson tint, while the spiky flower, like an inverted tassel, is one of the most delicate and fragile-looking growths imaginable, being of a faint yellowish-green colour, and each spicule is tipped with a golden point.

In the neighbourhood of such a tree, the air is fragrant with the sweet aroma of the bud and flowers. A clove before it is dried is a beautiful thing, and it only attains the deep chocolate colour of the commercial spice after exposure in the sun for several days.

There are two distinct details of the embryo flower or bud which are picked as being of commercial value. These are the actual bud or clove and its stem. The former is of course the most important and costly, while the stem is used solely for distillation purposes, in order to obtain the valuable essential oil of cloves.

The harvesting of the clove crop is in more senses than one a difficult and troublesome matter. The harvest generally commences in July, and with a heavy crop extends to the following February. This long period of harvest entails an adequate and organised labour supply, a consummation difficult to achieve in Africa. Moreover, as only the buds of the flower are of any value, it requires some prevision to arrange for the small army of pickers to be ready at those localities where the buds are sufficiently matured for collection.

The actual process of picking the cloves has to be done with care, but here again there is considerable room for improvement in the methods now adopted. The difficulty is largely due to the great height and the general structure of the tree itself. The clove, with its adherent stem, has to be picked by hand, and it is still an unsolved problem how to reach the bunches of cloves which grow at the extremities of the thin branches. Formerly, as may be seen from the engraving illustrating clove picking on the Zanzibar Government currency notes, a rough wooden scaffold was employed to reach the clove clusters, but this system has entirely died out, partly owing no doubt to the increased height of the trees, and partly on account of the labour entailed by moving the heavy structure from one tree to another.

The present method is for the pickers to climb into the tree, and reach the cloves by standing on the branches. This would be efficacious if the branches themselves were of any strength, but the contrary is the case, and so in the process of picking, the trees often become greatly damaged by the branches being broken. A worse evil is the method adopted by the pickers if left to their own devices. As the cloves are difficult to reach, the picker, to save himself trouble, breaks off entire boughs upon which the clove clusters grow, and then proceeds to pick off the cloves at his leisure seated comfortably on the ground. A plantation which has undergone this process is a sorry sight, the trees having a lacerated appearance, while the ground in the vicinity is strewn with piles of dead branches.

The cloves when being picked are placed in a cloth tied round the shoulders of the picker, who, after descending, proceeds to separate the cloves from the stems. The workers are paid according to the quantity of cloves picked, and an industrious picker can earn as much as two or three rupees daily. Government now regulates both the standard measures used to ascertain the quantity collected and also the prices to be paid the workers. Before this was undertaken, the Arab plantation owners—incredibly ignorant as to the benefits of mutual co-operation against the picker—were wont to entice labour on to their shambas by employing a measure of less contents than those of their neighbours. When this process of diminution reached the limit, the plantation owners went to the other extreme, and began to outbid their neighbours in the wages paid. The result was that they paid exorbitant wages for a very small measure of cloves.

The annual yield of each tree varies greatly, but it is generally calculated that 5 lb. weight of dried cloves should be obtained annually from a good tree in suitable soil.

On the Government plantations there are 81,889 clove trees. In a bad season such as 1910–11 proved to be, the average yield per tree was only 0·88 lb. The following harvest, the yield per tree was as much as 7·22 lb., the 3,090 trees on the famous Dunga estate giving during that season as much as 13·59 lb. per tree.

The cloves and stems after being picked are next dried in the sun. This is effected by their being spread on large mats placed upon a cement or concrete platform raised slightly above the ground-level.

Whenever rain threatens, and daily at sundown, the cloves are collected and placed under shelter for the night, and the mats are rolled up and stowed away until the following day. In the process of drying, the pinkish flush of the newly picked clove and stems fades, and is replaced by the final tinge of deep brown of the clove of commerce.

Sun-drying is the only method adopted in the Zanzibar dominions, but it would appear that in the Dutch East Indies the clove is dried first of all over a slow wood fire, prior to being placed in the sun. In favour of this double process of desiccation, it is claimed that the clove does not become shrivelled in appearance, and that the essential oil is not unduly evaporated, with the result that the full value of the spice is not depreciated.

Cloves and clove stems are of course kept entirely distinct, both during the drying and packing processes. The spice is packed for shipment in matting bags, which are made by the Mshihiri Arabs resident in Zanzibar town. Each bag or bundle, when ready to be exported, contains 140 lb. of dried cloves.

Before considering what becomes of all the cloves, it may be explained at this juncture that if the unopened bud of the clove-flower is not picked—and of course a very great number are left on the tree—the process of nature continues and the bud develops into a yellowish-white-tinted blossom. This is, as already remarked, a very delicate growth, in form like a small and most fragile brush, each bristle tipped with a golden coloured knob, and the whole held together by the crimson calyx—a very charming object. The calyx in due course swells, and the seed enlarges into a big ovoid crimson berry, similar in appearance to the hip of the briar rose. This seed pod is called " mother of clove," and contains one or two seeds, from which clove trees may be generated. Commercially " mother of clove " is of no value.

The following table shows how the cloves exported from the dominions of His Highness the Sultan of Zanzibar were disposed of during the years 1914, 1915, 1916, and 1917.

	1914. tons.	1915. tons.	1916. tons.	1917. tons.
United Kingdom	1,394	3,427	3,061	1,557
India	3,330	5,015	4,067	4,350
Aden	46	40	123	162
Australia	28	31	32	130
France	173	639	423	23
United States	1,562	2,000	959	811
Italy	49	71	260	27
China	10	53	27	12
Germany	864	—	—	—
Austria	42	—	—	—
TOTAL	7,576	11,350	9,054	7,640

From the above it will be observed that as regards cloves, India is the best customer of Zanzibar, taking nearly half the clove output, while the United Kingdom is an easy second.

The clove crop is always a variable one, as the above totals indicate, but it may generally be anticipated that every third year the crop is an abundant one. Fortunately this capriciousness of output does not generally affect every portion of the two islands at the same time, otherwise during some seasons there would be scarcely any cloves at all, while in other years the harvest would be so heavy as to exceed the demand. It often happens that when the crop is a small one in Pemba, a good harvest is experienced in Zanzibar, and *vice versa*. Similarly a small crop in certain areas of both islands may be counterbalanced by a substantial output in other plantations. This variability in production extends even to individual trees in the same plantation, but the owner may rest assured that if during one season his trees fail to give him a good return, they will recompense him with an increased crop in the course of the next harvest, provided he attends to their welfare by regularly cleaning his plantations. This essential condition to ensure the continued prosperity of Zanzibar is just the one which is most likely to be ignored, and indeed the apathy of the Arab landowner with regard to his clove trees is the ominous cloud on the horizon which may eventually cause the wreck of the clove industry.

The islands of Zanzibar and Pemba were planted out with the magnificent plantations of cloves which now supply the world with this spice by slave labour, and the estates were maintained in order and extended by similar machinery. When these means were no longer available, the estates became neglected, and many of the owners took the line of least resistance and mortgaged their properties to the Indian moneylenders. The Arab, generous to a high degree, but lacking business acumen, soon fell into the toils, and many are now so deeply involved in debt that they no longer take much interest in their plantations, inasmuch as any produce derived therefrom goes to pay the interest due for accommodation received in the past. Sufficient return is at present obtainable from these derelict estates to pay the mortgagee his dues, but in a great many instances little is done to improve or regenerate these valuable and unique properties.

Under the beneficent autocracy of the old regime, the Sultans by their personal influence simply compelled their Arab subjects to maintain their properties in proper order, while under the modern regime of personal freedom the executive endeavour to stave off impending disaster by means of the lengthy processes of the law.

From the table showing the production of cloves in the Sultanate, it will be observed that something like 10,000 tons of cloves are exported annually from Zanzibar. This is an enormous quantity, and it may well be asked what the world does with it all.

The most valuable product obtained from the clove by distillation is a volatile oil of cloves, of which the most important constituent is phenol eugenol, upon the quantity of which the value of the oil depends. The clove is remarkable among other plants for the great quantity of essential oil it contains, the yield being seldom under 15 per cent. and very frequently as much as 18 per cent. The " clove stems," which are also a commercial product of the tree, yield 6 per cent. of oil.[1]

Oil of cloves is extensively used in many industries and is also employed in pharmacy. As regards its commercial uses, eugenol forms the basis of nearly all perfumery, and the oil, which has a very large commercial importance, is largely employed in the preparation of liqueurs : while the clove itself is utilised as a condiment and a flavouring agent in culinary operations and in confectionery.

It is to be regretted that the clove is not more extensively used in the domestic economy of the household, for it is essentially tonic and antiseptic in its action. No rat or mouse will touch a clove.

As a preserver of teeth from decay, as a purifier of the mouth, and a preventive of sore throat it is far more efficacious and pleasant than the host of advertised drugs,

[1] *The Chemistry of Essential Oils*, by Ernest J. Parry. (Scott, Greenwood & Sons. London, 1908.)

while its sweet fragrance, reminiscent of the Isles of the
Sun in the Azanian Sea, imparts a sense of reassuring whole-
someness and freshness to the wardrobe or linen cupboard
in which a few are placed.   Nothing accentuates or brings
out the subtle aroma of good tobacco   whether cigar, cigarette, or pipe—better than the presence of a few well-dried
cloves in the cigar or cigarette box.

The clove is probably seen at its worst when used in the
conventional manner beloved of English cooks.   The process of boiling the spice with fruit reduces it to a sodden
and acrid object, bereft of its true aromatic sweetness.   To
fully appreciate a clove it must be in a perfectly dry state
with all its fragrance and valuable antiseptic constituents
still intact within it.

A word of warning may be given with respect to the
practice of mixing " spent " cloves with real cloves.   " Spent "
cloves are those which have undergone the process of distillation and from which all the valuable oil has been extracted.   Such a " clove " is one in appearance only, and
in nothing else.   As a spice or for any other purpose it is of
course useless.

This trick of first distilling the cloves and then palming
off the worthless residue as genuine spice is stated to be
commonly practised in Germany.   In any case the fraud is
a European one, for no distillation of the spice takes place
in Zanzibar.

CHAPTER XXI

THE ISLAND OF PEMBA

1

THE Arabs call Pemba *El Huthera*, or the Green Island: and indeed it is the Emerald Island of the Indian Ocean, not in a political sense, but in a spectacular one, for viewed from the sea it forms a charming picture of undulating hills covered with dense masses of vegetation, comprising forest trees, clove plantations, and orange and palm groves. Unlike Zanzibar Island, where the highland is some distance from the coast, the green hills of Pemba rise abruptly from the sea, and this gives to the island an appearance of altitude and diversified scenery which is lacking in the sister island.

The coast, moreover, is broken into numerous deep inlets, and the sea thus penetrating far into the heart of the island affords many beautiful and diversified views of land and sea. Archipelagoes of small verdant islets are scattered along the western coast, and give additional charm to the prospect. Pemba is certainly a beautiful island.

The island is considerably smaller than Zanzibar, being forty-two miles from north to south, and its width varies from fourteen miles to five or six miles.

It lies to the north-east of Zanzibar, and the channel which separates the two islands is about twenty-eight miles broad. It is thirty-six miles from the mainland, the mountains of which are clearly visible during fine weather.

The geological structure of the island is similar to that of Zanzibar, being of coral limestone in various stages of modification.

The argillaceous red earth, so common in Zanzibar, is evident everywhere in Pemba, the hill-masses being composed almost entirely of it, and it is this loamy earth which forms the most favourable soil for the cultivation of the clove tree, for which particular spice Pemba is famous.

Sometimes, owing to its comparative remoteness, Pemba is not always given sufficient credit for its contribution to the wealth and prosperity of the Zanzibar Sultanate, for there is no doubt that the former island produces a greater abundance of cloves than Zanzibar. Thus, while in the season of 1914–15 Zanzibar Island produced in round figures 6,700,000 lb. of cloves, Pemba delivered 11,000,000 lb. ; again, in the harvest of 1915–16, Zanzibar's contribution was 4,600,000 lb., while 22,000,000 lb. came from little Pemba. It will be clear from the above figures that Pemba soil is admirably suited for the cultivation of cloves.

The most diversified portion of the island is situated in the south-west, and the whole of this region is devoted to the cultivation of cloves. Towards the east coast the height of the hills diminishes, and evidences of the sub-structure of the island becomes apparent in outcrops of coralline limestone rock.

In this respect Zanzibar and Pemba are similar, for in both islands the more hilly and fertile country lies contiguous and parallel to the west coast, while the eastern regions are largely composed of unproductive coralline rock.

The east coast of the island is edged with a narrow fringing reef, formed probably by the erosion of the coralline cliffs by the action of the waves. In Zanzibar, this outlying reef is from one to two miles in breadth, but in Pemba it seldom extends seaward for more than a mile.

A great portion of the east coast of Pemba is charming, and unlike the corresponding part of Zanzibar is easily traversed. The scenery is prettier and more diversified than in the latter island. Even within the limits of the coral-rag country, one traverses in Pemba a fruitful country of good soil, of peaceful, well-kept villages inhabited by happy and contented people. Fat cattle browse on the slopes of the basin-like valleys, at the bottom of which the green rice fields lie. Stretches of open grass land relieve the monotony of the eternal coco-nut groves, and " over the edge of the purple down " one glimpses the dark blue of the open sea.

Pools and lakelets of clear fresh water, covered with hundreds of white and blue water-lilies, and edged with grass as short and green as that of meadow-land in England, afford a sense of coolness and relief after the heat and glare of dusty Zanzibar.

The climate of Pemba is considered harmful for continued residence by Europeans, but those quartered in the island only suffer from the ailments inseparable from life in a tropical country. Most Europeans suffer from the usual touch of malarial fever of a mild type : and from a health point of view the climate of Pemba differs but little from that of Zanzibar. What does adversely affect the health in such a place as Pemba is not so much the climatic influences as the effect of a somewhat lonely existence without social amenities, and without the possibility of associating frequently with one's fellow-men. Some persons are so constituted that they are quite content with their own society, and are ever finding employment in new directions for their minds and hands : but all are not of this type, and it is the man without resources who must live in a crowd that finds Pemba uncongenial as a place of residence.

The rainfall of Pemba is greater than that of Zanzibar; for instance, in 1915, 67 inches fell in Pemba, while 52·87 inches were recorded in Zanzibar. On the other hand, the average annual temperature is considerably lower in Pemba, as the following figures will show :

	Max.	Min.
Zanzibar	85·7	77·1
Pemba	81	70·3

The historical vicissitudes of Pemba are obscure, but it is obvious that they must coincide in a great measure with those of the larger island of Zanzibar. Pemba lies farther from the continent, and is more remote than Zanzibar. This is not altogether due to mere mileage, for the actual sea channel which separates the two islands from Africa differs only in breadth by about twelve miles, but these extra miles cause Pemba to be just off the track as well as out of view of vessels passing up and down the coast between Mombasa and Mafia. On the other hand, Zanzibar blocks the way, and cannot very well be avoided, while Pemba lies out of sight in the offing.

As far as the identification of the two islands with the ancient Menouthias of Ptolemy and the *Periplus* is concerned, the above consideration leads one to select Zanzibar rather than Pemba, for there is no doubt that the accessibility of the former island is greater, and is situated in a better position to command the adjacent littoral of the mainland.

That this is so is evident from the past annals of the Azanian coast up to the present time. The history of Pemba is insular, that of Zanzibar is continental.

Pemba is only sixty miles from Mombasa, and its past history has been modified and moulded to some extent by the proximity of the latter important port. That this has been the case, the historical records of the east coast of Africa from the advent of the Portuguese to the coming of the Omân Sultans to Zanzibar demonstrates, and prior to that period circumstances no doubt tended in the same direction.

Pemba has participated in the fluctuating fortunes of East Africa, and she has been subject with the other islands and ports of the littoral to the diverse alien dominations which, since the commencement of the Christian era, have for varying epochs manifested themselves on the coast.

When the ancient Sabaeans held sway over the Azanian coast as far south as the lost town of Rhapta, and Menouthias attracted the Greek and Arab traders from the Red Sea, Pemba must have shared in the trade of the coast, and later, when the Arabs, unified under the banners of Islam, swept through northern and eastern Africa, the Emerald Island of the Indian Ocean received her quota of devout Moslems. Five hundred years later, when Kilwa the Great rose to fame and power, we know that both Zanzibar and Pemba came under that domination, and shared its prosperity.

During the occupation of the Azanian regions by Portugal, the island certainly became Portuguese in the sixteenth century, only at a still later date to fall again under the traditional influence of the rulers of Omân.

The revolt of the Mombasa Arabs against Omân in the eighteenth century brought Pemba once more into close association with Mombasa, until in 1822 she was constrained by force of arms to submit to the Imams of Muscat and Sultans of Zanzibar, whose flag still dominates her.

Closely associated with the history of Pemba are the numerous ruins which are scattered around her coasts.

Compared with the famous ruins of the world they are as nothing, but insignificant as they are, they bear witness to the fact that Pemba has a history, although no written word of it has filtered down to us through the ages.

It may be said at once that as far as can at present be ascertained the ruins in Pemba relate, on a conservative estimate, to the period of the later Middle Ages (twelfth, thirteenth, fourteenth and fifteenth centuries), when the prosperity of the Persian and Arab settlements of the East African coast was at its zenith.

The ruins are not, of course, of African origin, but were built by aliens, who colonised and traded for ivory, slaves, gold, and tortoiseshell, commodities which Africa through the centuries has supplied to the world on such a lavish scale. It is more than probable that the ruins which we see to-day may but mark the sites of still more ancient settlements, and as regards Pemba there appear to be some grounds for believing that more than one race occupied at different epochs the ruined towns which to-day lie nearly forgotten and hidden in her jungles.

II

The two chief settlements in Pemba are at Chake and Weti, both situated on the west coast. These two little towns possess a good water supply derived from two small running streams in the neighbourhood. There are no rivers in the island, although many of the valleys have fresh water running through them, but they are streams of insignificant dimensions, and the majority become lost, ere they reach the sea, in mangrove creeks.

In addition to the two towns above mentioned there is the small Government station at Mkoani in the south-west corner of the island, and considerable native populations congregate in and around the villages of Kengheja, Mtangani, Jambagone in the south, and at Mtangatwani, Chwaka, and Sisini in the north.

Chake, or Chake-Chake, is the largest town in the island, and, if so grandiloquent a term may be applied to it, the "commercial capital" of Pemba. The present population consists of four or five Europeans, 100 British Indians, and 1,000 Arabs and Swahilis.

There are two aspects of Chake. The distant one lends enchantment to the place, and viewed from the opening of Chake Bay it is one of the prettiest-situated towns that I know. The wide entrance to the bay gradually converges wedgewise, until in the dim distance the sea appears to lose itself in the green hills of the land. At the very apex of the watery wedge lies the white town of Chake, standing well above the sea, in a smother of verdure. Any town would look beautiful set in such surroundings.

The other aspect—the near view—is not so entrancing! Having arrived at the end of the wedge-shaped bay, a very muddy creek is encountered, from which at low tide all the water drains out, leaving a mile or so of oozy mud to be traversed; sometimes the town can be approached by transhipping into a canoe, at other times it is best to get through the mud on donkey-back; if all else fails, one has to walk. If the founder of Chake sought to select a spot difficult of access, he succeeded in attaining his end.

The town itself is built on the extreme summit of a ridge surrounded on all sides but one by mangrove swamps. The most interesting feature of the town is the remains of the old Portuguese fort, which commands the landing-place, and is used at present as the district prison. Formerly it was a much more extensive range of buildings, and Burton, writing of his visit in 1857, mentions a round tower as well as the existing rectangular tower. The former tower and much of the fortress walls are no more, having been demolished to make room for the erection of police lines and a Government hospital. It was during this demolition that a gold ring set with a green stone [1] was found in the debris of the walls.

In former times Chake must have been almost impregnable, thanks to the muddy creek and the surrounding swamps. About a mile to the north-west of the town, it is stated that an old Portuguese battery existed, and that the guns are still lying in the bush. At the time of my visit, the jungle was so dense that investigations were difficult, but the discovery of an iron cannon ball evidently of ancient make, in the locality where the battery is said to be, lends some confirmation to the tradition.

On the seaward side of Chake, at a spot where the bay narrows, lies Banani, the head-quarters of the Friends' Industrial Mission. It is beautifully situated amidst plantations of coco-nut and clove trees, and on the estate many emaneipated slaves and their descendants reside.

At the southern point which marks the commencement of Chake Bay is an important Government plantation, and on the estate is a large, old-fashioned Arab mansion which overlooks the sea. Although the house is only about five miles, as the crow flies, from the town of Chake, the place is only approachable by sea, and it is one of the most isolated and lonely spots imaginable. It is said to be haunted, and nothing will induce an Arab or native to sleep in this otherwise eligible mansion : indeed, I believe there are a good many Europeans who have hesitated to do so. The accounts of the actual manifestations differ, but appear to range from footsteps on the stairs to the apparition of a shrouded figure which lurks amidst the dark shadows of the verandah.

About eleven miles to the west of Chake lies a small pear-shaped uninhabited island named Mesali. It is about one mile long and half a mile broad. This islet is referred to by some people as " Captain Kidd's Island," and there is a tradition that it was here that the famous pirate had a depot and buried his treasure. Save for rumour, there is no evidence to show that Captain Kidd ever landed there, but

---

[1] The ring passed into the possession of Archdeacon Farler, who always wore it, but since his death trace of the ring has been lost.

OLD PORTUGUESE FORT, CHAKE-CHAKE, PEMBA.

there is some reason to believe that he did at one time have his head-quarters either in Pemba or on one of the numerous islets along its coast.[1]

With reference to this pirate's connection with Pemba, Burton wrote : " In A.D. 1698 the bold buccaneer Captain Kidd here buried his blood-stained hoards of gold and jewels, the plunder of India and of the further Orient. The people have found pots of ' nuggets,' probably intended for buttons, in order that the pirate might wear his wealth. Thus it is that the modern skipper (1857) landing at Madagascar or other robber haunts of the older day, still frequently witnesses the disappearance of his brass buttons, whilst the edge of a knife resting against his throat secures the quiescence essential to the rapid performance of the operation." [2]

I am not aware on what evidence Baumann and Burton make their assertions relative to Captain Kidd and Pemba, or to the people having found " pots of nuggets " : but this last statement does explain the action of the Zanzibar natives during the visit of H.M.S. *Leopard* and *Orestes* in 1799, in the method of doing business as related by Lieutenant Bissel of the *Leopard*.

Extracts from Bissel's journal have already been given in a previous chapter, and the reader will remember the statement that the Zanzibaris would not accept a guinea in payment for their wares, but readily took a brass button. This certainly looks as if they had heard of gold buttons !

Inquiries at the present time (1918) regarding the finding of " pots of nuggets " by natives meet with no success, and the tradition has evidently quite died out. A story was extant, however, some years ago to the effect that an aged native living in a remote village in the south of Pemba was wont to relate that one night a boat rowed by white men had arrived on the coast near his village ; that they had proceeded to a large baobab tree in the jungle, upon which a cross had been cut by some unknown person long before : that these Europeans had dug at the foot of this tree, and as a result had disclosed a large bowl or dish made of silver

[1] Dr. Oscar Baumann in *Die Insel Pemba*. (Leipsig, 1899.)
[2] *Zanzibar : City, Island, and Coast*, by Richard F. Burton. (London, 1872.)

full of money—another version says that a chest full of money was found—that they carried this treasure down to their boat and disappeared as secretly as they had come. What the exact truth about this episode is will never be ascertained, but it is quite possible that some such incident really happened long ago, and the story has been handed down from father to son, and from generation to generation. In any case it is not a story a native living in a remote corner of Pemba is likely to have invented by himself.

Captain Kidd may of course have made Pemba his base of operations for a time, but from all accounts he was only a comparatively short time filibustering in the Indian Ocean. Apart from this, I have never been able to understand why pirates should have " buried their treasure " : I should have thought that it would have been so much safer on board their own ships under their personal protection. To bury rich silks, for instance, in a tropical island would mean the destruction of the fabric in a few weeks. To conceal " pots of nuggets " would lead to the risk of any disaffected member of the crew deserting, and helping himself at his leisure to the hidden treasure.

The movements of Captain Kidd are fairly well known. His ship the *Adventure* was launched at Deptford in December 1695. He left England in February 1696, and was at the Comoro Islands a year later. He careened ship at Mohilla, one of the Comoro group, and it is stated that he lost fifty of his men in a week, presumably from fever or cholera. At Johanna, another of the Comoro Islands, he found four East Indiamen outward bound filling up with water. These he did not molest, as they were heavily armed.

After cleaning the hull of the *Adventure*, he left on April 25th, 1697, for India, via the Red Sea. This course would have led him past Pemba, although the usual track of the East Indiamen bound for Surat lay some hundred miles to the eastward of that island. Captain Kidd, however, could not have lingered long off Pemba, for after lying off the entrance of the Red Sea with the intention of intercepting the Mocha Fleet he proceeded to the coast of India, and arrived there on September 9th, 1697. He watered at " Carwarr " (Kathiawar ?), and then proceeded to the

Malabar coast, where he intercepted various ships, among them being a rich prize belonging to a Khoja Indian. It was during these operations that he killed one of his crew named William Moore, by hitting him on the head with " a certain wooden bucket, bound with iron hoops, of the value of eightpence." The murder of this man formed one of the counts with which Kidd was eventually charged.

The prizes he obtained are stated to have been taken to St. Marie in Madagascar. This place was the pirate strong-hold of the Indian Seas, and thither resorted all the well-known European buccaneers. No doubt they had their secret haunts elsewhere, but St. Marie was the common resort of most of them at the period of which we are now speaking. The proclamation of November 29th, 1698, by the English Government, offering certain terms of surrender to the filibusterers of the Indian Ocean, refers to " all the pyrates settled in Madagascar."

A misfortune happened to Kidd on his arrival at St. Marie, for ninety of his crew deserted, and went over to the *Moca* frigate, under the command of Captain Culliford, a real pirate of the most brutal character, who a few days later sailed for the Red Sea, " out against all nations."

Kidd, much embarrassed, sailed for England, and finally surrendered himself to Lord Bellamont, the Governor of New England in August 1699, so it will be seen that he was only in the Indian Ocean for a period of eighteen months. He was hanged with one of his crew at Execution Dock on the Thames, on May 23rd, 1701, the rope breaking the first time.

Culliford, who appears to have been a much more villainous and desperate character, was eventually pardoned.

Although Captain Kidd himself may not have resorted to Pemba, it is highly probable that some of the numerous pirates who haunted the Indian Ocean during the sixteenth, seventeenth, and eighteenth centuries did so. The numbers and audacity of these ruffians—both European and Asiatic—during the above-mentioned period is scarcely credible, and the pirate problem became a really serious one. The pirates feared nothing, and instances of French and Dutch men-o'-war being captured are on record.

In 1720, Captain Mackra, commanding one of the East India Company's ships,[1] had a tremendous fight off the Comoros with two vessels manned by European pirates, and although he killed nearly one hundred of them, he had to surrender his ship, and barely escaped with his life. Captain England, who commanded the pirates, was deprived of his command by his own men, owing to his endeavours to save the life of Captain Mackra.

It is related that on one occasion H.M.S. *Centurion*, a 50-gun frigate, was attacked by mistake, under the impression that she was disabled, but on this occasion the pirates received the lesson of their lives!

So much for Captain Kidd and the pirates of the Indian Ocean. After this long digression let us return to Pemba.

III

The only other town of any importance in Pemba Island is Weti, fifteen miles to the north of Chake. A great deal of money has been spent in developing Weti in the hope that the insalubrious Chake might be abandoned, but at present the commercial element prefers the latter place, so European officials are still doomed to reside there.

Weti has a population of about 600 souls, and contains no feature of interest. It is situated on the edge of a cliff of sandy loam about 50 feet in height, which is washed by the waters of Weti Creek.

About a mile from the town is the islet of Mtambwe Kuu with a small native population. On this islet, which is barely 800 yards in length and only 400 yards broad, there are indications of stone buildings, both on the shore and along the steeply scarped plateau which forms the centre of the island. The history of these works is entirely unknown, but the most remarkable factor concerning this isle is that the population is in possession of quantities of Chinese

---

[1] In 1730 most of the East India Company vessels were of 500 tons only. The crew numbered 92, and the ships carried 30 guns—generally 18-pounders or long 12- and 6-pounders. At the close of the eighteenth century the ships were larger and ranged from 1,200 tons. Some carried forty-four 18-pounders.

porcelain-ware, some of which has been stated by the authorities of the Victoria and Albert Museum to be of seventeenth-century manufacture, while other specimens produced by the natives are of Leeds and Staffordshire ware of the early nineteenth century.

The natives explain their possession of this pottery by stating that they or their ancestors found the specimens in the sand at a certain place on the sea-beach of their island.

The spot referred to is strewn with innumerable fragments of Arabian or Syrian glass vessels, and of broken pottery, including specimens of the ancient Chinese Celadon-glazed ware of the Ming dynasty. In addition to the pottery fragments numbers of antique beads composed of polished and faceted semi-precious stones are found, and it may be mentioned that when inspecting this part of the beach I picked up on the sand a red carnelian ring stone, together with fragments of gold jewellery.

How this variety of articles, including pottery of the fifteenth century, comes to be concentrated on this tiny and remote islet of Mtambwe Kuu, whither Europeans seldom come, is at present a mystery. That it was occupied at one time by some superior race is evident from the remains of the masonry work and the vestiges of cement which still exist, and one can only suggest that, as in the case of other ruins in the Zanzibar Protectorate, it was for several hundred years a depot—probably fortified—where foreign traders stored their goods, which they used in barter for the ivory and other merchandise of the mainland.

Such island-depots would only have been necessary at the period prior to the establishment of permanent trading stations and cities on the continental littoral, and it would therefore appear probable that the masonry remains at Mtambwe, and at other similar island depots, are of ancient date.

To account for the existence of the late medieval and more modern pottery, including the Leeds and Staffordshire ware of the late eighteenth or early nineteenth century, one must turn for explanation to the presence of British, Indian, and Arab vessels in Pemba waters, either as traders or, in the case of early British pottery, to the visits of surveying-ships of the Royal Navy or Indian Marine, which did as a matter of fact visit Pemba in about 1822.

The fact that specimens of early Staffordshire ware can be produced at the present day unbroken, at a place like Mtambwe Kuu, after being in the possession of natives for one hundred years or so, at first appears improbable, but their existence can be accounted for, owing to the natives themselves having their own fashions in China ware, and preferring these latter to the patterns they are not used to. It is, for instance, quite comprehensible that a native would find very little use for a lustre-ware mug with a handle, and this being so, it would be put away in some dark corner of his hut, and remain there until some European came along ready to give the owner a few rupees for it. In some instances the pottery may have been found in the sand of the beach, but it seems more likely that these specimens have come into the possession of the present owners through their ancestors, and have remained unused. The natives of Mtambwe are too primitive and their island is too far removed from association with Europeans to raise any doubts as to their good faith in the matter, but it is certainly a curious fact that in this small islet alone these specimens of antique and early English pottery, not to mention the remnants of Persian and Arab glass-ware, are to be found.

Mkoani, a small port in the south-western corner of the island, is the only other Government station where a European resides. From this place a very large quantity of cloves is exported.

The population of Pemba Island is estimated to number 80,000, and of this total only about twenty are Europeans, who are employed either in the Government service or as workers in the Anglican or Quaker Missions.

As in Zanzibar Island it is not always easy to distinguish the difference in physical traits between the original inhabitants and the mixed breed known as Swahili. The so-called Wapemba are of doubtful origin, and it appears likely that the majority are descended from some tribe originating from the mainland of Africa. It will be remembered that Barreto de Rezende, writing in 1635, tells us that the population of Pemba consisted of " Moors and natives of Africa," the

A PEMBA BULL-FIGHT, A RELIC OF THE OLD PORTUGUESE OCCUPATION.

319

latter having been brought to the island by the former, to assist in cultivation. It is generally considered that the Wahadimu of Zanzibar and the Wapemba are akin, and from Rezende's account there can be little doubt but that both these sections of the population of the Zanzibar Protectorate are mainly African. If indeed there ever was an aboriginal race inhabiting the island, any individual and racial characteristics have been merged into the common type of the Swahili.

The Wapemba, like the Wahadimu of Zanzibar, claim descent from the Shirazi settlers of old time, and from the numerous Shirazian ruins in the island it is not difficult to perceive that in their veins there may be a strain of alien blood derived from the sojourn in their midst of Semitic and possibly Aryan races.

The people of Pemba still retain among their amusements a most interesting memento of the occupation of the island by the Portuguese during the sixteenth and seventeenth centuries. This consists in a bull-fight evidently based on the Iberian model, and carried out with many of the accompaniments of the real thing. For instance, elaborate grandstands are erected for the more important spectators, and the safety of the ladies is ensured by their being penned together in a strongly constructed stockade. The attack, too, on the bull is undertaken with the aid of cloths, which are fluttered in front of him, and the native matadors seek to induce the admiration of the onlookers by posturing and even kneeling before the bull in a spirit of bravado, precisely as is done in modern bull-fights in Portugal. It must be admitted that the chief performers at these entertainments exhibit a high degree of skill and agility in eluding the rushes of the bull at the last moment, and it is only occasionally that the latter has the satisfaction of getting his attack home on the chin or on the softer portions of the toreador's anatomy. I presume it is needless to remark that the bull, which is always a young one without horns, is not killed, tortured, or injured in any way, and the limit of his martyrdom is a mild bewilderment at the antics of the " bull-fighters," who endeavour to bestir him to make an occasional rush in their direction. The whole affair is

merely a romp or " rag," and the utmost damage that is
done is when some dusky toreador trips up, and for a moment
lies prone and open to the attack of the bull. Such a mishap creates roars of laughter, while the ladies in their enclosure redouble their shouts and applause, and the native
band of musicians add to the general din.

Like their cousins the Wahadimu and Watumbatu of
Zanzibar Island, the people of Pemba are of a retiring disposition, and it is soon apparent to the visitor that the
latter possess characteristics which are lacking in the mixed
races which compose the population of Zanzibar. The true
Wapemba are independent, and the younger men, while
perfectly respectful to Europeans, give evidence of a high
spirit, and even of a good-natured rowdiness when excited,
which is in marked contrast to the general apathy of the
Zanzibar youth.

The method of cheering or rather of giving vocal expression to the exuberance of their feelings may be mentioned, as
it certainly differs from that generally in vogue among the
inhabitants of the Central African region. When a number
of young Wapemba are highly excited they suddenly run
together, and when thus clustered round each other and
with their heads almost in contact they utter a series of
loud yelps, not unlike the barking of dogs. They then rush
off for about fifty yards, cluster together again and repeat
the performance.

Since the Portuguese quitted the island at the close of
the seventeenth century or during the early years of the
eighteenth century, the people of Pemba have seen but
little of Europeans, and they have had less opportunity than
the Swahili of Zanzibar or Mombasa of enlarging their under-
standings or views of life by contact with other races. One
consequence is that they have retained to a great extent
beliefs and practices which in more civilised places inspire
but a limited credence, and it is certain that any proselytising
their old Portuguese masters may have indulged in has left
no mark upon the morals or beliefs of the people.

In fact, the natives of Pemba possess a sinister reputation
as to their dealings in both white and black magic ; and such
is the repute of their wizards, that it is commonly asserted

that natives from other parts of Africa resort to the island for the purpose of being initiated into the higher and more subtle branches of the black art. From all accounts the witchcraft practised in Pemba is more than the mere " Mumbo-Jumbo " and charlatanism of the ordinary African medicine-man, and it appears to involve all classes of the native population, while in certain instances Europeans are reputed to have experienced evidences of the malign influences which deeply permeate native existence in Pemba.

In writing on a subject such as this, it is of course easy to belittle the seriousness of the whole matter, and it is on the other hand as easy to exaggerate its importance, but the fact remains that the belief in the existence of an advanced form of wizardry in Pemba is firmly established in the native mind both in the island and in Zanzibar.

When a whole population live under the spell and apprehension of a widely diffused and powerful influence in which they firmly believe, it is obvious that definite evidence of malpractices is hard to obtain, for the native police are afraid to take action against the heads of the confederacy, for by so doing they imagine that they will inevitably run the risk of invoking upon themselves and families the vengeance of the masters of magic. The lower-class Arabs and Indians similarly prefer to let sleeping dogs lie, and thus efforts to ascertain the full extent of the evil are thwarted at the initial stages.

Magic as organised in Pemba appears to be divided into three classes or grades. In the first we have the " medicine man," the word " medicine " being used in its widest sense, and signifying the exercise of white magic. This includes the concocting of love philtres, charms, and amulets, the exercise of geomancy, the forecasting of propitious days for social events, the dispensing of " medicine " to keep thieves away, and the sale of other compounds to make thieves invisible while engaged in their nefarious occupations. Added to these practices the medicine man would probably be ready to advise as to the recovery of stolen property, and to point out the person responsible for the death of cattle or other domestic afflictions, and in addition he might also be prevailed upon to cast spells on people to their detriment.

The next class of wizard is more dangerous and malevolent. He is the Mchawi or wizard if a man, and witch if a woman. They are supposed to work in societies, and they are the ministers of evil, who keep alive the belief in devil worship, which cult is understood to be so prevalent in Pemba.

The Mchawi have assimilated a certain amount of the magic lore of Arabia and the East, and have grafted it to the knowledge which has been handed down to them from their African ancestors. Thus we find in their practices much reminiscent of the horrible and foul customs common to the witch doctors of Africa, as, for instance, the exhumation of the dead, the eating of putrid human flesh, and the making of potent charms from disinterred corpses.

Their meetings are reputed to be held at night, and they are said to be summoned to their unholy feasts by the cry of the owl, or in Africa by the bark of the fox. It has been asserted on good authority that in Pemba the members of these societies have a curious and weird custom of assembling in large numbers at night, and barking like dogs for several hours without ceasing, with the idea apparently of scaring away strangers—including Europeans of course—from the vicinity of their haunts.

This class of wizard is said to prepare charms and poison from corpses, by hanging the body to a tree until it become putrid, and then with the rotten flesh and the brains compounding their filthy concoctions. The poison thus obtained is supposed to be of the most potent type, and it and other charms are stated to be sent for occasionally by persons in Zanzibar for evil purposes.

Added to the dispensing of charms and poisons, the Mchawi possess hypnotic power in varying degree, and it is probably the exercise of this power which is their most important asset in maintaining their hold over their victims, and in perpetuating and enhancing their reputations.

Among the Pemba people witchcraft is said to be hereditary, and it is common to both sexes, those possessing diabolical powers being known instinctively to each other.

Thus mutually attracted, they mate, and sometimes transmit their magical powers to their offspring.

Among the native beliefs concerning these Pemba wizards are that they possess the power of making themselves invisible, and that they can travel great distances in a fraction of time, riding on a straw both by land and sea. This is strangely similar to the witch's broomstick of Europe. They are also credited with the power of themselves assuming or of changing another person into the form of some animal.[1]

Should any person wish to join the fraternity, he is first obliged to take a fearful oath not to divulge any of the secrets of the brotherhood. No one can be admitted unless married, and he must have children or relatives near akin, for he is bound to give one of his family as a sacrifice when ever required to do so. At his initiation he is taken to a burial-ground, and is forced to lie in an open grave with a dead body by his side : if he passes through this ordeal and other nerve-racking tests without flinching, he is further initiated into the deeper mysteries of the cult.

The most significant manifestation of the grip which sorcery and black magic have on the bulk of the population of Pemba is stated to be the existence of guilds composed of those who believe, practise, or tolerate devil-worship. As may be supposed, natives who have become Christians in Pemba are peculiarly liable to persecution and annoyance at the hands of the master-wizards, and it is when such cases occur that some of the truth concerning the prevalence of belief in witchcraft comes to light. Occasionally cases have occurred when Christian natives have reverted to paganism, and have themselves become initiated members of these witch guilds. As such, they, with their intelligence sharpened by the education imparted by a mission, prove to be the most dangerous and unscrupulous type of guild member. Nominally the bulk of the people of Pemba profess to be Moslems, but to some extent at any rate their belief is believed to be obscured and partially nullified by the credence they give to witchcraft and to the practices arising therefrom. In some instances their religion may be said to be a form of devil-worship, and it is stated by those who

---

[1] This is a universal belief among the natives of Central Africa.

have made a special study of the subject that both Arabs and Indians alike rely on its powers and share its mysteries.

It is obvious that extreme caution is necessary in dealing with witchcraft cases in the law courts, for an acquittal simply implies to the native mind that the magical powers of the accused are more potent than the European magistrate who administers the law of the land.

The stable product of Pemba is of course the clove, and the greater portion of the western side of the island is covered with plantations of this spice tree. In no part of the world do cloves grow with greater luxuriance or in greater profusion than in Pemba. The clove harvest is a busy time, and to cope with a large crop, thousands of natives are sent from Zanzibar to assist the local pickers. Many of the trees now bearing are eighty or ninety years old, for, as already related, Pemba escaped the great cyclone of 1872 which devastated the clove plantations of Zanzibar.

The coco-nut palm continues to grow in favour in Pemba, and the export of copra is increasing every year. This is regarded as a somewhat unfortunate sign, for it means that instead of maintaining the clove plantations upon which the whole prosperity of the Sultanate depends, the Arab and native plantation owners are turning their attention to the easily cultivated and accommodating coco-nut.

There is a diminutive variety of coco-nut palm which grows in Pemba. It is a pretty and well-proportioned little palm, and the nuts, which are of a beautiful golden colour, often grow as low as 8 or 12 feet from the ground.

Among other specimens of Palmaceae in Pemba are the areca nut (*Areca catechu*), the doom palm (*Hyphoene thebaica*), the wild date (*Phoenix senegalensis*), from the leaves of which fine mats are made, and the West African oil palm (*Elaeis guineensis*), which grows half-wild in the bush. A feature of the Pemba landscape is the palmyra or borassus palm (*Dis chrostachysutans*, Benth.) which grows to an enormous size. They appear to thrive equally well on the small coralline islets which fringe the coast, as in the interior of the island. They form conspicuous clumps, and seem to be always in evidence in the vicinity of the groups of ruins ; but whether their growth in these localities is primarily due to the ancient inhabitants of the ruined towns, or is merely a coincidence, it is difficult to state. Another beautiful palm which is common in Pemba is the raphia (*Raphia pedunculata*).

The orange, various varieties of citron, the jack fruit, and the mango flourish, as do also the sugar-cane, tobacco, and the usual grain and root crops which are cultivated in Zanzibar.

As we have seen, Pemba was famous when the Portuguese were in occupation, during the sixteenth and seventeenth centuries, for its rice, and as recently as the early years of the nineteenth century the island used to export a considerable quantity to Zanzibar. Rice is a troublesome crop to grow, owing to the amount of watching it requires to prevent the depredations of the small " rice bird." The natives of Pemba use various devices to frighten away these and other raiders, and in addition to scarecrows of the universal pattern they employ, with much skill, a sling for the casting of clay pellets. These slings are woven from dried grasses or rushes, and are so manipulated as to crack like a whip when the missile is thrown.

At one time it was hoped that pearl fisheries would prove profitable in Pemba waters, and considerable investigation work was undertaken at considerable expense, but the enterprise was dropped as the reports were unsatisfactory as to the variety of oyster which is found, and as to the prospects of obtaining pearls of value. As in Zanzibar, pearls are occasionally obtained, but they are small and of a poor colour.

CHAPTER XXII

THE NATURAL HISTORY OF ZANZIBAR AND PEMBA

By W. Mansfield-Aders, Ph.D., F.Z.S.

THE visitor to Zanzibar who expects to find an island teeming with animal life is speedily disillusioned. The island fauna is marked by its paucity and lack of gay-coloured forms in contrast to the more abundant animal life of the mainland, and the majority of mammals and birds which do occur are common to the coast from Mombasa to Daresalaam. The fauna of Zanzibar and Pemba has been studied in former years by a number of naturalists, among whom stands out the name of Sir John Kirk, who did so much to advance our knowledge of the African coast fauna and flora.

Among the mammals of Zanzibar three species of monkeys are found, one of them of great interest—the *Colobus kirkii* —a species now considered to be almost extinct in Zanzibar. The chief characteristics of *Colobus kirkii* are that it is smaller than the mainland *Colobus*, and its peculiar colouring, which I venture to describe in full. Its nose and lips are white, its face black ; from the sides of the throat a ring of white hair extends under the ears ; the crown and the back of the head are covered with reddish hair, the shoulders are black, the back reddish-brown, the tail red and towards the tip yellowish, the throat, breast, and abdomen are greyish white.

The majority of the specimens sent to Europe were obtained in the south-east of Zanzibar Island near Jambiani. The Colobi are all arboreal and show a marked partiality for small thickets.

The Colobus lives almost entirely on leaves and a few

COLOBUS KIRKII MONKEY, A RARE SPECIES

THE ELEPHANT-SHREW OF ZANZIBAR.

unripe fruits, refusing to eat any animal food or ripe fruit. These monkeys have not thrived hitherto in captivity, probably on account of an unsuitable diet, but one which I have had in my possession for some months has done well on a diet of various leaves and unripe guavas.

The Blue Monkey (*Cercopithecus albigularis*) is common in many parts of the island, generally living in small, dense copses : on account of their sombre colouring and retiring habits they are not easily detected, but on the approach of man to their haunts they emit a loud guttural bark, instantly betraying their whereabouts. These monkeys abound on the island of Tumbatu, and do an immense amount of damage to the millet and maize crops. The little Grey Monkey (*Cercopithecus rufoviridis*) or "Tumbili" of the natives, rare in Zanzibar, is quite common in Pemba. They make charming pets, and a number have been taken to Europe.

There are at least two species of Galagos (the commonest is *Galago garnetti*), more commonly called Lemurs, found in the Protectorate. I am inclined to believe that there is a certain amount of seasonal variation in their colouring which makes the recognition of species difficult : when they descend to the ground they sit up on their haunches, and move by jumping on their hind legs like Jerboas. The Galagos are interesting as being the only Lemuroids not inhabitants of Madagascar ; they are widely distributed in Africa, ranging from Senegambia to Abyssinia, and as far south as Natal. They are called by the natives " Komba," and occur even in the heart of Zanzibar town, their peculiar strident night-cry being somewhat disturbing. These little creatures are very inquisitive, often venturing on to verandahs and entering rooms. They have a great liking for fermented coco-nut sap called *tembo-kali*, and this powerful intoxicant is often their undoing. The natives place bowls of the sweet-smelling liquor under trees, and the Galagos, thus led into temptation, scramble down, get drunk and incapable, and are easily captured.

Wild pigs are common throughout the two islands, and do great damage to native crops.

The Wild Pig of Zanzibar Island is the common red bush-pig of Africa (*Potamochoerus africanus*) ; the general colouring is reddish, and full-grown specimens have a long blackish-grey mane, and warty knobs on the cheeks above the corner teeth. The young, as usual in all species of wild pig, show pale-brown longitudinal stripes, a characteristic which disappears after the first few months of life.

On the island of Pemba black pigs are found, probably the descendants of a domesticated species left by the Portuguese. I have examined a number of their young and found no trace of striping, though Darwin states that pigs which had run wild in Jamaica had resumed this aboriginal characteristic.

Two small antelopes locally known by the native name " Paa " occur. One of them, *Nesotragus moschatus*, is common in several parts of the island and is also found on many of the small islets near Zanzibar.

A larger one belonging to the Duiker family (*Cephalophus adersi*) is a rare species inhabiting the Chwaka district. At present it is only recorded from the Zanzibar Protectorate. This species has been recently described by Mr. Oldfield Thomas, of the British Museum; the following is an extract from his paper:

" General colour of withers and nape dark brown, which gradually becomes more rufous on the shoulders and flanks. Under surface whitish ; a mesial rufous patch on the chest. Fore limbs with the rufous of the shoulders passing down without interruption, but on the hind quarters there is a broad whitish band, running across the outer side of the hips and separating the chestnut red of the rump from the rather pale red of the legs ; this band is more or less rufous white where it commences on the sides above the inguinal glands, but becomes nearly pure white posteriorly, where it contrasts prominently with the mahogany-red rump. Tail, without tuft, about two inches long, the tuft well marked, its hairs rather more than an inch long, wholly white, though there is a narrow rufous line running along the tip of the tail basally."

One of the most interesting mammals is the Tree-Coney (*Dendrohyrax neumanni*). This peculiar animal abounds on the islands of Tumbatu and Fundo, and is also found on the coralline rocky plains of the main islands. This species, sombre in colour, is not unlike a large rabbit, and can always be recognised by a patch of greyish hairs on the middle of the back. They are extremely difficult to detect, generally hiding in dense trees, closely assimilating to the colour, and almost seeming to be a part of the branch on which they crouch down with their pad-like feet tucked under them. At night they sleep in holes in trees. Their food consists of tender young plant shoots. From a zoological point of view these animals are of great interest : they have a certain resemblance to rodents, but in reality are closely allied to the Rhinoceros by their dentition, and in the reduction of the digits of the foreleg to four, and of the hindleg to three.

The large carnivora are represented in the Protectorate by the Leopard. In certain parts of the island these animals are still fairly abundant, and take toll of the native goats. The natives, as in other parts of Africa, build large wooden traps, and when an unfortunate leopard is captured, its eyes are generally seared before it is dispatched.

The Civet Cat (*Viverra orientalis*) is quite common. The pelt is thick and coarse, and a long erectile mane extends from the neck to the base of the tail ; the general colour is grey with black spots which form badly defined transverse stripes.

The slender-bodied Genet Cat (*Viverra megaspila*) with its conspicuous spotted marking is quite common : it is much smaller than the Civet.

The Mungoose (*Herpestes gracilis*), called by the natives " Cheche," is abundant everywhere ; this small mammal is far oftener seen than any of those previously mentioned, especially towards sunset, when it moves about freely and seems quite fearless of man.

The striped or Zebra-Mungoose (*Crossarchus fasciatus*), the " Mcheiro" of the Swahili, has been recorded; but as these animals are imported in numbers from the coast as pets, I am inclined to think that the few which have been observed are escaped individuals.

The Bdeogale (*Bdeogale tenuis*), a curious mungoose-like mammal, is quite common round Zanzibar town. Its chief characteristic is that the digits are reduced to four on both fore and hind limbs. Its diet consists chiefly of large land-snails.

The rodents of the Protectorate are not very numerous, comprising only one species of squirrel, a giant rat, and the usual ubiquitous house-rats and mice. The Squirrel (*Paraxerus palliatus lastii*) is a pretty little creature with a greyish back and red bushy tail ; it occurs chiefly in the south of Zanzibar Island. For a long time I was anxious to obtain a live specimen, but all the efforts of my collectors failed. Eventually I was driven to try an ordinary rat-cage suitably baited, and, much to my surprise, four fine squirrels were captured.

The Giant Rat (*Cricetomys gabianus*) or *buku* of the natives is a loathsome, foul-pelted creature ; some of them measure nearly 3 feet from snout to end of tail.

The insectivora are represented by three species. The large Elephant-Shrew (*Rhynchocyon adersi*), the most handsome species, was first found in the south of Zanzibar Island and proved to be new to science. The colouring of this weird animal is remarkable. The crest on its head is of deep chocolate-maroon, the shoulders dark brown, the hind quarters and back deep black, the long snout rufous. These shrews are very retiring in their habits, living in dense bush.

Another small Shrew is *Petrodomus sultani*, a species somewhat rarer than the former, and lighter in colour.

A little Shrew-Mouse (*Pachyura murina*) is a common denizen of the town, living in association with the common house-rats.

A remarkable sight towards sunset is the flighting of the large, ungainly Flying Foxes (*Pteropidae*) from the islets in the harbour to the main island, to feed on the various fruits, and to return at the first sign of dawn. Thousands have their habitat on Bat Island, a small coral islet overgrown with bush in Zanzibar Harbour, where if disturbed in the daytime they darken the sky by their numbers, uttering strident squeaks of resentment. The females carry their young in a most humanlike fashion clasped to their breasts. The natives of Pemba are extremely fond of the flesh, considering it a great delicacy. There are two common species (*Pteropus voetzkowi* and *Eidolon helvum*), the larger with a beautiful russet-brown fur, and a smaller variety with a greyish fur. There are many varieties of bats, and among them a small species (*Hipposideros commersoni*) of quaint appearance, with peculiar foliated outgrowths around the nostrils.

The birds of the island comprise many beautifully coloured tropical forms. In the town gardens, and almost as common as the house-sparrow in England, is the pretty little Java Sparrow, imported from India many years ago. This bird has become very tame and domesticated, nesting in close proximity to man, sometimes even in the gutters of houses. The Southern Sparrow (*Passer diffusus*) is also frequently met in the town, but its distribution is nothing like so general as the former species. The most ubiquitous of all the town birds is the Indian Crow (*Corvus splendens*), originally imported from India, it is said, by the Parsees for local towers of silence which they proposed to build ; the erection of these towers was forbidden by the reigning Sultan when he learned to what use the birds were to be put, and Zanzibar was left with its Indian Crow.

The large black-and-white African Crow (*Corvus scapulatus*), so common in the country districts, seldom dares to enter the town, having been driven out by his Indian cousin.

Layard's Bulbul (*Pycnonotus layardi*) abounds in all the town gardens ; it is a gregarious and cheerful individual with a monotonous voice, except in the breeding season, when it has a short beautiful song.

The most noticeable and beautiful of all our small birds are the Sunbirds, with their metallic glistening plumage resembling the humming-birds of America. In all gardens these pretty little creatures flit here and there. The male bird of one species (*Cinnyris gutturalis*) has a brilliant red-coloured throat and breast, the female being of a sombre earth-colour, a great contrast to her brilliantly coloured mate. Others are exceedingly small with a brilliant green iridescent plumage. They feed on nectar of flowers, and occasionally on insects. The bills in some species are long and much curved ; the tongue is cylindrical and tubular, eminently suitable for inserting into blossoms to suck up the sweet nectar. During the breeding season they have quite a sweet song, their usual note being a loud and shrill chirp. The nest—a very beautiful object—is suspended from the extremity of a branch : it is pear-shaped and built of grass ornamented with bits of lichen and fibres of plants.

The Fire-Throated Finch (*Pytelia afra*), gentle and very confiding in its habits, is fairly common in open wooded spaces, frequenting bushes and rarely descending to the ground.

The Lesser Tawny Pipit (*Anthus rufulus*), which at first sight by its colouring and habits reminds one of the larks at home, is met with in all open grassy spaces busily hunting, usually in pairs, on the ground for insects. Its song is short and sweet, generally uttered from a branch of a tree. Whydah's Pin-Tailed Finch or Widow Bird (*Vidua serena*) is a conspicuous bird, and is to be seen at all seasons of the year around the town. The male, during the breeding season, has an enormously long tail, the female being dull-coloured with no such appendage. In his courting, the male, who is polygamous, rises into the air, hovers with outstretched wings above the hen, and utters loud twitterings. As far as my experience goes the finches feed entirely on seeds.

The small Love Bird (*Agapornis cana*) is rarely seen in the town, except on the Residency lawn, where it is a constant visitor ; it is a charming pet and lives well in captivity.

The African Roller (*Eurystomus afer*) frequently mistaken for a jay, is often noticed sitting alert like a sentinel on some outstanding bough : suddenly with a swift dart he is seen to pounce on some unfortunate insect, instantly returning to his perch.

The Long-Tailed Roller (*Coracias caudatus*) is generally considered to be the most beautiful bird in the island with its brilliant blue and green colouring and long spatular-shaped tail feathers. The Rollers are often mistaken for jays.

Another very pretty bird is the Long-Tailed Bee-Eater (*Merops persicus*). It is fond of alighting on bare trees, thus producing a startling effect with its brilliant colour.

As in all parts of the world, there are a number of beautiful swallows, the prettiest being the Isabelle (*Hirundo puella*) with its speckled breast and copper-coloured head.

The game birds of the island are none too plentiful, and offer no great attraction to the sportsman, especially he who has wielded a gun on the mainland. The most sought after are guinea-fowls ; of these as far as my experience goes there is only one species (*Numida mitrata*). A number of vulturine guinea-fowls have been imported from the coast, but I have been unable to obtain any authentic records as to their having become merged into the fauna of the Protectorate.

Numida mitrata is to be found on the open coral moorlands or *wanda* country, feeding chiefly in or near the millet fields. The shooting of the guinea-fowl is an arduous undertaking, and generally results in a small bag and boots torn to strips by the razor-like points of the coral rag.

The Spur-Winged Plover (*Hoplopterus* sp.) is very plentiful at certain seasons of the year on the rocky plains in the centre of the island and affords fair sport.

The Pigmy Goose (*Nettapus auritus*) with its gay plumage occurs on various swamps, but is by no means abundant.

Curlew and Whimbrel are extremely shy and very difficult to approach : they abound all along the coast, and in mangrove swamps, and in their company are seen numbers of Curlew-Sanderling, Ring-Plovers, Dotterels and Greenshanks, and an occasional Oyster-Catcher.

The Fruit or Green Pigeon (*Vinago delalandei*) occurs, but its distribution is very local and limited. These birds have a fondness for perching in large bare trees such as the silk-cotton tree. As their name implies, they feed chiefly on wild fruits. This pigeon is much sought after, its flesh being most delicate. There are a number of pigeons and doves, including the Turtle-Dove (*Turtur capricola*) the Half-Collared Turtle-Dove (*Turtur semitorquata*), and the ubiquitous little Spot-Winged Dove (*Chalcopelia afra*), so named from the patch of coppery-green feathers in its wings ; the last-named species is solitary, and very shy, flying away with rapidity when alarmed. Its melancholy cry is one of the commonest bird calls.

The Half-Collared Turtle-Dove, or *Hua* of the Swahilis, is

to be found everywhere; its characteristic cry is said by the natives to resemble the following phrase, " *kuku mfupa tupu mimi nyama tupu* " (the chicken is all skin and bone; I am all flesh).

Among the migrant game birds are the Giant Snipe (*Gallinago major*), and its constant companion, the Painted Snipe (*Rhynchaea capensis*); both are occasional visitors, and a few have been shot after the rains in swamps close to Zanzibar town. On some of the pools both in Zanzibar and Pemba a few ducks are to be seen from time to time. The little Button Quail (*Turnix lepurana*) is, like the snipe, an occasional immigrant. I have never seen any species of Francolin, although a variety (*Francolinus kirkii*) is supposed to exist.

The Herons, which include the Egrets, comprise a number of species. The commonest of all is the Reef Heron (*Ardea gularis*). The bird abounds on all sandy flats along the coast, and is also a common denizen of the mangrove swamps. Its general colouring is slate-grey with a white throat and yellow toes, but a pure white and a speckled species also occur.

The True Egret (*Herodias alba*) is also to be found on both islands, but is by no means common.

An interesting and easy way to study bird life in Zanzibar is to visit one of the marshes close to the town. The bird lover at once notices stalking round the edges the common blue Reef Heron, moving slowly and deliberately. Perching on low trees or shrubs is the shy and wary Squacco Heron (*Ardeola ralloides*), conspicuous with its white throat, wings, and tail, and occasionally as its companion the rare Pigmy Bittern (*Ardetta minuta*).

The next bird to attract attention is the tiny crested Malachite Kingfisher, perhaps the most beautiful of all our local birds. With a sudden dart and very rapid flight a streak of blue and red hovers for a moment over the water, dives, and quickly returns to its perch on some bush at the edge of the swamp.

The common Pied Kingfisher (*Ceryle rudis*), a study in black and white, lifts itself into the air with outstretched wings, hovers for a few seconds, then drops vertically down-

wards to the water, and if fortunate rises with a fish in its
beak. The African Jacana or Lily Trotter (*Phyllopezus
africanus*) with its enormously long toes is seen tripping
over the leaves of the various aquatic plants. On suspicion
of danger it crouches or partially submerges, and if molested
rises reluctantly and scuttles over the water with trailing
legs, uttering its loud, harsh cry. It feeds chiefly on insects
and small molluscs. Its general colouring is a deep
maroon-brown, the frontal shield being a piece of bare skin
light blue in colour at the base of the beak.

Allen's Purple Gallinule (*Porphyrio alleni*) is also a swamp
lover. It is easily recognised by its coral-red feet and
beak, its general colour being a mixture of blue shading
to black.

The Little Grebe or Dabchick (*Podicipes fluviatalis*), a bird
ranging over Europe, Asia, and Africa, is somewhat difficult
to distinguish, diving at the slightest alarm and appearing
again some distance away without leaving a ripple. Its
note is a harsh croak, its general colouring dusky brown
above, silvery white beneath. The reeds surrounding the
swamp are alive with gay-coloured finches and other small
birds, the most notable being the Bishop Bird (*Pyromelana
flammiceps*) which is of the Weaver Tribe. This charming
little bird has a flashing red gorget and scarlet head and
beak, the underside being an inky black. The Weaver
Finches are very sociable, numbers being seen together flitting hither and thither perching on the extremities of the
reeds, which often break under their weight. Their nests
are retort-shaped, and made of a mass of roughish grass
lined with feathers, down, and wool. A smaller species with
the same habits is the Black-Bellied Bishop Bird (*Pyromelana
nigriventer*), whose colouring, however, is nothing like so
conspicuous as that of his larger brother. Of all the Weaver
Birds, the most abundant in Zanzibar is the small orange
species (*Hyphantornis aureoflavus*). These canary-like little
birds live in vast colonies, building dome-shaped nests, hundreds of which may be seen hanging from the leaves of
coco-nut palms. They are most destructive to crops, and
in harvest time descend in countless numbers on to the rice
fields.

Among the commoner and more conspicuous birds of the Sultanate is the Lesser Hornbill (*Lophoceros melanoleucus*) ; this bird, with its slow, heavy flight, seeming almost to be weighed down by its huge bill, is very local in its distribution, and I have only seen it in the extreme south of the island of Zanzibar, where it is plentiful.   In the same distriet, but far commoner in Pemba, is the only Parrot of any size, the Dusky-Headed Parrot (*Poecephalus fuscicapillus*) ; its general ground-colour is green and its head brown.   These parrots fly with great rapidity, and are extremely difficult to recognise on the wing ; they are fond of congregating in bare trees, thus enabling the bird-lover to observe them at leisure.   One of the commonest birds in the Protectorate is the large brownish-coloured Lark-Heeled Cuckoo (*Centropus superciliosus*), the *Tipputibi* of the natives, which with its long tail may be seen sailing with outstretched wings across an open space to alight immediately in some dense bush, where in spite of its size it is not easy to follow.   I have dissected a number of these birds, and found the stomach full of various plant bugs and grasshoppers, thereby proving their great use to the agriculturist.

The Bronze Cuckoo (*Chrysococcyx cupreus*) with its metallic green colouring is a beautiful object.   The natives maintain that it lays its eggs in the nests of Weavers, but this I doubt, as most of the Weavers feed their young on grain and the Cuckoo is insectivorous.

One of the prettiest of the small birds is the Paradise Flycatcher (*Tersiphone cristata*), which has a black crest on its head, and dark russet-brown plumage, the tail being of a similar colour and of great length.   The Red-Headed Woodpecker (*Dendropicus zanzibaricus*) is only very occasionally seen, being most retiring in its habits.   Its most noticeable feature is a red patch of feathers at the base of the head, and its speckled plumage recalls its cousins in Europe.   Another rare bird is the Glossy Starling (*Lamprocolius* sp.) with its wonderful iridescent plumage.   I have only seen a few on the east coast of the island.   The noisy and gregarious Woodhoope (*Irrisor erythrorhynchus*) foregathers in noisy gossiping groups on coco-nut trees.   Their piercing, laugh-like note is accompanied by most amusing bowings.   Their plumage is a beautiful iridescent blue-black ; their long tail is blue speckled with white, and their red beak long and curved.

The ubiquitous Barn Owl (*Strix flammea*), its plumage identical with that of the British bird, is found everywhere

The Nightjar (*Cuprimulgus fossei*), with its wide gaping mouth and soft brownish colouring, is a common sight at dusk, flitting silently a short distance and alighting again immediately.

The Kingfishers are well represented, and I have already described two species in my account of the bird life which can be observed near the fresh-water pools.

The Striped Kingfishes (*Halcyon cheliculensis*) is a solitary little fellow, with somewhat sombre colouring, very fond of perching on telephone wires, and is a true land Kingfisher feeding on insects ; another species, more brilliant and much rarer, is the Senegal Kingfisher (*Halcyon senegalensis*), conspicuous by its red beak.   It is a lover of wet, swampy ground, and, like the Striped Kingfisher, is insectivorous.

The Black Drongo (*Buchanga assimilis*), with its markedly forked tail and glossy black plumage, is common.   These birds are generally seen in pairs, and are fond of settling on exposed or dead branches of trees.   After the burning of grass by the natives they flock to the spot to feed on the innumerable insects which have been driven forth by the smoke.

The common scavenging birds are the African Black-and-White Crow (*Corvus scapulatus*) and the Egyptian Kite (*Milvus aegyptius*).   The former is common everywhere ; the latter with its soaring flight is to be seen any day sailing over the harbour.   The sacred Ibis (*Ibis aethiopica*) is an occasional migrant.   One was shot close to the town by my collector, who was attracted to the bird's haunt by its weirdly querulous cry.

Two species of eagles occur—one large speckled brown, and the common whitish Fish Eagle.

Among the reptilia of the Protectorate there are, fortunately, very few poisonous snakes ; the only one I have noticed is the Black-Throated Cobra (*Naja nigricollis*), which is common in the island of Pemba, but of which very few specimens have been obtained from Zanzibar.   This cobra

22

is extremely fierce when cornered, rearing and expanding its hood, and has also the unpleasant habit of spitting venom, which it ejects in the form of a fine spray, straight at the face of its aggressor.

Other species of venomous snakes have been recorded, namely, *Elapechis niger*, and one species of ground-adder (*Atractaspis irregularis*), but I have never found them and surmise they are not plentiful. The Puff Adder (*Bitis arietans*) one of man's deadliest foes, and so common in Africa, happily does not seem to exist in Zanzibar. There are a number of small harmless grass-snakes which, as in other parts of Africa, are considered venomous by the natives. A very beautiful species is the Green Tree-Snake (*Philothamnus semivariegatus*), whose long tail is whip-like and admirably adapted for its arboreal life. The common House-Snake (*Boodon lienatus*) is ubiquitous.

Pythons, the " Chatu " of the natives, are common, and specimens measuring up to 15 feet have been obtained from various localities. They are also found on some of the smaller islands in the harbour and off the coast.

Among the lizards figures the large Monitor (*Varranus niloticus*), commonly and wrongly called an Iguana; some of these attain a length of 4 feet. The skin is very prettily marked, being a greenish grey above, with darker reticulation, and yellowish ocellated spots on the back and limbs. This monitor is semi-aquatic, being generally found in reeds and bush near swamps. Natives hunt and kill them, as they are great chicken robbers. There are no other interesting lizards except the small Geckos, so common on the walls and ceilings of our houses. Probably two species of Chameleons exist ; the natives are absurdly frightened of them, believing them to be most venomous. Crocodiles, so far as my experience goes, are not indigenous in the Protectorate. Recently a large specimen measuring 7 feet 11 inches was found and shot on the sea-beach at Chwaka, a village on the east coast of Zanzibar Island. There has been much discussion as to how this monster arrived there, and I. personally think it was washed over from the African mainland.

As in all tropical seas, there are numbers of beautifully coloured fish, the most striking being the Parrot Wrasses.

W. Mansfield-Aders.

THE " NGURU
(*Acanthocybium Commersoni*).

W. Mansfield-Aders.

THE " KOLI-KOLI "
(*Caranx sp.*).

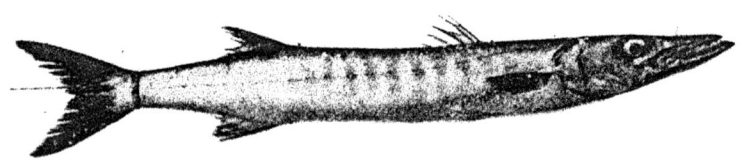

W. Mansfield-Aders.

THE BARRACOUTA
(*Sphyræna sp.*).

Among the game fish are the Horse-Mackerels and the Barra-couta, which afford excellent sport for the fisherman. The best fighter is the " Nguru " (*Acanthocybium commersoni*) ; many of them weigh 50 lb. or more, and put up a game struggle when caught with a rod and tarpon tackle. The " Kolikoli," a smaller species of Horse-Mackerel, is also a plucky fighter. The Horse-Mackerels are sold daily in the Zanzibar fish-markets, their flesh being firm and of excellent flavour. They are caught by the natives by trolling from dhows, and sometimes in drift nets. Large Whip-Rays are common in shallow water ; they are great enemies of the oyster beds. Their flesh, although coarse, is much relished by the natives. Sharks of considerable size are often caught, and there is a great trade in dried shark, a special market being set aside for the sale of this evil-smelling commodity. Hammer-Head Sharks are common.

Large Sea-Eels, often mistaken for sea-snakes, belonging to the family *Muraena* abound in rocky holes ; some of them are wonderfully marked with intricate patterns of lines and circular spots. They are armed with formidable pointed teeth, and have been known to attack human beings. Among other denizens of the sea are the Turtles. The Hawksbill Turtle (*Chelonia imbicata*), the carapace of which is the tortoise-shell of commerce, is occasionally captured. The Green or Edible Turtle (*Chelone mydas*) is common near the coast, and visits the adjacent uninhabited islets to lay its eggs. Among molluscans, nearly all of which are eaten by the natives, a small Rock Oyster and the true Pearl Oyster (*Margaratifera vulgaris*) are abundant, and small seed-pearls are often found.

Cassis rufa, a large shell, the lips of which are of a rich red colour, is very common. These shells are collected, and exported to Italy for cameo-cutting, under the trade name of Bull's Mouth.

The Sea Slugs or *Holothurians*, the *bêche-de-mer* of commerce, abound on all sandy beaches. A small colony of Chinamen have settled in Pemba, who collect and dry these delicacies for export to their native country.

A number of edible crustaceans occur : the most sought after are crawfish, crabs, and prawns, all of which are very palatable.

PART III

CHAPTER XXIII

THE RUINS OF ZANZIBAR AND PEMBA

1

BEFORE describing the ruins in the islands of Zanzibar and Pemba a word of warning is desirable, lest anticipation run too high.

They are not ruins great in extent ; they are not massive ruins ; they are not beautiful—save with the beauty which is one of the attributes of age : in fact, compared with the great ruins of the world they are very humble ruins. And yet they are of interest, because their history is that of Zanzibar, and these ruined towns—the very names of which are now forgotten—hold within their confines the secrets of the past, and as we all know,

It is the mystery of the unknown that fascinates us.

And besides, it is not so easy nowadays to light upon groups of ruins, even although they may be only some six hundred years old, which have never been examined, never excavated, and possibly in some instances never seen by European eyes.

Insignificant as these ruins are, the " mystery of the unknown " enshrouds them; and while their full history still remains to be written, the following description of their present condition will at least furnish an interim record, until opportunity occurs for their thorough and systematic exploration.

It may be remarked at once that the ruins about to be described are chiefly those of towns founded by Persian and Arabian settlers during the twelfth and subsequent centuries—a period when the Persian-founded kingdom of

Kilwa, and the numerous other sultanates scattered along the Azanian coast, attained their greatest prosperity.

There is no need here to reiterate all that has been said already concerning the commercial relations which existed between these African coast-towns and Asia. Slaves, ivory, and gold were among the products which Africa has supplied to the Eastern world from the earliest times ; and the gold-trade of Sofala was a lure which induced Asia, and at a later period Europe, to turn their attention to the east coast of Africa, with the result that while the gold-argosies passed northwards along the coast with their treasure, the prosperity and affluence of the Azanian coast-cities waxed great, for each ruler levied a tax in kind, as a return for the accommodation and shelter their harbours afforded to the treasure-fleets from Sofala.

We have already seen from the *Periplus of the Erythraean Sea*, and from the works of Claudius Ptolemy, that important trade-emporia existed upon the Azanian coast during the first century of the Christian era, and the incursion and immigrations of Persians and Arabs in the tenth century merely perpetuated or re-established these ancient trade-centres.

It is known as a historical fact that during the middle of the thirteenth century trade was extremely active on the west coast of India and in the Arabian Seas, and it would have been strange if East Africa had not shared in the general extension of commerce at this period. There is indeed evidence that a Chinese fleet paid a visit to the Azanian coast about A.D. 1270, and also at subsequent dates : and the tangible evidences of the direct connection of China with East Africa during the later Middle Ages are to be found in the numerous Chinese coins which are, from time to time, picked up on the coast, as well as in the vast quantity of Chinese pottery which litters every ruined site.

Dr. Friedrich Hirch, of Munich, has assigned dates to many of these Chinese coins discovered on the East African coast, and the periods in question range from the K'ai-yuan Dynasty of A.D. 713–742 to that of Shau-hing between A.D. 1131 and 1163.

As pointed out in a previous chapter, it is probable that while comparatively remote islands, as Zanzibar and Pemba, would be selected by new-comers for settlement, they would also be the first places to be abandoned when conditions of trade and of existence became more settled and established on the mainland.

If this is true, then it appears likely that there may have been settlements on Zanzibar and Pemba before the cities on the continent were founded.   This idea obtains some degree of confirmation by the native tradition that the town on Tumbatu Island was built before a settlement was made at Kilwa.   This latter place, the capital of an important State, was, we know, founded in A.D. 975, and Mogdishu and Brawa probably before that date.

However this may be, the reasons which induced settlement on such islands as Zanzibar and Pemba are fairly evident.

With regard to the navigation of the East African coast, the periodical monsoons are the dominant factor, and there can be no doubt but that ships from India and the East sailed southwards to Azania during the season of the northeast trades, and returned home during the south-west monsoon, even as hundreds of native craft do at the present day.

Vessels from the Persian Gulf, Arabia, India, and even from the Far East came with trade-goods to obtain ivory and other produce from the negro races inhabiting the coast.   It was not a matter, as at present, of calling at a coast-port, taking on board a cargo, and sailing home again in a few weeks.

Under modern conditions, native ships either find their cargoes waiting for them or the merchandise they seek can be purchased at the hundred-and-one stores which stock nearly every class of commodity the Western world supplies. In ancient times, however, the traders came with their goods, and their first efforts were directed towards obtaining the goodwill and friendship of the native chiefs and sultans, who controlled the coast-ports and the routes to the interior of the continent.

It will be remembered that the author of the *Periplus*

tells us that wine was brought in ships from Egypt, not, he explains, for sale, but solely for the purpose of cajoling and obtaining the goodwill of the negro chiefs. After a period of negotiation, it may be assumed that ivory and other produce began slowly to arrive from the interior ; and during the process of bargaining and collecting merchandise, the ship and its cargo of trade-goods must always have been liable to attack by the coast-natives, or by some treacherous chief. The ship, before starting on her return voyage, would certainly have to be careened and her hull cleaned, a proceeding fraught with peril if the natives were inclined to be hostile. Moreover, the ports on the Azanian coast must have possessed, under the conditions then existing, many disadvantages for a prolonged stay.

Lamu, Mombasa, Kilwa, and others were just traps if the chiefs of those places were treacherously inclined. A vessel once inside these havens could never leave without the sanction of the local ruler : and it is evident that a trading vessel was in constant danger as long as she was liable to the whims and guile of the negro potentates, who before the Arab and Persian settlement dominated the coast.

The way out of these difficulties was obvious, and traders from Asia and Egypt found, in such islands as Zanzibar and Pemba, the safety which the coast-ports often failed to afford.

The situations of the two islands referred to were almost ideal as trading centres for the African coast. Seyyid Said of Omân realised this fact nearly a thousand years after the first Arabian and Persian settlers had done so, and to-day the advantages of Zanzibar as the chief trade-port of the east coast is still patent to all.

To seafaring people the distance to the mainland was as nothing, and yet their ships and their merchandise were safe from attack from the negro. The islands, too, possessed excellent harbours, and plenty of good drinking water. If there were indigenous inhabitants they were not numerous, and in any case the many small islets off the coasts of Zanzibar and Pemba afforded excellent sites for defensive works. Fish, turtle, and probably some game were always obtainable ; the soil was fruitful ; and lastly, but not least, the climate was infinitely more healthy for a prolonged sojourn than that of the mainland.

No wonder, then, that the early traders from Asia founded towns and trade-depots in Zanzibar and Pemba.

At these depots their trade-goods for barter were stored, and the ivory and slaves and other produce which they sought up and down the coast were collected ready for shipment. It may be supposed that their ships were either dismantled and laid up, until the time came for the return voyage, as is the case-to-day, or perhaps, after discharging their cargoes of trade-goods, they sailed home again, to return in due course with further supplies.

The island-depots, in course of time, became permanent stations with a permanent population. With regard to these ancient settlements in Zanzibar and Pemba, there is no doubt about the permanency of occupation. The towns, it is evident from the ruins, were of an enduring and substantial character. The houses were well built of stone and mortar, and certainly some were more than one story in height. Large mosques of elaborately finished masonry are a feature of these ruined towns, while the attention paid to the sanitation of the dwelling-houses clearly indicates that the dwellers had attained a high state of civilisation.

That they possessed beautiful articles in their houses is also manifest, from the innumerable pieces of ancient Chinese pottery, and of Syrian and Arabian glass vessels of all shapes, sizes, and colours which now cover the sea-beaches in the vicinity of the ruins ; while the fragments of finely wrought gold ornaments which have been picked up at these sites testify to the wealth and refinement of these ancient settlers.

These fragments of pottery are a valuable aid, as indicating the period during which the towns were thriving. The authorities of the Ceramic Department of the Victoria and Albert Museum have very kindly undertaken the examination of a considerable collection of pottery obtained from the ruined sites, and have identified much of the Celadon glazed-ware as being of the Sung and Ming Dynasties. The first of these periods extends from A.D. 960 to 1279, and the Ming period to 1368. The reader will no doubt appreciate the fact that these evidences as to the antiquity of the Pemba ruins confirms in a remarkable manner what has already been written on the subject.

Another proof of the permanency of these towns is the care bestowed on the burial of the dead, as testified by the existence of elaborate tombs, upon which much skill and care have evidently been lavished.

The first settlements were no doubt on a small scale, and the buildings and store-houses were probably built of perishable material, just as to-day the pioneer colonist builds for himself first the wattle-and-daub hut, to be replaced at a later date by a more permanent and extensive home.

Apart from the general excellence of the workmanship displayed in these ruined towns, two reasons may be adduced which account for the preservation of these ancient Persian and Arab buildings in the jungles of Zanzibar and Pemba.

In the first place the better-preserved remains are built on strata of perfectly drained porous coralline-limestone rock, with the result that the foundations of the buildings are as stable and firm as on the day they were erected. The second factor which has ensured the preservation of these old Persian towns may be looked for in the hardening process which affects the material of which the buildings are composed.

Coralline limestone has a marked propensity to harden with age and exposure to the elements. When excavated from the quarry, the stone is soft, but after some years it becomes extremely hard. The reasons which induce this alteration are chemical ones, and are perfectly well known.[1]

Numerous examples of this induration are common. For instance, the surface of the coral " rag " country is so hard

---

[1] Crossland, in his *Desert and Water Gardens of the Red Sea*, explains the chemical reaction very clearly as follows :

" The continual wetting by spray or rain and drying under the tropical sun has a very marked effect in hardening and consolidating elevated coral or coral sand. The upper parts are dissolved, and as the water sinks into the porous corals, and becomes super-saturated with lime, the latter is crystallised out, thus filling up all cavities with crystalline limestone. Thus in the end the highly porous heterogeneous limestone becomes a rock of exceeding hardness, crystalline and homogeneous."

He points out that the extent of this hardness can be demonstrated by striking the once soft rock with a hammer, when a " clear bell note " is produced.

as to make walking over it even in boots almost impossible ; and if the piles of coralline limestone stacked for purposes of road repairs in the open air by the roadside be examined, it will be found that the once soft and crumbly stone has become crystallised, and of such an intense hardness as to lacerate the hand unless picked up with care.

This process of hardening occurs in buildings composed of coralline limestone and lime-mortar which are exposed for a long time to the air and rain [1]: so that, although such a building will in a very short space of time assume a most venerable and aged appearance, it will, if it survives its first century or two, become so intensely hard and tough as to almost defy time and the elements.

This is certainly the case in some of the existing buildings in the older groups of ruins in Pemba, and I have little doubt but that the ruined buildings in the deserted towns in Pemba are contemporary with the founding of the settlements.   In confirmation of this opinion we may refer to the existing fabric of a ruined mosque in Pemba Island, on the walls of which some one has scratched an invocation and affixed the date of A.D. 1414.   Further reference is made to this particular mosque on a subsequent page, but for purposes of our comparison it will suffice to realise that the building must have been standing 500 years ago.

The fact is, that apart from the toughening process which all limestone work exposed to the atmosphere undergoes, the equable temperature experienced throughout the years at sea-level in these tropical latitudes has little or no disintegrating effect upon masonry once hardened by exposure.

Of course a saturated sub-soil, which causes foundations to sag and sink, soon destroys any kind of building, but a coral island is probably better drained than any other locality in the world, owing to the porosity of the fundamental stratum ; and in this respect the chances are that

---

[1] This process of hardening limestone by exposure is so well known in Zanzibar that it was the custom among Arabs to spread the building of their houses over a period of years, in order to ensure that the foundations especially should remain exposed to the rain and sun for at least one season.   An Arab never finished his house at once, for the longer he took over it, the stronger he knew it would be.

foundations of ancient buildings built on coral-rock will remain sound for centuries.

II

The following list indicates the most important ruins situated within the dominions of His Highness the Sultan of Zanzibar : [1]

IN ZANZIBAR ISLAND

1. The ruined town on Tumbatu Island.
2. The ruined houses at Mgogoni or Mvuleni.
3. Some ruined buildings at Kisimkazi.
4. A small ruined mosque at Chwaka.
5. Unguja Kuu (Old Zanzibar).

IN PEMBA ISLAND

1. The Ndagoni Group.
2. The Pujini Group.
3. The Chwaka Group.
4. Mtambwe Kuu (the Isle of Mystery).
5. The mosque at Msuka Mjini.
6. The mosque at Chaoni.
7. The mosque at Verani.
8. The mosque on Fundo Island.
9. The mosque at Kijiweni.
10. The mosque at Shengeju.
11. The mosque at Mandani, near Ole.
12. " The Lonely Tomb " at Vitongoje.
13. The mosque at Mtangani.
14. The mosque at Kiwani.
15. The ruin on Makongwe Island.

It will be observed that there are more ruins in Pemba Island than in Zanzibar, and it appears that in ancient times the former island was more favoured for colonisation than the latter. The exact reason for this preference is not

[1] No account has been taken of modern ruins at Mtoni, Marahubi, Dunga, Kidichi, or Masingini, etc., all of which are situated in Zanzibar Island.

clear, but it may be surmised that Pemba was more attractive to the early Persian and Arab colonists and traders as being rather more remote from the mainland, and therefore less liable to attack, or the greater fertility of Pemba may have appealed to them ; on the other hand, it is possible that owing to the denser population of Zanzibar, ancient ruins may have been more completely destroyed. The temptation to utilise the material of ancient buildings is as potent in Zanzibar as it is—or let us hope, was—the case in Europe.

The architecture of the more important ruins is of a distinctive character, and may be conveniently referred to as the Shirazian style. The name Shiraz is employed by the Arabs and Swahilis at the present time to denote ancient Persian, and a large proportion of the native population of Zanzibar and Pemba claim to be of Shirazian or ancient Persian descent.

There can be little doubt that the Persians, or Shirazis, who arrived on the east coast of Africa at a very early date —Professor Stulhmann, for instance, says towards the close of the sixth century—introduced the art of building in stone, the production of lime and cement, wood-carving, and the weaving of cotton. During the period from the ninth to the twelfth century they built many mosques, both on the Azanian coast as well as in such islands as Zanzibar, Pemba, and Mafia, and they reached the height of their fame towards the close of the fourteenth century.[1]

The chief characteristics of their architectural style are the pointed arch, the free employment of dressed limestone for the edgings of pillars and doorways, the utilisation of squared roof and floor beams, the rectangular wall-recess as distinct from the rounded or pointed recesses of the Arabian style, the rectangular window, and the peaked and divided keystone—a very distinctive feature. It may be noted also that the stone courses and mouldings of their doorways and arches are invariably cut at less than a right angle—generally 85°.

Apart from these typical characteristics, the refinement

[1] Stulhmann, *Handwerk und Industrie in Ostafrika.*

of design marks the Shirazian work as different from all other styles met with in buildings in East Africa.

Persian work did not long survive in Africa, for it became modified by the introduction of Arab influences, both as regards design and execution. Fortunately there are examples of good Shirazian work still to be found in some of the ruins of Pemba, and attention will be directed to these features in the following chapters. The definite substitution of the South Arabian cult can be traced clearly in the architecture of the various groups of ruins in Pemba, and leaves scarcely any doubt that the original Persian colonists were succeeded by the less highly cultured Semitic races of South Arabia.

In classifying the ruins of Zanzibar and Pemba according to their architectural styles, we find that the oldest are the most artistic, being of Shirazian design; this architectural period was succeeded by what may be called the Arab-Shirazian epoch, which in turn gave way to the cruder Arab-African. It is worthy of note that nearly every ruined town in the Sultanate is built on an island, or on a peninsula which is nearly surrounded by the sea at high tide.

In nearly every instance it is evident that the guiding principle which governed the selection of the site was safety from attack, and this fact is suggestive of the political conditions which existed at the time the several towns in Pemba were founded. Judged by other considerations many of the sites, however excellent they may have been as defensive posts, could scarcely have been very convenient for the bulk of their populations, for barely one town—and some of them must have had some thousands of inhabitants if the inevitable slave population is included in the total—possessed any water supply save from a few shallow wells or possibly from storage tanks. The town on Tumbatu is an excellent example of this, and most of the domestic water must have been obtained from a spring on the main island of Zanzibar, and brought over to the town in boats.

The evidences of human occupation of the ruins at present forthcoming consist of : 1. Beads ; 2. Fragments of Chinese pottery ; 3. Fragments of Syrian or Arabian glass ; 4. Fragments of Persian earthenware ; 5. Fragments of gold jewellery and some small portions of copper or bronze, which may have been coins or personal ornaments.

Beads.—These are found in considerable profusion at Ndagoni, partly owing (no doubt) to the encroaching sea having washed a large portion of the ancient town away, and thus disclosing the treasures of graves and kitchen middens on the sea-shore.

The beads are not only found in large numbers, but in great variety as well, and many of them are of considerable beauty. The best beads, which are obviously not of modern manufacture, are made from semi-precious stones, such as amethyst, garnet, quartz crystal, red and white carnelian, onyx, agate, and chalcedony, and are chiefly found at Mtambwe Kuu and Ndagoni. All these are carefully polished, pierced, and in some cases faceted, the result of much skilled labour.

Mention may also be made here of the quartz crystal pendant-shaped ornaments, which may have been used as earrings or as a necklet. These crystal pendant-drops are more than an inch in length and are carefully cut and polished. That these ornaments are of great age is evident from their worn and battered appearance.

There is little doubt but that the red carnelian and chalcedony beads of the more valuable kind originally came from India, for Portuguese travellers at the commencement of the sixteenth century give us a good deal of information concerning the carnelian bead-trade of Hindustan.

Thus Duarte Barbosa, who wrote a description of the Malabar coast in about 1512, speaking of " the great city of Cambay," says that in the city were " great lapidaries, and imitators of precious stones of all kinds, and makers of false pearls which seem real . . . and they make beads of great size, brown, yellow, blue, and coloured, which they export to all parts. . . ."

With regard to the carnelian beads the same author tells us " that beyond Cambay there is an inland town called Limadura, where there is a stone from which they make beads for Berberia. It is," he says, " a stone as white as milk, and has some red in it, and with fire they heighten the colour, and they extract it in large blocks. In these places

23

there are great artists, who manufacture and pierce these beads in various fashions, oval, octagonal, round,[1] and of other shapes : and with this stone they make rings, buttons, and knife handles. And the Cambay merchants go and buy them there, and they string them and take them away to sell in the Red Sea . . . and they also carry them throughout all Arabia, Persia, Nubia. . . . They also find in this town much chalcedony. They make beads of it, and other things which they wear about them, so that they touch the skin, as they say it is good for chastity. These stones are of little value there, for there are many of them."

Writing concerning the trade of Aden, Barbosa says that ships from Somaliland used to come over to Aden and carry away merchandise from Cambay, and " also carnelian beads, and other large and small beads, perforated for stringing, with which they trade in Arabia Felix, and in the country of Prester John."

He also tells us that at " Xeher " or " Shehir " (Mshihiri) on the Hadramaut coast, " Moors of Cambay and Malabar " bring merchandise, and among it " Granates [garnets] on strings, and several other jewels of small value."

Among the many varieties of beads found at Mtambwe Kuu are polished and faceted " granates," ready pierced for threading.

It will be seen from the above extracts that there is every probability that the agate, carnelian, and chalcedony beads found in the vicinity of the ancient towns of Pemba originally came from Cambay in India, but it must not be supposed that they were necessarily brought to Pemba during the comparatively recent period when Barbosa wrote his account. They are probably much older, for it is well known that the carnelian trade of North-western India dates back to Roman times, and the author of the *Periplus*[2] mentions that from the port of Barygaza (the modern Broach on the Gulf of Cambay) were exported in his time (the first century of the Christian era) " agate and carnelian." So it is clear that the Cambay carnelian trade is of very ancient date.

[1] Exactly the shapes of the carnelian beads found in Pemba.
[2] Translation by Wilfred H. Schoff. (Longmans, Green & Co., London, 1912.)

It is of interest to note that among the Zimbabwe exhibits in the Cape Town Museum are several specimens of red carnelian beads, similar in shape and size to those found in Pemba. The museum authorities consider that these beads date from the eleventh to the fifteenth century.[1]

Besides carnelian beads, pierced amethysts and garnets and great quantities of glass beads are also found at certain states of the tide at the ruined towns in Pemba. They are generally considered to be of Arabian or Persian manufacture, and to date from the twelfth to the fifteenth century ; although some specimens may be considerably older and date from the Ptolemaic period.

The most common bead found at Ndagoni is a large, irregularly shaped, bluish-green glass bead of a distinctive character. After heavy rain they may be picked up on the sea-beach by hundreds. That they are of somewhat archaic manufacture is evident from the irregularity of their shape and size. Many of them appear to have become distorted in the process of being made.[2]

The question is often asked how the existence of such quantities of beads in the sea-sands of Pemba can be accounted for.

The suggestions generally put forward in reply are :

1. That they formed a portion of a cargo of a wrecked ship.

2. That they have been washed out of ancient graves by the encroaching sea.

3. That they are the remains of some propitiatory or thank-offering made by the former inhabitants of the ruins, to the sea.

4. That a bead factory or depot existed at the towns where beads are now found, and that the encroaching sea has liberated the beads.

---

[1] Carnelian beads of rather rough manufacture have also been found in Eastern Pondoland near the mouth of the Msinkulu River, and at other places in South Africa. The museum authorities consider them to be of Persian manufacture.

[2] I am informed that the beads found at the ruins in Pemba are exactly similar to those found at Zimbabwe and at other ruins in Rhodesia. This association between the great and famous ruins of Zimbabwe and those of Pemba opens out a very interesting line of conjecture.

With reference to the above propositions, it will be realised of course that beads formed until quite recent times
—and in fact to some extent form still—the chief currency of
native Africa : and everything from a tusk of ivory to a
cob of Indian corn had to be paid for in beads, cloth, and
in more recent times by brass wire and gunpowder, so there
is nothing inherently extraordinary that beads should be
found at the sites of these ancient and deserted trading-
stations. The only surprising thing about them is that they
should be found concentrated in particular spots on the
sea-shore.

With regard to the above suggestions as to how the beads
came in their present position, all are reasonable except
perhaps the first. It would be too remarkable a coincidence
that ships had run ashore, and been wrecked exactly opposite most of the towns of Pemba and Zanzibar. It is, moreover, reasonable to suppose that had they run ashore as is
suggested, the cargo would have been saved and taken
out of them, for all the sites where beads are found are on
the shore of a harbour, and the sea in these sheltered tropical
waters is never rough enough to break up a ship. At these
" bead-sites," the sea is seldom rougher than the Serpen-
tine.

The fourth explanation seems the most probable, and it
possesses none of the objections of the previous ones. It
not only accounts for the glass beads, but also for the glass
fragments, some of which, especially at the Ndagoni ruins,
appear to be, not pieces of glass vessels, but melted fragments and slag from crucibles used in the manufacture of
the blue beads.

It is worthy of note that at Mogdishu, in Italian Somaliland, one of the oldest Persian or Arab settlements on the
coast, complete apparatus for the manufacture of glass
beads, such as crucibles, paste for making beads, glass stems,
and coloured beads have actually been discovered.[1]

If a glass-bead manufactory existed at Mogdishu, there is
no reason why similar establishments should not have been
erected elsewhere : although it is as well to restate the fact
that while the existence of bead factories will explain the

[1] Justus Strandes, *Die Portugiesenzeit von Deutsch-und-Englisch-Ostafrika.*

presence of special varieties of beads at these old ruins, it must not be concluded that they account for all such deposits.

As already observed, the carnelian, chalcedony, garnet, amethyst, and the more elaborate and expensive varieties are almost certainly of Indian manufacture.

Fragments of Chinese Pottery.—A special interest attaches to these fragments, for from them a close approximation of the period during which the ancient towns in Pemba existed may be deduced. These pieces of porcelain occur in considerable quantities, especially on the sea-beaches at Ndagoni and at Mtambwe Kuu, the Isle of Mystery : and the authorities of the Ceramic Department of the Victoria and Albert Museum have very kindly examined a large assortment of fragments from these sites, and reference to the subjoined list of specimens retained by the department will indicate better than elaborate descriptions the type of pottery found, and the periods assigned to the various specimens.

CHINESE POTTERY, ETC., FROM PEMBA

Portion of a dish, blue and white porcelain, seventeenth or eighteenth century.

Portion of a dish, blue and white porcelain, floral design, eighteenth century.

Bowl, blue and white porcelain, floral design, eighteenth century.

Bowl in fragments, cream-coloured Ting ware, Sung dynasty (A.D. 960–1279).

Two fragments of rims of dishes, dark grey stone ware, brownish celadon glaze. Sung or Ming dynasty.

Base of a bowl, incised ornament, greyish celadon glaze. Sung dynasty.

Fragment of a base of a bowl, incised ornament, greyish celadon glaze. Sung dynasty.

Fragment of a base of a bowl, greyish celadon. Sung dynasty.

Base of a bowl, impressed fish, celadon glaze. Ming dynasty (A.D. 1368–1644).

Two fragments of fluted dishes, celadon glaze. Ming dynasty.

Fragment of bowl, relief ornament inside, celadon glaze. Ming dynasty.

Five fragments of vessels, celadon glaze, Ming dynasty.

Three fragments, cream-coloured Ting ware, probably Sung dynasty.

Seven fragments, blue and white porcelain, seventeenth or eighteenth century.

One fragment, brown-glazed earthenware, probably Persian.

Five fragments red earthenware with sgraffiato decoration, Persian, fourteenth or fifteenth century.

Fragment of stone-ware vessel, studs in relief, dark brown glaze, Chinese.

Fragment of red earthenware, mottled blue glaze, Persian (?).

Two spindle-whorls (?) cut from Persian pottery.

Fragment red earthenware with relief decoration, Indian (?).

Fragment earthenware, blue glaze with lustre decoration, thirteenth or fourteenth century.

Six fragments of glass, green, light blue, and amethyst colour. Arab or Syrian.

Portions of similar Chinese pottery belonging to the Ming dynasty have been found, it is understood, at Zimbabwe, and certainly along the littoral of East Africa. The variety of markings and pattern is very great; and from the quantities which strew the beaches and ruined sites, the importation of china ware to East Africa during the later Middle Ages must have been on an extensive scale.

Much of the pottery found at various places on the East African coast, and also at the ruins in Zanzibar and Pemba, cannot be included with the older and rarer specimens referred to above. It is of later date, and, as will be seen from the list of the Victoria and Albert Museum, belongs to the seventeenth and eighteenth centuries. In some instances this more recent ware may have come from Persia.

With regard to this Persian-made pottery, it may be of

interest to quote the following extract from E. Sykes's *Persia and Its People*:

" Early in the seventeenth century, Shah Abbas imported Chinese workmen into his country to teach his subjects the art of making porcelain, and the Chinese influence is very strong in the designs on this ware. Chinese marks are also copied, so that to scratch an article is sometimes the only means of proving it to be of Persian manufacture, for the Chinese glaze, hard as iron, will take no mark."

Strandes also points out that much of the porcelain which is collected in East Africa is frequently brought from the interior of Persia, but that rare specimens of really antique specimens of Chinese and Persian ware may still be obtained in East Africa. Professor Stulhmann, writing on the same topic, states that he considers the celadon-glaze plates and bowls, used in ancient times for tomb decoration in Eastern Africa, were brought direct from China.

The practice of decorating tombs and mosques with plates and bowls embedded in the walls must be considered as typical of the Shirazian cult, although the custom was adopted for tombs at a later period by the Arabs, and continues to some extent in Zanzibar at the present day.

Unfortunately, not a single specimen of antique porcelain remains *in situ* in the ruins in Pemba and Zanzibar Islands at the present time, all having been extracted, in the majority of instances I believe by natives, who hoped to utilise them for domestic purposes. As a matter of fact, the bowls were fixed into their places in the walls with such iron-hard cement that it is improbable that many specimens have ever been picked out intact. This view is confirmed by finding in the soil beneath the mosque wall at Chwaka, in Pemba, several fragments of antique celadon-ware, with cement still adhering to them, which had evidently been picked out from the wall above and broken in the process.

It is evident that the most ancient tombs at Ndagoni, at Chwaka, and at other places in Pemba were originally decorated with porcelain bowls, for the hollows in the walls and the cement which held the bowls in position are still clearly visible.

Arabian and Syrian Glass.—Quantities of coloured glass

fragments are found on the beach at Ndagoni, and in lesser degree at some of the other ruined settlements.

Hitherto no unbroken specimen of glass utensil has, so far as I am aware, been found, but the patterns and markings on some of the pieces, and the thinness of the glass itself, clearly indicate that there must have been many beautiful vessels of glass in use in these old towns. Most of the glass is either green or blue, but some crimson pieces—evidently portions of a large bowl—have been found at Ndagoni. Pieces of small perfume bottles, necks of clear-glass bottles, bases of dark-green vases are not infrequently picked up, and these show clearly that the original inhabitants must have possessed refined and cultivated tastes. The Phoenicians, and the Arabs after them, were of course famous for their glass, so there is no mystery as to the presence of antique glassware in the vicinity of the old ruins in Pemba Island.

Glazed Persian Earthenware.—From the museum list it will be seen that a fragment of an earthenware vessel covered with blue glaze, and with lustre decoration, is considered as belonging to the thirteenth or fourteenth century. This piece was found on the sea-beach at the Ndagoni ruins, amidst hundreds of fragments of earthenware vessels. Most of these vessels were glazed on one side only, and many were decorated with incised patterns of foliage, and occasionally with representations of fish.

Connected with these glazed earthenware fragments are the spindle-whorls referred to in the museum list. These " whorls " are really discs cut from the ancient pottery, and perforated through the centre with a hole. The diameter of these discs is about 1½ inch, but some are smaller. A large number of similar whorls are displayed in the Cape Town Museum in the Zimbabwe exhibit.

The presence of these pottery discs on the sea-shore in Pemba is interesting, for as an ornament they could have only appealed to a race of little culture or refinement, and certainly not to the people who were capable of building such refined and well-designed edifices as are found in the deserted towns in Pemba. Their existence may be explained by the assumption that, after the final abandonment of the old towns by the race which built them, the ruins were in course of time occupied or frequented by some African race —possibly slaves of the original settlers—who manufactured for themselves these discs from the fragments of ancient Persian pottery lying on the beach. Another explanation is that the discs were made by Persian or Arab colonists from the broken pottery, as a medium of barter with the savage pagans of the mainland.

Primitive beads made of chalk, wood, soapstone (steatite) are also picked up in the sand at Ndagoni, and it may reasonably be assumed that whoever made the pottery discs made these rough beads as well.

Up to the present time no coins have been discovered at any of the ruined sites in Zanzibar or Pemba. That such exist must, I think, be obvious, when it is remembered that these towns were occupied for centuries by people who, from the evidence of their architectural tastes alone, must have belonged to civilised and cultured races.

The absence of coins in Zanzibar and Pemba is the more strange as thousands of copper coins have been picked up on the sea-beach at a certain spot in Mafia Island, 120 miles to the south of Zanzibar. The coins in question are found on the sea-shore in the vicinity of some ruined masonry buildings which are submerged at high tide. Literally thousands —perhaps tens of thousands—of these copper coins have been apparently washed out of this submerged town, and now strew the sands. The coins have not as yet been critically examined, but they appear to be those of the ancient " kings " of Kilwa. That they are of great age is evident from the fact that many of the inscriptions are in the archaic Kufic character, which was used on many Oriental coins from the seventh to the thirteenth century of the Christian era.

It is to be hoped that systematic excavation and exploration of the ruins in Zanzibar and Pemba will disclose not only ancient coins, but many other interesting articles, although it must not be anticipated that the finds will be of great intrinsic value. It is as well to mention this point in order to prevent disappointment. It must be borne in mind that, however extensive and well built these settlements may have been, they were but colonial towns—outposts of some imperial enterprise controlled under the aegis of the transient autocracies of Western Asia. That they were affluent and prosperous settlements is, I think, beyond question, for the very multiplication of these towns and sultanates on the Azanian coast go to prove this; but although the mosques and buildings which comprise them were permanent, and built to last, it may be anticipated that the rulers and governors, as well as those of the wealthier commercial classes who had their temporary residence in these island-towns, did not bring with them their most valued possessions from their homes in distant Persia or in far-off Arabia.

They, like the modern colonial official, were but birds of passage, and no doubt looked forward to the day when they could leave Old Africa for ever, and betake themselves with their families and household gods to their own homeland, to enjoy there the fruits of their labours.

CHAPTER XXIV

THE NDAGONI RUINS, PEMBA

I

THE Ndagoni ruins are the most interesting within the Zanzibar Protectorate. This is partly due to the fact that certain remarkable tombs are comprised within the group, and partly because the style of architecture and the general refinement displayed make it evident that the builders must have been a civilised and cultured race. Who they were, whence they came, whither they went, is not known with certainty, but it is generally supposed that the original builders and settlers were either Persians from the shores of the Persian Gulf, or Arabs from Mesopotamia, or from South Arabia. In all likelihood both Persians and Arabs exercised at different epochs preponderating influences at this and other settlements in Zanzibar and Pemba.

The remains of this ruined and deserted town, the very name of which is now forgotten, are situated at the western extremity of Ras Mkumbuu, a strangely attenuated peninsula, which projects from the western coast of the island of Pemba. So narrow is this curious-shaped peninsula in parts, that it appears likely that the extremity upon which the ruins are situated may indeed have been an island in former times, and a very little digging would certainly effect the transformation.

The ancient buildings are situated on the very edge of the sea, and it is evident that at Ndagoni, as in other places on the western coasts of Zanzibar and Pemba Islands, the sea is steadily encroaching, so that some of the walls and tombs, undermined by the advancing tide, lie prone on the sand, and washed by high tides.

In this connection, the native tradition may be mentioned, that not so very long ago a wall or building, belonging to the ancient town, was visible under the sea. A further story is current, that a pillar or tower stood, many years ago, projecting from the sea close to the existing ruins.

The ruins are to-day entirely hidden from view, both from the sea and land sides by dense forest ; and it is to be feared that this growth has done much damage to the old buildings. Creepers of every size have wound themselves round the walls, while large trees are growing within the empty and roofless rooms, which once, no doubt, echoed with the voices and laughter of children. There are no less than six large forest trees, besides palms and ferns, growing in the interior of the mosque.

In this dense forest the ruins of Ndagoni extend along the sea-beach, and at the back of the town rises a low, flat-topped hill with a precipitous scarp dropping sharply to the sea. The whole of this eminence is now covered with long grass, forest trees, and clumps of Borassus palms, but it is certainly a site suggestive of defensive works, commanding as it does the roadstead and the town at its foot. That some fort or acropolis existed on this summit seems the more likely, as at Mtambwe Kuu, another ancient port some eighteen miles to the north of Ndagoni, a similar table-topped hill dominates the harbour and on its summit there are vestiges of masonry walls which may, from their position on the very edge of the cliff, represent the remains of defensive works.

The following list indicates the principal and characteristic features worthy of note at Ndagoni :

1. The pillared tombs.
2. The mosque.
3. The house of the stone recess.
4. The hidden ruin.

The pillared tombs are the most interesting features of the Ndagoni ruins, not only because they are probably the most ancient remains to be found in the country, but also

A PILLARED TOMB AT NDAGONI, PEMBA.

because nowhere else in the whole of the East African region are so many to be found clustered in one place.

Each grave is surrounded by a wall from 4 to 6 feet in height, and from the top of this encircling wall rises a remarkable masonry pillar or stele 15 feet in height. Some of the pillars are plain and without embellishment, while others either have Chinese bowls or plates cemented into their surfaces, or are decorated near the summit by rectangular or arched panels incised in the stone.

At Ndagoni in 1916 there were still three of these pillars standing intact on the enclosing walls of their respective tombs, while in the case of several other mausolea the pillars had fallen, and lay prone and shattered. The grave within the wall is marked with a masonry head and foot stone, connected with a curb. Every grave lies due west and east, with the pillar at the eastern end. In no case has any inscription been discovered.

The most carefully built specimen of these mausolea is that depicted in the accompanying illustration, and although the pillar is in a very insecure condition, and a great portion of the encircling wall has collapsed, it may be accepted as a type of these pillared tombs. The top of the pillar in the specimen here illustrated is 15 feet 6 inches from the ground-level. The pillar is rectangular, and has on its face, near the summit, four incised panels, which, under the influence of Time and Nature, have turned a beautiful pinkish tint.

There are indications that the tops of the pillars were embellished with some ornament, but of what precise pattern is not clear. The corners or edges of the pillar are formed of carefully cut limestone, and this work is so well done that even to-day, after the stress of centuries, the joints will, in many instances, scarcely allow the insertion of a visiting card.

The frequent use of cut and dressed stone is one of the distinctive characteristics of the Ndagoni ruins. It is employed in all classes of buildings, and indicates alike the permanency of the settlement and the skill and artistic perception of the race who made such free use of this building medium. The material utilised for this purpose is coralline limestone, and exposure to the atmosphere for prolonged periods has imparted to it a mellowed pinkish hue : this colouring, coupled with the weathered masonry, from which spring innumerable ferns, gives to these ruins in the Ndagoni forest a most attractive and unique appearance.

Near the base of the pillar of this typical tomb is the concave impression of a bowl, which once had ornamented the grave in accordance with what was evidently the usual practice. There are similar marks in other tombs, but the porcelain vessels have, alas ! all disappeared. During my second visit to these ruins in 1915, I noticed that a portion of a bowl still remained cemented in its column. Attempts had evidently been made to extract it long ago, but the cement had proved too strong, and the bowl had been so damaged as to cause the despoiler to desist. There was, however, sufficient of the bowl left *in situ* to make it worth while to remove it, in the hope that expert examination might afford some clue to the history and period of the whole group of ruins.

This bowl, with other specimens of pottery from the Pemba ruins, is now in the collection of the Victoria and Albert Museum, and has been kindly examined by Mr. Bernard Rackham, the well-known expert, who is in charge of the galleries of the Ceramic Department of the National Collection. He is of opinion that the bowl is a specimen of cream-coloured Ting ware of the Sung dynasty (A.D. 960,–1279).

This piece of evidence is of the greatest value in affording some idea of the age of the mausolea at Ndagoni : and it is a coincidence worthy of note that it was during the above period the Chinese visited the east coast of Africa.[1]

The fact that a specimen of pottery of a particular period is found cemented into a ruined wall cannot of course be accepted as absolutely conclusive evidence that the ruined wall is of the same age as the pottery ; but the presumption that such is the case is strengthened in the case of the Pemba ruins by the present-day practice among the natives of Zanzibar of decorating their family tombs with crockery. In these cases, the native invariably uses modern plates and

[1] Dr. Franz Stuhlmann, *Handwerk und Industrie in Ostafrika.* (Hamburg, 1910.)

saucers of European make, purchased straight from the bazaar. The Swahili not only prefers the gaudy modern patterns, but obviously does not possess—any more, it may be presumed, than did the tomb builders of Ndagoni—a supply of antique bowls and plates with which to decorate the graves of their relations.

This custom of embedding porcelain plates and bowls into tombs, and around the kiblas of ancient mosques, is believed to be of Persian origin ; and it was practised not only in Zanzibar and Pemba, but also at the ancient settlements on the Azanian coast. Such decorations are found at Kilwa Kissiwani, at Lamu, and at other places which came under Shirazian influence. It is of interest to note that a similar practice of building plates into walls occurs in Asia Minor.

A characteristic form of embellishment used freely on the more carefully built graves at Ndagoni is either the chevron pattern or the rope device, so called from its similarity to a cord or cable. This pattern is cut in stone, and is generally used as a course above and below the " pigeon-holes."

These devices—the chevron and the rope patterns—are also found in the Chwaka and Tumbatu ruins, and it is of interest to observe that this embellishment is also employed in the ruins at Great Zimbabwe in Rhodesia, and on some of the steatite articles which have been found there.[1]

The dense forest shown in the illustration of these tombs will indicate the growth which now conceals from view this once busy town ; and until some clearing had been effected, it was impossible even to penetrate into the ruins, or to examine them with any degree of facility.

Such growth adds very much to the beauty and romantic aspect of the ruins and their surroundings, and it is pleasant to see the brilliant sunshine strike through the green canopy of trees, and dapple the grey walls with a mellow light : but it is very bad for the old buildings. A judicious clearing under sympathetic supervision is required : I say European supervision, because a native left to his own devices will

---

[1] In the Zimbabwe exhibit at the Cape Town Museum, there is a large and elaborately carved bowl of soapstone, which is freely decorated with this " rope " pattern.

fell trees without much thought where they are likely to fall, and considerable damage has already been done to the ruins in this way.

There are, in this group of ruins, altogether thirteen pillared graves, which can be recognised as such. All are encircled by the usual walled enclosure, and in the majority of cases remnants of the characteristic pillar or column can be found.

It is now time to place on record the little that is known concerning this particular type of mausoleum. The form is so unusual and distinctive that it might be thought there could be no difficulty in identifying it with a definite period, and with a particular race ; but at present such is not the case, and even the authorities of the British Museum are unable to tell us what people built the tombs, or when they were erected.

Tombs of similar form have been found in " German " East Africa near the coast at Tongoni, and they have been described and depicted by Burton in 1857,[1] and by Professor Franz Stulhmann in 1910.[2]

The pillared tomb alluded to by Burton is specially interesting, because it contained the only inscription which has ever been found connected with this particular style of sepulchre. It was situated on the African mainland at Tongoni, a small native haven to the south of Tanga, and due west of the ruins at Ndagoni in Pemba Island. The Tongoni ruins appear to have been similar in every detail to those at Ndagoni ; and Burton's description of them might very well apply to the Pemba ruins. Native rumour, he tells us, avers that a large city existed near Tongoni, now covered by the sea. Up a neighbouring creek Burton found other ruins, the architectural features of which denoted " a race far superior to the present owners of the land." A city was once there, and the explorer found remnants of mosques of solid and handsome structure, with columns of neatly cut coralline blocks, and elaborate mihrabs. In the neighbouring cemetery, he was shown a number of tombs, and " each of the principal mausolea had its tall stele of cut

---

[1] *Zanzibar: City, Island and Coast.* (London, 1872.)
[2] *Handwerk und Industrie in Ostafrika.* (Hamburg.)

coralline, denoting, like the Egyptian and Syrian Shahadah, the position of the corpse's head."

In one of these tombs he found a Persian glazed tile, with a portion of an inscription in Persian characters, which read,

" *Shid i raushan.* . . ." (The bright sun. . . .)

The natives held that the men of Ajem (Persia) once ruled the land, but Burton concluded that " the tile, like two China platters also mortared into the Shahadah," was evidently " an importation from the far north." What he meant by the "far north," or to whom he intended to refer, is not clear.

The pillared tomb mentioned by Stulhmann was also at Tongoni, and may have been identical with Burton's, as the illustration shows that formerly two bowls or platters had been cemented in the pillar. The Shirazi tomb illustrated by Stulhmann is not in so good a state of preservation as those in Pemba, and many of the graceful features of the Ndagoni tombs are lacking. The German author is of opinion that the first immigration of Persians to the coast of East Africa took place in the seventh and eighth centuries, and he considers that in all Shirazi tombs one of the outstanding characteristics is the four or eight-sided pillar, which is often, he states, surmounted by a peculiar excrescence of probably phallic significance. In some instances, he remarks, the columns are quite short, but in ancient tombs they are almost invariably lofty.

II

The next building which demands, and indeed deserves, attention is the ruined mosque at Ndagoni. This, even in its ruined and decayed condition, is a pleasing structure, and Time and Nature have imparted to it a certain mellowed sanctity of aspect which is very attractive. It is roofless, but some half-dozen forest trees grow within the circuit of its walls, and spread a canopy of green leaves overhead. Through this cool roof the sun strikes and illuminates en-

24

ticingly the columned interior, draped with a profusion of ferns and creepers.

The cemented walls too, have assumed in many places a decided blue tint; while the stone blocks which edge the pillars and buttresses have been coloured by the ages a dull pink hue. This soft colouring, mingling with the orchids and palms which sprout from the walls, makes this structure a singularly pleasing ruin. There is nothing dank and mildewy about the Ndagoni mosque.

I cannot do better in my endeavour to explain the attractiveness of this ruin, and at the same time to exhibit the refined style of architecture typical, not only of the mosque, but also of the buildings at Ndagoni, than to refer the reader to the accompanying illustration of an arched doorway which gives access to the mosque.

Regarded as a whole,[1] this arched doorway betokens a singular sense of refinement, and the touch of a master-hand.

Through the doorway on the right can be seen two of the twelve interior pillars, which originally supported the roof; and also the stems of some areca-nut palms.

On entering the mosque, the first thing that strikes the visitor is the difference of level between the south and north ends; and it is evident that the present floor-level is not the original one, for the fall of the roof and the domes has filled up the interior of the building, to a depth of nearly 3 feet.

The kibla, or mihrab, which takes the place in a mosque of the altar of a Christian place of worship, calls for no particular remark. It is a plain, substantial arched recess in the northern wall, and indicates the direction of Mecca. It is worthy of remark that neither the kibla nor the walls of the mosque show any indications of having been decorated with Chinese porcelain or other pottery. This fact appears to me to be one of the many indications that the mosque was not contemporary with, but of a later period than, the pillared tombs already alluded to.

To the westward of the kibla, a rectangular doorway, half

---

[1] It may be pointed out that the true proportion of the doorway is not really displayed in the illustration, as the threshold was found covered with 18 inches of soil, and indications of this excavation can be observed in the illustration.

A DOORWAY OF THE MOSQUE, NDAGONI, PEMBA.

buried in debris, was discovered. The debris at this spot
was cleared away, and a flight of stone stairs partly built
in the thickness of the wall was uncovered. These steps
must have led, it is apparent, to the summit of the minaret.

    •   •   •   •   •   •

If one happens to be in the ruined mosque at sundown,
it does not require a very vivid imagination to picture in
the growing shadows the figure of an aged Muezzin—dead
these five hundred years—descending this very stairway from
the summit of the minaret, where, facing Mecca, he had
summoned the faithful to prayer, and had proclaimed to the
world the solemn truth which still thrills the heart of Islam :

" GOD is great !   There is but One GOD ! "

And if the illusion is complete, one can hear the hum of the
adjoining town, the songs and shouts from the ships anchored
in the roadstead, due to sail on the morrow, homeward
bound, deep-laden with rich cargoes of African gold and
ivory, of slaves and spice.

And the aged Muezzin, a wraith in the deepening shadows,
slowly lights, one by one, the hanging lamps within the
mosque for evening prayer : and the momentary vision of
the past vanishes, as the chill night-breeze sweeps through
the empty aisles.

    •   •   •   •   -   -

Only the lower portion of the minaret tower remains, but
its substantial character is certainly suggestive of a lofty
structure. As the mosque is built on the very edge of the
shore, this minaret, in its perfect state, must have been a
very prominent object viewed from the sea.

Within the mosque, ten of the twelve rectangular pillars
which supported the roof are still standing. They are of
massive structure, and the edges of each are composed of
sharply cut blocks of pink-hued limestone. Of the nature
of the roof it is impossible now to write with certainty, but
it may be assumed with some confidence that the original
roof consisted of a series of domes, of a similar character to
those Shirazian mosques which still possess roofs, *e.g.* at

Kilwa Kisiwani in " German " East Africa, and at Chwaka in Pemba.

Thus, Dr. Strandes, describing one of the Shirazian mosques at Kilwa, says that :

" the whole construction consisted of nine cupolas in three rows, supported by pillars and the exterior walls. The central cupola is surmounted by a column of phallic shape. . . . The pillars and framework of the wall apertures are constructed of hewn stone, and the whole proportions show a wonderful harmony."

Again, Professor Franz Stulhmann writes on the same subject :

" During the period from the ninth to the twelfth centuries, the Shirazis built many mosques, decorated with artistic pillars and cupolas. In a mosque at Kilwa Kissiwani, there are forty columns arranged in four rows . . . the columns divide the mosque into squares, each surmounted by a cupola. . . . The characteristics of these buildings is the use of well-hewn sandstone, which was used for the lintels of the doors, the framework of the windows, and the kibla. . . ."

Leaving the mosque and turning our steps eastward, we pass again the columned tombs, and a few paces beyond the last of these mausolea we approach a ruined stone building, which I have designated, for purposes of easy identification, " the house of the stone recess." It is rather a melancholy ruin at present, hidden from the sun and sky by overhanging trees ; and its rooms are carpeted with dead and decaying leaves. The plan of the house, as far as it is now traceable, does not appear to have been of great extent : and its close proximity to the row of mausolea leads one to surmise whether the house or the tombs were built first. The site appears highly undesirable for such a building.

The building is worthy of note for a finely designed dressed-stone recess, let into one of the walls near the entrance doorway. I select this architectural item among others in the Ndagoni ruins as indicating the cultured artistic sense which must have influenced the builders of these ancient structures. Like the arched doorway of the mosque, this wall-recess is simple almost to bareness, and yet viewed as a whole it will be evident, I think, that its proportions are perfectly balanced, and its very severity of design acecn-tuates—if it does not actually create—the impression of a stately massiveness, combined with elegance.

Another building which may be briefly referred to is " the house of the cistern." This is one of the largest houses in the group of ruins, although now merely a shell of walls remains. It is situated on the very edge of the low cliff or bank which rises from the sea-beach. Attention is directed to this building, because it is illustrative of the conditions of life under which the original dwellers in Ndagoni lived.

There are numerous remains of buildings and enclosure-walls connected with this group of ruins scattered along the sea-front and in the forest behind ; but they call for no particular remark. They nearly all display the same careful workmanship, and the frequent employment of well-dressed stone as a building material.

In the ruins adjoining " the house of the cistern " the walls are provided with rectangular recesses, which, as explained in a previous chapter, are generally associated with the style of architecture known as Shirazian.

During my visit to Ndagoni in 1916, a new ruin was found in a clump of forest trees, about 250 yards to the north-west of the mosque. The existence of this building had been kept secret by the local natives ; but an isolated patch of virgin forest generally conceals something of in-terest, and a visit to this clump not only added another item to the Ndagoni group of ruins, but showed that the town was more extensive than at first supposed.

An interesting feature connected with this "hidden ruin " is that the building is erected on a raised flat-topped bank or platform, 7 or 8 feet in height. Judging by a mas-sive pair of stone-edged gate-posts, and the remains of an arched entrance-gate, " the hidden ruin " must have been, in its prime, one of the most important and largest buildings in the whole settlement. Vestiges of masonry near by are suggestive of a flight of steps which lead down from the entrance gate towards the sea.

On the inside of the massive doorway is a well-built deep rectangular niche of dressed stone. The contents of this recess at the time of my visit showed that the local natives, who, as already stated, had never mentioned this ruin, were in the habit of making propitiatory offerings to the spirits which haunt the place, for in it were oblations of a small piece of paper, some sugar, dates, sweetmeats, and a broken potsherd containing some charcoal.

Another patch of forest close to " the hidden ruin " suggested other remains, and as the trees spring from a mound of earth, it is fairly certain that another large building once existed at this spot. The remains of a stone grave close by strengthens this supposition.

This brief description of some of the chief features of the ruins at Ndagoni emphasises the need for further exploration and excavation of the site. With our incomplete knowledge of the place, it can only be surmised that this now ruined town was founded between the tenth and fourteenth centuries, probably by some Aryan race from Media, or by Arabs from Mesopotamia or Arabia.

It is clear that an immense amount of care and labour must have been expended in the building of the town. It was no mushroom settlement of adventurers—here to-day and gone to-morrow ; and the obvious permanency of the place, with its inevitable succession of inhabitants, raises nopes and anticipations that, lying buried beneath the soil, is the evidence in the form of coins and ornaments, and of the flotsam and jetsam of centuries of human occupancy, which will make clear the past history of this forgotten town.

CHAPTER XXV

THE PUJINI RUINS

THE nameless ruined citadel and port known to-day as Pujini is situated on the east coast of Pemba Island, 7¼ miles from the town of Chake. A special measure of interest is attached to these ruins, owing to their situation on the eastern coast of the island.

The characteristic of the Pujini site is its aloofness, and there can be little doubt but that one of the main principles which governed its selection was a desire for concealment. In this respect, it differs from every other ruined settlement and town in the Sultanate.

The sites of these latter were no doubt chosen with a view to defence, and to ensure security against land and sea attack, but it would seem that in no case was the factor of deliberate concealment entertained in their inception.

Most of these ancient towns are built on the water-edge : and at the period when they flourished, and were busy centres of trade, their existence must have been apparent far out at sea. They were, for the most part, cities set upon a hill. Their safety was ensured by their insular position, while shoals and reefs on the seaside added to their security from piratical and other hostile attacks : but in every case the open sea was attainable, without risk, by the ships which frequented their ports.

The principles which appear to have governed the selection of the Pujini citadel site differ from those of the ports alluded to above.

In the first place, Pujini is built on the dangerous east coast—a coast which even in these days of steam is shunned by vessels. The general character of the east coast of

Zanzibar Island has already been referred to in a previous chapter : and it will suffice to remark here, that the dangers of the east coast of Zanzibar are intensified in that of Pemba. Deep water is found close to the shore, but of such profundity as to afford a vessel no holding-ground, while the rollers of the Indian Ocean break with unchecked force on the coral reefs, which run parallel to the shore. Pujini can only be reached from the sea through a narrow gap in this fringe of iron-hard rocks, and this narrow passage could only have been navigated at great risk, even in the less boisterous months of the year.

Then again, the town and citadel were built at the extremity of a creek, which to-day is not suited for navigation. This drawback may of course have been less pronounced when the citadel was founded ; for it is possible that the creek may have silted up in recent times.

At the present time, the sea only reaches Pujini citadel at spring tides, and even then the water is too shallow to permit of the arrival of even a small dhow. The conjecture that ships could at one time come up to the citadel walls receives some confirmation from the native tradition that a channel or canal was cut by the original builders to enable vessels to reach the fortress. In fact, there are distinct traces of such a canal, about 15 feet wide and 10 feet deep, along the northern wall of the citadel ; but whether this was a portion of the channel cut to enable sea-going craft to reach the settlement, or was merely a part of the moat, which undoubtedly surrounded the main position, must remain for the present a matter of conjecture.

The ruins lie in a dense patch of forest, which completely conceals them from outside. The roar of the breakers on the reefs at the mouth of the creek can be heard, although no sight of the sea is obtainable through the dense vegetation.

Little has hitherto been known concerning these ruins, and few Europeans have visited them. Those who have done so have been much handicapped by the thick growth which smothers the site, and no excavation, survey, or even systematic inspection has been possible, prior to the author's visits in 1915 and the following years.

The Pujini ruins, as at present disclosed, consist of the citadel (within the circuit of which lie several buildings), the foundations of a mosque, and a few graves. The site occupied by the town—if such ever existed—has not yet been traced.

The citadel is formed by a massive earthen rampart, 15 to 20 feet in thickness, faced on the outside by a masonry wall 3 feet thick. The portion of this outer wall which is still standing is at least 15 feet in height, and is surmounted by a masonry breastwork, decorated with pinnacles at intervals of 9 feet.

In some places, the top of the rampart is 20 feet above the outside ground-level. The inner side of the encircling rampart is also retained by a masonry wall, about 10 feet in height, and access to the rampart top is obtained from the interior of the citadel, by means of flights of masonry steps.

Remains of a tower, with walls 51 inches in thickness at the north-west corner of the citadel, affords good grounds for the belief that similar towers stood at each corner of the fort; and from the general lie of the land, it would appear that the place was surrounded by the sea, at any rate at high tides.

Within the fortified enclosure lie numerous buildings, among which, one more elaborate and extensive in plan than the rest may be presumed to have been the palace or residence of the governor or ruler.

Outside the citadel walls are traces of a large mosque, and this structure affords some confirmation of the tradition that a large town was situated in the vicinity. As already stated, the only traces of human occupation, outside the citadel, are a few graves and a well-head.

It would be fruitless and tedious to describe every architectural detail of the remains at Pujini, so only those possessing any feature of interest are comprised in the subjoined list :

1. The pinnacled parapet and rampart wall.
2. The stairway leading to the ramparts.
3. The fallen arch.
4. The subterranean chamber.
5. The shrine.
6. The reception hall.
7. The pool of the blue water-lilies.

Access to the ruins is obtained at the south-west corner of the citadel. Here the parapet is only about 10 feet above the present level of the moat, which is partially filled up with debris at this spot. Traversing the western rampart in a northerly direction, a break in the line, and a re-entering angle, suggest the existence of a gateway with flanking towers, and immediately beyond this point a position of the original walls surmounted with its loop-holed breastwork is reached. Here we gather a very good idea of the aspect and style of the whole of the Pujini fortress, before it fell into ruin. The height of the wall at present visible is 11 feet, but its base is hidden by large accumulations of debris and soil, and this prevents its full height being appreciated. The height of the pinnacled parapet which tops the rampart is about 22 feet above the level of the encircling creek, so that in its original condition the citadel viewed from a distance must have presented quite an imposing appearance.

Each pinnacle is pierced with a loophole (6 inches square), while 30 inches below the top of the parapet a platform for the match-lock men and archers is provided. As this ramp or platform is only 30 inches broad, it seems improbable that any form of artillery was employed on the rampart for defensive purposes. This point is of importance, as likely to assist us in our attempt to fix the approximate age of the ruins. I have assumed that the loopholes were intended for some kind of firearm, because apertures only 6 inches square could scarcely have been of any use to javelin-men or archers.

If then, as seems likely, the Pujini loopholes were made for firearms, it may be assumed that they were not constructed prior to A.D. 1400.

The pattern of the pinnacles is worthy of notice, as differing from the usual Omân-Arab crenellations, exemplified in the architecture of Arab buildings in Zanzibar.

Thirty yards from the north-western corner of the citadel, along the northern wall, are the remains of a substantial masonry stairway, which gives access from the interior of the citadel to the rampart.

The accompanying illustration indicates the nature of

"THE STAIRWAY TO THE RAMPART," PUJINI CITADEL, PEMBA.

379

this structure, and the romantic surroundings in which it is situated.   On the outer side of the rampart at this point lies what is evidently the remains of an artificially cut channel or canal, and it was here, according to native theory, that ships came and unloaded their cargoes, the merchandise in question being carried down the stairway into the citadel.

The " fallen arch" is connected with a confused mass of buildings within the citadel enclosure.   What cause has led to the demolition of this substantial arch is not apparent, but only half of it now exists.   It is only of interest as being the sole specimen of an arch in the entire group of ruins.

No other structure at Pujini emphasises more strongly and emphatically the gulf which exists between the Pujini style of architecture and technique and that which is displayed at the ruined Shirazian town of Ndagoni.   The difference is too apparent to escape the notice of the most casual observer.

At Pujini, plaster and stucco take the place of carved stone ; crumbling muddy mortar is substituted for iron-hard cement.   Here at Pujini we encounter another race. Those who founded Pujini would not have been capable of building Ndagoni, and the builders of the latter town would not have demeaned their art by erecting such crude edifices as constitute Pujini.

Leaving this broken arch we next come to the subterranean chamber.   This is situated within the citadel enclosure, near the centre of the western wall.   Prior to excavation, the shaft from which the chamber opens appeared to be a rectangular well-head, filled nearly to the top with soil and debris.   On this being removed to a depth of about 10 feet, the commencement of what appears to be a passage or a lateral chamber, opening out from the main shaft, was disclosed.   Nothing of importance was discovered in the debris removed from the perpendicular shaft, except a quantity of ox-bones, fragments of two platters, stated by the Ceramic Department of the Victoria and Albert Museum to be of celadon glaze-ware of the Sung or Ming dynasties, and some common unglazed potsherds of a bright-red hue.

The chamber or passage at the bottom of the main shaft was cleared laterally for a few feet, when two buttress-pillars cut from the rock were met with. The tops of these pillars were cut to receive a squared wooden transom, and the inevitable conclusion arrived at was that the pillars were the lintels of a doorway which gave access to the main shaft from a passage or subterranean chamber which still remains to be explored.

In addition to a variety of rough potsherds and ox-bones mentioned above, a curved iron knife-blade with its sharp edge on the concave side, and a small strip of bronze or copper, perforated at one end, were found. The interesting feature connected with this latter article is that there is an inscription in Persian characters on each side. One of these inscriptions is too worn to be legible, but that on the other side is stated by Mirza Ali, His Highness the Sultan's interpreter, to read,

'A man must bear his own misfortunes."

Sir Hercules Read of the British Museum, who kindly examined this article, considers it to be a key of a native lock of a pattern not uncommon in the East.

The fact that the walls of this inner subterranean chamber have been embellished with cut buttress-pillars makes it clear that it was deliberately fashioned, and its concrete roof is not merely the foundations of some building erected above it. That it was a well seems unlikely, for in that case, there would appear to be no reason for the existence of the lateral chamber which opens from the bottom of the main shaft.

It is not improbable that this subterranean room may have been a tomb or treasure chamber ; but if so, it had apparently never been used as such, or it had been rifled of its contents prior to my visit.

The next feature of interest I have called the " shrine,'' but the precise significance of this subterranean chamber is obscure, although there are resemblances to the underground chamber already described. The "shrine" is situated in the north-eastern corner of the citadel enclosure, and in close proximity to a number of buildings which for facility of reference I have called " the palace." When first visited in

1915, all that was apparent was the main shaft, which it was observed was apse-shaped, and not circular or rectangular.

The walls of the shaft were found to be carefully plastered, while in the centre of the wall of the apse a large bas-relief of a horn or trumpet was disclosed. Six inches below this device was an arched recess or niche in the wall, possibly used for a lamp. The walls were further decorated with raised ridges on either side of the emblem of the horn. The only article found in the debris from this chamber was a fragment of green celadon-glazed pottery.

It is evident that originally the main shaft was covered by a domed roof, which may have projected above the ground-level. At the bottom of the shaft, facing the royal emblem of the horn,[1] a flight of masonry steps led upwards to the open air.

This flight of steps was excavated, and it was then possible to descend from the ground-level, down these steps, to the bottom of the " shrine." The steps, of which there are fourteen, are broad, and covered with cement plaster, which had been preserved intact by the superimposed covering of soil and debris.

At the base of the stairway and in contact with the door posts, a large cone-shaped object, about 2 feet in height and 18 inches in diameter, fashioned from limestone and covered with a thick layer of cement, was discovered. It had probably formed the terminal decoration over the doorway, or had fallen from the summit of the cupola which may have formed the roof of this subterranean chamber. As it lay on the stairway side of the entrance, and not, within the chamber, the first proposition is the most probable.

It will be seen from the above description that this "shrine" is of rather an elaborate nature, and much care was evidently spent in its construction. The large number of bones of oxen, broken potsherds, remnants of wood fires, and two fragments of boat-shaped lamps of coarse earthenware

---

[1] For further information regarding the significance of the horn as the emblem of chiefship and sovereignty in East Africa, see Chapter XXVI.

which were found in removing the debris from the stairway, are certainly suggestive of funeral rites.

Near the " shrine " lies " the reception hall." This is a name chosen rather for identification purposes, than from any knowledge as to the use this extensive gallery was originally put to. It lies westward of the " shrine " just described, and runs parallel to the northern rampart of the citadel. It is evidently a portion of the palace and is in an almost entirely ruinous condition. The outstanding features of this hall are the bases of at least three broad windows in the north wall, and eight very massive but roughly built pillars forming an arcade, which extends along the entire length of the fabric on its southern side. No excavation of this gallery was attempted : it was cleared of a dense mass of vegetation, photographed, and surveyed. Its dimensions, as far as could be ascertained, are 150 feet in length and 25 feet broad. There are some indications which suggest that this extensive structure may have been double-storied.

The Pool of the Blue Water-lilies.—This small lakelet, situated about 200 yards to the south of the ruined citadel, is a charming feature in the vicinity of the patch of forest which conceals the ruins of Pujini.

The natives who reside near by state that the pool never dries, and from it they have for generations obtained their water. Whether this lakelet existed when the adjacent citadel was founded, it is of course impossible to say, but its existence would most·certainly have influenced those who sought for a suitable site for their stronghold and town in a portion of the island where good water is none too plentiful. The supply of water in the pool is no doubt largely derived from rain, but its perennial character inclines one to think that perhaps it is also fed from a spring. In any case, its existence lends an air of beauty and freshness to Pujini, which is not easily forgotten. But the most pleasing feature of the pool is that the whole expanse is covered with the floating leaves and blossoms of thousands of white and blue water-lilies. On the banks a good deal of rice is grown, and the vivid green of this crop contrasts effectively with the clear water, and the darker fringe of palm trees, which encircle this miniature lake.

The ruins of Pujini are pleasantly associated with memories of a brilliant sun, a summer sky, a cool south-west breeze, and the pool of the blue water-lilies.

With this brief description of some of the chief features of the Pujini ruins, it remains to make some comments on the group in general.

In the first place it can be confidently stated that the ruins differ in character and in detail from the other groups in the Sultanate. Whether they are of earlier or later date cannot be definitely asserted, but excavation and examination of the site will no doubt afford evidence on this point.

In the meantime it is evident that the Pujini buildings are of cruder workmanship, and although they display a certain massiveness, both the masonry and the material used are of inferior quality. The rubble-work is irregular, large rocks and small stones, with a preponderance of the latter, being apparently utilised indiscriminately together. The binding material, chiefly composed of lime mortar often mixed with red clay, is inferior in strength and quality. Most of the walls, especially the thicker ones, display an absence of bonding ; and it is evident in several instances that they have been built up from both sides simultaneously, without ensuring cohesion through the thickness of the wall by the use of " headers." The consequence has been that at certain places one face of the wall has fallen, leaving the shell of the other side standing. This poor standard of building shows that either the builders were indifferent workmen or else that the edifices were erected in a hurry.

The foundations, moreover, lack strength, as may be seen in the case of the massive pillars of the reception hall, which, while intact themselves, have snapped short off at the base, and fallen prone.

The citadel walls, too, have similarly been pushed out by the " thrust " of the earthen rampart behind them, except at the spot where a few yards of pinnacled breastwork still stand intact. This ruinous condition may be partly attributable to local climatic conditions. As already explained elsewhere, lime mortar and coralline limestone have a tendency to harden when exposed to tropical atmospheric conditions, but when buried for centuries in damp soil, the tendency of calcareous formations, whether natural or artificial, is all the other way.

Pujini is not founded on a coral foundation, but on the silt, sand, and humus of a creek, and in this respect its permanency has been detrimentally affected in comparison with the ruins in other localities. For this reason alone it seems unlikely that Pujini can be of great antiquity.

In general design and technique, the Pujini buildings differ, in a marked manner, when compared with the other groups of ruins in Zanzibar and Pemba. In only two instances is dressed stone utilised in the construction of doorways, pillars, stairways, or arches at Pujini, and these two exceptions are of minor importance. In all cases, every detail of construction is finished off with coarse plaster, in the style generally associated with the building efforts of South Arabia, or with the degenerate methods which gradually perverted the true Shirazian school, after long contact with Africa.

There is no direct evidence as to the age or period of the Pujini ruins. The crudeness of their construction may of course be due to the archaism of their builders, but I do not think so. The evidence which is available leads to the conclusion that they are of no great antiquity.

The fact has already been mentioned that loopholes exist in the masonry breastwork which surmounts the citadel walls ; and it has been pointed out that in all probability they were intended for some kind of firearm. If this assumption is correct, it is evident that they must have been constructed subsequent to the period when hand-firearms were first employed.

This epoch is generally assumed to have been during the fourteenth century. Gunpowder had been known to the Chinese from time immemorial, and had been discovered by the Arabs as early as the eleventh century, and through their agency was introduced at a later period into Europe.

Until the commencement of the fourteenth century, gunpowder had not been employed for throwing projectiles.

Towards the close of the fifteenth century, bombards and

hand-cannon were in use ; for in 1476 the Swiss Army possessed 6,000 culverins or hand-cannon, and ten years later the English Yeomen of the Guard were similarly armed.[1]

But if the evidence afforded by the loopholes on Pujini rampart is accepted too readily as determining the age of the citadel, we may fall into error, for it is of course possible that they were constructed long after the main fortress had been founded. So without some confirmatory evidence it cannot be definitely asserted that the Pujini citadel could not have been constructed prior to the fourteenth century ; although from the general aspect of the ruins, I conjecture, apart from the evidence of the loopholes, that such was probably the case, and conclude that the age of Pujini does not exceed four hundred years.

Some confirmation as to the comparatively recent antiquity of these ruins may be found in the fact that I picked out from the mortar of a wall of one of the cluster of ruined buildings within the citadel a small fragment of Chinese pottery, probably dating from the sixteenth or seventeenth century. This piece of porcelain had evidently been mixed up with the mortar with which the wall had been constructed ; and when I saw it, it was firmly imbedded therein. It was on the outside of the wall about 4 feet from the ground, so there is no question that it had become lodged in the wall inadvertently, at a date subsequent to the erection of the wall in question.

It is fairly evident that the particular edifice in which this fragment of pottery was found could not have been erected prior to A.D. 1500, and probably considerably later. The house in question is one of many of similar style and design, and the find certainly confirms in a somewhat cogent manner the estimate of the age of the Pujini group, as determined by the loopholes in the walls of the citadel.

Sir Richard Burton relates that when he visited Pemba in 1857, he was informed, while at Chake-Chake, that there were ruins about a day's march away from that town, and that the remains of two steeples of a Christian church were still to be seen. Burton evidently concluded that the ruins were of Portuguese origin, and he tells us that he did not

[1] *Encyclopaedia Britannica.*

visit them, as he took no interest in looking at Portuguese remains.

These ruins thus referred to must have been those now known as Pujini, but I think he was mistaken in concluding that they were of Portuguese origin, for they are, without doubt, of Asiatic—probably South Arabian—design, and this view is strengthened by the undoubted Afric-Arabian emblem of the royal horn, or *siwa*, which embellishes the wall of the elaborate well or shrine, to which reference has already been made.

That the Portuguese during their long occupancy of Pemba may have had a garrison stationed at Pujini citadel, to watch the east coast of the island, is more than likely ; but that they built churches there, there is nothing now to show.

There seem to be no indications of any such structures in the existing ruins, nor do the local natives preserve any tradition that such buildings ever existed.

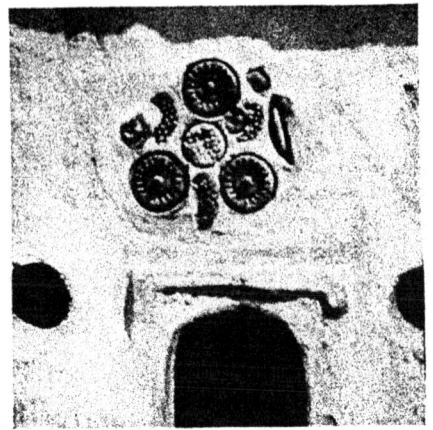

ASTRONOMICAL DESIGN ON TOMB AT ZANZIBAR.

STONE FRETWORK.

CHAPTER XXVI

THE CHWAKA RUINS

THE group of ruins known as Chwaka is situated in the extreme north-eastern part of Pemba Island, nine miles from the little town of Weti.

The founders of ancient Chwaka placed their stronghold on a prominent eminence at the southern end of a long creek, and in the days of its prosperity it must have presented an imposing and effective appearance to those who approached it from the sea.

The site was well and skilfully chosen, and the intricacies of the navigation of the deep inlet upon which the town was built practically secured it from any attack by sea. It moreover possessed a good supply of fresh water, derived from a rivulet which skirts the southern extremity of the settlement and debouches into the creek close to the town. So on the east the peninsula upon which the town was erected is bounded by the creek, and on the west by the rivulet and a swampy valley, difficult of access to an armed force of any size.

The ruins are to-day buried in a dense mass of forest growth, and doubtless many of the ancient buildings have long ago succumbed to the damp, and to the clinging creepers, and lie buried deep in the rich humus of the forest.

Nevertheless there remain some interesting buildings of a character which tends to indicate that Chwaka in its prime must have been a large and important port.

Unfortunately other agencies than those of Nature have been at work in the demolition of the old town. In the eighteenth century the Mazrui Arabs from Mombasa established a fortress about a mile to the north of the Chwaka ruins, and there is every reason to think that they utilised much of the material of the ancient settlement for the erection of their stronghold across the valley. Fortunately, superstitious fears appear to have prevented them from destroying the mosques and some of the tombs on the ancient site, and it is these remains which it is proposed to describe in the present chapter.

The following list comprises the most interesting remains of the Chwaka ruins :

1. The small mosque.
2. Haruni's tomb.
3. The "great" mosque.

The Chwaka ruins are conveniently approached by land; and on nearing the site, one sees ahead the forest-capped eminence which conceals the site of the ancient town. The forest looks dark and mysterious, in strange contrast to the sunny landscape around.

The road leads at first through pleasant coco-nut palm groves, and cheerful-looking hamlets of native huts. When close to the ruins, one enters a saucer-shaped shallow valley, through which a stream meanders. All around the grass is lush and green, and pools covered with water-lilies impart a pleasant sense of coolness to the scene. As we proceed a heron slowly rises from the reeds and sails away towards the south. A few fat oxen revel belly-deep in the rich grasslands which border the stream, while immediately in front rises the ridge with its dark covering of forest.

This calm Arcadian scene, brilliant with sun, and cooled with a gentle breeze, aids us to attune our minds to contemplate with sympathetic interest the relics of a people long since dead, and whose identity has been forgotten.

We arrive at length at the foot of the eminence upon which the ruins stand ; and the path, freshly cleared for our convenience—for normally the native prefers to leave the harmless spirits of the dead severely alone—leads with a sharp rise up the steep bluff to the plateau, and we plunge at once into the cool damp glades of the forest. It is nearing noon, and the streaks of sunshine strike through the leaves overhead, and illuminate with dappled patches of gold the dead leaves underfoot.

The path winds like a snake through the trees—for what native ever yet made a path straight between two points ?—until a sudden turn brings us face to face with the ruins of a small mosque.

Native tradition affirms that this building was erected by a devoted wife to the memory of her husband, who was a ruler or prince of the ancient colony. The fact that this story of the founding of this mosque exists confirms in a measure the impression gained from an inspection of the building that it is not of extreme antiquity. This is the only ruin in Pemba, so far as I am aware, to which is attached a more or less definite account of its origin. The history of the foundation of the other ruined buildings throughout the island appears to be entirely unknown, save the universal legend that they were the handiwork of the Shirazi or ancient Persian settlers. But as regards this small mosque at Chwaka, not only is the above tale regarding its foundation current, but the name—" Miskiti cha Chiroko "—by which it is known locally tends to indicate that its erection could not have been so very long ago. " Miskiti cha Chiroko " signifies literally " the mosque of the pea," from the tradition that a species of small pea called *chiroko* was mixed with the mortar with the idea of rendering it extremely hard and tough.

The general style of this mosque is Shirazian, but of a late and modified type. The two entrance doors in the eastern wall are arched and edged with dressed stone, but, like the kibla recess within, are of poor design. The three central pillars which support the roof are octagonal—not rectangular as in the older buildings—and their dimensions are out of proportion to the small size of the building. The most interesting feature, however, of this mosque is the three existing cupolas or domes which form the roof. This is the only ruined building in Pemba with the domed roof practically intact.

The roof appears to be in imminent danger of falling, for it is wrenched away from its supporting pillars and is poised in a very precarious manner. One of the four cupolas has already collapsed, and a slight earth tremor, or a further subsidence of the foundations, will surely complete the inevitable downfall of the whole structure. Beyond the usual water cistern used for ablutions before prayer, there are no other signs of graves or buildings in the immediate vicinity of this little mosque.

Continuing our way along the forest path, we next come to the best-known feature of the Chwaka ruins, known as " Haruni's Tomb."

Who Haroun—or, as the softer-toned Kiswahili has it, " Haruni "—was, is not very clear ; but tradition asserts that he was a Shirazian Prince of Chwaka, and lies buried in the grave we see before us. There is a certain fascination about Haruni's tomb which is difficult to express in words. An air of calmness and serenity envelops it, and a sense of beauty and restfulness hallows it.

One has seen older, more elaborate, and more beautiful graves, but few engender the same subtle influence which seems to emanate from the rough-built tomb beneath which Haruni sleeps.

Possibly the loneliness of the grave in the sunny forest glade may account for our mood, or perhaps it may only be a predilection for the mystery of the unknown ; but however that may be, it is significant that the most unimaginative and matter-of-fact visitor generally admits that Haruni's tomb is " rather nice."

The tomb is of the pattern which in previous pages has been referred to as a " pillared tomb," for at the grave-head a tall stele or column rises from the top of the encircling wall. The style in its earlier types is supposed to be Persian or Shirazian, but it is probable that Haruni's grave is of more recent date, for there are signs that the original design has been modified by Arab influence.

The accompanying illustration shows Haruni's tomb in its present condition, and it will also afford the reader some idea of the forest scenery in which the ruins of old Chwaka lie hidden.

As in tombs of this pattern, the actual grave is surrounded by a wall, upon the eastern end of which rises a lofty pillar, and in the wall opposite is the doorway, which gives access to the interior of the enclosure.

There are some interesting details in the structure of this

HARUNI'S TOMB, CHIWAKA.

particular tomb which deserve attention, if only to demonstrate the modifications which Arab influence has imposed
upon the original design.

The pillar, for instance, is no longer rectangular, but ten-
sided, and the outside of it is decorated with numerous
sunken panels, some of which are surmounted with the
trefoil or saracenic arch. There is, too, a niche over the
grave-head, but it is the rounded Arab recess and not
rectangular or pointed as in the earlier tombs.

An interesting detail over the niche is the emblem, fashioned
in bas-relief, of the sun-disc, a device so pregnant and suggestive of the ancient worship of the sun, prevalent in
pre-Islamic times in Southern Arabia, in Chaldea and Iran.

This representation of the forms of the sun and moon
upon the walls of mosques and tombs in Zanzibar is of
archæological interest, for it reminds us that the religion
of the ancient Sabeans of South-west Arabia, who were so
closely associated with the Azanian coasts and its islands
from the earliest times, consisted in the worship of the
heavenly bodies.[1]

This cult, that eminent Orientalist the late Professor Palmer
opines, came originally from Chaldea, but, as in so many
other religions, its primitive simplicity became corrupted,
and at the period of the Mahomedan Revelation had
absorbed a number of new deities, with many meaningless
and superstitious rites.

In the Koran the following allusion [2] to King Solomon
and the Queen of Sheba indicates that the latter and her
people, viz. the Sabeans of South Arabia, worshipped the
sun, and, as we have already seen, the heavenly bodies.

" . . . And he [the lapwing[3]] tarried not long, and said
[to King Solomon], ' I have compassed what ye compassed
not : for I bring you from Sheba a sure information : verily
I found a woman ruling over them, and she was given all
things, and she had a mighty throne ; and I found her and
her people adoring the sun instead of God, for Satan had

---

[1] The name Sabean may be derived from the Hebrew *tsaba*, " a host or
multitude," as in Genesis ii 1. Thus the meaning may be " those that worship the host of heaven." See Hugbes's Dictionary of Islam.

[2] The *Koran*, chapter xxvii., " The Chapter of the Ant."

[3] The modern hoopoe.

made seemly to them their works, and turned them from
the path, so that they are not guided.   ' "

On the outside of Haruni's tomb, close to the entrance
aperture, are three other designs, sculptured on the wall,
which are worthy of close inspection.

These devices are carefully moulded in relief, and represent a sun-disc, a horn complete with its baldrick, and
what I conjecture to represent a diadem or crown. Unfortunately the moulding of this last design has partially
crumbled away, and identification is difficult.

These emblems on the wall of the tomb probably denote,
like the armorial bearings on Western graves, the royal or
princely rank of the deceased.

The history of the adoption and significance of the
trumpet or horn, by the ancient Arab and Persian colonists
of Azania, has yet to be written. It would make an interesting subject for special study, for there is little doubt
but that it was an emblem pregnant with meaning, the full
significance of which we have failed to realise.

Every one who was any knowledge of the past history of
the East African coast knows full well that every petty
Sultan owned a horn of ivory or of wood, which, like the
crown and sword of state, testified and marked him of royal
position.

The horn, or *siwa*, of the Swahili has for many centuries
been the emblem of royalty on the Azanian coast among the
Persian and Arab communities settled there, and one of the
first experiences of Vasco da Gama and his crew on arrival
at Malindi, during his pioneer voyage from Lisbon to the
Indies, was the music played in his honour by the musicians
of the local " king " of that place.

The anonymous narrator of that memorable voyage relates that at a reception held in honour of the Portuguese
Admiral, " there were many anafils,[1] and two trumpets of
ivory richly carved, and of the size of a man, which were
blown from a hole in the side, and made sweet harmony with
the anafils."[2]

[1] Probably the Swahili *zomari*, a kind of clarionet.
[2] *Journal of the First Voyage of Vasco da Gama*, 1497-1499, translated by
E. G. Ravenstein. (Hakluyt Society.)

The translator of the above extract quotes Sir John Kirk as saying :

" . . . The royal trumpet, or *siwa*, was peculiar to the cities ruled by the descendants of the Persians of Shiraz, who settled on this coast [East Africa] in the eleventh and twelfth centuries. They are of ivory or copper or wood, and consisted of three pieces. The ivory or copper was sometimes most elaborately carved, and bore Arabic texts."

There still exist at some of the towns of East Africa the ancient royal horns of the early Arabian and Persian colonists, and those who are acquainted with Zanzibar will not require to be reminded of the two sacred *siwa*, or trumpets, which belonged to the Mwenyi Mkuu, or Lord of Dunga, and with what veneration they were regarded by his subjects.[1]

But the fact that the horn was emblematic of royalty and sovereignty is by no means confined to East Africa; and the farther one probes back into the past, the more striking becomes the part which the trumpet and horn have played in the history of diverse nations, at different epochs in the history of the world.

In the sculptures of Babylon and Nineveh, for instance, the Assyrian Hercules Nin is represented as a giant, attacking and killing a bull ; and the god, adorned with the bull's horns as a trophy, is again depicted killing a lion. As pointed out by Mr. Hislop, this feat of strength is probably the origin of the significance of a horn, as a symbol of power and sovereignty, throughout the world.[2]

The word " crown," that supreme emblem of royalty, is derived from the Assyrian *krn* meaning a " horn " : and the title " Cronus," accorded to the Assyrian god Bel, simply means " the horned one."[3]

The Latin word *corona* is, of course, of similar origin, and, as pointed out by Garnier, indicates the points or " horns " by which crowns are surmounted.

So much for the horn as an emblem of domination when the world was young : but what of it in more recent times ?

---

[1] These two horns, which are of wood, are now kept at the British Residency, Zanzibar.
[2] *The Worship of the Dead*, by Garnier.   [3] *Ibid.*

The horn or trumpet is stated to have been the first musical instrument evolved by man, and of a surety it appears to have appealed to humanity in all ages and in all stages of human development. And yet in its present form, which differs but little from the original design, it must still be regarded as a primitive instrument. How strange it is that its limited notes can appeal so stirringly to the human mind as typical of majesty, of the dread of kings, of terror, of power, of uplifting, of glory, and of joy. Is not the whole human race to be awakened by the trump, reverberating through the aisles of the universe, on the Last Day?

How well one can visualise, in the ancient Hebrew worship of Jehovah, the priests " blowing up the trumpets in the new moon "! And the sun worshippers of old Iran, long before the Arab conquest, heralding with their enormous trumpets, from their city gates, the rising sun.[1]

From the early days of Islam, the horn or the trumpet has been the emblem of command, especially in a military sense. Thus when El-Aziz-Billah, the Fatimite Caliph of Egypt, invaded Syria in the tenth century, he was accompanied by 500 trumpets, each representing the chief commanders of his host.

And to-day, in this modern twentieth century, which we consider so prosaic and unromantic when compared with those misty epochs of the past, how could we get on without our trumpets and our horns? It really rather startles one, when one realises how the blare of the trumpet still thrills us. Even to-day it is the indispensable accompaniment of royal state. The royal heralds with their trumpets echoing down the royal gallery announce the Sovereign's approach. They announce his accession, they announce his demise!

---

[1] " From the days of Jamshid, who built the palaces still called by his name near Shiraz, every great city has enjoyed the privilege of hearing music, which is played from a gateway to usher in the rising sun, and to play out the setting sun.

" Indeed it is evident that this music is of great antiquity. The instruments consist of kettle drums of a large size, and long trumpets quite six feet long. When I hear the music I feel I am an Irani, whose history goes back to the days when the sun was worshipped."—*The Glory of the Shia World*, translated by Major P. Sykes. (MacMillan & Co., London.)

MULLION-WINDOW OF RUINED MOSQUE, MSUKA, PEMBA.

DECORATIONS ON HARUNI'S TOMB.

Every military guard has its bugler, and the importance of the salute rendered by the guard just depends whether it is accompanied by a flourish on the bugle or not.

We need not pursue the matter further. Whether in war or peace, the horn or trumpet seems to be still indispensable to humanity; and as in the ages past when it denoted the domination of the Assyrian deity, so later it was the emblem of royalty sculptured on the lonely grave of Haruni, the Shirazian prince in far-distant Pemba.

As already stated, the significance of the third emblem on Haruni's tomb at Chwaka is obscure.

The device has become broken and indistinct, and it is difficult to say precisely what it represents. It might be many things. It might be the small targe or shield of rhinoceros hide, decorated with silver, which Arabs from Omân used to carry. The sun disc, and the royal horn, are not uncommon devices in the ruins of Pemba, but nothing has yet been discovered, either in Zanzibar or Pemba, similar to the third bas-relief on Haruni's tomb. My own impression is that it represents a diadem or princely head-dress such as was worn by Persians, for apart from the general shape there is a mark on the uninjured portion of the sculpture distinctly suggestive of a decoration of precious stones. If it is not an ornamental head-covering, then it may be the peaked or plumed casque of a warrior.

Some fifty yards to the south-east of Haruni's tomb we come to the "great" mosque. The qualifying prefix is only used in a comparative sense to differentiate this mosque from the small mosque we have already alluded to.

The "great" mosque, although not very extensive, is a substantial and elaborately constructed edifice, and standing as it does on a small eminence, it must have picturesquely dominated the town, and have been a prominent landmark from the sea.

The chief feature of interest in this edifice is the interior of the northern wall, which is, or rather was, decorated with numerous porcelain bowls cemented into the wall over the kibla recess. Only the depressions now remain to mark the former position of this China ware. Some may, during the course of years, have fallen out, but undoubtedly the majority have been picked out, probably by natives, and occasionally by European visitors.

As a rule these bowls are fixed into position with a cement of such extreme hardness that it is almost impossible to extract the pottery without breaking it : and of course directly it is cracked in the process of extraction, a native has no further use for it. That this view is correct is proved by the fact that on the soil at the foot of the wall being excavated, the broken fragments of some of the original bowls were disclosed, with the cement still adhering on the outside.

The ware thus recovered proved to be celadon-glaze pottery of the Ming dynasty, while some of the fragments with incised patterns on the inside of the bowls are adjudged to date from the Sung dynasty (A.D. 960–1279).

In addition to these decorations of pottery—a characteristic feature of Shirazian architecture—the wall is further embellished with three stone discs surrounded with a cable-pattern edging. The largest of these discs, which is placed immediately over the point of the kibla arch, may have represented the sun, while the two other discs on either side may have been intended for the moon, although it is curious that the centre and right-hand disc are of the same pattern, while the left one is embellished with an extra ring.

The scheme of decoration further comprises a free use of stone courses, decorated with the chevron or double-cable device, inserted between the clustered columns of the arched recess, and also as a border to the two rectangular recesses on either side of the kibla.

The general aspect of the kibla arch and its decoration is pleasing, even in its present ruinous and despoiled condition, and the " great " mosque at Chwaka must be admitted to be the most elaborate example of late Shirazian work which exists in the Zanzibar Sultanate.

It is the desire of all good Mahomedans to be buried in the vicinity of a mosque, just as Christians are laid to rest in the hallowed ground around their churches : so we find around the Chwaka mosque various stone enclosures containing ancient graves. Immediately at the back of the mosque are the remains of a very large pillared tomb, evi-

dently the grave of a personage of great importance. Unfortunately the pillar now lies prone and in pieces, and the
fabric of the mausoleum is in a ruinous condition. There
appear to be no inscriptions or emblems, such as decorate
the tomb of Haruni, on any of these graves clustered outside
the mosque, and they appear to be of greater age than that
of Haruni. Some undoubtedly at one time were ornamented with high pillars, while some of the humbler ones
appear never to have been so decorated.

Lying scattered in the forest around the mosque are
some remains of substantially built houses, probably of a
residential character. Some wells, thirty or forty feet deep,
are also met with, and no doubt a systematic inspection of
the whole site would reveal other interesting remains. The
natives, who take a pride in the ruins of the mosques, seem
disinclined themselves to explore deeper into the forest in
search of other ruins. They suggest that wild bees will
attack the searchers, but in reality of course they fear to
disturb or annoy the spirits of the place by penetrating into
their forest-domain : and they are apprehensive that they
might incur the displeasure of the jinns, if they introduced
strangers into the sacred places.

With so few facts available it is not easy to offer any
opinion as to the age of the ruins at Chwaka. The pottery
hitherto discovered ranges from the tenth to the fifteenth
century, and it may be assumed, pending further exploration,
that it was during that period that the town was flourishing,
although there is little doubt but that it was occupied as a
permanent settlement at a much later date.

It is certain that much care and labour has been expended
in the construction of the mosques and tombs, and of the
permanent nature of the settlement in general there can
be no doubt—in fact, everything points to an occupancy of
centuries.

CHAPTER XXVII

THE RUINS ON TUMBATU ISLAND

THIS group of ruins is situated at the south-eastern corner of Tumbatu Island, which is separated from the main island of Zanzibar by a sea-channel some three miles wide.

Tumbatu is a low-lying coral islet, about five miles in length from north to south, and about one mile in breadth. It is situated off the north-west corner of the parent island, and at its highest point attains a height of fifty feet above sea-level. It is covered with coarse grasses and with a variety of bushes and scrub, through which are interpersed larger trees, while in the vicinity of the native villages and clearings we of course come across the ubiquitous coco-nut palm.

The ruins which are described in this chapter lie scattered irregularly along the sea-edge, on the summit of a low coralline cliff, twelve feet above high-water mark. Owing to this impermeable rampart, the sea has been unable to encroach upon or destroy any portion of the town, as has been the case at most of the ruined sites in Zanzibar and Pemba.

Ruins were previously known to exist at this particular spot in Tumbatu, and Burton tells us that he inquired as to the whereabouts of " the fort built by the Arabs," but he could not obtain any information on the subject. He apparently did not see any of the ruins which are dealt with in this chapter. It was not until 1916 that any attempt was made to clear the remains of this ancient town from the enveloping mass of vegetation which hid it from view. Even now much remains to be done, in order to ascertain the full extent of the ruins, for the natives of the island assert that the remains of stone build-mgs lie scattered in every direction, and extend at intervals along the sea-coast for some miles.

Enough of the ruins have been disclosed, however, to indicate clearly that this forgotten and unnamed town must have been of considerable size and importance ; in fact, the Tumbatu group of ruins is the largest and most extensive of any yet discovered in Zanzibar and Pemba Islands, and must have surpassed in size the ancient settlement of Ndagoni. Of course the true extent of the latter place will never be known, so much of it having been washed away by the encroaching sea; but judging by the number and extent of the ruins, there is little doubt but that Tumbatu was considerably larger. In both cases the stone-built ruins which we see to-day could have formed but a portion of the towns, and it may be conjectured that Tumbatu must have been at least four times the size of Ndagoni. In addition to the stone houses, there were hundreds, probably thousands of houses of less durable material, just as is the case in the towns of Zanzibar and Mombasa to-day.

The ruins at Ndagoni extend along the sea-front for less than half a mile, while those at Tumbatu, so far as at present ascertained, stretch for some two miles. By this it must not be understood that an unbroken line of ruined buildings exists within that distance : such is not the case, but within that limit, remains of substantial stone houses and walls are scattered at varying intervals.

Before proceeding to describe the main features of the ruins, it may be observed that they are composed of coral-line limestone, probably obtained from some local quarry. The buildings are constructed of rubble-work, bound together with lime-mortar. Certain distinctive features of the work enable us to classify the ruins as belonging to the Shirazian type, and to differentiate them from the Afro-Arabian style, which is chiefly in evidence among the edifices built in Zanzibar during the last two centuries.

As already pointed out elsewhere, the Shirazian characteristics are the graceful pointed arch of dressed limestone blocks, the mouldings and courses of which are generally cut to an angle less than a right angle (viz. 85°), the peaked and divided keystones of the arches, the coigns of dressed stone, the rectangular wall-recesses, and the use of the cable and chevron design for decorative purposes.

Associated with these evidences of origin may be noted the high standard of design and technique which is evident in the crumbling remnants of these old Shirazian towns. Following the plan adopted in previous chapters, it is proposed to deal only with those features of the ruins which may be considered of general interest, or which are typical of the group. In the following pages I shall therefore briefly refer to the following :

1. The mosque.
2. The (so-called) palace.
3. The buried arch.
4. The subterranean chamber.

The Mosque.—This is the best-preserved building in the ruins. It is situated within a few feet of the sea, on the top of a small eminence which rises from the sea-beach. This proximity to the sea is significant, as indicating that the builders belonged to a race who had command of the sea. The mosque even to-day is plainly visible from the main island of Zanzibar, and the town of which it formed a part must have similarly been manifest to all who approached it by sea.

The chief feature of interest in the mosque is the range of four arched doorways in its eastern wall. These doorways gave access to a side mosque or chapel, which adjoins the main body of the large mosque. The doorways are worthy of attention, as typical of the best characteristics of the Shirazian style of architecture, and in proportion and design they would not disgrace some famous Gothic gateways of Europe. The mention of Europe reminds one of the fact that it was not until the twelfth century that Europe adopted the pointed arch from the East.

This arcade of four graceful arches at Tumbatu does not appear to have constituted the true entrance of the mosque, but merely the dividing line between the aisle of the main building and the smaller side mosque. The outer wall of the main fabric has fallen, and left the arcade exposed to view.

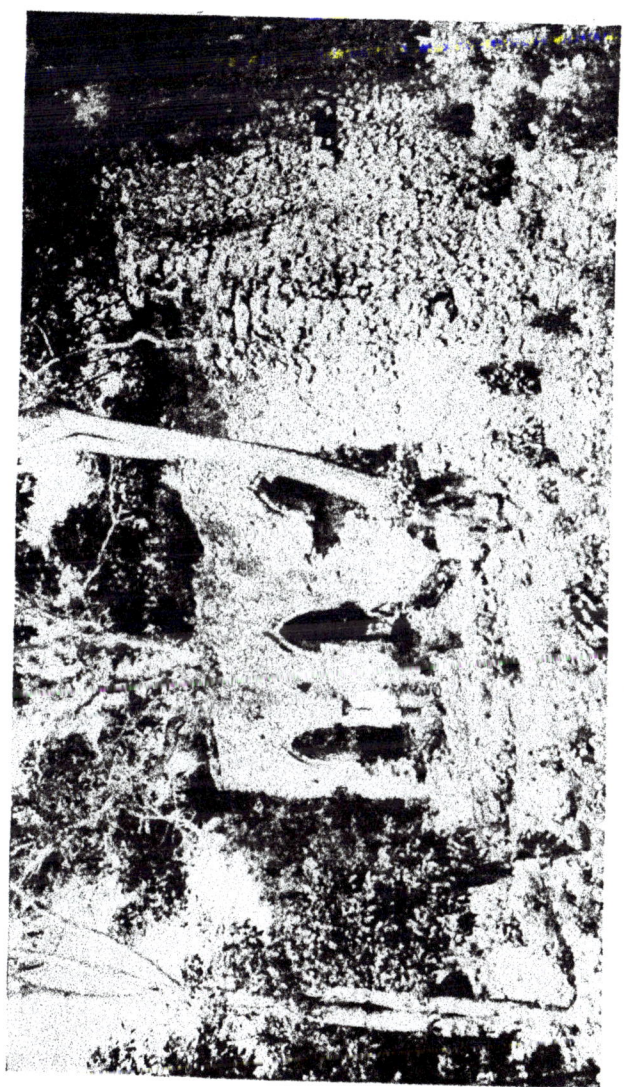

RUINED MOSQUE OF TUMBAT

The Tumbatu mosque is not of great size, being only fifty feet square, but it possesses a rather unusual feature in the form of a side mosque.

The modern natives of Tumbatu suggest that this side mosque was used by women for their devotions, but other Moslems whom I have consulted on this point appear to consider such a provision unlikely. However, it appears possible that the Tumbatu islanders may be correct in their assumption, for although women are as a rule expected to pray at home, in some few mosques they are admitted to a part specially reserved and screened off for their sole use. Thus in the mosque at Sitta Zainab in Cairo, women are admitted to such a reserved area, and in Jerusalem in the Aksa mosque a latticed balcony is provided for the use of Moslem women.

If the side mosque at Tumbatu was indeed intended for women's use, then the twelfth-century dwellers of Tumbatu appear to have been considerably more liberal-minded with regard to the spiritual needs of their womenfolk than the Moslem of to-day.

Another explanation of the existence of this side mosque is that it constituted the original building, and the larger fabric now adjoining it was constructed at a later date to accommodate an increased number of worshippers. That the two mosques were built at different times is fairly evident from the obvious break in the continuity of the masonry work, but it is difficult to determine which was the first to be erected.

The " Women's Mosque " contains an attractive feature. This is a very ruinous, but beautifully proportioned kibla in the northern wall, and one can well understand that the designer of the arcade already referred to also planned and erected this arched recess.

To-day we see it battered and crumbling, but in its decrepitude the touch of the true artist in stone is evident in its perfect proportion and grace of design. It is composed of the roughest blocks of rock, there is no embellishment whatever, and yet its merit is obvious.

Scattered irregularly in the bush around the mosque lie numerous remains of buildings and walls of all dimensions.

26

Some were obviously residential houses, while in other cases many of the walls are of great length, and indicate the sites, it may be supposed, of gardens or courtyards. The buildings appear to have been erected on no regular plan, and are dotted about seemingly without any relation to each other. Occasionally one comes across two buildings parallel to each other, and the space between them may have been a lane or alley in the city, but at present it is not possible to reconstruct the plan of the town with any degree of accuracy.

This lack of system in town-planning is of course quite in accord with Eastern ideals, and those who have lived in Oriental towns realise that this system of narrow streets is not altogether to be condemned, for it ensures that the population can move about and transact their business in the grateful shade of the houses. The city of Zanzibar, with its tortuous streets, exemplifies this advantage clearly. It is only when the European health fanatic enters the arena, imbued with the idea of teaching the benighted Oriental the proper way to lay out a town, that the cool, shady streets are turned into broad, blinding, dusty, sun-roasted, straight-as-an-arrow roadways.

Next to the mosque one of the most important ruins is that situated at the southern extremity of the ruins, some half a mile from the mosque. It is called by the local natives the " King's Palace," but except that the walls are more substantial than those of other ruins, and the extent of ground over which the remains are scattered is considerable, there is little to indicate the nature of the ruined edifice. It is finely situated on the very edge of the low coral cliff, and is fully open to the fresh south-west trade-winds which blow for the greater part of the year.

It is not possible to ascertain the original plan of the building, for the ruins consist of a maze of broken walls and blocks of masonry heaped together, and scattered throughout the surrounding bush. That the edifice was of considerable size is evident, and that it was at least two stories in height is probable. A row of basement chambers and vestiges of a drainage system is all that is now recognisable of the " King's Palace."

The local natives, who take a great interest in these ruins, state that it was in this palace that Yussuf, the founder of the town and father of the builder of Kilwa, lived.

This story is, of course, but a tradition, but it is well to bear in mind, before entirely rejecting it, that the Tumbatu islanders are notorious for their aloofness and their disinclination to associate with the ordinary Swahili of Zanzibar. It is in places like Tumbatu, where intercourse with the outside world is discouraged, that tradition may very often be founded on a substratum of truth.

About 250 yards to the north of the " palace," and 70 yards from the sea-shore, stands what I have for facility of reference named the " buried arch."

At this point the ground rises in a gentle slope from the sea, and the arch stands thus on a slight eminence. The archway is half buried—and thus prevented from falling—in the debris and ruin of the edifice of which it formed a part. What the nature of the building originally was, it is without further excavation impossible to assert, but that it was of some pretension is evident from the height of the standing wall.

The arch is well constructed of sharply dressed limestone, and is decorated freely with the favourite chevron pattern, which is found so widely distributed among the ruins attributed to the Persians in Africa.

There is little doubt that between the " King's Palace " and this fallen arch, and again between the arch and the mosque, remains of other buildings exist, but the whole site requires to be carefully cleared of vegetation—a laborious and recurrent task—before a clear idea of the full extent of the town—one might almost be excused for writing " city " —can be obtained.

About 100 yards to the west of the mosque are the remains of two extensive buildings standing close together. They are surrounded by an enclosing wall, one side of which is 70 feet in length, so that the areas enclosed are considerable. The natives suggest that these godowns and buildings may represent the site of the custom sheds, where goods and merchandise were stored ; and as they are situated exactly opposite the only feasible landing-place, the conjecture is certainly reasonable. In any case the designation of " Custom House " will serve for their future identification.

Northward of the Custom House and the mosque lie a number of ruins, some evidently houses, which may have been, from indications in the walls, double-storied, and furnished with wide verandahs. In one of these houses, which lies a little way back from the sea-front, is a well-preserved rectangular wall-recess, which served originally as a cupboard or shelf. Reference has already been made to these characteristic wall-recesses, which are quite a feature in the ruined houses of Zanzibar and Pemba, and which are a prominent feature in every Arab house.

There is a marked and typical distinction between the recesses found in ancient Shirazian buildings, and those met with in Arab houses. The former, as already explained, are rectangular, with a vertical division down the centre, while the latter are often of great size, and extend from the floor to the ceiling of a room. They are invariably arched at the top, and are divided horizontally by two or three teak shelves. The Arabs adorn these enormous recesses or niches in their rooms with porcelain vases, clocks, and other less-valuable articles.

The square or rectangular recess is not Arabic, but of Shirazian design, and is found in conjunction with the graceful pointed arches of the latter cult.

Among the many ruins to the north of the central mosque may be mentioned a high mound surrounded by the traces of a substantial wall, which suggests the possibility of a tower—perhaps a lighthouse—having once occupied the site.

The most northerly ruin at present disclosed in the Tumbatu group is built on the very edge of the coral cliff, and from its position and its general elaborate plan may have been the " fort " (inquired for by Burton) which guarded the roadstead and the town.

An interesting feature of this building is the subterranean chamber beneath it. This room now lies open to the sky, and is partially filled with broken fragments of masonry and other debris. It is not very large, being only about 10 feet long by 8 feet broad, but that it was of some importance·

is evidenced from the fact that access down to it was through a stone doorway of dressed stone. The walls are plastered, and as it must have been excavated out of the hard coralline rock on which the town is built, it is clear that considerable labour must have been expended upon it. The exact uses to which this underground chamber was put can of course only be a matter of conjecture, but it obviously could be utilised either as a dungeon or a treasure chamber.

At present no systematic excavations have been made at the Tumbatu ruins, so the list of articles found merely comprise a few beads of poor make and a fragment of Chinese pottery with celadon glaze, probably of the Ming dynasty period. This latter specimen was found in the vicinity of the mosque, and as it has cement adhering to the base, it may be assumed that it originally decorated the inside of the mosque or some tomb. It is a curious fact that hitherto no graves or mausolea have been discovered, except a few rather vague and inconspicuous vestiges near the northern end of the mosque. It may be that the whereabouts of the ancient burial-ground has been deliberately concealed by the Tumbatu islanders—not at all an unlikely contingency.

The question of beads found at Tumbatu, and at other ruined sites, has been dealt with elsewhere, so it remains to remark that only a few small beads have been discovered at Tumbatu, and these do not in any way compare with the beauty and variety of the beads found at the ruins in Pemba Island.

How old are the Tumbatu ruins ?

It must be confessed that a definite reply cannot be given to this question.

The very name of the town is forgotten, and there is little or no evidence at present forthcoming upon which to base a definite pronouncement as to who built the town, or at what date.

We know that the Arab geographer Yakut, who wrote in the thirteenth century, mentions that the people of the island of " Tumbat " were already Moslems at that period. This piece of information is interesting and important, as affording some definite basis from which to start.

Now " Tumbat " is a small coral islet, and although our geographer does not specifically mention the existence of a town, it is, I think, evident that the only justification for referring to such a small islet off the African coast, or for having any cognisance of its existence at all, would have been the fact that an important town and port existed on it. The islet is only 3,619 acres in extent, and there is certainly no reason to suppose that there is another ruined town on it.

It is then, I think, a fair and reasonable conclusion that the ruined town we see to-day was the identical " Tumbat " referred to by Yakut 700 years ago. I do not mean to imply that all the buildings which exist to-day are 700 years old, although I am quite ready to believe that some at least may be.

Associated with the name of " Tumbat," Yakut refers to the island of Lendguja, obviously identical with " Unguja," the modern Swahili name for Zanzibar. He tells us that the people of the island of Lendguja were wont to go to Tumbatu, to seek shelter and safety. The inference is clear, that in case of attack—possibly by pirates or slavers—the native population of Zanzibar Island used to cross over to the important town of Tumbatu, and seek shelter behind its fortifications.

It was at the period Yakut wrote that the Persian colonies on the Azanian coast were nearing the height of their prosperity ; and Kilwa, the mistress of the East African littoral, was outdistancing all competitors in wealth and influence, owing to the control she possessed over the Sofala gold trade.

It is manifest therefore that when Yakut wrote, the city of Tumbat must have been flourishing, and it is clear that by A.D. 1500—that is, at the time the Portuguese arrived in the Indian Ocean—the town of Tumbatu had, either been deserted as we find it to-day, or had sunk into insignificance.

Why this conclusion ? Because, had it retained any of its ancient importance, the Portuguese would most certainly have visited it, and would have recorded doing so : whereas we know that they ignored Zanzibar, and passed it by in silence. Their records are full of references to Kilwa, Sofala, Mombasa, and Malindi, but never a word of Tumbatu.

Even if Tumbatu is meant when the name " Zanzibar " is employed, it is evident that such casual mention can only have been applied to an insignificant place, bereft of all importance.

Tumbatu in its prime must have been, as can be seen from its ruins, one of the largest towns on the Azanian coast, and the only logical deduction we can draw is that it was flourishing when Yakut alluded to it in about A.D. 1220, and had become deserted or nearly so by A.D. 1500.

The natives of Tumbatu, a conservative and exclusive people, state that Tumbatu city was built before Kilwa was founded. This latter town was built in about A.D. 975, so there is nothing improbable, supposing the native tradition is well founded, in the conjecture that Tumbatu town was commenced as early as or even earlier than A.D. 900. This date would only allow three centuries for the town to have attained sufficient importance to have been worthy of mention by an Arab geographer in 1220 A.D. ; and it is evident, from the substantial nature of the buildings, that the town was of no mushroom growth, but must represent an occupancy of many centuries. As already observed, the first settlers would confine themselves to building houses of wood and clay, in precisely the same way as any modern pioneer—be he white or coloured—provides accommodation for himself in a new country. It is only those who succeed the pioneers, who think of erecting improved dwellings and comfortable houses of stone.

The better preservation of the buildings at Tumbatu, than at other ruined sites in Pemba, is easily accounted for by the fact that the Tumbatu town is built on a foundation of hard porous coral-rock. The consequence is, that the ground is perfectly drained, and cannot become waterlogged. Moreover the soil is so infertile and scanty, that forest growth will not thrive thereon : and as a result the ruins have been left free from those disintegrating agencies which in a more fertile and damper situation undermine the stability of ancient buildings.

A feature of the other ruined groups in Pemba Island is the quantity of pottery, glass, and beads of different patterns which are found in their vicinity. At Tumbatu similar remains, eloquent of a prolonged human occupancy, are conspicuous by their absence : or, the situation may be more accurately defined by saying that the middens and rubbish heaps of the town have not yet been located. At Tumbatu much of the foreshore is bare coral rock, and if the town refuse and broken crockery have in the past been consigned to the waves, it is probable that the fragments would be washed away into deep water by the strong currents which sweep through the sea-channel opposite the settlement.

At the other ruined towns in the Sultanate there is always a sandy beach or a backwater creek, where fragments of pottery and the like are retained and held back : and again, in most instances, the foreshore has been washed away by the encroaching sea, thus setting free the secrets of the town and graveyards.

Tumbatu, however, is built on an inviolable rampart of coral rock, and the sea has not been able to expose, during the centuries, its hidden treasures, and strew them on the beach.

CHAPTER XXVIII

SOME OTHER RUINS : IN PEMBA

1

BESIDES the groups of ruins which have been described in previous chapters, there are various isolated structures of ancient date which deserve notice ; not only on account of the interest which attaches to them architecturally, but to the mystery of their existence, in lonely and unexpected situations.

For instance, one can well understand the existence of a mosque or several mosques, in a group of ruins which was evidently once upon a time a town ; but when one comes across such an edifice, standing entirely by itself, in the midst of the jungle, without a trace or vestige of any other building in its vicinity, the desire to ascertain something of its history becomes intense, and one longs to know why the local natives still refer to the particular spot as " the town," where no town is !

So it is with the solitary stone house on the very edge of the cliff at Makongwe Island, or the lonely grave and the unfinished wall constructed on the inhospitable east coast of Pemba. What is their history and who built them ?

The first mentioned of these remains is a ruined mosque situated about a mile from the most northerly point of Pemba Island. It is not built on the shore, but lies almost half-way between the east and west coast of the great horn of land which terminates in Cape Kigomasha.

It was by chance that the ruin in question was rediscovered in 1916, and it is possible that no European had seen this particular mosque prior to that occasion.

It lies in dense bush, quite remote from any path or track ; and had not a fisherman mentioned its existence, it would still be lying unknown to Europeans at the present time.

There are several points of interest connected with this particular building, and in some respects it is unique among the ruins of Zanzibar and Pemba.

Its name is Msuka Mjini—that is, Msuka town—but, as already stated, there are no ruins save the mosque, and no vestige of a settlement. The forest and jungle close in upon the ancient structure, and large forest trees grow within the circuit of its walls, which they are slowly pulling to pieces.

Of the mosque, nothing remains but the outside walls and a deep well, on the southern side of the building. The kibla in the north wall is intact, and is interesting as possessing a rounded instead of a pointed arch. This fact inclines one to believe that the mosque is of Arabian rather than of Shirazian design : and with reference to this point, it may be remarked that the arch is not truly semicircular, but is of an elongated or oval shape. There is no doubt that this ovoid shape is intentional, for similarly formed arches are met with in the ruins at Kua, in the island of Mafia : in fact, it appears highly probable that the mosque at Msuka Mjini in Pemba and the ruined town at Kua are closely associated, for the style of the architecture in both places is, in many features, identical.

This adds greatly to the interest of the Msuka mosque, for here in the midst of an island, scattered with ruins which are typically Shirazian, we find this solitary specimen of another cult.

Within the recess of this kibla at Msuka was discovered an invocation in Arabic, scribbled on the plaster of the wall. Fortunately the writer of the prayer was inspired to add a date, and this alone makes the Msuka mosque unique among the ruins of Zanzibar and Pemba.

The fact that the invocation has been written on the wall within the kibla recess has preserved it intact from the rain and storms of centuries.

The translation as given below was made on the spot

RUINED MOSQUE, MSUKA, PEMB

11

by Sheikh Saleh-bin-Ali-bin-Saleh, Arabic interpreter to the British Resident, and runs as follows :

" In the name of God, He is All-Living. The Lord of those who have passed before, and of those who are to come —and Peace, the year 816."

The year 816 of the Hejira is equivalent to Anno Domini 1414.

So here at once, in addition to a very pious sentiment expressed in poetical language, we obtain an almost positive proof that the mosque was standing in A.D. 1414. From the fact that the invocation is scratched in the plaster of the wall, it may reasonably be inferred that the mosque at the time was a ruin, and therefore is considerably older than the date specified above. Apart from other considerations, a definite idea is obtained of the aspect of a building at least 500 years old. This mosque is very substantially and massively built, as can be seen from the illustration showing the oval-arched kibla.

To the right of the kibla recess will be seen the trunk of a big tree, the roots of which almost entirely hide the two stone steps which formed the pulpit, or *mimbar*, from which certain exhortations are wont to be delivered in Moslem fanes during prayer time on Fridays.

On the left of the recess will be noticed a small and tastefully designed niche, decorated round the edge with a number of hieroglyphics. In all so-called Shirazian mosques, built during the Persian occupation, the niches on either side of the kiblas are invariably rectangular, so this circular arched recess is something quite distinctive and unusual among the ancient buildings of the Zanzibar Sultanate.

A word must now be said regarding the pattern incised on the border which surrounds the niche. In connection with this device, it must be explained that in the southern wall of this mosque are the remains of a mullion window, constructed of cut and dressed stone ; and on this stone window frame are a series of signs or hieroglyphics, similar to those which surround the kibla recess.

In no other building, either in Zanzibar or Pemba, are similar devices to be found. In this respect the Msuka mosque again differs from all others.

What the hieroglyphics mean or represent has not yet
been determined, but it appears probable that they are
more than a chance pattern cut at random.   If the illustration of the mullion window-frame be referred to, it will
be observed that there are at least nine distinct and separate
symbols, most of which are reproduced, on the border
around the kibla niche.

The question as to the significance of these symbols at
Msuka requires careful investigation : for an important and
highly interesting link in the past history of Pemba may
be forged if these hieroglyphics prove to be really decipher-
able, or can be associated with any particular race of people
from Asia.

II

The Lonely Tomb at Vitongoje.—Vitongoje is the name of
a sparsely inhabited locality on the east coast of Pemba,
due eastward from the town of Chake.   The villages of this
area lie some distance from the coast, which is fringed for a
depth of a mile or two inland with an almost impenetrable
belt of dense thickets.   The soil is infertile, and the narrow
paths which traverse this wild bit of country are rendered
difficult and unpleasant by the constant protrusion of masses
and lumps of sharp coral rock.

The " bush " comes down to the sea-beach, and a few
hundred yards off-shore runs the line of coral reef, upon
which the rollers of the Indian Ocean break.   At high tide
the waves wash over this barrier, and sweep with tremendous
force up to the sandy beaches and low coral cliffs.   Altogether the locality known as Vitongoje is inhospitable, and
the coast is dangerous to all kinds of navigation.

It is on a stretch of sandy beach, lying between the dense
jungle and the breakers of the sea, that " the lonely tomb "
is situated.

No one knows who lies buried beneath it, or the reason of
its being located on the sea-shore.   But it is not only the
grave which calls for attention : for about 100 yards to
the south of this tomb is a very massive low stone wall,

which is obviously the commencement of some important undertaking. The wall or rampart, as it exists to-day, is about 100 yards in length, and it is not built in a straight line, but in a series of angles as if for purposes of defence. It is evidently in an unfinished condition.

What, then, is the explanation of the existence of this solitary grave, and the massive but incomplete wall on the sea-shore, in this remote and inhospitable region of Pemba ? It is impossible to say with certainty : but the native tradition appears to offer a likely solution of the problem.

They assert that long ago strangers from some distant country landed at this little inlet on the east coast of Pemba Island, and determined to found and build a city and a fortress.

The work was begun, and was progressing in a satisfactory manner, when suddenly their king or chief sickened and died. They buried him on the sea-shore, and leaving their work unfinished, as we see it to-day, they took to their ships and sailed away, no one knows whither.

That is the explanation given by the local natives of the lonely tomb on the sea-shore at Vitongoje.

That the unfinished wall was the commencement of a fort, or of a town wall, seems probable ; for it is planned so as to command and protect the landing-place and the shipping lying in the little bay. That the strangers were numerous appears likely, for the amount of work actually effected, and the prospective work in view, could only have been accomplished with the aid of many labourers.

What the inducements were which decided these immigrants to make their home at Vitongoje are not clear. The fact that the grave of their chief is on the beach itself points to the probability that the place, when they arrived, was entirely uninhabited, and that the thick, impenetrable bush came down to the very edge of the sea-shore, in precisely the manner it does at the present time.

Perhaps the party of Persian or Arab adventurers, driven from their homes by political or religious stress, had sailed for Africa, as many had done before, to seek new homes in the southern El Dorado of the Indian Ocean, and were driven by storms or unfavourable winds to this lonely spot on the coast of Pemba. Here, perhaps, some of their ships had been wrecked, or run aground, and, weary of their wanderings and hardships, they determined to build for themselves a home. Fever may have thinned their ranks, and when at last their chief succumbed, the fear of the encircling jungle seized the survivors, and they fled from the accursed spot.

Or it may have been that the new-comers were attacked and killed by the aboriginal natives who lurked in the bush.

Whatever the truth may be, some tragedy occurred, as is evident from the unfinished wall, the piles of material, the broken water-jars, and the lonely tomb on the sea-shore.

The Ruined Mosques at Chaoni, Mtangani, and Kiwani. —For purposes of record, it is desirable to mention these three mosques, situated in Pemba, although it is not considered necessary to describe them in detail. They are, in fact, all typical specimens of the smaller Shirazian mosque, and probably date from the thirteenth or fourteenth century.

The first-named is situated on the west coast of Pemba, while the other two are on the south-eastern coast of the island ; and the presence of these and other ruins indicates very clearly the extent to which the immigration of an alien race into Pemba at some period of its history had taken place.

Scattered about the island are not only ruined towns, but even, in remote localities such as Kiwani, substantial and well-built stone mosques are to be found. These mosques clearly demonstrate that a considerable population existed near them, and the very stability of the structures themselves prove, too, the permanency of this foreign occupation.

Perhaps it may again be emphasised that these stone buildings are entirely beyond the capability of the present native population to produce. These people regard them as the work of some other and strange race ; for the native of Eastern African extraction has no conception of the use of stone or mortar for building : his own requirements in architecture being satisfied with the ordinary erection of a wooden framework, tied together with coir fibre, and covered with red clay. If he lives in a locality where there is a stone outcrop, or if a ruin is handy, he may embody into the wooden framework of his house lumps of coral rock, prior to the application of the red clay, but that is the extent of his architectural efforts, especially in Pemba.

At the base of the bluff upon which the mosque at Chaoni is built are large quantities of broken pottery and porcelain ; and from this debris, pieces of cream-coloured Ting-ware of an early date have been picked up.

The mosque at Mtangani, on the east coast of Pemba, is also typical of the Shirazian style. It possesses the characteristic point-arched kibla, and two well-proportioned stone niches on either side. On the outside wall of this building, and close to the main entrance, are the marks of two bowls or saucers, previously embedded in the wall : but both pieces of pottery themselves are, however, unfortunately missing.

Two and a half miles to the south of Mtangani is the ruined mosque of Kiwani, another undoubted proof that at this latter place, also, was settled a colony of strangers.

It is when contemplating these evidences of former occupatiou, at a small and remote place like Kiwani, that the reality of this colonisation of Pemba, in former times, by some foreign race, is brought home to the modern visitor.

One can well understand the founding of towns and seaports by Persian and other Asiatics, for purposes of trade and commerce, but it is not so easy to comprehend the establishing of such settlements as must have existed at Kiwani, Mtangani, and other remote places. There could have been but little trade in such places, even supposing that there was a fairly dense aboriginal population. And yet we find these civilised strangers—we are bound to call people civilised who could build so beautifully and strongly in stone—settled permanently in the remote corners of Pemba, and leaving behind them, as memorials of their occupation, these stone temples, with their graceful doorways and their dressed-stone embellishments.

COMPARED with Pemba, the Island of Zanzibar is poor in ruins, and there are no series of mosques and groups of ruins dotted over the country to show that at any period the island was extensively colonised by strangers.

There is of course no doubt that the town on Tumbatu Island was founded and inhabited by aliens from Asia : but with this one great exception, actual evidence of ancient settlements is almost wanting.

Those remains which do exist will be briefly described in the following pages.

Unguja Kuu (Old Zanzibar).—One of the most interesting localities connected with the past history of Zanzibar is of course the site of the old native capital of the island at Unguja Kuu.

Unguja Kuu as seen from the sea is not imposing. All that meets the eye is a long low stretch of sandy beach, fringed with a dense mass of coco-nut palms. On the edge of the beach is one solitary house. To land, except at high tide, is a difficult matter, owing to the extreme shallowness of the water close to the shore. Far from this fact engendering any doubt as to whether the old town really existed on this particular site, the contrary is the case, for the first thought of the inhabitants of seaside towns in the past was to ensure their safety from attack, and the last thing they sought was a locality where deep water was contiguous to the shore. The sea, it must be remembered, was in ancient times the resort of slavers and pirates of all nationalities, and it was a supreme necessity for shore folk to sacrifice convenience, so as to preserve themselves and their town from sudden raids.

Hence there is nothing strange in the inhabitants of Unguja Kuu having selected a site for their homes which precluded landing from the sea except in the smallest of boats, and then only at high tides.

While therefore an uncompromising coral-reef protected

Old Zanzibar from the seaside, a creek ran up at the back of the settlement, and served to protect the vessels belonging to the inhabitants. This harbour is still used by native craft, differing no doubt but little in appearance from those which Ravasco seized 400 years ago, when he made his unprovoked attack on Unguja Kuu. In spite of the assertion of the headman and the villagers that no such things as beads or glass existed, a superficial search of the foreshore of the harbour at low tide, at the time of my visit, disclosed numerous fragments of Arabian and Syrian glass, pieces of glazed and coloured pottery, and some beads, all tokens of ancient occupation.

Of the old town itself only one or two possible vestiges are to be found. Close to the landing-beach there is a short length of loosely built wall, asserted by the natives to be the remains of a mosque. Close by, some green-glazed earthenware pottery was picked up. A few yards southward of the mosque, and close to the sea-shore, is a masonry-built well in a good state of preservation. There is nothing to show its age, except the native statement that it had been built by the Persians : and this appears likely from the known fact that the town rapidly declined after its destruction by Cabeira in 1653, and it is therefore improbable that so elaborate a well was constructed subsequent to that date.

If this is so, it may be possible that it was from this very well on the sea-shore that Sir James Lancaster refilled the water-casks of the *Edward Bonaventure*, while *en route* for the Indies in 1591.

About 40 yards from the well is a low mound, pointed out by the natives as being the place where several gold coins of extreme antiquity were found during Seyyid Majid's reign in 1866. This find of coins is well known in Zanzibar, and it is probably the same discovery which is referred to by Livingstone, who was at Zanzibar at the time. He states, it will be remembered, that the coins had inscriptions in the ancient Cufic character,[1] which was used on coins

---

[1] So-called from the ancient city of Kufa, or Cufa, near Bagdad, famous for the expert writers of this epigraphic script. The Koran was originally written in the Cufic character, and it was not until the tenth century that the cursive Arabic used to-day was introduced.

from the seventh until the thirteenth century. After the discovery Seyyid Majid is said to have had the whole site of Unguja Kuu dug over, in the hope of unearthing further treasure, but without success. As already remarked, the discovery of these ancient coins at Unguja Kuu is certainly significant that the original town was of great antiquity, for it must be remembered that to neither Arab nor Swahili would ancient coins appeal merely because of their antiquity, and therefore as such it is very unlikely they would be hoarded.

Kisimkazi, or, to give it its full native name, Kisimkazi-Diambani, is situated on the coast ten miles to the south of Unguja Kuu. From the sea it is even more unapproachable than the latter place, owing to the fact that at Kisimkazi there is no creek or harbour; and although there is deep water off the town, the intervening reef is very rough and unpropitious for landing. And yet it is believed that this town was once the capital of the southern portion of Zanzibar Island; and from the existing ruins which are described below, it must have been a centre of some importance.

The most important and interesting feature at Kisimkazi is undoubtedly the ancient mosque, situated a stone's-throw from the sea-shore.

The main fabric of the outer walls affords unmistakable evidence that the building is of Shirazian origin. Much has been modified and altered, but not even the horror of the modern corrugated-iron roof, and the " restorations " of the interior, can conceal the ancient dressed stone coigns and buttresses of the original edifice.

In the interior is a very ornate kibla fashioned in the form of a lance-shaped trefoil arch, and elaborately decorated with small clustered columns.

Close to the kibla is an Arabic inscription which states that the mosque was restored and repaired in A.D. 1772.

On each side of the kibla and extending along the northern wall is an ornamental frieze formed by a series of trefoil arches cut in relief, and in conjunction with this arcade are five small stone rosettes, possibly meant to represent the five planets.

Over this frieze is the most interesting feature of the

building—a feature which makes the mosque at Kisimkazi unique in Zanzibar, and, as far as I am aware, among the towns of the whole coast of Eastern Africa. This is a lengthy Cufic inscription. The lettering is clearly and deeply cut in blocks of stone, and the inscription extends not only along the wall, but follows the recess of the kibla.

Unfortunately the inscription has not yet been deciphered, for there is no one in Zanzibar of sufficient erudition to read the ancient characters in which it is carved; and although the people of Kisimkazi are very tolerant in allowing Europeans to enter the mosque to inspect the interior, there are obvious difficulties which prevent a " squeeze " or an adequate photograph of the inscription being taken.

The only other item of archæological interest at Kisimkazi is a ruined walled enclosure about fifty paces square, constructed of masonry close to the sea-shore, and about 100 yards south of the mosque. Its position immediately over-looking the landing-place suggests that it was a fort, and the remains of a rectangular turret-like chamber at the south-west corner certainly tends to confirm this impression. Portions of the southern and eastern walls, which attain in some places a height of 10 to 12 feet, are still standing, but it must be admitted that their thinness, and the absence of loopholes, raise doubts as to the original use of this walled enclosure. In any case it is evident that if it was built as a defensive work, it must have been prior to the introduction of any form of artillery.

Native tradition is entirely silent as to the origin of the ruins at Kisimkazi, but it is clear from the Cufic inscription in the mosque, and from the style of architecture, that the place must be of considerable antiquity. Personally I have little doubt that the group belongs to the series of stone-built towns which mark the colonising enterprises along the Azanian coasts of Asiatic emigrants from Mesopotamia or the Persian Gulf from the ninth century onwards.

APPENDIX

LIST OF THE MORE IMPORTANT WORKS WHICH HAVE BEEN CONSULTED IN CONNECTION WITH THE PRESENT VOLUME

" The Penetration of Arabia," by D. G. Hogarth (Lawrence & Bullen, Ltd. : London, 1904).

" A Handbook of the Swahili Language," by Edward Steere (S.P.C.K. : London, 1913).

" An-Nahlah."—Arab Periodical (London).

" The Colonisation of Africa," by Sir Harry Johnston (The University Press: Cambridge, 1899).

" Imams and Seyyids of Omân," by Salil-ibn-Razik, translated by George P. Badger (Hakluyt Society: London, 1871).

" The Sources of the Nile," by Charles T. Beke (James Madden & Co. : London, 1860).

" L'Afrique Orientale," by M. Guillain (Arthur Bertrand : Paris).

" Voyages of Sir James Lancaster to the East Indies " (Hakluyt Society : London).

" The History and Ethnography of Africa south of the Zambezi," by G. McC. Theal (George Allen & Unwin, Ltd. : London, 1910).

" The Partition of Africa," by J. Scott-Keltie (Edward Stanford: London, 1893).

" Die Portugiesenzeit von Deutsch-und-Englisch-Ostafrika," by Justus Strandes (Berlin, 1899).

" Cholera Epidemics in East Africa," by James Christie.

" The African Pilot."

" Dictionary of Islam," by Hughes (London, 1895).

" The Worship of the Dead," by Garnier.

" The Chemistry of Essential Oils," by Ernest J. Parry (Scott Greenwood & Sons : London, 1908).

" Persia and its People," by E. Sykes.

" A Journal of the First Voyage of Vasco da Gama, 1497–1499," translated by E. G. Ravenstein (Hakluyt Society: London).

" Journal of the Royal Asiatic Society " (London).

" Medieval Rhodesia," by David Randall-Maciver (Macmillan & Co. : London, 1906).

" Prehistoric Rhodesia," by Hall.

" Les Prairies d'Or," by Masudi, translated from the Arabic by C. Barbier de Meynard & Pavet de Courteille (Paris, 1861).

" A Description of the Coasts of East Africa and Malabar in the beginning of the Sixteenth Century," by Duarte Barbosa.

" Les Origines de la Cartographie Portugaise," by Jean Denuce (1908).

" Travels of Ibn Batuta," translated by the Reverend S. Lee (1829).

" Sailing Ships and their Story," by E. Keble Chatterton.

" Ships and Ways of Other Days," by E. Keble Chatterton (Sidgwick & Jackson, Ltd. : London).

" The Old East Indiamen," by E. Keble Chatterton (T. Werner Laurie & Co. : London).

" A Literary History of the Arabs," by R. Nicholson.

" Zanzibar : City, Island, and Coast," by R. Burton (Tinsley Bros. : London, 1872).

" The Real Captain Kidd," by Sir Cornelius Neale Dalton, K.C.M.G., C.B. (William Heinemann : London).

" Desert and Water Gardens of the Red Sea," by C. Crossland.

" The Coral Reefs of Zanzibar," by Cyril Crossland, B.A. (Proceedings of the Cambridge Philosophical Society : 1902).

" Travels in British East Africa and Zanzibar and Pemba," by W. W. FitzGerald (Chapman & Hall : London, 1898).

" Handwerk und Industrie in Ostafrika," by Dr. Franz Stuhlmann (Hamburg, 1910).

" The Qur'an," by E. H. Palmer (Clarendon Press : Oxford, 1900).

" The Glory of the Shia World," translated by Major P. Sykes (Macmillan & Co. : London).

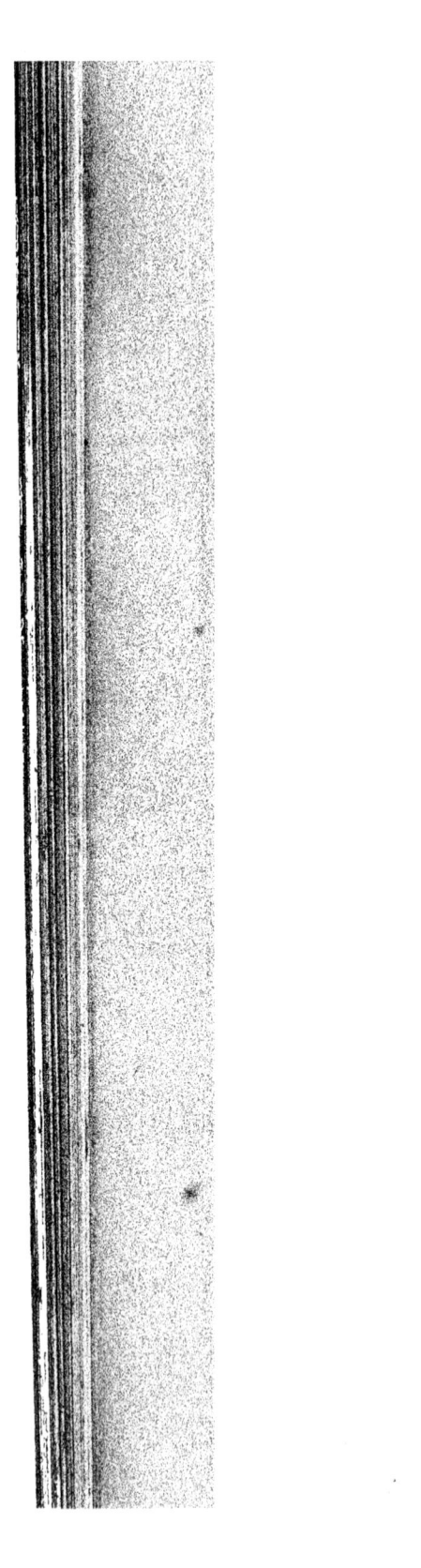

INDEX

CPSIA information can be obtained at www.ICGtesting.com
Printed in the USA
BVOW02s1232141215

430229BV00021B/550/P